Gender in Transitional Justice

Governance and Limited Statehood Series

Series editors:

Thomas Risse, Professor of International Politics, Freie Universität Berlin, Germany

Ursula Lehmkuhl, Professor of Modern History, Freie Universität Berlin, Germany

This ground-breaking monograph series showcases cutting edge research on the transformation of governance in countries with weak state institutions. Combining theoretically-informed and empirically grounded scholarship, it challenges the conventional governance discourse which is biased towards modern developed nation-states. Instead, the series focuses on governance in Africa, Asia and Latin America including transnational and transregional dimensions.

Located at the intersection of global governance and international relations, on the one hand, and comparative politics, area studies, international law, history, and development studies, on the other, this innovative series helps to challenge fundamental assumptions about governance in the social sciences.

Titles include:

Susanne Buckley-Zistel and Ruth Stanley (*editors*)
GENDER IN TRANSITIONAL JUSTICE

Amichai Magen, Thomas Risse and Michael A. McFaul (*editors*)
PROMOTING DEMOCRACY AND THE RULE OF LAW
American and European Strategies

Governance and Limited Statehood Series
Series Standing Order ISBN 978–0–230–23597–7 (hardback) and
ISBN 978–0–230–23598–4 (paperback)

You can receive future titles in this series as they are published by placing a standing order. Please contact your bookseller or, in case of difficulty, write to us at the address below with your name and address, the title of the series and one of the ISBNs quoted above.

Customer Services Department, Macmillan Distribution Ltd., Houndmills, Basingstoke, Hampshire RG21 6Xs, England

Gender in Transitional Justice

Edited by

Susanne Buckley-Zistel
Professor of Peace and Conflict Studies,
Center for Conflict Studies,
Philipps University Marburg, Germany

and

Ruth Stanley
Research Associate,
Center for Conflict Studies,
Philipps University Marburg, Germany

palgrave
macmillan

First published 2012 by
PALGRAVE MACMILLAN

Palgrave Macmillan in the UK is an imprint of Macmillan Publishers Limited, registered in England, company number 785998, of Houndmills, Basingstoke, Hampshire RG21 6XS.

Palgrave Macmillan in the US is a division of St Martin's Press LLC, 175 Fifth Avenue, New York, NY 10010.

Palgrave Macmillan is the global academic imprint of the above companies and has companies and representatives throughout the world.

Palgrave® and Macmillan® are registered trademarks in the United States, the United Kingdom, Europe and other countries.

ISBN: 978–0–230–24622–5

This book is printed on paper suitable for recycling and made from fully managed and sustained forest sources. Logging, pulping and manufacturing processes are expected to conform to the environmental regulations of the country of origin.

A catalogue record for this book is available from the British Library.

A catalog record for this book is available from the Library of Congress.

10 9 8 7 6 5 4 3 2 1
21 20 19 18 17 16 15 14 13 12

Printed and bound in the United States of America

Contents

Part IV Politics of Justice and Reconciliation

Contributors

Susanne Buckley-Zistel is Professor of Peace and Conflict Studies at the Center for Conflict Studies, Philipps University of Marburg. She has previously held positions at King's College London, the Peace Research Institute in Frankfurt, and the Free University of Berlin. She has published on issues pertaining to transitional justice and conflict transformation, with a particular focus on Rwanda and Uganda. Her research interests include dealing with the past, gender, post-structural theory, and the nexus between peace and development assistance. She is the author of *Conflict Transformation and Social Change in Uganda* (2008) and co-editor of the volume *Nach Krieg, Gewalt, und Repression: Von schwierigen Umgang mit der Vergangenheit* (2011).

Louise Chappell is Professor and Australian Research Council Future Fellow in the School of Social Sciences and International Studies at the University of New South Wales. She researches and teaches in the areas of human rights, gender and political institutions, and comparative Australian politics and has published widely on gender and politics. Her current research project focuses on an evaluation of gender justice and the International Criminal Court. She is the author of *Gendering Government: Feminist Engagement with the State* (2002), *The Politics of Women's Interests* (2006, co-edited with Lisa Hill), *'No Fit Place for Women'? Women and Politics in New South Wales 1856–2006* (2006, co-edited with Deborah Brennan), and *The Politics of Human Rights in Australia* (2009, with John Chesterman and Lisa Hill).

Nikita Dhawan is Junior Professor for Political Science at the Goethe University of Frankfurt, with a research focus on gender and postcolonial studies. In spring 2008, she was a visiting scholar at Columbia University, New York. In 2006–7 she was Maria-Goeppert-Mayer Guest Professor at the Carl von Ossietzky University of Oldenburg. She has written extensively on the ethics of non-violence, postcolonial feminism, queer diasporas, and decolonization and democratization. She is the author of *Impossible Speech: On the Politics of Silence and Violence* (2007) and *Postkoloniale Theorie: Eine kritische Einführung* (2005, with María do Mar Castro Varela) and co-editor of *Hegemony and Heteronormativity: Revisiting 'the Political' in Queer Politics* (2011, with María do Mar Castro Varela and Antke Engel).

Rirhandu Mageza-Barthel is working on gender and postcolonial studies in the Cluster of Excellence 'The Formation of Normative Orders' at the Goethe University of Frankfurt. She is a doctoral candidate in the Faculty of Social Sciences. Amongst other things she has conducted extended research visits to Rwanda and has also been a Visiting Researcher at the Primedia Unit for Holocaust and Genocide Studies, University of South Africa. Her focus areas are international politics, peace and conflict studies, and gender and women's studies, with an emphasis on the socio-political relations of countries in the Global South.

Fionnuala Ní Aoláin is the Dorsey and Whitney Chair in Law at the University of Minnesota Law School and Professor of Law at the University of Ulster's Transitional Justice Institute in Belfast, which she co-founded. She has been a visiting professor at the University of Minnesota Law School (2003–4), Harvard Law School (1993–4), Columbia Law School (1994–6), and the School of International and Public Affairs, Columbia University (1996–2000), as well as an associate professor of law at the Hebrew University in Jerusalem (1997–9) and a visiting fellow at Princeton University (2001–2). Her teaching and research interests are in the fields of international law, human rights law, national security law, and feminist legal theory, and she has published extensively on emergency powers, conflict regulation, transitional justice, and sex-based violence in times of war, including *Gender and the Post-Conflict Process* (2010, with Naomi Cahn and Dina Francesca Haynes), *Law in Times of Crisis: Emergency Powers in Theory and Practice* (2006), and *The Politics of Force: Conflict Management and State Violence in Northern Ireland* (2000).

Catherine O'Rourke is Lecturer in Human Rights and International Law and Gender Research Coordinator at the Transitional Justice Institute, University of Ulster. She has been a visiting scholar at the American University School of International Service, Washington DC, and a visiting researcher at the law schools of Universidad Diego Portales in Santiago, Chile, and Universidad de los Andes in Bogotá, Colombia. Her doctoral work examined feminist engagement with, and gendered outcomes of, transitional justice in Chile, Northern Ireland, and Colombia, and she was awarded the 2010 Basil Chubb Prize by the Political Studies Association of Ireland for the best thesis produced in an Irish university in any field of politics. Her research interests include gender and transitional justice, the human rights of women, women's movements in transitional societies, peace agreements, and socio-legal research methodologies. She has published widely, including in the *International Journal of Transitional Justice, International and Comparative Law Quarterly,* and *International Political Science Review.*

Elisabeth Porter is Professor and Lecturer in Politics and International Relations at the University of South Australia. Before this she was head of the School of International Studies at the University of South Australia. She has been research director at the International Conflict Research Centre (INCORE) in Northern Ireland, a centre linked with the UN University. She has also taught at Flinders University of South Australia, the University of Ulster, and Southern Cross University. Her books include *Women, Peace and Security: Good Practices* (forthcoming), *Peacebuilding: Women in International Perspective* (2007, 2008), *Feminist Perspectives on Ethics* (1999), *Building Good Families in a Changing World* (1995), and *Women and Moral Identities* (1991). Her co-edited books include *Mediation in the Asia-Pacific Region: Transforming Conflicts and Building Peace* (2009), *Activating Human Rights* (2006), and *Researching Conflict in Africa* (2005).

Romi Sigsworth is Senior Researcher in the Gender Based Violence Programme at the Centre for the Study of Violence and Reconciliation (CSVR), South Africa. Before joining CSVR she worked as the managing editor of the medical ethics journals *Bioethics* and *Developing World Bioethics.* Her research interests include the gendered nature of xenophobia in South Africa, the attrition of rape cases in the South African criminal justice system, the nature and causes of sexual violence in South Africa, and the impact of culture on sexual offending in South Africa. She is the author of *Gender-Based Violence in Transition* (2008) and the co-author of *The Gendered Nature of Xenophobia in South Africa* (2008).

Ruth Stanley is Research Associate at the Center for Conflict Studies, Philipps University of Marburg. Prior to this she was Reader in Politics at the Institute of Political Science, Free University of Berlin, where she also directed a research project on security sector reform and on the governance of public security in Argentina and Mexico, funded by the German Research Association. Following the first democratic elections in the German Democratic Republic (GDR), she was a member of the Policy Planning Staff of the GDR Foreign Ministry, and prior to that, she worked at the Peace Research Centre CIP-FUHEM in Madrid. Her doctoral thesis, a historical study of the effects of scientific migration on weapons proliferation, was awarded the Rudolf Kellerman Prize for the best German-language work in the field of technology history. Her research interests include democratization and human rights, peace and conflict research, security governance, and gender issues, and she has published widely on these topics.

Silke Studzinsky has worked for more than 17 years as a criminal defence lawyer and as a legal representative for civil parties before criminal courts in Germany and elsewhere in Europe. One of her main areas of work is fostering the rights of victims of sexual violence, sexual abuse, trafficking, and racial discrimination inside and outside the courtroom. She joined the Association of European Democratic Lawyers in 2000 and acted as their secretary general from 2005 until the end of 2007. She organized and participated in several human rights missions and trial observations and delegations in Turkey, Spain, Greece, Israel, South Korea, and Kashmir. Since February 2008, she has been working with the support of the Civil Peace Service of the German Development Organization in Cambodia to represent civil parties before the Extraordinary Chambers in the Courts of Cambodia (ECCC).

Nahla Valji is Programme Specialist on the Rule of Law at UNIFEM (United Nations Development Fund for Women, now part of UN Women). She was a senior project manager in the Transitional Justice Programme at the Centre for the Study of Violence and Reconciliation in Cape Town, South Africa, where she managed the African Transitional Justice Research Network. She is the co-founder and managing editor of the *International Journal of Transitional Justice*. Her recent publications include the UNIFEM report *A Window of Opportunity: Making Transitional Justice Work for Women* (2010).

Angelika von Wahl is Associate Professor in the Program of International Affairs at Lafayette College. She studies comparative and international politics with an emphasis on social policy and gender in post-industrial states. Her recent comparative research focuses on human rights and reparations. She has published three books, and numerous articles in journals, such as *West European Politics, Social Politics, German Politics and Society*. One forthcoming article in *German Politics* (Special Issue) discusses intersectionality and female leadership. One of her recently published articles is 'The Politics of Reparations: Why, When and How Democratic Governments Get Involved' (*Historical Justice in International Perspective*, 2008).

Magdalena Zolkos is Research Fellow in Political Theory with the Centre for Citizenship and Public Policy at the University of Western Sydney.

She holds an MA in Scandinavian Studies from the University of Danzig and a PhD from the Department of Political Science of the University of Copenhagen. She researches and teaches within the areas of contemporary political theory, gender and politics, and discourse theory. Her publication record includes book chapters and academic articles in *European Legacy, Studies in Social and Political Thought, International Journal of Transitional Justice* on the critique of reconciliation, collective trauma, testimony and witnessing, postmodern subjectivity, and post-apocalyptic political thought. She is the author of *Reconciling Community and Subjective Life: Trauma Testimony as Political Theorizing in the Work of Jean Amery and Imre Kertesz* (2010).

Introduction: Gender in Transitional Justice

Susanne Buckley-Zistel and Magdalena Zolkos

'I cannot even kill a chicken. If there is a person who says that a woman – a mother – killed, then I'll confront that person' (Pauline Nyiramasuhuko, cited in Landesman, 2002). These are the words of Pauline Nyiramasuhuko, who currently stands trial before the UN International Criminal Tribunal for Rwanda (ICTR), which has been established to prosecute crimes committed during the 1994 genocide. Together with her son, she is accused of genocide, crimes against humanity, and rape. Nyiramasuhuko is the first women to be tried by the ICTR.

Nyiramasuhuko's case is challenging on a number of counts. First, it draws attention to the rampant violence against women during conflict and to the specific forms of violence to which women, in particular, are subjected. Secondly, the charges against her challenge the conventional view that women have been solely the victims, and not the perpetrators, of massive human rights abuses and genocidal events – a view that reflects deeper assumptions about gender roles and that is echoed in Nyiramasuhuko's own words cited above. The aim of this volume is to explore these multifaceted and interrelated roles of women, and men, and how they manifest themselves in the context of transitional justice (TJ).

Transitional justice refers to processes of dealing with the aftermath of violent conflicts and systematic human rights abuses in order to provide conditions for a peaceful future. It makes use of a number of instruments and mechanisms, including national and international tribunals, truth commissions, memory work, reparations and institutional reforms, which aim at uncovering the truth about past crimes, putting past wrongs right, holding perpetrators accountable, vindicating the dignity of victims-survivors and contributing to reconciliation (Minow, 1998).[1]

In regard to its temporal focus, TJ is at one and the same time oriented towards the past, present, and future. As a past-oriented practice, it addresses wrongs that have been committed during a conflict; as a present-oriented practice, it establishes a new ethical and institutional framework of post-authoritarian and/or transitional politics for interpreting the past and, through this, it seeks to prevent the *future* occurrence of gross injustices and violence. In recent decades the concept of TJ has acquired a central place in transitional and democratic discourses, as well as in sociological, political and legal academic research.

In the initial stages of the development of the TJ field, its gendered dimensions were largely unrecognized and they have remained under-researched. The relatively few studies that exist on the question of gender in TJ have focused almost exclusively on women as victims of sexualized violence. As critics of that tendency have pointed out, this has created the problematic possibility that women's and men's experiences of violence and repression would be reduced to a single thematic aspect, and stereotypical gender categories would be perpetuated, rather than identified and challenged, within the TJ literature.

This volume seeks to move the analysis beyond the tendency to equate gender with questions of (often narrowly understood) sexual violence, and to contribute to the emergence of more inclusive and complex studies of the cross-section of gender and TJ. It builds on the assumption that gender cannot be accommodated within TJ as a descriptive category of the victims, but that it has the potential to transform, or at least reformulate, some of the most rudimentary questions of the TJ field: Whose justice – and for whom? What is the transition to? How can one negotiate between the Western ideas of justice that animate the TJ project (and thus the implied global transmission of hegemonic values) on the one hand and its impact on local needs and the culturally situated understandings and practices of gender on the other? What is the significance of the TJ processes for the shape of social gender relations in post-transitional phases? Is there a need for a broader conception of TJ, which would encompass economic, social and cultural human rights, in order for TJ to contribute to greater gender equality? In short, incorporating a gender perspective not only with regard to the topics of TJ, but also into the very texture of its analytical framework requires a more fundamental reflection on the underlying theoretical, political and ideological premises of the TJ project, as well as an analysis of the gender implications of their alternative formulations. To place the category of gender at the heart of the study of TJ thus implies exposition of (often unarticulated, but assumed) ideas about the specifically *transitional* nature of justice in this project and its function.

Historical development of transitional justice

While the genealogy of transitional justice points to the war crimes trials in Nuremberg and Tokyo following the Second World War, the concept first became widely used in 1990s to describe judicial and non-judicial mechanisms of accountability introduced in the period of transformation from authoritarian to democratic government, or from a conflict society to a post-conflict society, in order to address earlier violations of human rights. As such, TJ discussions have dovetailed with the wider debates about democratization, peace-building, socio-economic transformations and state-building, in post-conflict and post-authoritarian societies (Teitel, 2003: 69). The proponents of TJ have argued that the pursuit of past-oriented justice is crucial for the achievement of democratic consolidation. However, others have problematized what they have seen as the politicization of justice within the TJ project (especially some of its more punitive forms) as a potential impediment to the democratization process. Suffice it to say that since its emergence and implementation in a variety of socio-political situations, TJ has been positioned in a close, but complicated relationship to democratic transition (see for example Leebaw, 2008).

TJ is based on the assumption that the transition to peace after violent conflicts or authoritarian rule requires a clean break from past injustices so as to prevent their recurrence. Historically, the concept and the academic discussion of TJ has evolved dialogically. After the Second World War, the objective of the Nuremberg Trials and Tokyo Tribunal (as well as the specific death camp trials, the Nanjing Tribunal, and many others) was to judge Nazi German and Imperial Japanese leaders and officials for war crimes and gross human rights violations committed during the war. The broader intention of the trials was encapsulated by the phrase 'never again' – namely to prevent the future recurrence of such genocidal events as the Holocaust. Subsequently, during the Cold War period, defined by the central concerns for regime stabilization and balance of power, there were few continuations of the national and international accountability trend initiated by the post-war tribunals. However, the lost momentum of TJ was regained in the late 1970s and early 1980s with the events in Southern Europe (the 1975 trials in Greece of members of the military juntas and others accused of serious human rights violations during that country's military dictatorship), and Latin America (the 1985 Trial of the Juntas in Argentina, against leading members of the military government that held power from 1976 until 1983). The end of the Cold War also marked the growing use of public commissions focused on discovering and disclosing systematic human rights abuses among the affected populations, such as the Argentine Commission on Disappeared Persons (CONADEP). In many cases, this aim was linked with promoting societal reconciliation, such as the Chilean and post-apartheid South African truth and reconciliation commissions. Despite the Greek and Argentine cases mentioned above, criminal trials of the perpetrators of human rights abuses were used rather sparingly, in part because of the very high political costs attached. More recently, with the establishment of the International Criminal Court (ICC) in 2002, this element of TJ has regained prominence, turning criminal justice into a central component of the repertoire of measures employed within the framework. At the same time, while students of TJ were initially concerned mainly with its judicial and non-judicial tools at a macro level, including national or international tribunals and truth commissions, recently the attention has been broadened to include micro levels focusing on victims and their subjective experiences and concerns.[2]

This short historical sketch shows that the emergence of the TJ concept has been contingent upon political changes in the post-war era, which have fuelled its specific development and have made it into a 'global', though not homogeneous, project. In particular, crucial for the current paradigmatic shaping of TJ has been the worldwide trend towards democratization after the Second World War (Germany, Italy, Japan), especially since the mid-1970s (Southern Europe), spreading more widely since the beginning of the 1990s (most of Latin America, parts of Africa and Asia). Not only has the transition from authoritarian rule to democracy created public openings and fora for the investigation of a violent past, but such inquiry has also become part and parcel of the strategies of legitimizing the new regime and underlining its discontinuity with the previous authoritarian rule. In a number of cases, the concept of democratic transition has been closely intertwined with liberal values formed at the conjunction of the approaches of 'dealing with the past' and of enforcing the rule of law (Forsberg, 2001: 57). This includes arguments about accountability for past human rights violations. In the post-Cold War world the 'evangelical optimism of liberalism' (Hazan, 2007: 10) and its (specifically defined) pursuit of justice following violent conflict has thus gained new momentum and widespread validity. Consequently, there has been a need for a critical analysis of TJ that would problematize both its idea of the subject of justice (and what it means to do *justice* for the *past*), and the assumptions about the democratic implications of TJ. Such a critique by no means implies a rejection of TJ. Rather, while it acknowledges its significance and potential for streaming individual perspectives of human suffering into the field of politics, it seeks to dissect and complicate the ideological assumptions of TJ.

At the same time as the 1990s marked an era of increased human rights focus in international affairs, the decade also witnessed events spurred by violent nationalism and ethnic conflict in the former Yugoslavia, Rwanda, Sierra Leone, and elsewhere (Forsberg, 2001: 57). These events have challenged the liberal 'neutral' idea of the subject of TJ by highlighting the significance of gender, age, race, and ethnicity for understanding specific victimization patterns. Ruti G. Teitel argues that the global dissemination of the TJ idea as an appropriate response to the intensifying political instabilities and violence has nowadays made TJ the rule rather than the exception (Teitel, 2003: 71). Others have even spoken of a 'mantra' of TJ (Hazan, 2007). All this suggests that through the global propagation of liberal norms, practices and institutions, the demand for accountability for past human rights abuses is not solely a domain of national governments, but has become part of the discourse of an international responsibility.

Gender in transitional justice – state of the art

The field of TJ has been recently enriched through the systematic impact of gender analysis with the effect of problematizing its legal theoretical assumptions, mechanisms of operation and societal outcomes. In that context, the project of *gendering* TJ has defined a number of approaches insofar as it has reflected the polysemy of both the notion of 'gender' and of 'justice'.

First, at the most basic level, *gendering* TJ has connoted critical attempts of identifying and addressing the exclusion, or insufficient inclusion, of women within (inter) national TJ frameworks. Here, gender has been understood as synonymous with the social category of women, and its primary critique has been directed at the systemic acts of privileging and universalizing male perspectives, and, consequently, rendering female perspectives inferior, irrelevant or invisible (Minow, 1998; Valji, 2009; Askin, 2003). As Christine Bell and Catherine O'Rourke have emphasized (2007), the exclusion of women from early and more traditional forms of transitional justice had to do largely with the underrepresentation of women in peace negotiations and peace agreements, and/or with the male bias in the formation and operation of the justice-seeking institutions in post-conflict contexts. The exclusion meant that not only did women's potential to contribute to reconstructive processes remained unutilized, but also that their suffering during the conflict, which took a variety of forms, was not recognized (Turshen et al., 2001; Chinkin, 2003; Bunch, 2005). In response to the under-involvement and under-representation of women in transitional justice, the dominant liberal institutional approaches advocated policies and practices of gender mainstreaming (Rosser, 2007).

Characteristically, within the initial attempts of gendering TJ, the topic of sexual violence has acquired noticeable significance (Seifert, 1996; Copelon, 1995; Cahn, 2005). While this focus can be seen as a necessary corrective to the general tendency to ignore or de-emphasize sexual aspects of war violence, some feminist scholars have stressed certain problems with it. They have included (a) over-identifying women with the sexual domain and with the category of victims (Campbell, 2004; Mertus, 2004); (b) making a distinction between war-time and peace-time (and domestic) sexual violence; and (c) excluding from the gendered frame of analysis instances of sexual violence against men (Oosterhoffet et al., 2004; Sivakumaran, 2007).

At the level of analysis of the international jurisprudence and international legal practice, there have been numerous contributions, coming both from the liberal institutional position and from the critical feminist stance, to the debates on categorizing different forms of sexual violence, including rape, sexual enslavement and trafficking, impregnation, sterilization, and enforced prostitution, as war crimes. This included analysis and discussions of the gendered mandate of the ICTY (International Criminal Tribunal for the Former Yugoslavia) and ICTR (International Criminal Tribunal for Rwanda) (Tiemessen, 2004; Engle, 2005; Campbell, 2007; Wells, 2005); the Rome Statute and the practice of the ICC (Boon, 2001; Oosterveld, 2005); the truth and reconciliation commissions in Haiti, Sierra Leone, East Timor, and others (Shaw, 2005; Bastick, 2008); and gendered violence not only during conflict, but also during the transition phase (Ní Aoláin, 2006). Gendered scholarship of TJ has also identified issues relevant for women's well-being in the functioning of courtrooms and in the legal enforcement mechanisms. These include the questions of the status of victims-witnesses, interviewing methods, admission of evidence, protection and support of victims of sexual violence to prevent re-traumatization, and their social reintegration (Campbell, 2004; Dembour and Haslam, 2004; Kelsall and Stepakoff, 2007).

A further body of analysis, associated above all with the work of Ruth Rubio-Marín, focuses on reparations. It analyses the specific forms of victimization of women (as well as how, even when women are subject to the same violations as men, these violations may impact them very differently in view of cultural gender assumptions), in order to understand their specific needs for redress. Rubio-Marín also addresses the question of why women appear to favour specific remedies over others and the extent to which reparations programmes need to be tailored accordingly (Rubio-Marín, 2006: 7). More recent studies have stressed the need for sensitivity to the differential impact of institutional reforms in the security sector on women and men, with a focus on recognizing and addressing the specific security needs of women (DCAF, 2008; OECD, 2009).

Another approach to gendering transitional justice has focused on discourses of femininity and masculinity, rather than on the socio-political and legal categories of women. It has conditioned the emergence of a sub-field of academic literature on transitional justice that criticizes traditional ('masculine') conceptions of law and accountability, and interrogated different cultural forms of the nexus between masculinity and violence. A number of texts have advocated deeper atunement to more 'feminine' modes of achieving justice and seeking healing, for example through production of familial narratives (Ross, 2003; van der Merwe and Gobodo-Madikizela, 2007). Others have produced studies of violence, both during and after a war or civil conflict, as a social practice deeply embedded in the hegemonic discourses of masculinity (Wetherell and Edley, 1999; Hamber, 2007). Often connected to critical evaluation of the gendered construction of the mandate and practice of the South African Truth and Reconciliation Commission, these approaches have emphasized that the nature of gendered exclusions in transitional justice settings has been conceptual, rather than merely situational. As a result, female experiences, stories and perspectives have been deemed irrelevant (Ross, 2003). Other critical studies have stressed the need for greater intersectional and cultural sensitivity in the analysis of gender issues, especially, but not exclusively, in regard to the victimization of indigenous women, as opposed to statistical identification of women's under-representation (Ní Aoláin and Rooney, 2007).

To sum up, these two gender-centred approaches to transitional justice emphasize the under-visibility and under-privileging of women on the one hand, and the social-discursive constructions of femininity and masculinity on the other. Importantly, they seek to transform transitional justice and critique selected aspects of its implementation, but affirm its project in general. In contrast, another critical feminist approach has suggested that transitional justice is deeply, even intrinsically, implicated in the patriarchal and neo-liberal structures of governance. The nature of this post-Marxist feminist unease with transitional justice has had to do with the fact that it connotes a process of transition from 'male-defined political violence' to 'liberal democratic frameworks', both of which, though for different reasons, have been found problematic (Bell and O'Rourke, 2007: 23). Critical feminist contributors to the debates of transitional justice have pointed out the limits of the liberal feminist advocacy of breaking the silence and invisibility of women. Katherine M. Franke has argued (2006: 823) that one should be wary of the appropriation of women's 'stories, memories and experience' within the dominant and only seemingly ideologically neutral liberal democratic institutions. She views with some discomfort the possibilities of 'popular identification with selected aspects of women's suffering', where, in particular, 'their sexual violation can stand for the nation's violation as a whole' (Franke, 2006). Franke thus expresses concern that the focus on the harms suffered by women will be instrumentalized in the service of an essentially patriarchal, albeit newly democratic state.

A gendered critique of transitional justice

One crucial aspect of incorporating gender in an analysis of TJ is that it can serve as a powerful critical tool. In a similar vein, Ann Tickner argues that a feminist research agenda incorporates 'a distinctive methodological perspective that fundamentally challenges the often unseen androcentric or masculine biases in the way that knowledge has traditionally been constructed in all the disciplines' (Tickner, 2005: 3). A critical gender analysis poses a number of significant questions to TJ: to what extent, and how, are concepts of justice, in our case transitional justice, mediated and normed by gender? And, in turn, to what extent, and how, does TJ mediate and norm what we understand as gender? Does TJ hold the potential to challenge and subvert gender concepts and gender relations that evolve around privilege and hierarchy and potentially contribute to gender justice? Against this backdrop, we use feminism as a methodology to critically assess the underlying notions of TJ frameworks. In doing so, we do not necessarily propose new perspectives and arguments on transitional justice. We seek to piece them together in a way that criticizes the dominant discourse of TJ *per se*. Importantly, our reflections in this introduction rely on a selective overview of notions and practices of transitional justice since our objective is not so much to paint a complete picture, but to point towards tendencies in need of further research. Our argument, moreover, betrays a slight bias towards particular instruments, namely tribunals and truth commissions, reflecting the dominant tendencies in both transitional justice theory and practice.

Similarly to Kirsten Campbell (2007), we argue that the 'gendered' character of transitional justice has been particularly conspicuous in two domains. First, in its constitutive definitions about what constitutes crimes in need of rectification through TJ; and, second, in its applied norms and understandings about what constitutes an adequate practice of *doing justice* for historical violence, abuse, or systemic injustice (Campbell, 2007: 420). Following Bourdieu, Campbell argues that entering into a particular field of social practice – in our case the social practice of TJ – implies tactical acceptance of its fundamental law. For example, specific human rights abuses can only be addressed according to the norms or logic internal to the human rights discourse. Accordingly, transitional justice deals with any emerging difficulties through recourse to its own rules, norms, and conventions, and it does not – in fact it *cannot* – rely on a logic that lies beyond its normative remit. In other words, in a TJ process, the actors involved (such as the parties to a conflict, external promoters and donors, staff and supporters, and so on) consider their situation, and indeed their own identities, from *within* the TJ discourse.

What are these normative remits that determine the scope of TJ practice? What delineates what lies at the centre of its discourse, and what resides at the peripheries? What is constructed as 'invisible' or 'silent'? With Campbell's dual analytical frame in mind, the following section firstly considers what constitutes a crime and, secondly, asks what constitutes an adequate practice to render (transitional) justice.

What constitutes a crime in transitional justice?

This discussion begins with the question what kind of crimes are being addressed by transitional justice frameworks in order to analyse how they are mediated and normed by gender. It will argue that there is a process of selection at work, which is highly andocentric. To begin, generally the systematic and extensive war crimes, crimes against humanity, as well as genocide have been considered to be crimes of such a massive scale that they require exceptional measures (including TJ). For example, the statutes of the tribunals for Rwanda, former Yugoslavia, and Sierra Leone included in the category of crimes in their jurisdiction murder, extermination, slavery, deportation, imprisonment, torture, and rape if and when these actions were executed systematically and on a large scale, in particular against civilian populations (Bell, 2009).

According to Ní Aoláin, *within* TJ frameworks certain kinds of bodily harms are considered to be more significant than others (Ní Aoláin, 2009: 1061). In its early days, TJ was characterized by a focus on political and civil rights violations perpetuated against men in the context of repression and civil wars, ignoring the often highly gendered use of violence. Meanwhile, as a result of changes of perception in international law, the scope of what constitutes a crime has been expanded to include sexual and gender-based violence against women and men. More precisely, the Geneva Conventions of 1949 referred to rape as an attack on the honour of women, thereby ignoring the practice of sexualized violence against men, but failed to define rape as constituting a grave breach of the Conventions, a lacuna with important consequences for the obligation to prosecute such crimes. While this definition was repeated in the Additional Protocols to the Geneva Conventions of 1977, more recent developments in international law have moved beyond this limited conceptualization of gender-based crimes. Due to landmark decisions by the ICTY and ICTR there has been an important shift towards rendering sexual and sexualized crimes in the context of war and massive human rights abuses crimes against humanity and genocide crimes.[3] Similarly, early truth commissions in Latin America did not pay special attention to gendered versions of truths while the commissions for Guatemala, South Africa and Peru included gender in their analysis, even though it was not part of their official mandate (Valji, 2006: 6–7). More recently, the truth commissions of Haiti, Sierra Leone, and Timor-Leste incorporated gender and sexual violence in their mandate turning it into a critical aspect of their investigations. These normative shifts are significant in respect of what these TJ frameworks count as a crime in need of rectification.

And yet, notwithstanding these important achievements, the inclusion of sexualized violence in legal prosecution, truth commissions, and beyond is a mixed blessing since it reduces women to targets of one particular crime and constructs them as perpetual victims, fixing their social positions and political identities in the newly emerging society as passive, inferior, vulnerable, and in need of (male) protection. As argued by Franke:

> To the extent that criminal tribunals tend to expect and solicit testimony of sexual violation from female witnesses, women become

> figured in collective memory as particular sorts of victims that encourage popular identification with selected aspects of women's experience. (Franke, 2006: 825)

Without diminishing the importance of prosecuting sexualized violence, Franke draws attention to the fact that this selectivity of sexual crimes might have a counterproductive impact for wider questions of gender justice (Franke, 2006). To focus only on sexual crimes is highly selective on the basis of a particular image of femininity, namely peacefulness and non-aggressiveness, and this leads to insufficient consideration of women's role as political agents and, consequently, also as perpetrators of violence and atrocities (such as indicated in the quotation opening this chapter). In Liberia, for instance, the truth commission emphasized the plight of women as victims of violent attacks while failing to draw attention to the fact that a comparatively large section of the combatant forces consisted of women.[4] Accordingly, their crimes remained unrecognized. In doing so, the truth commission's findings undermined women's agency and capacity to independently make political decisions, framing them as passive objects, and rendering them as victims (this time not of sexual abuse but of degradation).

A further moment of selectivity concerns the privileging of political and civil rights over economics, social and economic rights. For, as pointed out by Nahla Valji (2007: 11), the new laws against sexual violence reduce the experience of women during repression and violent conflict to that of sexual crimes even though women are subjected to various forms of non-direct, structural violence such as exclusion, marginalization, and discrimination. This manifests itself in, inter alia, eroding social services and family structures, displacement and flight, poverty, and starvation which are, to a large extent, consequences of systematic and unequal power relations extenuated in times of crises, yet do not fall within the responsibility of most TJ frameworks.[5] Valji thus stresses that justice, where addressed, is often narrowly defined and does not comprise gender justice and a wider transformation of power asymmetries in a post-conflict society.

Regarding the selection of spheres and spaces in which crimes need to occur in order to fall into the remit of transitional justice frameworks, the focus is on abuses perpetuated in public by combatants or security forces (and occasionally civilians drawn into combat) against other combatants or civilians. For many women, though, the experience of violence during repression or war is confined to the supposedly safe space of the home, and is often perpetuated by relatives and spouses.[6]

In this context, a category on which the liberal composition of TJ is predicated is the distinction between public and private social spaces where the focus on the public nature of the crime may tend, albeit inadvertently, to downplay the seriousness of similar crimes perpetrated in the 'private' context.

A further conceptual feature of TJ has been challenged by feminist perspectives, namely the dichotomy between 'before' and 'after' war violence (Hansen, 2001). In the words of Rosemary Nagy:

> Transitional justice...implies a fixed interregnum period with a distinct end; it bridges a violent or repressive past and a peaceful, democratic future. Notions of 'breaking with the past' and 'never again', which align with the dominant transitional mechanisms, mould a definitive sense of 'now' and 'then'. (Nagy, 2008: 280)

Gender analysis undermines this distinction in two ways. First, the structural violence experienced in times of crisis, as referred to above, persists after repression or violent conflict so that there is no peaceful aftermath for women (Turshen et al., 2001). Women, in particular, suffer from the lack of security impinging on the roles they can assume in public life, the absence of men in their households, the consequences of unwanted pregnancies, HIV/AIDS infections, or the responsibility of heading a household at a very early age. Second, for many women, and at times men, the experience of direct, physical violence does not stop with the signing of a peace accord or truce. Instead, violence continues in a variety of forms, often in the private realm of home and family due to manifold reasons including extreme stress; the desire of men to (re)assert their masculinity against a backdrop of eroding social structures; unemployment; and the loss of self-worth in a post-conflict society (Hamber, 2007). Valji thus concludes that 'the removal of wartime rape from the continuum of violence against women in which it is inherently a part...reinforces a false dichotomy of conflict / post-conflict' (Valji, 2007: 12),[7] calling into question a very central element of transition justice, which is that there is a simple transition from violence to peace.

It is, moreover, assumed that sexual violence is only a criminal offence when committed in times of war or repression. To give an example, in the Foca case the ICTY held that the act of rape also constituted torture in the circumstances of the case, stating that it would be difficult to conceive of a situation where the use of rape by one warring party against another would *not* constitute torture. The focus in this case was entirely on the political nature of the event. What of rape outside of this specific context of war, which feminists have long argued can constitute torture in certain circumstances? By so emphasizing the specific situation of war, the decision seems to suggest that it is precisely, even uniquely, this context that is determinative of rape as torture, relegating rape in peace-time, by implicit definition, to a lesser level in the hierarchy of crime.

In addition, whether or not a crime is recognized and addressed within the TJ mechanisms in place depends on what subjects have been given the victim status. In other words, not all crimes of all subjects are considered to be appropriate crimes in the TJ processes. Even a cursory look into that matter reveals that there is a system of crime gradation at play in the TJ discourses. To be granted the victim status often depends on the opportunity structures that constrain and enable the agency of subjects, such as being heard as claimants in tribunals. If such opportunity structures are not in place, for instance due to social stigma and taboo as is often the case with sexual and gender-related crimes, those who had been harmed remain powerless within the available system of justice. For instance, as illustrated in Chapter 7 by Angelika von Wahl, even though persecution of homosexuals in Nazi Germany was a widespread and systematic strategy (including their incarceration in death camps), they have only recently been successful in lobbying for compensation (of a symbolic nature). Similarly, Silke Studzinsky's Chapter 3 in this volume reveals how prosecution strategies operate to deny justice to victims of gender-based violence seeking redress before the Extraordinary Chambers in the Courts of Cambodia (ECCC), the special court set up to try grave human rights violations committed by the Khmer Rouge regime. Likewise, Asian women forced into sexual slavery by Japanese soldiers during World war II (as well as Chinese and other Asian women) – the euphemistically called 'comfort women' – have not been given any form of material or symbolic compensation by Japan, in spite of the recommendations of the UN Report on Japan's liability and guilt. In fact, it was not until the 1980s that Korean Women's Movement managed to publicize the war practice of imprisoning and sexually exploiting the 'comfort women' and to break its taboos and silencing. In this sense, one must be alert that the TJ framework will inevitably produce and reproduce already existing hierarchies, norms and perceptions regarding the recognition of gendered (and other) crimes.

Finally, it is not only sexual or gender-based violence, economic, social, and cultural rights or particular victims groups that fall outside the borders of what constitutes a crime in TJ. Through its focus on immediate agency, the concept fails more generally to address complex issues of complicity. These include the widespread tolerance or approval of gross human rights violations on the part of the population, as well as the economic, moral, and military support of external actors. For example, certain Western powers' support for the apartheid regime of South Africa, or the military and economic assistance Latin American dictatorships received from the United States, although both may be crucial to the repressive regime's survival. Here, too, the operation of the mechanism of inclusion and exclusion determines what counts as right or wrong. Critically, it has been noted that the criminalization of certain acts through transitional justice implies that other forms of violations and killings are being de-criminalized, that is they are considered to be legitimated forms. By focusing on extreme manifestations of violence, TJ frameworks have the potential to conceal that death and pain are characteristics of any war and violent conflicts. They suggest that violence is justifiable as long as it adheres to 'our' (mostly Western) social conventions of what constitutes crime and human rights abuse in international law. Non-sanctioned violence comes to count as acceptable and there is no space for more radical voices that demand that the use of violence as such be outlawed. Rather, war persists in prescribed 'sanitized' forms; that is through international rules of conduct during military operations (Dauphine, 2008).

What constitutes an appropriate way of rendering transitional justice?

According to Nagy, '[t]he question today is not *whether* something should be done after atrocity but *how* it should be done' (Nagy, 2008: 276). With TJ being a burgeoning industry, a series of instruments have been developed and refined to deal with the past including, inter alia, tribunals, truth commissions, memory work, public apologies, and reparations. The aim of this section is to discuss some of these instruments, albeit selectively, in order to analyse what gender norms TJ measures embody, and whether they hold the potential to challenge and subvert social gender concepts and gender relations.

Generally, it can be noted that there is a tendency towards legalistic approaches in transitional justice. This is, inter alia, driven by international donors and the international community, as manifested in recent tribunals in and/or for the former Yugoslavia, Rwanda, Sierra Leone, and Cambodia, as well as the ICC. Yet why have legal responses to systematic human rights abuses gained such a prominence? Barbara

Oomen suggests that the answer lies in the fact that law is often deemed to be neutral, universal, and apolitical (in particular when compared to highly politicized responses such as military or diplomatic interventions), and that it seems like the safest and most cost effective way of engaging with a country (2005: 893). To illustrate her point she refers to the ongoing wars in the Democratic Republic of Congo and Northern Uganda, and one could add Darfur, where the international community has been extremely hesitant to engage, yet where the ICC has endorsed investigations.

And yet, far from being neutral, universal, and apolitical, international law is firmly situated in a modern, Western tradition as it has emerged over space and time. One aspect of this development is the emergence of boundaries that determine dichotomies such as law/violence, civilization/savage, inside/outside and male/female (Buchanan and Johnson, 2005: 133). To pick up the latter point, law has been criticized from a feminist perspective for excluding women in its procedures, as well as for privileging the interests of men (Charlesworth and Chinkin, 2000). It has been described as:

> a particularly masculinist practice, elevating rationality and objectivity over context and nuance, preferring process to substance, master-narrative to nuance, and being generally ill suited to the kind of empathic listening that would transform the speaking self into a healing self. (Franke, 2006: 825)

Without essentializing femininity, it has been argued that many women would assume a different, less positivistic, and more interpretative perspective (Tickner, 2005), raising serious questions regarding the usefulness of positivist, legalist approaches for women.

In addition, as mentioned in the previous section, legalistic approaches in international law are based on individual, civil, and political rights, the prosecution of which is, in many cases, relevant for men as victims of direct violence during conflict or repression. In contrast, economic, social, and cultural rights which address structural violence tend to be relevant for both men and women, yet they are not subject to legal inquiries in crime tribunals thereby limiting the adequacy of these mechanisms as ways of rendering justice for women in particular.[8] Since women often suffer differently from the experience of violence then men, challenging structural violence and its ramifications is particularly relevant in order to change prevailing power asymmetries, to prevent future harm, and to further gender justice.

Another seemingly appropriate way of dealing with the past is influenced by the desire of *laying it to rest*. 'We needed to acknowledge that we had a horrendous past', declared the chairman of the South African Truth and Reconciliation Commission, Desmond Tutu. 'We needed to look the beast in the eye, so that the past wouldn't hold us hostage anymore.' In some cases acknowledgement and confrontation with the past takes place in truth commissions, at times with the added intention to contribute to national reconciliation such as in Sierra Leone and South Africa. Since, compared to courts and tribunals, truth commissions have a stronger focus on victims as well as on collecting multiple perspectives, they are considered to be more sensitive to gender concerns and, as indicated above, increasingly consider them in their analysis. At times, though, this is hampered by the publicity-focused function of the hearings (although testimonies sometimes may be given in private). Publicity collides with the fact that there is often a culture of silence around sexual abuse, in particular, since women fear stigma and being ostracized by their communities, as well as for being shamed and blamed for becoming the (bush) wives of rebels (Dougherty, 2004: 50). However, truth commissions require this triangular communicative structure of commissioner, witness, and audience since the truth is not revealed for its own sake but for informing, if not influencing, the public about the past, be it through public hearings or published reports (Buckley-Zistel, 2011).

Truth commissions as well as other TJ instruments frequently promote a justice and reconciliation discourse that serves to frame individual statements and testimonies to 'fit' this meta-narrative. To put it in the language of a Foucauldian analysis, this discourse 'disciplines' individuals to produce statements and testimonies within particular 'restorative governmentalities' (Pavlich, 2005: 108), and as such it forms the subject positions of victims, perpetrators, bystanders, and so on. Yet what if people who experienced extreme injustices refuse to take this path, maintain their anger, and seek to dissent from the meta-narratives of justice and reconciliation? What if their stories do not fit? Are there possibilities of rebellion against the 'hegemonies' of the dominant transitional discourses and of reclaiming, publicly, 'disobedient' or 'contumacious' testimonies? Individuals might have the possibility to opt against participating in TJ initiatives; yet once they are participating it seems difficult not to succumb to the dominating discourse. For instance, testimonies of female survivors in South Africa and Peru reveal that their evidence about gender-based violence to truth commission hearings was taken up and spun by the commissioners who sought, inadvertently, to influence their framing of past and present along the lines of reconciliation (Garcia-Godos, 2008). Over the course of interviews, the way women referred to their experiences resembled more and more the discourse of the institutions. For some, silence seemed to be the only possibility to dissent from the seemingly appropriate way of dealing with the past (Motsemme, 2004; see also Zolkos in Chapter 9).

The field of transitional justice has incorporated two interconnected, yet potentially competing ideas of justice (Fraser, 1997; Fraser and Honneth, 2003; Franke, 2006). The first one points to *redistribution*, which connotes the re-organization of resources that can be both material (for example, post-conflict financial retributions or land claims) and symbolic. Here scholars have discussed the possibilities and limitations of the transitional justice framework to intervene in, and alleviate, the system of existing inequality, discrimination and dispossession through, inter alia, distribution of material reparations (Aguirre and Pietropaoli, 2008). The second idea of justice points to *recognition*, which includes acknowledgment of culpabilities and injuries; identification and categorization of victims, perpetrators, bystanders, and so on; and of the character of the acts of past violence and injustice. However, recognition in TJ extends beyond the categorization of past events to include the acknowledgment and assertion of current rights. As Rubio-Marín has noted with a view to reparations:

> they should be intended as acts of assertion of the rights themselves and thus, collectively speaking, as an exercise of creation (and not just validation) of the basis of legitimacy of a given political order that claims to be grounded in the respect for such rights and the recognition of its citizenry as equal rights holders. (Rubio-Marín, 2006: 25)

This is an aspect that carries the potential to contribute to more gender equality in a society.

Many efforts to render justice in times of transition have been highly 'medicalized' in their definition, for example in respect of their objectives of overcoming trauma and hurt; regaining dignity and self-esteem; rendering broken lives ('becoming whole again'); and/or finding personal closure. Set in the context of often divided societies, these objectives are promoted by slogans such as 'Revealing is Healing' in the case of the South African Truth and Reconciliation Commission, or 'The Truth Heals' as expressed on posters lobbying for the Rwandan Gacaca tribunals (Buckley-Zistel, 2005). There has been criticism that this approach pathologizes individuals as 'sick' victims in need of therapeutic assistance through TJ, or similar means such as trauma work, and so on, for both men and women. The goal is to turn them into healthy, functioning individuals and valuable members of a peaceful civil society (Pupavac, 2004: 383). This focus on the psychic life of the victims, and the rhetoric of 'harm' and 'hurt' that needs to be remedied, perpetuates a view of transitional society that revolves around a future-oriented restoration deeply transforming, and revitalizing, the community fabric.

And yet, medicalized language not only masks ethical and political decisions as 'technical necessities' (Pavlich, 2005: 35), but also defines what are the appropriate ways of *doing justice* for the past. Some critics have pointed out that by defining past violations and crimes (predominantly) in terms of the 'breakdown of pre-existing relationships between victims, offenders, and the community', these 'medicalized' discourses might inadvertently embrace the idea of the pre-conflict society as a 'coherent whole' and a 'relational equilibrium' (McLaughlin et al., 2003; Shriver, 2003: 25–44). This would undermine the possibility of more substantial social changes and gender justice post-conflict. As other critics have pointed out, in the transitional situation defined by the goals of communal repair, and by the restorative and reconciliatory impulse more generally, there is also a danger that those who suffered historical violence will be instrumentalized because of the high symbolic status of victimhood (Pavlich, 2005).

What is needed is a critical investigation into the ontological assumptions about the position of the 'victim' (as well as 'perpetrator', 'bystander', and so on) that are made within the present TJ frameworks regarding the outcome of this conceptualized transition. Otherwise, the social and political structures that affect the agency of these individuals remain unexamined, calling into question the direction and objectives of *transition* in TJ. This is particularly important since almost all violence that is subject to transitional justice occurs in the context of political confrontations through repression or violent conflict. That is, it has often been conditioned, if not provoked, by conflicts deeply embedded within social, political, and economic structures (Minow, 1998). What the therapeutic or legalist conceptions of TJ leave unchallenged are the structural conditions in which the individuals are placed. These structural conditions not only impacted on the emergence of violence in the first place, but also on what working through the past in light of TJ processes can actually achieve. This is, for instance, illustrated in the persecution of sexualized violence against women and men.[9] They fall prey to systematic attacks not as individuals, but because they represent specific positions within a society which the opponents seek to destroy. For women, this often equates with their roles as reproducers of a particular identity group, and as objects of 'possession' of their male family members who can be humiliated through the violation of spouses or daughters (Jacobsen et al., 2000: 2). For men, this leads to them being singled out as potential combatants and assumed carriers of the ethnic lineage, and their subsequent extermination, a practise for which the term gendercide has been coined (Warren, 1985). Given this social and political context of sexual and gender-based violence, there is a limit to what the persecution of individual acts can achieve (even though this may remain of significance to the men and women who were the targets of the acts).

Our introductory gendered analysis of what constitutes a crime for TJ frameworks, and of what is considered to be an appropriate way of rending justice for it, has suggested limits to the applicability of the TJ concept more generally. Revealing the contingent, as well as historically and culturally specific, character of the formation of gendered (and other) political subjects and subjectivities illustrates that systems of inclusion and exclusion are situated in space and time and can be understood both in terms of the global operations of power and of the local dynamics that determine how relevant norms are shaped, distributed and applied. In other words, what occurs with the social and ideological constructions of women and femininity, as well as of men and masculinity, in Transitional Justice is a process of drawing and re-drawing boundaries of *inside* and *outside* a community, demarcating those groups who have their rights considered and those who have not.

A gender perspective therefore unmasks and challenges the dualist thinking that has underpinned the formation of some of the central concepts of (international) politics such as inter alia national/international, private/public, or universal/particular. At an epistemic and academic level, this requires the re-evaluation of what has been conventionally defined as marginal or peripheral to the political domain, to questions of freedom and emancipation, and as an issue for political contestation. This calls for nothing short of 'a retheorization of the "political"', which also means 'problematization of sovereignty, of what it means for the self "to be in the world", how the self interacts with others, and how these complex relationships relate to the political problems of our time' (Jabri, 2004: 270).

In contrast to the assertion of the sovereign subject as *the* subject of international politics, the feminist ethics project (pursued by Jabri,

Hutchings, and others) works with the idea of a divided, multiple, and connected/relational self. Furthermore, critical gender analysis traces the processes whereby gendered subjectivity is constructed in social and political life, and how this subjectivity is formed and perpetuated though diverse systems of knowledge (Jabri in Hutchings et al., 2008: 166). It thus draws attention to the subjects at the margins of political communities – those that on the basis of gender, class, ethnicity, or other categories of social differentiation tend to be regarded as 'invisible' or 'silent', or unable to exert political participatory agency. Contributing to this is one of the objectives of this volume.

Structure of the book

We chose to call this volume 'Gender in Transitional Justice', with explicit reference to Ann Tickner's book 'Gender in International Relations' (Tickner, 1992). This was to highlight the fact that, although there is a paucity of gender analysis in the field, as well as a relative dearth of women as practitioners (although we do not equate one with the other), both the practice and the academic study of transitional justice is a thoroughly masculinized sphere of activity in which women's voices are considered 'inauthentic'... 'for it is in the way that we are taught to think about international politics [or transitional justice] that the attitudes... are shaped' (ibid.: 4).

In order to offer an alternative teaching, this volume is structured in four parts highlighting various aspects of gender in transitional justice. This begins with the first section on the correlation between retributive justice and gender justice, focusing on crime tribunals and their inclusion, as well as enforcement of, sexual and gender crimes. In the first chapter, Louise Chappell considers the role of the International Criminal Court (ICC) and the Rome Statute in helping to achieve a dual goal in the (gendered) transitional justice to address and account for past violence and injustice, and to open up new and peaceful possibilities of co-existence in the future. The conjunction of retributive and restorative elements has been integral to the formation of the Rome Statute and the ICC, which – in truly innovative ways – have built gender sensitivity into their structural and discursive logic. Chappell suggests that, so far, the ICC record in that domain has been rather miscellaneous and inconsistent. More specifically, while within the pursuits of retributive justice gender-related crimes and abuses have not been sufficiently or effectively prioritized by the ICC, within the restorative attempts of peace-building and community-building the ICC has had some recognizable successes in empowering the post-conflict gendered subjects.

Chappell's chapter offers a thorough presentation and analysis of both the ICC's functioning and activities, and of the secondary feminist engagement with this issue. What is equally important is that she indicates the problematic areas with the ICC practice, and poses key questions about the directions of its current and future development. At the level of juridical practice, it seems that the ICC has not lived up to the path-breaking legislation of the Rome Statute (an effect that had been exacerbated by the diffusion of the statute laws at the national levels). However, it would be a mistake to regard the ICC as a *failed project*. It still has possibilities for the provision of gendered transitional justice; especially if its future developments in that area will reflect the continuing support, pressure, and critique of invested agents, including numerous NGOs.

In Chapter 2, Fionnuala Ní Aoláin raises the question of under-enforcement in the context of gendering of transitional justice. Drawing on Lawrence Sanger's work on under-enforcement of constitutional norms, Ní Aoláin emphasizes that selective choices against upholding some norms in particular judicial settings result in a gap between *enforceability* (or validity) of a norm and its *enforcement*. Ní Aoláin also suggests that, in the context of transitional justice, this gap becomes particularly pronounced in cases that directly concern female populations.

The gendered under-enforcement is partly related to the *prima facie* exclusions of women from, or their under-representation in, peace agreements and treaties that initiate transitional justice processes. Next, there is a danger that the structures and hierarchies of the legal norms stipulated in these documents will either insufficiently recognize the specificity of the needs and priorities of women, or essentialize them. For instance, the under-representation of socio-economic and cultural concerns in peace accords and transitional agreements has been proven to affect women's situation in particularly acute ways. Finally, and more broadly, gendered under-enforcement in transitional contexts is also on account of the weakening of the societal ties and connections, and the precarious position of women during armed conflicts, and/or a result of non-democratic practices, political intimidation and repression, sexual violence, and so on. The gendered under-enforcement suggests that the idea of transitional justice should extend beyond processes of dealing with past human rights violations to include, inter alia, structural exclusions and entrenched inequalities.

Focusing on the work of the ECCC for the prosecution of crimes committed during the period of Democratic Kampuchea, in Chapter 3 Silke Studzinsky lists and analyses its challenges of dealing with sexual and gender-based crimes. In its attempt to transform Cambodia into an agrarian society, the Khmer Rouge undertook measures of radical social engineering that brought about displacement, persecution, widespread practicing of torture, famine, and mass killings in the period from 1975 until 1979. Studzinsky stresses in particular the Khmer Rouge goal to produce a 'gender-neutral' or 'gender-blind' society, where, inter alia, social and cultural expressions of 'femininity' were declared illegitimate and policed. In addition, there was a strictly enforced separation of males and females in public (and often private) spaces, which coincided with the practice of forced marriage. At the same time, the genocidal techniques employed by the Khmer Rouge included sexual crimes and violence against women, such as punitive genital mutilation, sexual assaults, sexual enslavement, and rape (of both females and males).

Studzinsky provides a thorough description of the structure and jurisdiction of the ECCC, as well as their critical gender analysis, and suggests that the ECCC has not been able to adequately address the gender-based crimes of the Khmer Rouge, especially sexual crimes, as crimes against humanity. Following the Rome Statute, the legal framework of the ECCC has regarded sexual crimes as synonymous to rape, thus unavoidably silencing the claims of sexual violence of any other character. In this context, one particular area in which the ECCC has been proven unable to criminalize the Khmer Rouge practices has been in the cases of forced marriage. In turn, force marriage has been regarded as related to *arranged marriage*, which is practiced in Cambodia. The legal framework of the ECCC has also required identification of the discriminatory intent for each crime, which has proven very difficult in the case of the sexual violence. In spite of some attempts to the contrary, the inadequate dealing of gender-oriented crimes of the Khmer Rouge regime by the ECCC within the contemporary domain of transitional justice means that it risks re-traumatizing its victims; marginalizing gendered subjects; and, potentially, negatively affecting the peace-building process.

Entitled *Transitional Justice and Social Change* the second part focuses on limits of the transformative potential of transitional justice in contributing to wider social transformation after violence. Chapter 4, by Romi Sigsworth and Nahla Valji, is based on the observation that sexual and gender-based violence against women does not begin with conflict or political instability and end with a transition to peace or democracy. Rather, violence often continues at levels similar to those experienced during the conflict. They argue that this violence is rooted in pre-conflict power relations and accelerated by the conflict, and that it leads to a reinforcement of women's subordination and their unequal role in the post-conflict society.

For Sigsworth and Valji the transitional justice mechanisms are limited by their gendered definitions of 'violation', 'political', and 'transition' and thus fail to respond to the challenge of political violence taking on a different form after the official ending of a conflict. In South Africa, which they use to illustrate their point, this primarily includes violence against women, both sexual and non-sexual, undermining the achievements of the end of apartheid. The authors refer to the construction of damaged, violent masculinities during apartheid, a culture of deeply rooted patriarchy, a perceived loss of masculine power, and feelings of vulnerability and insecurity as some of the causes for (the extreme level of) violence against women.

Crucially, in the context of South Africa and beyond, this violence impedes on the women's access to their rights as well as on their participation in broader development initiatives, their general productivity, mobilization capacity, and mobility within the country for fear of abuse. For the authors, this continued threat of insecurity to women, a substantial sections of the population, undermines the goals of transitional justice and leaves the most dominant structures of injustice in post-apartheid South Africa unchallenged. As a consequence, they advocate for the reconceptualization of transitional justice from the perspective of women's lived experiences and conclude with a number of suggestions as to how this can be encouraged, including a less punitive approach to sexual violence but one that understands both causes and consequences.

The starting point for Chapter 5, by Catherine O'Rourke, concerns the inadequacy of the legal frame for the conceptualization of the transitional justice field. This is, firstly, because the role of politics and the effects of political processes on this field have been significant. Scholars have pointed out possible or actual tensions between the legal and political approaches to transitional justice. Secondly, the legal frame of analysis does not permit a reflection on those societal consequences of transitional justice that are long-term and essentially *non-legal* in character. O'Rourke situates her analysis of gendered transitional justice in Chile and Colombia with that dual insight in view.

The chapter focuses on those cases that problematize gender-neutral conceptions of citizenship, including the women's social movements and politicization of motherhood in Pinochet's Chile (for example the establishment of the Mother Centres) which, during democratic transition and the operation of the Chilean National Truth and Reconciliation Commission (TRC), have been largely demobilized. O'Rourke undertakes a careful critical gender analysis of the 1991 Report of the TRC. In particular, she draws the readers' attention to the Report's focus on (and monetary entitlement of) those victims who, as result of physical violence, experienced loss of pregnancy. She problematizes the Report's recognition of the political subjectivity of selected women on the basis of (terminated) pregnancy. The language used in the Report suggests that fetal life be recognized as subject to torture.

O'Rourke then turns to another case, militarized citizens in Colombia, which demonstrates that, in some conflicts, violence permeates wide and diverse strata of society and becomes partly constitutive of gendered forms of identification (masculinity and femininity), which affect people's ordinary lives, and are not simply the 'state of war'. These are in turn highly consequential for both reparative and truth-telling institutions established in post-conflict Colombia. What O'Rourke's case analysis indicates is that the militarized and violent forms of masculinity that emerged in the wake of the conflict have in fact been reinscribed through transitional justice mechanisms, which have been premised on selective and gender-neutral conception of citizenship. If these post-conflict attempts to deliver justice to the victims of military conflicts are to be truly *transitional*, they must address, as O'Rourke concludes, 'disarming the hegemonic form of masculinity that privileges and sustains violence in the conduct of social relations', and not exclusively in the situation of war.

Part III contains two chapters on the potentials and limits of agency in transitional justice processes, and begins with Rirhandu Mageza-Barthel on women movements in post-genocide Rwanda. Against the backdrop of the highly gendered violence during the 1994 genocide, she analyses how, in the transition phase, women asserted their presence through interfering in the drafting of legislation to, first, prosecute sexualized violence committed in the course of the massacres, and, second, to change legislation about property and land inheritance. Central to her analysis is not punitive or restorative justice, but the lobbying of interest groups regarding legal reforms affecting transitional as well as gender justice. Importantly, particularly in relation to the chapter of Sigsworth and Valji on South Africa, her case illustrates a significant shift from women being passive victims (of genocide crimes) to becoming active agents in changing the socio-political and legal post-conflict landscape.

The foundation of this intervention, Mageza-Barthel argues, are the international gender frameworks that have emerged as a result of women's activism in the 1990s. Especially central here are the UN gender norms, the Convention on the Elimination of All Forms of Discrimination against Women (CEDAW), and the 1995 Beijing Declaration and its Platform for Action (PFA), since these provide women in general, and of Rwanda in particular, with a range of tools for political action. And yet, the domestification of the norms has proven difficult in the Rwandan context so that women resort instead to massive lobbying on various fronts to raise awareness about the gender-insensitive nature of the drafted bills. They have done so through pooling their resources under the guise of women's organizations and in cooperation with the parliamentarian women group as well as the Government of Rwanda and its Ministry of Gender, Family and Social Affairs.

As a result of the women's interventions, sexual crimes are now legally persecuted and categorized amongst the most serious genocide-related crimes, and the new Matrimonial Regimes Law treats men and women equally for the first time in the country's history. Moreover, Rwanda is today the only country in the world to surpass gender parity in parliament. Despite these achievements, though, Mageza-Barthel points out that women in Rwanda still suffer disproportionately from marginalization, poverty, and destitution related to their experience during the genocide and beyond, and that gender justice seems far off.

While most of the chapters of this volume focus on transitional justice and gender in terms of the relation between women and men, the contribution of Angelika von Wahl opens the scope by including the aspect of sexual identity. Her concern, in Chapter 7, is to illustrate how some groups of victims are excluded from making their claim to symbolic or material reparations after experiencing human rights abuses because of the feature of their identity for which they were being persecuted. In order to highlight the political, social, and legal challenges of gay men she compares the struggle for restitution of homosexual victims of Nazi crimes with those of Jewish victims of the Holocaust. Significantly, even though both crimes – albeit very different in scope and extent – occurred at the same time, in the same country, and were perpetuated by the same regime, they were treated differently. Based on a theoretical framework of social movement research, von Wahl analyses the respective struggles for symbolic and material compensation to demonstrate why and how the efforts of gay men failed while those of the Jewish community were successful. She concludes that, in contrast to Jews, after the end of National Socialism homosexual victims did not receive any political support by the new West German government, or by the Allies, by the courts, the media, or society. In fact, their criminalization continued under West German law until 1969, undermining any efforts to legally organize as claimants groups and to struggle for material or symbolic reparations. Gay men did not have the opportunity to share their experiences, to pool their resources, or to develop a collective identity rendering reparation claims impossible. The situation improved from the 1970s onwards leading eventually to the, by no means uncontested, construction of the Berlin Memorial for Gays Persecuted by the Nazis in 2008. The comparison of gay men with Jews thus reveals that not all victims of human rights abuses are allocated the same status, but that it depends on the availability of political opportunity structures to be identified as 'victims' and to have an impact on the transitional justice process.

In the final section of this volume we raise the question about the politics of justice and reconciliation from local to post-colonial perspectives. Firstly, in Chapter 8, Elisabeth Porter analyses inclusivity in gender in transitional justice solutions implemented in Timor-Leste in the wake of the 1974–99 conflict. Importantly, the Timorese Commission for Reception, Truth and Reconciliation (CAVR), established in 2001 under the auspices of the UN Transitional Administration in East Timor (UNTAET), has highlighted the gendered nature of the investigated crimes and abuses. In particular, the emphasis has been placed on integrating the gender-sensitive approach of the commission's work and the post-conflict and peace-building measures introduced in Timor. Porter recognizes that 'gendering' violence and suffering during the military occupation, whilst necessary, is also very complex and cannot be based on the dualistic opposition of 'men' and 'women'. At the same time, there is a suggested connection between the forms of aggression and use of force during the conflict and some of the deeply embedded and socially sanctioned models of masculine behaviour of 'warriors' or 'protectors'.

Porter describes the UNTAET initiative to integrate gender perspectives within its transitional justice approach, including a unit called Gendered Affairs (though of nominal value due to underfunding), and the implementation of training programmes for women aimed at increasing their political engagement. Within its truth investigations and re-integrative and victim-focused activities, CAVR adopted a deliberately gendered approach, which Porter documents and analyses in detail. In particular, she points to three significant areas in CAVR's functioning and findings: the link between gender-based violence and sexual crime; the carefully balanced proportion (and equal validation) of male and female testimonies; and the deliberate practice of 'careful listening' to gendered voices of the CAVR members. As Porter convincingly demonstrates, CAVR's gendered approach to transitional justice has been a significant attempt at constructing a more nuanced and sensitive engagement with socio-political and socio-psychological complexities of the victimization of women and men in the conflict (even if its practical consequences have remained somewhat opaque). Making a case for a broad conception of justice within the transitional frameworks, Porter concludes that while CAVR has succeeded at gender *inclusion*, the *effectiveness* of its approach has been limited.

Following this, in Chapter 9, Zolkos examines the case of the 1990s trials in Germany of women from the former Federal Republic of Germany (FRG) who were accused of espionage for the East German Stasi. Elaborate strategies of sexual blackmail and/or seduction were developed by Stasi agents to acquire the cooperation of women working for the West German state administration or foreign embassies in Bonn. Zolkos develops a critique of the normative public discourse of the trials, drawing on critical theoretical approaches from Foucault and Butler. She examines the strategies of the transitional German state of appropriating and working through the meanings of female body and intimate life as an element of post-authoritarian justice. The suggestion is that the matrix of seduction / espionage into which the lives of these women were discursively inscribed meant that, rather than being excluded from the process of reunification and reconciliation, the female body had became central to the process of justice. The female body was politically emblematic in the process of punitive and redemptive re-signification insofar as its 'contamination', 'abjection', and 'betrayal' could be re-figured within the emerging political community. Zolkos reflects critically on the impulse of making the intimate life and gendered body the crux of justice and reconciliation, and explores both the problematic implications of reducing complex subjectivities to the standpoint of the 'victim', and the violent potentialities that are lurking in the politics of transitional justice.

Last but not least, in Chapter 10, Nikita Dhawan invites us to take a critical look at the theory and practice of transitional justice from a post-colonial, feminist perspective. In her chapter, she offers a critical engagement with Western notions such as justice and equality by asking to what extent they are enabling and disenfranchising particular communities, and if and how they serve to re-inscribe hegemonic power relations between dispersers and receivers of 'justice'. Regarding gender-based violence, as central to this volume, this is most poignantly summarised by Gayatri Spivak's remark about white men saving brown women, the politics of which are also explored. For Dhawan, prevailing norms of recognition determine what counts as just or unjust in transitional justice discourses, defining who is listened to and who has the power to listen. In order to deconstruct this condition, she calls for a genealogical analysis to assess how recognition is historically constructed and articulated, so that existing norms can be rendered more inclusive as well as to enable new norms to emerge.

Beginning with a historical contextualisation of law and frames of justice, she examines how a profoundly Western understanding of justice in the field of transitional justice can turn into a travelling norm and absorb ascriptions beyond its remit, in particular from those at the receiving end of justice. Against this backdrop, she contemplates how to address issues of justice without being trapped by either universalism or relativism. She closes with a Derridian reading of justice as a utopian concept which is perpetually deferred without ever achieving closure. This, she argues, requires the permanent vigilance of those who disperse transitional justice.

In this volume, only some key connectional and empirical issues pertaining to gender and transitional justice are covered. With such interest in the topic, and the numbers of publications increasing, the debate will be alive for some time, and remain intriguing by the various facets it might take. Important lacuna are, as identified in the chapter by Sigsworth and Valji, the analysis of the correlation between hegemonic masculinities and gender-based violence, as well as more research on men as victims of sexual and gender-based violence and agents in TJ processes in general. Moreover, the gaze of researchers tends to focus on distant abuses and modes of transitional justice, whilst ignoring what is happening in their own vicinities. It is hoped, therefore, that this volume will stimulate further research and discussion on gender in transitional justice.

Notes

Susanne Buckley-Zistel would like to thank Steffen Hamborg for his invaluable assistance in compiling this volume.

1. For an extensive list of aims see Crocker (1998: 496).
2. For examples see Cohen (2001); de Greiff (2006); Edkins (2003); Rombouts (2002); Vandeginste (2003).

3. However, despite these legal achievements the prosecution of sexualized violence against women remains exceptional (see Ní Aoláin in this volume) while male victims-survivors are frequently excluded from programmes and projects. This aspect is painfully illustrated in a documentary released by the Uganda-based research institute Refugee Law Project entitled 'Gender against Men' which inter alia portrays an man who had experienced sexual violence, but when I tried to report it to a health agency they were only interested in the abuse of his daughter.
4. Young female combatants comprised about 30–40 per cent of all the fighting forces in the country (Sherif, 2008).
5. One exception is the Timorese Commission for Reception, Truth and Reconciliation in which sexual violence as well as the abuse of socio-economic rights have been considered (see Porter in this volume). Similarly, the Moroccan truth commission emphasized that women had been collectively suffering from structural violence.
6. This point is powerfully illustrated in the chapter by Romy Sigsworth and Nahla Valji in this volume.
7. See also Sigsworth and Valji illustrate this topic in Chapter 4 on South Africa.
8. As the case of the Moroccan Equity and Reconciliation Commission illustrates, these rights might be addressed by reparations recommended in the final report of a truth commission.
9. See Graham, 2006.

References

D. Aguirre and I. Pietropaoli (2008) 'Gender Equality, Development and Transitional Justice: The Case of Nepal', *International Journal of Transitional Justice*, Vol. 2 No. 3, 356–77.

K. Askin (2003) 'The Quest for Post-Conflict Gender Justice', *Columbia Journal of Transitional Law*, Vol. 41 No. 3, 509–21.

M. Bastick (2008) *Integrating Gender in Post-Conflict Security Sector Reform* (Geneva: DCAF Publications).

C. Bell (2009) 'The "New Law" of Transitional Justice' in K. Ambos, J. Large and M. Wierda (eds.) *Building a Future on Peace and Justice: Studies on Transitional Justice, Peace and Development: The Nuremberg Declaration on Peace and Justice* (Berlin and Heidelberg: Springer-Verlag), pp. 105–26.

C. Bell and C. O'Rourke (2007) 'Does Feminism Need a Theory of Transitional Justice? An Introductory Essay', *International Journal of Transitional Justice*, Vol. 1 No. 1, 23–44.

K. Boon (2001) 'Rape and Forced Pregnancy under the ICC Statute: Human Dignity, Autonomy, and Consent', *Columbia Human Rights Review*, Vol. 32, 625–75.

R. Buchanan and R. Johnson (2005) 'The "Unforgiven" Sources of International Law: Nation-Building, Violence, and Gender in the West(ern)' in D. Buss and A. Manji (eds) *International Law: Modern Feminist Approaches* (Oxford: Hart Publishing), pp. 135–58.

S. Buckley-Zistel (2011) 'Narration und Transition Vom Umgang mit der Vergangenheit in Wahrheitskommissionen' in S. Ferhadbegović and B. Weiffen (eds) *Bürgerkriege erzählen* (Konstanz: University of Konstanz Press), 289-302.

S. Buckley-Zistel (2005) '"The Truth Heals?" Gacaca Jurisdictions and the Consolidation of Peace in Rwanda', *Die Friedens-Warte*, Vol. 80 Nos. 1–2, 113–29.

C. Bunch (2005) 'Peace, Human Rights and Women's Peace Activism: Feminist Readings' in R. Coomaraswamy and D. Fonseka (eds) *Peace Work: Women, Armed Conflict and Negotiation* (New Delhi: Women Unlimited).

N. Cahn (2005) 'Beyond Retribution and Impunity: Responding to War Crimes of Sexual Violence', *Stanford Journal of Civil Rights & Civil Liberties*, Vol. 1 No. 1, 217.

K. Campbell (2007) 'The Gender of Transitional Justice: Law, Sexual Violence and the International Criminal Tribunal for the Former Yugoslavia', *International Journal of Transitional Justice*, Vol. 1 No. 3, 411–32.

K. Campbell (2004) 'The Trauma of Justice: Sexual Violence, Crimes Against Humanity and the International Criminal Tribunal for the Former Yugoslavia', *Social and Legal Studies*, Vol. 13 No. 3, 329–50.

H. Charlesworth and C. Chinkin (2000) *The Boundaries of International Law: a Feminist Analysis* (Manchester: Manchester University Press).

C. Chinkin (2003) 'Gender, Human Rights and Peace Agreements', *Ohio State Journal of Dispute Resolution*, Vol. 18 No. 3, 867–86.

S. Cohen (2001) *States of Denial: Knowing about Atrocities and Suffering* (Cambridge: Polity Press).

R. Copelon (1995) 'Women and War Crimes', *St. John's Law Review*, Vol. 69, 61–8.

D. A. Crocker (1998) 'Transitional Justice and International Civil Society: Toward a Normative Framework', *Constellations*, Vol. 5 No. 4, 492–517.

E. Dauphine (2008) 'War Crimes and the Ruin of Law', *Millennium – Journal of International Studies*, Vol. 37 No. 1, 49–67.

DCAF/INSTRAW/ODIHR (2008), Security Sector Reform and Gender, Practice Note 1, available at http://www.osce.org/publications/odihr/2008/02/29669_1030_en.pdf (accessed 17 December 2010).

M. B. Dembour and E. Haslam (2004) 'Silencing Hearings? Victim-Witnesses at War Crimes Trials', *European Journal of International Law*, Vol. 15 No. 1, 151–77.

B. Dougherty (2004) 'Searching for Answers: Sierra Leone's Truth & Reconciliation Commission African Studies Quarterly', Vol. 8 No. 1, 39–65.

J. Edkins (2003) *Trauma and the Memory of Politics* (Cambridge: Cambridge University Press).

K. Engle (2005) 'Feminism and its (Dis)contents: Criminalizing Wartime Rape in Bosnia and Herzegovina', *American Journal of International Law*, Vol. 99, 778–816.

T. Forsberg (2001) 'The Philosophy and Practice of Dealing with the Past: Some Conceptual and Normative Issues' in N. Biggar (ed.) *Burying the Past: Making Peace and Doing Justice after Civil Conflict* (Washington: Georgetown University Press), pp. 57–72.

K. M. Franke (2006) 'Gendered Subject of Transitional Justice', *Columbia Journal of Gender and Law*, Vol. 15, 813–28.

N. Fraser (1997) *Justice Interruptus: Critical Reflections on the 'Postsocialist' Condition* (London: Routledge).

N. Fraser and A. Honneth (2003) *Redistribution or Recognition?: A Political-Philosophical Exchange* (London: Verso).

J. Garcia-Godos (2008) 'Victim Reparations in the Peruvian Truth Commission and the Challenges to Historical Interpretation', *International Journal of Transitional Justice*, Vol. 2 No. 1, 63–82.

R. Graham (2006) 'Male Rape and the Careful Construction of the Male Victim', *Social and Legal Studies*, Vol. 15 No. 2, 187–208.

P. de Greiff (ed.) (2006) *The Handbook of Reparations* (Oxford: Oxford University Press).

B. Hamber (2007) 'Masculinity and Transitional Justice: An Exploratory Essay', *International Journal of Transitional Justice*, Vol. 1, 375–90.

L. Hansen (2001) 'Gender, Nation, Rape: Bosnia and the Construction of Security', *International Feminist Journal of Politics*, Vol. 3.1, 55–75.

P. Hazan (2007) 'Das neue Mantra der Gerechtigkeit. Vom beschränkten Erfolg international verordneter Vergangenheitsbewältigung', *Der Überblick*, No. 1–2, 10–22.

K. Hutchings, M Zalewski, A. Tickner, C. Sylvester, M. Light, V. Jabri and F. Halliday (2008) 'Roundtable Discussion: Reflections on the Past, Prospects for the Future in Gender and International Relations', *Millennium – Journal of International Studies*, Vol. 37 No. 1, 153–79.

V. Jabri (2004) 'Feminist Ethics and Hegemonic Global Politics', *Alternatives, Global, Local, Political*, Vol. 29 No. 3, 265–84.

R. Jacobsen, S. Jacobs and S. Marchbank (2000) 'Introduction' in ibid. (eds.) *State of Conflict. Gender, Violence and Resistance* (London: Zed Books), pp. 1–24.

M. S. Kelsall and S. Stepakoff (2007) '"When We Wanted to Talk About Rape": Silencing Sexual Violence at the Special Court for Sierra Leone', *International Journal of Transitional Justice*, Vol. 1, 355–74.

P. Landesman (2002) 'A Woman's Work', *The New York Times*, 15 September 2002, available at http://www.jendajournal.com/vol2.1/landesman.pdf (accessed 20 October 2010).

B. A. Leebaw (2008) 'The Irreconcilable Goals of Transitional Justice', *Human Rights Quarterly*, Vol. 30.1, 95–118.

E. McLaughlin, R. Fergusson, G. Hughes and L. Westmarland (eds.) (2003) *Restorative Justice. Critical Issues* (London: SAGE Publications).

J. Mertus (2004) 'Shouting from the Bottom of a Well: the Impact of International Trials for Wartime Rape on Women's Agency', *International Feminist Journal of Politics*, Vol. 6, 110–29.

C. N. van der Merwe and P. Gobodo-Madikizela (2007) *Narrating Our Healing. Perspectives on Working Through Trauma* (Newcastle: Cambridge Scholars Press).

M. Minow (1998) *Between Vengeance and Forgiveness: Facing History after Genocide and Mass Violence* (Boston: Beacon Press).

N. Motsemme (2004). 'The Mute always Speak: On Women's Silence at the Truth and Reconciliation Commission', *Current Sociology*, Vol. 52 No. 5, 909–32.

R. Nagy (2008) 'Transitional Justice as Global Project: Critical Reflections', *Third World Quarterly*, Vol. 29 No. 2, 275–89.

F. Ní Aoláin (2009) 'Women, Security, and the Patriarchy of Internationalized Transitional Justice', *Human Rights Quarterly*, Vol. 31, 1055–85.

F. Ní Aoláin (2006) 'Political Violence and Gender During Times of Transition', *Columbia Journal of Gender and Law*, Vol. 15, 829–49.

F. Ní Aoláin and E. Rooney (2007) 'Underenforcement and Intersectionality: Gendered Aspects of Transition for Women', *International Journal of Transitional Justice*, Vol. 1 No. 3, 338–54.

OECD-Development Assistance Committee (2009): *OECD DAC Handbook on Security System Reform – Integrating Gender Awareness and Equality* (Paris: OECD).

B. Oomen (2005) 'Donor-Driven Justice and its Discontents: The Case of Rwanda', *Development and Change*, Vol. 36 No. 5, 887–910.

P. Oosterhoff, P. Zwanikken and E. Ketting (2004) 'Sexual Torture of Men in Croatia and Other Conflict Situations: An Open Secret', *Reproductive Health Matters*, Vol. 12 No. 23, 68–77.

V. Oosterveld (2005) 'The Definition of "Gender" in the Rome Statute of the International Criminal Court: A Step Backwards?', *Harvard Human Rights Journal*, Vol. 18, 55–84.

G. Pavlich (2005) *Governing Paradoxes of Restorative Justice* (London: Glasshouse Press).

V. Pupavac (2004) 'International Therapeutic Peace and Justice in Bosnia', *Social and Legal Studies*, Vol. 13 No. 3, 377–402.

H. Rombouts (2002) 'Importance and Difficulties of Victim-Based Research in Post-Conflict Societies', *European Journal of Crime, Criminal Law and Criminal Justice*, Vol. 10 No. 2–3, 216–32.

F. C. Ross (2003) *Bearing Witness: Women and the Truth and Reconciliation Commission in South Africa* (London: Pluto Press).

E. Rosser (2007) 'Depoliticised Speech and Sexed Visibility: Women, Gender and Sexual Violence in the 1999 Guatemalan Comisión para el Esclarecimiento Histórico Report', *International Journal of Transitional Justice*, Vol. 1, 391–410.

R. Rubio-Marín (2006) 'The Gender of Reparations: Setting the Agenda' in ibid. (ed.) *What happened to the Women? Gender and Reparations for Human Rights Violations* (New York: Social Science Research Council).

R. Seifert (1996) 'The Second Front: The Logic of Sexual Violence in Wars', *Women's Studies International Forum*, Vol. 19, 35–43.

R. Shaw (2005) *Rethinking Truth and Reconciliation: Lessons from Sierra Leone* (Washington DC: United States Institute of Peace).

A. Sherif (2008) 'Reintegration of Female War-affected and Ex-combatants in Liberia', *Conflict Trends*, Vol. 3, 26–33, available at http://www.crea-africa.org/mediaresources/files/Documentos/DDHH/Reintegraci%C3%B3n%20mujeres%20Liberia.pdf (accessed 7 December 2010).

D. W. Shriver (2003) 'Where and When in Political Life is Justice Served by Forgiveness', in N. Biggar (ed.) *Burying the past: making peace and doing justice after civil conflict* (Washington: Georgetown University Press), pp. 25–44.

S. Sivakumaran (2007) 'Sexual Violence against Men in Armed Conflict', *European Journal of International Law*, Vol. 18 No. 2, 253–76.

R. G. Teitel (2003) 'Transitional Justice Genealogy', *Harvard Human Rights Journal*, Vol. 69 No. 16, 69–94.

J. A. Tickner (2005) 'What Is Your Research Program? Some Feminist Answers to International Relations Methodological Questions', *International Studies Quarterly*, Vol. 49, 1–21.

J. A. Tickner (1992) *Gender in International Relations: feminists perspectives on achieving global security* (New York: Columbia University Press).

A. E. Tiemessen (2004) 'After Arusha: Gacaca Justice in Post-Genocide Rwanda', *African Studies Quarterly*, Vol. 8 No. 1, 57–73.

M. Turshen, S. Meintjes and A. Pillay (2001) 'There Is No Aftermath for Women' in S. Meintjes, M. Turshen and A. Pillay (eds) *The Aftermath: Women in Postconflict Transformation* (London: Zed Books).

N. Valji (2009) 'Gender Justice and Reconciliation' in K. Ambos, J. Large and M. Wierda (eds.) *Building a Future on Peace and Justice: Studies on Transitional Justice, Peace and Development The Nuremberg Declaration on Peace and Justice* (Berlin and Heidelberg: Springer-Verlag), pp. 217–36.

N. Valji (2007) 'Gender Justice and Reconciliation', *Dialogue on Globalization*, No. 35 / November 2007 (Berlin: Friedrich-Ebert-Stiftung).

N. Valji (2006) *Truth Commissions and Gender: Principles, Policies and Procedures* (New York: ICTJ).

S. Vandeginste (2003) 'Reparation' in D. Bloomfield, T. Barnes and L. Huyse (eds) *Reconciliation After Violent Conflict: A Handbook* (Stockholm: International Institute for Democracy and Electoral Assistance), pp. 145–62.

M. A. Warren (1985) *Gendercide: The Implications of Sex Selection* (Lanham: Rowman & Littlefield Publishers).

S. L. Wells (2005) 'Gender, Sexual Violence and Prospects for Justice at the Gacaca Courts in Rwanda', *Southern California Review of Law and Women's Studies*, Vol. 14, 167–96.

M. Wetherell and N. Edley (1999) 'Negotiating Hegemonic Masculinity: Imaginary Positions and Psycho-discursive Practices', *Feminism & Psychology*, Vol. 9 No. 3, 335–56.

Part I

Retributive Justice and Gender Justice

1

The Role of the ICC in Transitional Gender Justice: Capacity and Limitations

Louise Chappell

According to feminist legal scholar, Katherine Franke, the main objective of transitional justice is to 'honor the injuries and crimes of the past while creating the possibilities for new ways of being the future' (Franke, 2006: 823). The International Criminal Court (ICC), and the Rome Statute which underlies it, has an important role to play in this process. By combining elements of both a traditional, retrospective retributive justice approach alongside forward-looking restorative measures, it attempts to remove the 'impunity gap', which has existed under domestic and international law for the perpetrators of the most egregious crimes at the same time as offering victims/survivors of war torn communities new avenues for rebuilding their lives.

The retributive and restorative aspects of the International Criminal Court stand to provide an important new venue, especially for victims/survivors of gender-based violence. One of the most innovative features of the Rome Statute, upon which the ICC is built, is its sophisticated articulation of those crimes experienced by women in times of war and conflict, and its provision of the most comprehensive recognition of those crimes as war crimes and crimes against humanity. How well has the promise of the ICC system, in its initial phase, to advance gender justice been matched by the reality? What do the early outcomes of the Court's practice suggest about the role it might play in future in advancing retributive and restorative justice for women victims of sexual violence in transitional contexts? This chapter argues that ICC has produced mixed outcomes in these areas. In terms of the retributive aspect, the Court has been slow to prosecute gender-based crimes while states have been reluctant to implement the Rome Statute including its gender elements. More promising has been the Court's efforts in capacity building in conflict and post-conflict situations. Both the Court itself, and the extensive civil society network surrounding it, have made an important contribution to reconstructive efforts within transitional justice contexts, including with victims/survivors of gender-based crimes.

This chapter commences with an outline of the features of the ICC as they relate to transitional justice, and highlights some of the challenges confronting the Court in advancing these features over its first eight years of operation. It then turns to the question of gender and transitional justice, and considers the potential of the Court to advance gender justice in post-conflict settings. It analyses the ICC's treatment of gender-based crimes in its initial prosecutorial actions and considers the challenges of implementing the Rome Statute, including its gender articles, at the domestic level. Finally, it assesses the Court's involvement in restorative justice strategies and how these might impact gender equality in post-conflict settings.

The ICC and transitional justice

The ICC is a new and a unique international legal institution. Its uniqueness has a number of dimensions. While its unique gender aspects will be discussed in detail below, it is important here to look at its political dimension. The ICC operates in the context of an international relations system, where the norm of state sovereignty takes precedence. This reality constrains the Court in a number of respects. The Court's operations are limited by the support it receives from the international community in general and states parties in particular. It is as strong, or as weak, as states enable it to be. The Court is a body, and the Rome Statute is an instrument, built on political consensus and diplomatic agreement. As Schiff notes, the Court is 'an amalgam of normative commitments, legal understandings, political interests, diplomatic bargains, and organization dynamics' (Schiff, 2008: 3). As a creature of politics, it is limited in a number of respects including its jurisdiction both concerning the nature of the crimes over which it can adjudicate,[1] and its capacity to intervene in the affairs of states.[2] Aside from Security Council referrals, the ICC can only intervene in a state when it is 'unable or unwilling' to address a crime falling under its jurisdiction. Furthermore, without access to an international enforcement agency, the Court depends on states parties to co-operate to surrender those it has indicted, or for the accused to hand themselves over to the ICC (which has occurred on one occasion to date). The ICC has a restricted budget; one which relies entirely on the voluntary contributions of member states. Financial constraints present a stark reality for the ICC in terms of the number of trials it can run at any one time, and its ability to provide protection for witnesses and intermediaries in conflict situations.

Another interesting dimension of the ICC is that it merges 'old' and 'new' justice norms, practices, and processes (Schiff, 2008). These two faces of the Court mean that it is best to conceive it as operating as a system, rather than as a single legal entity. Most of the attention on the ICC to date has been on its role in bringing to trial perpetrators of war crimes, crimes against humanity, and genocide at The Hague. However, for the reasons noted above, it is unable to try every perpetrator of the crimes under its jurisdiction. The ICC will need, to use Franke's terms, to 'settle for a minority of cases that can be used to establish important precedent, identify important kingpins or masterminds of the violence, or, in many cases, whomever they can get their hands on' (Franke, 2006: 821). Restrictions on its capacity to conduct trials, and the 'complementarity compromise' struck during the 1998 Rome Conference to establish the ICC, mean that the ICC is equally interested in ensuring that state parties implement domestic legislation to bring their countries in line with the Rome Statute, and maintain judicial systems through which perpetrators of these crimes can be prosecuted. The principle of complementarity means the ICC can only operate as a Court of last resort, while state parties to the Rome Statute become the primary venue for prosecuting war crimes and crimes against humanity. Furthermore, through its outreach activities, the ICC seeks to foster an understanding of the Court, a respect for the rule of law, and training in and support for international legal norms. Together, the Court's work in The Hague, its complementarity principles, and outreach activities combine to create the ICC *system*.

Each of these features of the ICC system is directly relevant to states in transition. In its retributive justice mode, the ICC, like the International Criminal Tribunals for Rwanda (ICTR) and for the former Yugoslavia (ICTY) which preceded it, offers an avenue through which victims/survivors in transitional contexts can pursue individual perpetrators of crimes. It does this first, and foremost, through international prosecutions at The Hague. For citizens in ICC member states without a functioning legal system, or one riddled with corruption, the Court provides an important site for independent legal hearings. Through trials at The Hague, the Court aims to provide the highest standard of legal protection, both in terms of the codification of crimes found in the Rome

Statute, and the rights of accused and victims appearing before the Court; standards that are often lacking in domestic settings, especially those emerging from conflict. Civil society groups maintain pressure on the Court to be accountable for its actions (or inactions, as the case may be); something not always possible in transitional contexts (see for example Amnesty International, 2009; Human Rights Watch, 2009).

The second way in which the ICC can contribute to advancing retributive justice in transitional contexts is through prosecutions under the codes of the Rome Statute at the local level. Through its 'complementarity' provisions (Articles 1,17–20) – which oblige state parties to introduce implementing legislation to bring local legal codes into alignment with the Rome Statute – the Statute seeks to diffuse the highest standards of international law to domestic jurisdictions (Warbrick and McGoldrick, 2001; Robinson, 2008). In introducing such a provision, the international community recognized that there are advantages in holding trials in the state where an alleged crime was committed, not least because, as Broomhall notes, 'the proceedings have the greatest legitimacy and the greatest impact in the eyes of the society most immediately interested in them' (2003: 84). By introducing the standards of international law, the Rome Statute seeks to challenge common problems in transitional contexts, including the hang-over of power relations from a previous regime, where police and judicial systems are inherited and judicial capacity is limited (Schiff, 2008). It is envisaged that the diffusion of the Rome Statute to the local level, and the role played by the ICC in determining whether a state is capable of carrying out a fair trial, and that proceedings are consistent with principles of due process, will combine to reinforce higher standards of justice at the local level than would otherwise occur (Ellis, 2008).

As critics have long pointed out, retributive justice alone cannot answer all transitional justice questions (see for example Aukerman, 2002). Those framing the Rome Statute were alert to the limitations of traditional justice approaches, demonstrated so clearly in the criticisms of the ICTY and ICTR both of which initially had very poor relations within the relevant transitional countries, and made certain that the ICC would also operate with restorative justice measures in mind (see Schiff, 2008: 59–60). Some of these measures relate to the trial proceedings, especially expanding access to the Court for victims, which is an important feature of restorative justice models. For instance, the Statute includes provisions allowing victims to 'present their views and concerns at all stages of the proceedings' (ICC, 2007); a measure which is uncommon in traditional trial proceedings. Furthermore, strict provisions are in place under Article 68 for victim protection, including for victims of sexually based crimes, both in the courtroom and on the ground. Importantly, under Article 75, there is also a redistributive element to the victim provisions, enabling them to seek 'restitution, compensation and rehabilitation' for crimes committed under the Statute. As will be discussed further below, these reparations have the potential to make an important contribution to rebuilding efforts in post-conflict contexts, including for women who have been victims of gender-based violence.

The Rome Statute provides a clear role for the Registry to conduct outreach activities. It is responsible for ensuring that the Court is 'public and transparent with respect to the populations concerned by the crimes being prosecuted' (Schabas, 2007: 360). Through its outreach strategy, the Court has 'put in place mechanisms to ensure that affected communities can understand and follow the Court through the different phases of its activities' (ICC, 2006: 3). The objectives of these are to:

- provide accurate and comprehensive information to affected communities regarding the Court's role and activities
- promote greater understanding of the Court's role during the various stages of proceedings with a view to increasing support among the population for their conduct
- foster greater participation of local communities in the activities of the Court
- respond to the concerns and expectations expressed in general by affected communities and by particular groups within these communities
- counter misinformation
- promote access to and understanding of judicial proceedings among affected communities.

(ICC, 2006: 5)

The ICC's outreach activities are currently focused on the four countries where the Court is undertaking investigations, and focuses on engagement with victims, non-government organizations, the legal community, academics, and local media amongst others.

The attempt to blend old and new justice norms and practices in the Rome Statute is an acknowledgment of developments in approaches to justice in transitional contexts, especially in the former Yugoslavia and Rwanda. However, the blending of the two approaches is far from seamless, with evident tensions being played out between the two as the

ICC develops. Critics have emerged on both sides of the retributive/restorative dichotomy. Some argue that the international law principles underpinning the ICC are overly focused on 'the hegemonic values of Western punitive criminal justice, including a focus primarily on retribution and deterrence' (Lipscomb, 2006: 194–5). Such critics argue that the Court's focus on retributive justice does nothing to heal the deep wounds of conflict on the ground and, indeed, that the slow pace of international law and its inability to deal directly with the large numbers of perpetrators and victims can exacerbate them. Their point about the scope and pace of international law is certainly borne out in practice. In the first seven years of operation, the ICC had issued just 13 arrest warrants (with another under review). At the time of writing, the Court is yet to hand down one sentence. At least two accused, Germain Katanga and Mathieu Ngudjolo Chui, from the Democratic Republic of Congo (DRC) have been held in detention at The Hague for over four years awaiting the start of their trial. A second area of contention concerns the fact that, in its establishment phase, the ICC is seen to be operating on a double standard. It appears willing to investigate failed or transitional African nation states (the first four investigations are in the DRC, Uganda and Sudan [Darfur]), but not crimes committed by Western forces in Iraq or Afghanistan, or by Israel in Palestine (BBC World News, 2008).

At the base of much of this criticism is a deep divide over whether in conflict and post-conflict situations it is best to privilege peace or justice. Those who advance the former (see for instance Flint and De Waal, 2009; Bauman, 2008) argue that the focus on bringing to trial political leaders, such the recent indictment of Sudanese President Al-Bashir, severely disrupts delicate peace negotiations, and leaves those most vulnerable to human rights abuses by such regimes in even more peril. ICC defenders, on the other hand, refuse to concede arguments emphasizing peace over justice. Their response is that there can be 'no peace without justice'; it is only through the application of the rule of law, which is by its nature a drawn-out process, that a lasting peace can be achieved. On the Sudanese case specifically, the arguments of Al-Bashir and others for the need to 'put peace first', have been rejected by civil society groups as a political ploy used mostly by Al-Bashir supporters to avoid international scrutiny, including by the ICC (see FIDH, 2009: 15–16).

It is clear that the ICC is an imperfect institution operating within the confines of the current international relations system and attempting to balance two distinct approaches to justice. Despite its limitations, the Court and the Rome Statute do potentially provide a new arena through which to pursue justice for the most serious criminal acts, including, as we shall see, in the area of gender justice.

The ICC and transitional gender justice

Before looking at the gender justice elements of the ICC, it is necessary to locate these developments within the broader debates which are the focus of this book. This includes the ability of transitional justice mechanisms to take into account the reality of women's lives and the extent to which deeply entrenched stereotypes and prejudices about men's and women's roles in conflict and post-conflict environments are either maintained and reinforced, or potentially challenged, by transitional justice strategies. In particular, it is important to assess the extent to which international law, as it relates to transitional justice, is gendered.

There has been extensive debate between feminist legal scholars about how international law, and especially its retributive face, can contribute (or not) to advancing gender justice in transitional settings. There is agreement amongst these commentators that, traditionally, international law has incorporated women primarily as victims of armed conflict and as mothers, but never as independent actors. Women have not been entitled to the 'mainstream' protection afforded to men in similar circumstances, nor has the law taken into account their unique and varied experiences of, and participation in, armed conflict.

Moreover, the law has treated crimes commonly experienced by women, especially those of a sexually violent nature, as lesser crimes to those usually suffered by men. For instance, traditionally, international laws on rape have been treated as a crime of honour, not a grave breach of law; they have not been about protecting individual women from an act of violence, but about protecting men from insults inflicted on dependent women by other men (see Gardam and Jarvis, 2001).

A divide emerges in the literature about how to address the way international law has addressed and reinforced gender differences. One on side are those who strongly insist that gender-based crimes are equal in gravity to other war crimes and crimes against humanity, and that perpetrators of these crimes should be tried under international norms reflecting this fact (see for instance Copelon, 2000). Reiterating such a view, Condon argues:

> If a state fails to prosecute rapes committed in [conflict/post-conflict] circumstances either due to an ill working judicial system, lack of

> political will, or inherent legal bias against women, the international community has a duty, in addition to a practical interest in furthering deterrence, to prosecute and punish the rapist.

Others see little value in using international law in general, and international prosecutorial trials in particular, as a way to secure gender equality in post-conflict situations. Much of this critique centres on the argument that retributive trials compound the suffering of those who have experienced gender-based violence, and do little to advance gender equality in transitional contexts (for a discussion see Franke, 2006; Mertus, 2004). Looking at the ICTY and ICTR process, Franke makes the point that the women victims of sexual violence who testified before the tribunals did not enjoy a sense of justice for themselves. In her view, the 'translation of human suffering into the language of law and rights will always satisfy the interests of legal authorities more than those who are called to narrate their pain' (Franke, 2006: 821), a point strongly supported by Julie Mertus (2004).

Leading feminist legal scholars, Charlesworth and Chinkin (2000: 334) have other concerns about the application of international law, and the ICC in particular. Firstly, the use of international tribunals and the ICC to address the effects of conflict ignores the fact that violence against women in situations of armed conflict and in times of peace is 'part of the same spectrum of behaviour'. By focusing on violence in times of conflict, developments under international law do little to challenge the 'acceptability of violence and ... the private order of the domination of women' at other times. Second, in their view, international criminal law continues to employ a very limited understanding of women by emphasizing their sexual and reproductive identities. The emphasis on sexual violence, including acts of forced pregnancy, keeps women in the role of 'other'; identified only through their relationship with men and children. Finally, the social burden that falls on women in armed conflict remains unacknowledged, and women continue to be cast as passive victims rather than as survivors or agents of change. Gardam and Jarvis agree that recent advances do little to alter the negative social, economic, and health-related impact of armed conflict on women's experiences (2001: 229).

Despite the many critiques of the use of retributive international law to address women's justice in post-conflict environments, to date, the process of 'gendering' transitional justice has tended to concentrate on this area. According to Bell and O'Rourke, much of the effort has focused on recognizing gender-based crimes as amongst the most serious crimes of war; securing prosecutions for these war crimes; and reforming courtroom procedures in order to ensure that 'victims of sexual violence were not re-victimized by the adversarial legal process' (2007: 27). These objectives correspond closely to the initial efforts made by gender justice advocates in relation to the ICC. However, these advocates have also attempted to push the gendering of transitional justice through the ICC in a restorative direction by ensuring that the Rome Statute and the Court also takes gender into account in its outreach activities, including being sensitive to educating and empowering women in local communities. The following discussion looks at the capacity of the Court in extending a transitional gender justice in all of these areas, and assesses its achievements in its initial phase of operation in light of the critiques of such a strategy.

Prosecuting gender-based crimes

The current categories of crimes over which the ICC has jurisdiction (genocide, war crimes, and crimes against humanity) are not in themselves new. However, the Rome Statute extends these in various ways, including innovations in the articulation of the gender aspects of these crimes. The drafters of the Rome Statute were influenced both by the jurisprudence of the ad hoc tribunals, which had recognized rape as a form of genocide in the Rwandan *Akayesu* case therefore constituting a war crime (see Mackinnon, 2006), as well as the strong advocacy of gender justice proponents at the preparatory committees for the Statute and at the Rome Conference. The Women's Caucus for Gender Justice (WCGJ), which was the core advocacy body in these venues, had clearly defined goals in relation to the capacity of the ICC to bring to justice perpetrators of gender-based violence. It argued that the Statute should incorporate the full range of core crimes against women; recognize these crimes as among the gravest violations; and include an explicit direction to prevent all forms of discrimination in the application of the law (Facio, 2004: 324).

The WCGJ achieved success in these three areas as a result of its intense lobbying efforts. For the first time, the Statute codified a range of gender-based crimes as crimes against humanity and war crimes, thus constituting grave breaches of international law. Included under the category of war crimes are:

> Rape, sexual slavery, enforced prostitution, forced pregnancy, enforced sterilization, or any other form of sexual violence of comparable gravity. (Article 7 (h))[3]

The inclusion of the offences of sexual slavery and forced pregnancy as an element of war crimes and crimes against humanity[4] represents a transformation in the way international law represents and understands women's experience in situations of armed conflict. Women's rights activists also successfully advocated (for details see Chappell, 2008a; 2008b) to have the term gender defined for the first time in an international treaty, and to have it included it in Article 7 (h) as a ground for prosecution (alongside political, racial, religious and other such categories).[5] Further, Article 21, prohibiting discrimination based on gender in the application and interpretation of the Statute, reflected an attempt to integrate gender concerns more broadly within the operations of the ICC. Under the Rome Statute, the trial proceedings set out to provide the highest standards of justice. As noted above, it provided for victim access to proceedings and specific protection measures for those suffering gender-based violence.

Armed with this gender-sensitive Statute, how well has the Court reflected gender justice concerns in its initial prosecutions? The answer, it appears, is far from perfectly. In the first case to be tried before the Court, concerning DRC warlord Thomas Lubanga, the Office of the Prosecutor (OTP) failed to include charges of sexual violence, despite widespread evidence of the use of rape as a weapon of war (for details see WIGJ, 2009b; Schiff, 2008). Lubanga has been charged only with the crimes of conscripting and enlisting child soldiers. The OTP wrongfully assumed such a strategy would lead to a speedy trial and conviction, and dealt a major blow to gender justice advocates, such as the Women's Initiatives for Gender Justice (WIGJ). The Women's Initiatives sought approval, under Article 61, to present an amicus brief to the pre-trial chamber to have the charges amended to include acts of sexual violence.[6] While this request was disallowed, as the trial progressed it became evident through victim and witness testimony that the crime of sexual enslavement of girl soldiers was a feature of Lubanga's case (International Bar Association, 2009). The testimony of witnesses and victims in the prosecution stage of the trial included accounts of girls'...'[p]hysical and psychological suffering, injuries both external and internal, unwanted pregnancies, and rejection by their families and communities' (WIGJ, 2009a: 70). In the view of the WIGJ, the testimony presented by girl soldiers demonstrated that 'their vulnerability as girls was intentionally and systematically exploited, and as a result they have been denied the right to a childhood, to be schooled, a right to integrity, a right to reproductive health and sexual autonomy' (WIGJ, 2009a: 70).

There are important lessons emerging from this first trial. Of primary importance is the obvious need for the OTP to consider carefully the inclusion of gender-based crimes in initial charges where there is evidence for them; something it manifestly failed to do in this case. Its failure to address such crimes reinforces the impunity gap for the victims of gender-based crimes. It has also had another more immediate effect, which is to delay proceedings unnecessarily. Such delays are troubling for all victims remaining in the conflict zone, including those of sexually based violence, who are vulnerable to further attack by supporters of the accused. The development of this trial provides some grist to the mill of feminist critics of the inadequacy of retributive justice approaches – especially drawn-out international prosecutions – for addressing issues of violence against women (see for example Mertus, 2004).

On a more positive note, this case also demonstrates the importance of victim and witness testimony in terms of bringing to light the actual experiences of women and girls in conflict situations. According to the WIGJ, '[q]uestioning by Legal Representatives [of the victims] elicited important evidence for the Court about the impact of [Lubanga's] alleged crimes on victims, and in particular about the gender-based crimes that have been committed in the context of the charges against Lubanga' (2009a: 96). As a direct result of this testimony in July 2009, at the end of the prosecution's arguments, the trial chamber suspended proceedings to consider amending the crimes to include sexual enslavement. In December 2009, the Appeal Chamber disallowed a modification of the legal characterization of the facts in the case (see ICC, 2009c). This was not a welcome outcome for the victims of gender-based crimes in this case. However it is a significant move in other ways; it could be argued that the matter has raised the profile of gender-based crimes more generally, and reinforced the need for the OTP to pay more attention to such crimes in future. This case has also shown the value of victim testimony. And it does appear that interest in this avenue for participating in international trials is strong. Over the period 2005–09, 1814 applications were received from persons seeking to participate as victims, 43 per cent of which were successful (WIGJ, 2009a: 95) (the Court does not maintain a gender breakdown of the applications for Victim Status). In the *Katanga and Ngudjolo Chui* trial, which commenced in November 2009, 345 victims registered to participate.

The OTP does seem to have learnt some lessons from the Lubanga trial. In following cases to come before the Court concerning Jean-Pierre Bemba, relating to the situation in the Central African Republic

(CAR), and Germain Katanga and Mathieu Njudjolo, relating to the DRC, investigations into gender-based crimes have been conducted, evidence gathered, and charges of sexual violence have been laid (see ICC, 2009d). This is a step forward for gender justice, but the trials still have a long way to run. These proceedings will be a test of the ability of the OTP to gather evidence relating to gender-based crimes that is of a standard to secure a conviction, and of the Prosecutor's willingness to utilize the full range of sexual violence charges available under the Statute (see WIGJ, 2009d).

Given the few cases that have come before the ICC, it is still too early to make any assessment of the gendered nature of the jurisprudence to emerge from the Court. However, it will be interesting to closely watch its developments over time, especially given the fact that there is now a majority of women judges on the ICC bench (as of November 2009, 9 of the 16 judges were female). Such an outcome has not come about unassisted. Only after significant lobbying by gender advocates at the Rome Conference to determine the Statute, was a clause on 'fair' gender representation of judges included in the Statute. Achieving nominal gender equality is in itself an achievement given that the 15 member International Court of Justice has only ever had one permanent female judge, the current President, Rosalyn Higgins, while many of the state parties to the ICC themselves have very poor records of female judicial representation. Gaining substantive representation may not be quite so easy. Evidence from legal studies on gender and judging suggest that it is the commitment of men and women to a feminist politics, rather than the mere presence of women, that makes the difference (Hunter, 2008; Kenney, 2008). However, the insistence in the Statute that some judges, both male and female, have expertise in sexual violence makes it more likely that the ICC jurisprudence will be more sensitive to gender justice issues (see Chappell, 2010).

It is clear that, in the first years of the operation of the ICC, the prosecution strategy has not lived up to the full promise of the Rome Statute as far as gender justice is concerned. Formal recognition of gender-based crimes is one important step, but this means little unless the Prosecutor and, in future, the Judiciary are willing to carefully investigate, provide evidence for, and to convict those responsible for these acts. Taking the voice of victims and witnesses into account throughout the proceedings will be an important feature of the trial process. Retributive justice at the international level is only one part of the ICC system. However, domestic level prosecutions are equally, if not more, important.

Closing the gender crimes impunity gap at the national level

The ICC in The Hague is a court of last resort. It was the underlying intention of the Rome Conference to build a global criminal justice system whereby all states ratify and then, through the notion of complementarity, implement the provisions of the Rome Statute – including its gender provisions – into domestic law. Through this process, the Court seeks to act as a 'spur' to 'regular and effective enforcement of international criminal law by the jurisdictions closest to the events' (Broomhall, 2003: 84).

The Court is still a long way from achieving its objectives relating to state ratification and implementation. As at February 2010, there were 110 states parties to the Rome Statute, but they do not include key international players such as the USA, Russia, China, and Israel.[7] To date, the ICC has only achieved moderate success in having states adopt implementing legislation. With 110 state parties to the Statute as of November 2009, only 44 are known to have enacted complementarity legislation in full, with Amnesty International noting that many of the laws that have been enacted 'fall short of what is required by the Rome Statute and international law' (2009: 8). The stumbling blocks for ratification and implementation are numerous: lack of political will or priority; the unwillingness of the US to support the Court; and legal/technical difficulties (see Bekou and Shah, 2006). The willingness of the Court in 2009 to issue an arrest warrant for the current head of state of Sudan has further frustrated the ICC's ratification and implementation efforts, especially in Africa and the Middle East region. The evident loss of immunity for heads of state has converged with arguments about the Court's political bias to create widespread and strong resistance to the ICC in these regions (see Human Rights Watch, 2009).

The slow progress on implementation significantly reduces the transformative effect of the Rome Statute as far as transitional gender justice is concerned. Aside from the few cases that will be heard by the ICC, justice for gender-based crimes will be the responsibility of the states where they reside. So long as states who are parties to the ICC have no implementing legislation, women who experience gender-based war crimes and crimes against humanity will be unable to seek justice. But it is not only in those states without legislation where women are left unprotected. Indeed, a troubling pattern is starting to emerge whereby Rome Statue gender provisions are significantly diluted and/or only partially implemented in complementary legislation. For example, the

Australian legislation includes a narrower definition of rape than that in the Statute, and in Bosnia-Herzegovina, forced pregnancy, enforced sterilization, and any other form of sexual violence are omitted from war crimes. Several other states have also reduced the gender provisions of either or both crimes against humanity or war crimes (for example, Estonia and Brazil). However, it is also important to note that a number of states have taken the opportunity to include gender as a category under the definition of genocide which advances the crime further than provided in the Statute (for instance Australia, Colombia, Congo, Ecuador, Finland, and Portugal).

Adopting new definitions of crimes based on the Rome Statute is important to the advancement of gender justice at the national level. It is equally significant, given the nature of crimes committed against women in conflict situations, that national level criminal justice systems also provide for the level of witness protection provided for under the Statute, including careful evidence-gathering procedures which protect confidentiality, provision for in camera evidence and, if necessary, witness protection programmes. Such programmes are heavily resource intensive and there is a concern that, especially in conflict situations in less-developed states, there will be scant access to such services, leaving female witnesses exposed to reprisals. Another challenge, especially in common law countries, will be how to ensure implemented legislation allows for victims' involvement in trials. Victim access is a foreign concept in many countries and could result in resistance from those upholding existing legal norms.

Complementarity is a double-edged sword as far as expanding women's rights is concerned. Nested in a system that is structured by state sovereignty, the Rome Statute and the International Criminal Court provide states with the capacity to develop and expand their treatment of gender-based crimes through the reform of national law. The inclusion of gender under the crime of genocide in a number of countries appears to reflect this expansion. At the same time, it gives states the capacity to fragment new international legal norms and to work against the diffusion of new women's rights norms to the national level.

Outreach and capacity building

What of the ICC's ability to contribute to a redistributive gender justice? The Court's restorative character comes from its capacity to undertake outreach activities and to provide compensation to victims. Learning some important lessons from earlier international tribunals, the ICC has set out to develop a comprehensive outreach strategy, which includes gender-sensitive elements. As with other aspects of the Court's operation, despite its good intentions, its outreach efforts are hampered by a lack of resources. However, it does benefit greatly from the non-governmental organization (NGO) sector which co-operates with the Court to extend its reach. Women in conflict and post-conflict situations have begun to participate in these outreach activities, and in ways that enhance their representation in peace-building efforts.

The Registry, charged with carrying out the ICC's outreach activities, aims to overcome many of the shortfalls of the ICTY and ICTR operations, including engaging women in all activities on the ground in situation countries. Communicating and information sharing about ICC activities is a key component of the outreach strategy. The Registry has demonstrated sensitivity to the fact that women have particular communication needs due to their difficulty in accessing public information – including illiteracy, isolation, and so forth – and aims to make women's engagement easier. One way it strives to do this is through capacity building with women's community groups and NGOs, who, once educated about the Statute in general, and the gender provisions in particular, are able to pass the information on across the community (ICC, 2006). While the public documents of the Registry use the language of gender inclusiveness, the WIGJ, the gender watchdog on the Court, suggests that there is still much work to be done. It points to two particular needs: 1) providing enough Registry staff to 'ensure effective programs are developed to reach women and diverse sectors of communities in each of the four conflict situations' and 2) providing safe, alternative forums, especially for the discussion of gender-based crimes (WIGJ, 2009: 163).

A second important restorative aspect of the ICC concerns Article 75 of the Rome Statute allowing the Court to determine the scope and extent of any damage to victims and to order reparations in the form of 'restitution, compensation, and rehabilitation'. The cost of these reparations can come from two sources: a court order against a convicted person to pay damages, and the Trust Fund for Victims (TFV), which operates under the guidance of the Assembly of States Parties. Funds for the TFV are made through voluntary state contributions and at the end of 2009 totalled just over €3 million.

As the Court is still to make a conviction, no reparations have yet been paid to an individual. However, the TFV has begun distributing some of the funds for rehabilitation projects in the DRC and Uganda. During 2008–09, the TFV approved 30 projects in these regions at a cost of €1.3 million including the provision of psychological support and physical rehabilitation for victims of the conflicts. The TFV estimates that through these measures it will reach a combined total of 3.8 million direct and indirect victims (ICC, 2009e). As with the Court's outreach activities, the TFV is making an effort to make its operations gender-sensitive. In 2008, after lobbying from the WIGJ and other NGOs, the Board of Directors of the TFV launched a three year global campaign to assist 1.7 million victims of sexual violence under the jurisdiction of the Court. To date, the governments of Norway and Denmark and the Principality of Andorra have contributed a combined total of just over €700,000 toward the fund. As the WIGJ points out, current commitments fall well short of the TFV's goal (2009: 37). Nevertheless these earmarked funds have already been put to use in projects in the DRC, Uganda, and CAR. Importantly, from a redistributive perspective, amongst the projects are those to assist women and girls in developing income-generating activities to encourage social and economic integration, as well as micro-credit projects.

Neither the TFV nor the Registry expects to be able to carry out their outreach activities alone. Both emphasize the need to engage NGOs, local grassroots organizations, victims' groups, women's associations, and faith-based groups, who are rooted in their local communities (ICC, 2009e: 3). Indeed, since the time of its establishment, the ICC has relied heavily on the non-government sector in helping it to frame its mandate, structures, and activities. As Schiff states:

> Nongovernment organizations cajoled, lobbied, and in a myriad of ways pushed hard for the birth of the International Criminal Court, and now they are nurturing it, criticizing it, and sometimes acting as the Court's surrogates or agents, extending its reach. (2008: 144)

The Coalition of the ICC (CICC) – an umbrella body with over 2500 member organizations – operates to 'ensure that the Court is fair, effective and independent; make justice both visible and universal; and advance stronger national laws that deliver justice to victims of war crimes, crimes against humanity and genocide' (CICC, 2010). The Women's Initiatives for Gender Justice is a member of the CICC, working specifically with local women's groups in situation countries. The WIGJ provides a valuable example of the ways in which NGOs can extend the reach and the resources of the ICC in transitional contexts.

The WIGJ is an international NGO that advocates 'for inclusion of gender based crimes in the investigations and prosecutions of the ICC and...the rights of women victims/survivors of armed conflict throughout the justice process including through the Trust Fund for Victims'. It supports 'the use of international treaties, specifically the Rome Statute of the ICC, to advance women's rights and gender equality domestically' (WIGJ, 2010). Aside from monitoring the Court's activities, intervening as amicus curiae in ICC trials, and lobbying for the election of skilled feminist judges, the WIGJ also conducts field activities in each of the ICC four situation countries. Over the past five years, the WIGJ has provided training for local lawyers and women's groups on the ICC and the Rome Statute, produced materials in local languages to disseminate information about trials in The Hague, and supported the development of grassroots women's groups and networks between these groups and with other international NGOs. The Women's Initiatives have supported witnesses and intermediaries requiring protection, and assisted in the documenting and gathering of evidence about gender-based violence in each country (for details see WIGJ, 2010b).

A recent workshop held by the WIGJ in Northern Uganda provides an excellent example of the ways in which NGOs are supporting the work of the ICC in a transitional justice context. The meeting, held in July 2009, brought together 40 women's rights and peace activists from the North for training on the documentation of gender-based violence and the implementation of the Juba Peace Agreements, specifically the Agreement on Accountability and Reconciliation. A core aim of the workshop was to 'ensure women understand the agreements, have an established platform to influence their implementation and are ready to be active participants in the construction of justice, peace and reconciliation mechanisms' (WIGJ, 2009d). A feature of this meeting – and others conducted by the WIGJ in other contexts – was the involvement of senior government officials, in this case the Special War Crimes Division of the High Court of Uganda (WCD), as well as international representatives, including the Office of the High Commissioner for Human Rights.

According to the WIGJ's report on the meeting (WIGJ, 2009d), local women were able to identify their concerns about the peace process in the region and develop a platform for lobbying government officials. In particular, they wanted answers on 'accountability for state actors and for "peace spoilers"', who, in their view, had sabotaged earlier peace-building efforts. Women also pressed for the Special War Crimes Division of the High Court of Uganda to include all the provisions of the Rome Statute, and were especially concerned to ensure that it included those provisions which safeguard the legal rights of women and of victims/survivors. In addition, the participants raised the need for women to be full partners in the implementation of the Peace Agreement and to be appointed to senior levels of the institutions and bodies to be established in this process. These concerns were expressed directly to High Court officials in a question and answer session.

The involvement of the Women's Initiatives in the Uganda case highlights the way in which the ICC, through a third party, is able to contribute to restorative justice measures in transitional contexts. The WIGJ is just one organization engaged in these types of activities. Human Rights Watch, International Federation for Human Rights (FIDH), and regional chapters of the Coalition for the International Criminal Court, are a few of the many agencies who have conducted their own in-country training programmes, including in relation to the gender justice elements of the Statute, and capacity building with women's groups. Through such work, NGOs operate as a bridge between local communities and the Court. They transfer knowledge about the Court and further its outreach capacity. They provide a safe space for women to express their concerns not only about the operation of the Court, but more locally relevant peace processes, and a venue through which they can transmit their concerns to law makers. While tensions undoubtedly arise between NGOs and grassroots organizations about when and where to emphasize peace versus justice strategies in relation to local issues (see Schiff, 2008: 159), the development of a close, trusting, working relationship, such as that fostered by the WIGJ and women in Northern Uganda, can help work through and defuse some of these tensions. In sum, it is clear that NGOs are playing an essential role in extending the ICC's restorative justice capabilities, and in such a way as to advance a gender justice agenda that would not have otherwise been possible.

Conclusion

This chapter suggests that the gender justice outcomes of the Court in its initial stages are variable and patchy. Despite a groundbreaking Statute, the Court still demonstrates a number of the problems highlighted in earlier feminist critiques of international law. The trials are very slow; few perpetrators have come before the Court and, when they do, the prosecutorial team has shown it is not as alert as it should be in ensuring relevant and sufficient evidence is gathered in order to lay charges for gender-based crimes. Moreover, the diffusion of the Rome Statute to the national level has been slow, and states have frequently been unresponsive to implementing new norms of gender justice in domestic legislation. This leaves limited opportunities available to gender justice seekers to use the Statute in national trials and improve access to justice in transitional settings.

However, it would be a mistake for gender justice seekers to avoid the ICC. There are good reasons to remain optimistic about the potential of the Court and the Statute to improve women's access to justice. It is still early days, and it is clear that the Court is learning lessons from the first trials, and paying much closer attention to gender-based crimes in subsequent cases. The Court now has achieved gender equality on its bench and many of these judges are trained in issues related to gender-based violence. These attributes will never overcome all the difficulties of a retributive justice approach, but they will ensure that where gender justice is at issue, it will be treated with greater sophistication than in the past.

Where the Court may well make the greatest impact is through its restorative justice measures. In its own outreach activities, but especially through engagement with NGOs and grassroots organizations, the ICC can contribute to expanding the legal knowledge and political advocacy skills of gender justice advocates on the ground. Such capacity building measures have the potential to enhance efforts to obtain justice and secure peace, and ensure women have a much greater public role in rebuilding their societies.

The ICC has many 'critical friends', including the NGO community, who see it as an imperfect, but nonetheless important part of the 'incomplete and messy' framework of transitional justice (Franke, 2006; Lipscomb, 2006; Bell and O'Rourke, 2007: 42). The ability of the Court to offer gender justice seekers a resolution to past crimes and future security has only partially been fulfilled. However, with ongoing pressure and support, it does have the potential to contribute to the advancement of justice, and thus should be seen as an important feature of the 'tool box' available for addressing gender injustices in transitional settings.

Notes

Thanks to Rosemary Grey for her excellent research assistance.

1. It has jurisdiction over war crimes, crimes against humanity, and genocide. However, at the 1998 Rome Conference, states could not agree on a definition on the crime of aggression. As a result, the ICC does not have jurisdiction over this crime. Aggression was to be reconsidered at the seven year review conference held in May 2010.
2. According to Article 14 of the Rome Statute, the ICC has jurisdiction in 'a) a State on the territory of which the conduct in question occurred ... or

b) the State of which the person accused of the crime is a national'. Under Article 15, the Security Council can refer a case for investigation to the Prosecutor of a non-member state. This was the situation in relation to the investigation and subsequent issue in 2009 of a warrant for the arrest of President Al-Bashir of Sudan (for details see International Criminal Court, 2009).

3. Similar crimes are enumerated under the category of crimes against humanity (see Article 8 (b) (xxii)).
4. Features of the Balkan conflict and recognized by the ICTY as war crimes.
5. Gender based crimes were not included under Article 6 on Genocide, with some of the more optimistic gender justice advocates reasoning that it was unnecessary, having already been established as an element of that category of crime in the jurisprudence of the ad hoc tribunals.
6. An *amicus curiae* brief is a document filed in a court by someone who is not directly related to the case under consideration, such as an advocacy group like the WIGJ. The information provided in such a document can be useful for the judge evaluating the case, and it becomes part of the official case record.
7. For a list of states parties see: http://www.icc-cpi.int/Menus/ASP/states+parties/

References

Amnesty International (2009) *International Criminal Court: Concerns at the Eight Session of the Assembly of State Parties*. IOR 40/011/2009 (London: Amnesty International).

M. J. Aukerman (2002) 'Extraordinary Evil, Ordinary Crime: A Framework for Understanding Transitional Justice', *Harvard Human Rights Journal,* Vol. 15, 39–97.

O. Bekou and S. Sangeeta (2006) 'Realising the Potential of the International Criminal Court: The African Experience', *Human Rights Law Review,* Vol. 6 No. 3, 499–544.

C. Bell and C. O'Rourke (2007) 'Does Feminism Need a Theory of Transitional Justice? An Introductory Essay', *The International Journal of Transitional Justice,* Vol. 1, 23–44.

R. Brauman (2008) 'The ICC's Bashir Indictment: Law Against Peace', *World Politics Review,* available at http://www.worldpoliticsreview.com/article.aspx?id=2471 (accessed 12 February 2010).

BBC World News (2008) *Sudan lobbies against Bashir case,* available at http://news.bbc.co.uk/2/hi/7630071.stm (accessed 22 November 2009).

B. Broomhall (2003) *International Justice and the International Criminal Court* (Oxford: Oxford University Press).

L. Chappell (2010) 'Gender and Judging at the International Criminal Court', *Politics & Gender,* Vol. 6 No. 3, 484–95.

L. Chappell (2008a) 'Governing International Law through the International Criminal Court: A New Site for Gender Justice?' in S. Rai and S. Waylen (eds) *Global Governance: Feminist Perspectives* (Basingstoke and New York: Palgrave Macmillan).

L. Chappell (2008b) 'Women's Rights and Religious Opposition: The Politics of Gender at the International Criminal Court' in Y. Abu-Laban (ed.) *Gendering the Nation State: Canadian Comparative Perspectives* (Vancouver: University of British Columbia Press).

H. Charlesworth and C. Chinkin (2000) *The Boundaries of International Law: A Feminist Analysis* (Manchester: Manchester University Press).

E.-M. Condon (2008) 'The Incoherent International Jurisprudence of Rape' in M. S. Ellis and R. J. Goldstone (eds) *The International Criminal Court: Challenges to Achieving Justice and Accountability in the 21st Century* (New York: International Debate Education Association), pp. 200–13.

R. Copelon (2000) 'Gender Crimes as War Crimes: Integrating Crimes against Women into International Criminal Law', *McGill Law Journal*, Vol. 46, 217–40.

Coalition for the International Criminal Court (CICC) (2010) *About the Coalition*, available at http://www.iccnow.org/?mod=coalition (accessed 19 February 2010).

M. Ellis (2008) 'The International Criminal Court and Its Implication for Domestic Law and National Capacity Building' in M. S. Ellis and R. J. Goldstone (eds) *The International Criminal Court: Challenges to Achieving Justice and Accountability in the 21st Century* (New York: International Debate Education Association), pp. 85–114.

A. Facio (2004) 'All roads lead to Rome but some are bumpier than others' in S. Pickering and C. Lambert (eds) *Global Issues: Women and Justice* (Sydney: Federation Press).

FIDH (International Federation for Human Rights) (2009) *ICC: The International Criminal Court's First Years*. (Paris: FIDH).

J. Flint and A. de Waal (2009) 'To put justice before peace spells disaster for Sudan', *The Guardian*, 6 March, available at http://www.guardian.co.uk/commentisfree/2009/mar/06/sudan-war-crimes (accessed 22 November 2009).

K. M. Franke (2006) 'Gendered Subjects of Transitional Justice', *Columbia Journal of Gender and Law*, Vol. 15, 813–27.

J. G. Gardam and M. J. Jarvis (2001) *Women, Armed Conflict and International Law* (The Hague: Kluwer Law International).

Human Rights Watch (2009) *Human Rights Watch Memorandum for the Eighth Session of the International Criminal Court Assembly of States Parties* (New York: Human Rights Watch).

R. Hunter (2008) 'Can Feminist Judges Make a Difference?', *International Journal of the Legal Profession*, Vol. 15 No. 1, 7–36.

International Bar Association (2009) *First Challenges: An examination of recent landmark developments at the International Criminal Court* (London: IBA).

International Criminal Court (2009a) *Warrant of Arrest for Omar Hassan Ahmad Al Bashir*, ICC-02/05-01/09-1, available at http://www.icc-cpi.int/iccdocs/doc/doc639078.pdf (accessed 22 November 2009).

International Criminal Court (2009b) *Trust Fund for Victims: What we do*, available at http://www.icccpi.int/Menus/ICC/Structure+of+the+Court/Victims/Trust+Fund+for+Victims/What+we+do/ (accessed 20 November 2009).

International Criminal Court (2009c) *Appeals Chamber of the International Criminal Court reverses the decision on the change of the legal characterisation of the facts in the Lubanga Dyilo case*, Press Release: 8 December 2009, ICC-CPI-20091208-PR484, available at http://www.icc-cpi.int/menus/icc/situations (accessed 15 December 2009).

International Criminal Court (2009d) *All Situations*, available at http://www.icc-cpi.int/Menus/ICC/Situations+and+Cases/Situations (accessed 15 December 2009).

International Criminal Court (2009e) *Report to the Assembly of States Parties on the Activities and Projects of the Board of Directors of the Trust Fund for Victims for the Period 1 July 2008 to 30 June 2009*. ICC-ASP/8/18*.

International Criminal Court (2006) *Strategic Plan for Outreach of the International Criminal Court* ICC-ASP/5/12, available at http://www.icc-cpi.int/NR/rdonlyres/FB4C75CF-FD15-4B06-B1E3-E22618FB404C/185051/ICCASP512_English1.pdf (accessed 1 December 2010).

S. Kenny (2008) 'Thinking about gender and judging', *International Journal of the Legal Profession*, Vol. 15 No. 1, 87–110.

R. Lipscomb (2006) 'Restructuring the ICC Framework to Advance Transitional Justice: A Search for a Permanent Solution in Sudan', *Columbia Law Review*, Vol. 106, 182–212.

K. Mackinnon (2006) 'Defining Rape Internationally: A Comment on Akayesu', *Columbia Journal of Transnational Law*, Vol. 44 No.3, 940–58.

J. Mertus (2004) 'Shouting from the Bottom of a Well', *International Feminist Journal of Politics*, Vol. 6 No. 1, 110–28.

D. Robinson (2008) 'The Rome Statute and its Impact on National Law' in M. S. Ellis and R. J. Goldstone (eds) *The International Criminal Court: Challenges to Achieving Justice and Accountability in the 21st Century* (New York: International Debate Education Association).

W. A. Schabas (2007) *An Introduction to the International Criminal Court*, 3rd edn (Cambridge: Cambridge University Press).

B. N. Schiff (2008) *Building the International Criminal Court* (Cambridge: Cambridge University Press).

C. Warbrick and D. McGoldrick (2001) 'The Preparatory Commission for the International Criminal Court', *International and Comparative Law Quarterly*, Vol. 50, 420–35.

WIGJ (2010a) *Home Page*, available at http://www.iccwomen.org/ (accessed 18 February 2010).

WIGJ (2010b) *What We Do*, available at http://www.iccwomen.org/whatwedo/uganda/initiatives.php (accessed 19 February 2010). Women's Initiatives for Gender Justice (WIGJ (2009a) *Gender Report Card on the International Criminal Court 2009* (The Hague: WIGJ).

WIGJ (2009b) 'The Prosecutor v Thomas Lubanga Dyilo:: Trial finally under-way', *Legal Eye on the ICC*, Vol. 1, available at http://www.iccwomen.org/news/docs/LegalEye_Mar09/index.html#drc (accessed 30 November 2009).

WIGJ (2009c) *Statement on the ICC decision to omit charges for gender-based crimes against Jean-Pierre Bemba Gombo*, available at http://www.iccwomen.org/news/docs/Statement---PTC-Decision-on-Bemba.pdf (accessed 15 December 2009).

WIGJ (2009d) *Uganda: Women from the Greater North meet at the Women's Dialogue on Accountability and Reconciliation workshop in Soroti*, available at http://www.iccwomen.org/news/docs/WomVoices_July09/index.html#uganda1 (accessed 15 February 2010).

2
Gendered Under-Enforcement in the Transitional Justice Context

Fionnuala Ní Aoláin

The transitional justice field has been, throughout its relatively short development phase, de facto exclusionary to the issues and concerns of women. This is not to say that the broad issues that have dominated the field have not influenced women's lives (Bell, 2009a). Such core aspects of transitional justice's domain as criminal accountability, restorative justice, reconciliation, amnesty, and lustration invariably affect women individually and as a group. Nor has the impact of transitional justice been uniformly negative. For example, greater emphasis on, and attention to, criminal accountability for systematic human rights violations has also addressed some of the harms experienced by women and is a positive development (Askin, 2009). There is increased recognition, however, that, in its broadest sense, the discourse and the practice of transitional justice has failed to take into account the unique needs and issues that women face in conflicted and repressive societies (Bell et al., 2004; 2007). Encouragingly, there has been a growing literature and practice that recognizes the gendered lacunae of transitional justice theory and practice, and identifies pragmatic and transformative routes forward.

Drawing on previous work, this chapter further explores the gendered under-enforcement of change processes in transitional societies.[1] In doing so, the author acknowledges that the enforcement of women's rights and interests across multiple societies and legal dimensions is unreliable and patchy. Catherine O'Rourke reminds us that '[t]he problem ... is the limits of the legal imagination' (O'Rourke, 2008: 274), and advancement on the issues that affect women's social and legal status requires deep reflection on and subsequent action based upon the broader feminist critique of the limits of legalism and legal reform.[2] With that context in mind, we now focus attention on what happens to and for women in the transitional context. The transformative potential of political transition offers at least the possibility that women should do better from the deals struck, and that change might also implicate gendered change. The first section of this chapter draws conceptually on Lawrence Sager's seminal work on 'under-enforced constitutional norms' in the United States judicial context, and sets out a general framework to understand gendered under-enforcement. From this departure point, the chapter will explore causality for gender under-enforcement and examine how it manifests in specific forms. The second section explores the ways in which under-enforcement is evident in transitional contexts and mechanisms, with particular reference to negotiation processes and the exclusion of women from the sites of political agreement. This part also explores the link between presence, representation and the substantive content of transitional agreements. In the next section, the chapter will address the gendered consequences that flow from the consistent marginalization of and the limitation on transformative gender outcomes resulting from under-enforcement.

The gender dimensions of transition have, until relatively recently, been obscured by academic, political, and policy analyses. Presumptions of the positive benefits of transition for all (including women) have imbued the discourse.[3] Evident progress has been made in assessing the impact, form, and experience of transition for women (Orford, 2006; Ní Aoláin, 2006; Bell and O'Rourke, 2007). Current research includes the effect of truth recovery processes for women (Ní Aoláin and Turner, 2007; Nesiah, 2006) and the gendered dimensions of peace-making and peace processes (Bell, 2004). A substantial amount of recent literature has begun examining the accountability mechanisms in post-conflict societies and how they accommodate sexual violence experienced by women. This literature has allied with an increasingly vibrant analysis of reparations and their gendered effects (Chinkin and Paradine, 2001; Chinkin, 2009; Rubio-Marín, 2009). Despite these advances across a number of research and policy arenas, women remain at the margins of transitional processes and excluded from many of the benefits that accompany legal and political transformation.

Part one: under-enforcement – a general overview

The term under-enforcement has a specific meaning in the context of this analysis. The concept is identified as a particular feature of transitional implementation processes and is conceptually drawn from Lawrence Sager's seminal work on 'under-enforced constitutional norms' in the United States judicial context.[4] Sager's exploration of under-enforcement arises in the context of judicial interpretation when he posits that American courts (particularly the Supreme Court) have the legal capacity to interpret certain constitutional norms more fulsomely, but make selective choices not to do so. In his analysis, rights are viewed as having the capacity for variable degrees of fulfilment, and a more limited interpretation of any particular right's scope does not undo the core commitment to that rights' enforcement per se. In his influential article, Sager argues persuasively that the US federal judiciary 'sometimes decline[s] to uphold constitutionally based claims, not because of any reading of the relevant constitutional clause itself' (Sager, 1978: 1212), but because of competing 'institutional' interests, specifically deference to other branches of government. In this context, he asserts that a distinction should be drawn between the extent to which the federal judiciary may enforce the norm, and the extent to which the norm is otherwise valid and enforceable. This gap between the scope of a norm's potential meaning and its actual interpreted substance creates the context for Sager's reflection. This concept of under-enforcement, as first articulated in the context of American constitutional inquiry, becomes a useful conceptual mechanism to think more broadly about the phenomena of under-enforcement in other sites involving legal enforcement and interpretation.

The author has found Sager's construct a helpful means to think about the gap that frequently exists in the enforcement of agreements, treaties, and mechanisms that facilitate transitional processes in conflicted and post-authoritarian societies. This gap is particularly pronounced in relation to issues, mechanisms, and institutions that are most likely to affect the lived reality of women's lives. Under-enforcement is conceptually relevant to many transitional contexts because the mechanisms giving rise to transition are generally legal. Moreover, mechanisms of agreement such as accords and treaties have a quasi-constitutional quality. Hence, there is some useful conceptual application from theoretical analyses of malleable constitutional interpretation to the analysis of negotiated settlements from conflict and/or repression.

In the context of transitions from armed conflict to less violent political contestation, peace agreements are the primary vehicle containing the political bargain struck. As Christine Bell's path-breaking work on the legal nature of peace agreements confirms,[5] peace agreements are quintessentially legal and political documents (Bell, 2009a). In their legal dimensions, peace agreements and other political change agreements are subject to scrutiny on the basis of whether the parties do, in fact, adhere to the essential legal arrangements contained therein. Peace agreements give rise to a parallel set of uncertainties and ambiguities about the meaning and interpretation of terms, similar to the kinds of debates and contestations that arise in the legal interpretation of constitutional documents. There are, as a result, some conceptual and policy benefits to be gained from applying the insights of constitutional theorizing to the problems of enforcing peace agreements in transitional societies. As utilized in this chapter, under-enforcement contains an expression of the idea that while certain principles and norms are broadly accepted as forming the basis of legal action and state responsibility, in practice their full effects or promise may not be translated into legal obligations and structures. The gendered dimensions of this gap are what interest us most.

As Sager notes, an advantage to under-enforcement resulting from constitutional interpretation is that notwithstanding the fact of under-enforcement, a plausible and compelling argument can nevertheless be made that core (constitutional) norms are still being implemented. This facet is important as a matter of legitimacy. It is also central to maintaining rule of law claims by the state and the judiciary. In Sager's analysis, there is a spectrum of under-enforcement. Thus some norms will be interpreted more fully than others and judges will decide which norms are to be interpreted more broadly or more narrowly at any particular point. Identifying this continuum of adherence is important to understanding under-enforcement in the context of transition, and can help us explain why some parts of a peace treaty or political agreement are robustly implemented while others languish. Following Sager's line of argument, a certain degree of enforcement facilitates the legal and political argument that an essential value is still being utilized and implemented in law. The critical point is not the implementation of the norms per se, but the extent of application. An obvious caveat, of course, is that enforcement in Sager's context is through the courts, and involves the articulation of rights claims. Conversely, in the peace agreement context, the articulation of some rights may be part of the agreement to end hostilities between combatants, but more broadly the 'deal' involves a variety of political, legal, and social mechanisms, institutions, and commitments. In that sense the site under analysis here is evidently more fragmented than a singular constitutional document. Regarding peace agreements, the degree of application and implementation is critical for women. Self-evidently, significant empirically grounded work is necessary to address whether the patterns of under-enforcement across transitional societies reveal women experiencing disproportionate under-enforcement in specific ways that men do not, though some significant data already exists (Bell and O'Rourke, 2010).

In teasing out the concept and value of under-enforcement as a conceptual category to 'capture' what women experience in the transitional context, it is important to understand that, from the state perspective, there has been no formal negation of the values or principles in question. When a state is challenged as to whether a peace agreement or a political 'deal' is being implemented, there is a defensible position that legal obligations are being met. The state is therefore in a position to claim that legal implementation has followed the dictates of agreed principles, while in reality state practice may fall far short. This is not just an academic matter. Principles underpinning political transitions are invested with both internal and external political significance, and that substance is often a key feature of the acceptability and the long-term durability of the transitional deal. Perceived enforcement of a peace agreement is often what prevents a return to violence. How political figures, international interveners, and others describe the success or process of enforcement matters in practice. Thus, the political and legal spin on enforcement is often what keeps the peace, or maintains a political transfer in power. However valuable the maintenance of the transitional process, this chapter seeks to probe whether women benefit equally from the reality and the facades of enforcement in situations of transition.

Under-enforcement can occur for multiple reasons during transition. Clearly the transitional context for under-enforcement will be wider in scope than those identified in Sager's judicial model focused primarily on institutional competences and preferences (with an emphasis on the role of other branches of government in a federal system).[6] The myriad reasons for general under-enforcement of political agreements in transitional societies are manifold and are beyond the scope of this chapter. Understanding the totality of under-enforcement includes paying attention to the actors at the negotiation table and their relative political strengths and weaknesses; the degree to which external actors, including states and international institutions, support transition; the extremity of preceding violence and/or repression; and the economic and social capital capacity of the state, to mention just some important dimensions. Within the general causes of under-enforcement, there are elements with distinct and negative features, particularly pronounced for women, and some of these are explored in the next section, together with the suggestion that there are features of under-enforcement that are unique to gender or manifest in specific forms for women.

Part two: the forms and persistence of gendered under-enforcement

Under-enforcement is most marked in the areas of economic, social, political, and legal transformation that affect women, and as a result, under-enforcement takes on a remarkably gendered hue. In particular, as outlined in other contexts, transitional agreements tend to place a high premium on the narrow enforcement of civil and political rights, to the exclusion, or minimal inclusion, of broader concerns regarding economic and social rights.[7] Economic and social transformation provisions suffer from a lack of prioritization within the internal hierarchy of treaty documents, or may be acknowledged but not connected to any specific enforcement mechanisms. Moreover, violence against women and gendered harm has a low priority (or may not even be specifically articulated) in the transitional 'deals' that follow conflict or repression. More often than not, general principles that frame peace agreements are broadly articulated to include acceptance of violations of human rights across multiple arenas and a commitment to human rights protection (preambles are the favoured location). The placement and signalling around these issues, entitlements, and rights create the context from which gendered under-enforcement follow. In order to explain the causalities that under-pin under-enforcement, I begin by addressing the absence and exclusion of women in the sites where the 'deals' are made.

Presence, absence and exclusions

A key departure point for understanding under-enforcement is to see the way in which transition deals exclude or limit women's participation. It needs constant restatement that, across most jurisdictions, women are the group most historically marginalized and excluded from the peace-making, peace-building, and political change processes. While inclusion itself is not a panacea to the problem of under-enforcement, presence at least ensures that women's issues and concerns may appear in the substance of an agreement. Inclusion is a *sine qua non* to address the gender content problem, though we should not presume that the inclusion of (some) women will necessarily lead to greater protection for women's rights and interests.

Bell's three-pronged formulation outlining and assessing the modalities of peace-making, namely Pre-Agreement, Agreement, and

Implementation phases, provides a useful way to think about the way in which women are present and absent during processes of political change. It also forces us to see how under-enforcement is structurally built into the mechanics of political change agreements (Bell, 2009a).

First, pre-negotiation agreements invariably revolve around bringing perceived key political actors to the negotiation table. They can include broad context-setting initiatives as well as statements of principle. The pre-negotiation stage is likely to exclude women for a number of structural reasons. It is rarely a civil society dominated phase, but typically includes only state and non-state military actors at the highest echelons.[8] It is often secret in its operation, and, given the high value placed on the ending of public violence, the pre-negotiation phase tends to place disproportionate emphasis on the military outcomes perceived as essential to facilitate broader political engagement. This orientation de facto excludes women. Lasting political arrangements will follow from the principles set in this preliminary phase, that fundamentally affect women's lives. Notably these principle-setting mechanisms tend to have an intense focus on military and political values (ceasefires, amnesty, and political representation) and to exclude broader social, economic, or redistributive ideals.[9] This bias has long-term consequences for what women will gain in the deal that follows. It is one structural pre-curser to under-enforcement. When the 'deal' includes little to acknowledge women's needs and experiences, there is little to enforce (or under-enforce). Understanding these prima facie exclusions means that we ought to recognize the degree of under-enforcement as structurally dictated by the forms, timing and terms of the agreement made.

The second phase in negotiating peace agreements involves what Bell identifies as 'Substantive/Framework' agreements that 'aim to sustain ceasefires and provide a framework for governance that will address the root causes of the conflict'.[10] These documents are generally ambitious and far-reaching, tackling matters traditionally associated with peace agreements such as demilitarization, prisoner release, amnesty, the military's status, but also frequently addressing legal and political reform, social and economic reparation and reform, and institutional reform. Substantive agreements set out a framework for the exercise of power, as well as laying the groundwork for mandated government policies across a range of dimensions social, economic, and political.

Framework agreement phases are more likely to include women in at least some minimal, and public, form. This is often the most high profile phase of conflict negotiations and frequently involves international actors and agencies as they support a peace process forward. Local actors are typically under significant pressure to include women in order to legitimatize the negotiation process, even if women are not then actually given negotiation space to give voice to issues that affect them. For example, in East Timor following the UN Security Council's establishment of the United Nations Transitional Administration in East Timor (UNTAET), this international administrative structure was formally committed to, and worked with, local women's groups to bring about women's participation in the transitional administration and in constitutional drafting processes (UN Security Council, 1999). Participation does not however mean that substantive outcomes were drastically better for women across all markers.

Part of the reason for inclusion of women in the peace agreement contexts (and not in other broader regime change contexts) derives from United Nations Security Council Resolution 1325 which 'urges UN Member States to ensure increased representation of women at all decision-making levels…for the prevention, management and resolution of conflict' (UN Security Council, 2000: 1). The Resolution mandates that all actors involved in negotiating and implementing peace agreements adopt a gender perspective and therein provide a basis for attending to women's exclusion from, or under-representation in, negotiations (UN Security Council, 2000). But the attention to women's inclusion alone may be insufficient to address the multiple and subsequent contexts in the negotiation process which effectively sideline women's issues and interests. Gendered under-enforcement might then be conceptualized as a facet of the political bargaining that accompanies deal making, marking the space where women's issues fail to 'get on the table'. Ongoing research indicates that the implementation of Resolution 1325 does not, in fact, necessarily deliver better outcomes for women, and that comparison across peace negotiations and agreements empirically raises warning flags about the efficacy of 1325 in practice.[11] It is increasingly evident that the mere presence of women in decision-making contexts is a necessary but not sufficient condition to ensure transformative outcomes with gender as a measure.

Further high-level political visibility to women's experiences of the conflicted and post-conflict environment is found in UN Security Council Resolution 1820, which has not, in any sense, solved the problem.[12] The welcome emphasis on violence and its prevention in both resolutions does little to engage with the fundamental social and cultural contexts that support, create, and protect such practices. Furthermore, without a transformative social and economic agenda to accompany the rhetoric of impermissible acts, it is debatable what fundamental gender change is likely to be engineered. This critical view suggests that presence alone is unlikely to change the substantive content of transitional agreements. Rather, the negotiation process must necessarily include women, but needs to further encompass a deep and transformative vision of political change to impact on women's needs and address the harms women experience.

The third phase of agreements, identified by Bell's paradigm, is 'implementation agreements' which 'take forward and develop aspects of the framework, fleshing out their detail' (Bell, 2009a: 62–5). While Bell's focus is on peace agreements, her general point as to the nature of transition 'deals' holds true across a variety of political agreements. Outcomes are broadly worded treaty agreements that frequently avoid outlining the specific implementation measures necessary to transform principle to practice. The inherent and 'constructive ambiguity' of transition agreements is often the means to ensure that vastly opposing political entities agree to sign up to them (Bell and Cavanaugh, 1999: 1356). This means that much of the difficult work of real compromise can be left to the implementation phase, where both genuine opportunity and pitfalls exist for women.[13]

The purpose of implementation agreements is often technical. They can be seen as simply moving forward the work (with greater detail and clarity) to which the parties have previously agreed. In practice, their negotiation and content is far more contested. Often the opportunity to renegotiate offered by this kind of agreement means that parties view them as sites to revisit and regain losses (perceived or actual) in other parts of the negotiation process. Other times, the implementation phase actually does little to move the work forward, not because the implementation procedures are verbally or outwardly contested, but because political compromise underlies the negotiation process and there is little political will or unified approach to see the agreements through. They become agreements without any intention to perform.[14]

When the implementation phase is taken seriously by the society itself, then it can help in meaningful transformations that promote women's interests.[15] There are examples of the implementation phase as the context during which legal outcomes are more evidently advanced than in either pre or framework negotiations phase. Northern Ireland's ongoing negotiation of a Bill of Rights, and the South African Constitution, each involved a lengthy period of public consultation and engagement (Smith, 2004). Such participatory processes can be very effective in developing 'buy-in' as multiple constituencies not only connect to the mechanics of constitutional engagement (constitution making as a process), but are equally deeply involved in the contestation over what kind of social contract is sought and agreed upon by a society experiencing transformation. In this way, implementation can overcome the enforcement gap by grafting on substantive benefits to women. To get to that outcome, public consultation generally needs to be deep and meaningfully ordered and women's organizations require the supported capacity to cast themselves as central, rather than peripheral, stakeholders in the process of negotiations, impacting on the substance of the 'deal'.

The inclusion of women's interests and their representation is imperative in transitional settings. Transition agreements have a heightened importance in legal systems where the rule of law has been absent, denigrated, or manipulated to corrosive and authoritarian ends. In such contexts, there is a high degree of overlap between women's poor social, economic, and political standing and the legal apparatus which gives little value and meaningful protection to women. Peace agreements and/or broad political compacts hold potent symbolism in these contexts, particularly when they are held out by national and international elites as evidence of a new dispensation of rights and the remaking of law to that end. Lack of attention to women in these contexts has powerful representational and practical consequences. Moreover, in societies where rule of law is fragile or absent, there is evidence that customary institutions and practices clearly survive when formal legal structures collapse (especially in rural settings) (Isser et al., 2009). In this view, under-enforcement of the transitional agreement occurs from the praxis of poor or limited inclusion for women in all three phases of negotiation, allied with an assertion of domestic customary law that is antithetical to women's interests.

A broad swathe of research on the status and protection for women in customary and communal settings indicates real problems of equality, fairness, and entrenched gender bias.[16] Transitional agreements, if substantively engaged with women's concerns, constitute one means to address this deficit. For example, secular political documents play an important mediating role in providing a legal space in which customary and religious laws concerning women can be contested in a structured, rule driven forum. Secular documents may facilitate the creation of a contested legal space in which the values of equality, tolerance, and non-discrimination have legal potency, and can be articulated to respond to other culturally relativist values which invariably limit women's rights and opportunities. In this way, these political agreements should be valued not only in terms of their substantive content and their instrumentality, but as a means to open up a substantive space of contestation to women. The absence of women means that such capacity is much less likely to be sought or realized.

General international interest, allied with United Nations Security Council resolutions, raise several issues of concern to gender equality when considering the problems of under-enforcement already identified. Firstly, as noted above, the practicalities of enforcement are typically left to governmental officials and to the institutions established as a result of negotiations. As if to anticipate this problem, Resolution 1325 calls for an increase in the presence of women in 'all decision-making levels'. Resolution 1820 requests weaker 'consultation' in identified decision-making security contexts. The historical absence of women from these decisive sites, along with the interests they are deemed to represent, is usefully translated into an enforcement issue through these resolutions. But, as an enforcement issue, it remains divorced from the cultural and social realities that frame the capacity for women's meaningful inclusion. Specifically, economic realities such as poverty and refugee/internally displaced persons (IDP) status, allied with the broader burdens of care of women literally estop women from being present, and the issues which affect them most may be invisible to the male elites who generally undertake the negotiations. Moreover, the related question of which women should be deemed representative is vital to gendered outcomes, as explored below.

Fundamentally the most profound aspect of under-enforcement may be how women's presence in negotiations is conceptualized by the UN resolutions. Whilst 1325 and 1820 provide an important basis for attending to women's claims for inclusion, the resolutions suggest that a presence of women will improve the negotiations and subsequent chances of peace. Whilst this is obviously a strong strategic reason for women's participation in peace negotiations, it should be advanced with some caution. It implies that an additional expectation and responsibility may attach to the participation of women in these negotiations. It further suggests a conditional admission of women to negotiations that is not applied to men in these contexts. When women in conflicts come into public view they often do so as people uniquely able to overcome disdained, violent politics. This representation accords with the expectation and responsibility for making peace that frequently attaches to calls for women's admission to negotiations. It is as though women are admitted to conflict discourse, and to negotiations, as symbolic presences free of the brutality and messiness of conflicts and outside of the deep-rooted intersectional inequalities at their core. It does little to address what women bring (in addition) to the negotiation table.

Brittain reports that women artificially installed in negotiation teams have viewed their presence as 'window dressing' and become disillusioned. The inclusion strategy may provide short-term visible gains in a reported and applauded 'presence' of women in negotiations and may usefully highlight their erstwhile-unnoticed absence (Brittain, 2003). Claims that Resolution 1325 has thereby been effectively implemented are potentially damaging for women in these contexts who see their 'presence' as providing only the illusion of transformation. Presence may do little to affect substantive content or subsequent enforcement. This also strengthens the claim about the difficulty in addressing under-enforcement, when the evident retort may be that the presence of women gives cover to what follows, albeit negative. An externally imposed women's presence is no guarantee that issues pertaining to women's day-to-day lives will be addressed when it comes to the enforcement of what was agreed in negotiations. Indeed, a gender analysis of the key elements of strategic under-enforcement calls for a more subtle conceptualization of gender that intersects with group identities and provides a more nuanced articulation of gender roles in the transitional society.

To raise the question of women's absence in negotiations, ensuring that the interests of women and children are represented effectively when it comes to enforcement, risks falling into the conceptual trap of essentializing the woman who is absent. Furthermore, her capacities for building peace are uncritically presumed. This easily leads to the assumption that a 'presence' of women, of any women, in negotiations will address the gender gap and thereby positively change the process and its enforcement. However, when this solution is countenanced other questions arise with equally perplexing implications. For instance, which women should be present? Would any woman be able to 'represent' women's interests? Can only women represent these interests? In the context of violent political conflicts, in what ways may women's and men's 'interests' and experiences diverge, or be in dispute, or coalesce? Can legal formulation accord recognition to women's presence in this context? Are 'women's interests' in enforcement different from men's interests? How so?

The strategic answer provided to these complex and pragmatic questions remains the implementation of UN Security Council Resolution 1325, which requires the presence of women in delegations. In doing so, international mediation may be reflexively blinded to its own patriarchy, and to the reality that the presence of international male elites (equally unrepresentative) does little to communicate the necessity for profound reform across international institutions (as well as within the societies they support and engage).[17] International cajoling and oversight is part of a package that accompanies under-enforcement and allies with Sager's recognition that complex institutional choices and preferences undergird patterns of under-enforcement in the judicial sphere.

Gender regimes play a key role in under-enforcement, disadvantaging women in particular ways, and the poorest women more than others, across jurisdictions and contexts. First and foremost, women are either invisible or represented in a tokenistic presence in the transitional negotiations, and they are left out of account when it comes to legal enforcement of what was agreed. Gender regimes are constitutive of social identities and economic inequalities and not separable, and they structure the transition discourse such that 'certain kinds of questions' are precluded and certain kinds of narrative constructed. It is important to make visible how women are hailed into view in conflict discourses and then subsequently set aside. The initial hailing may be decisive at key moments when the presence of 'women' in the narrative confers legitimacy and authority, particularly to violent action taken by states on behalf of women, but from which women are normatively excluded. The presence of 'women' powerfully confers legitimacy and authority in contemporary war rhetoric.[18] Women are summoned into view, but also kept apart, noticeable by their erstwhile absence from the mainstream account. The 'women' of these legitimizing discourses are not the key actors, nor do they direct the action.[19] Many are further disadvantaged and disillusioned by under-enforcement of gender equality norms promised in transitional negotiations. The apparent powerlessness of women in this arena is at times strategically deployed in the management of the conflict to strong effect. To be on the side of 'women' and to have women onside appears to be an occasionally unassailable strategic position in the management of the discourse of modern conflicts.[20] This confirms the concern articulated in this chapter of the presumed value of transitions in general and to women in particular.

Rules to enforce

In assessing the legal forms of enforcement, one needs to pay particular attention to the structures and hierarchies of legal norms contained within peace agreements and other transitionary compacts. Here one has to play detective on the documents, matching the nature and form of the legal obligations with the political priorities of the parties. In doing so, recognition and caution should be exercised against the danger of grafting an essentialization of women's issues and needs onto such documents, and designating some issues as more important to women than others. Obviously, women and men have shared interests in ending communal violence and having more liberal rather than repressive political oversight. That stated, there is a considerable body of literature suggesting that women (when asked) articulate different priorities and needs over men in transitioning societies.[21] These priorities are little in evidence in the standard transitional agreement and, when they appear, tend to be aspirational rather than formally legally binding in nature. They may be found in the preamble to an agreement, or manifest as parts of the agreement without any enforcement provisions attached and no consequences for non-enforcement. Analysis of rule status to issue is a primary starting point in assessing what kind of 'bite' the legal rules on any given issue may have for women. Status translates to priority and thereafter funding in the transitional phase. Further empirical research is needed to ground these assertions, but there is reason to believe that women do not fare well in the legal hierarchy of transitional rules.

The status of the rules matter and are particularly relevant to women's experience of transition.[22] We know that peace treaties and other transitional compacts translate principles into legally binding obligations. In doing so, choices are made between which aspects of the agreement will have 'hard' law status, and will be translated into domestic law or follow with specific forms of agreed implementation, and which will be 'soft' law, remaining as aspirations or goals without formal measures to force compliance. This gap between 'soft' and 'hard' law has a distinct influence on the experience of women in transitional societies. The gap can be linked to the paucity of women in negotiation processes, and, if present, exacerbated by limited power and influence.

Norm privilege and under-enforcement

In conceptualizing gendered under-enforcement, reflection is required on the overwhelming emphasis on civil and political rights, illustrated by the calls for war crimes tribunals, in many transitional deals. While civil and political rights are foundational, their significance at the expense of other types of rights reflects a masculine construct of the priorities of government and law, and potentially has a negative impact on women's social, political, and economic status during the transition process. Without a broader lens on gendered reconstruction issues, minimal transformative possibilities open up to women, thus squandering the momentum and possibility of the massive transformative potential of the post-conflict process. Only with a broad framework will the measurement of what constitutes success for transitional justice actually encompass the experiences of women.

It is not that women and men in transitions are necessarily or always opposed in the expression of interests prioritized in negotiations from authoritarianism or conflict. Men and women have many interests in common in the enforceable outcomes of change processes. For instance, the implementation of human rights' legislation and programmes focusing on citizenship rights and democratic participation in the exercise of state power are crucial, especially to previously excluded groups. But, normatively, women are persistently the most excluded people within these groups and stand to profit most from any redistribution of state power and benefit gained in negotiations, provided these benefits are fully enforced. Chinkin's work on the lack of protection for economic, social, and cultural rights in post-conflict societies affirms the breadth of obstacles faced by women in asserting the need for economic provision and redistribution of resources (Chinkin, 2008). She makes the link between the failures of economic reform and centrality with broader limitations for the traditional spheres of transitional justice:

> It is our contention that failure to deliver economic, social and cultural rights through national legal frameworks in accordance with international standards undermines the sought-after stability and human security post-conflict (including food, health, gender and physical security), which in turn lessens the ability or willingness of victims and witnesses to participate in the formal processes of post-conflict justice. (Chinkin, 2008: 4)

In this context it is necessary to pay attention to, and benchmark, gender equality and social inclusion. The failure to do so, means that both dimensions may be subsequently stymied through under-enforcement. As Hamber has observed of the South African Truth and Reconciliation Commission (TRC), criticisms of the TRC's lack of focus on women's conflict experiences and the socio-economic harms of apartheid rightly point to the hidden political and social consequences of transitional processes (Hamber, 1998). The consequence of a bargaining dynamic around legal reform is significant and has gendered effects. What one might describe as the tension that exists between a need to maintain law's stability, while simultaneously acknowledging its failings during the previous regime, has resulted in a corresponding timidity in tackling fundamental issues of social transformation. Women experience the blunt edge of the hesitation.

Meaningful enforcement requires both the acknowledgement that women have particular needs, allied with hard hitting legally enforceable transformative action, in those spheres (social and economic) that have consistently been most resistant to legal regulation. Addressing equality, discrimination, and social status through political agreements requires encompassing both procedural and substantive equality, so that enforcement looks and feels radically different in terms of its impact on women in transitioning societies.

Group status, women and transition deals

A relevant dimension of under-enforcement for women is related to the broader context of transition. This context includes the causes of the conflict and/or the politics of the authoritarian transition.[23] Many post-conflict or post-authoritarian societies exhibit sharp differences between identifiable communities with regard to the confidence they display in legal structures and processes. Securing the commitment of such groups can be a central goal of many transitional processes, and viewed as critical to the success or failure of the peace agreement and political compact. Though this point is generally recognized in the analysis of minority or group political participation in the transformation of conflicted or repressive societies, no such presumption is applied to women and their degree of confidence or investment in legal and political systems per se (and as a result what needs to be done to re-engage and secure such confidence). Given the importance of legal enforcement to realizing the principles and formulae agreed through negotiated processes, the lack of attention to gaining the confidence of women in legal and political institutions is an illustration of the neglect of gender specific needs and outcomes. When the harms experienced by, and the needs of, women are not uppermost in the minds of those making the deals, one observes skewed outcomes.

In other words, minorities and/or other defined groups may have their needs writ large in the agreements made, and the (constructive) preoccupation of negotiators with their requirements then also frames how 'hard' and 'soft' rules are embedded in the legal formulae the agreements produce. This follows particularly where civil wars or low-intensity conflicts preceding transition have been motivated in part by contestation between majority and minority(s) about how much power should be shared, with whom, and for what compromises.

Equally we should bear in mind Conaghan's insights as to how gender is both 'ignored and enshrined' in legal discourse in ways that have specific real world impacts that disadvantage women in general (Conaghan, 2000). This conceptualization of gender as intersecting with other dimensions of inequality in state or regime formation, and in law, provides an important tool for understanding the dynamics of under-enforcement in transitions. These inbuilt biases are the bedrock upon which the further layers of relative disadvantage are built.

Finally, negotiation processes privilege elites, including both state and non-state actors. The very process of determining which groups are critical to enabling the end of conflict, or a changeover in power itself, determines the content of the negotiation process. This then determines the perception of whose needs should be recognized, and what compromises are necessary to maintain the presence and inclusion of certain groups. Women as a group never hold this privileged status as the deal-makers or enablers. As a result, there is a clear pre-determination as to status, inclusion, and compromise that sees gender inevitably sidelined. Groups of women, however, have worked strategically to use the division between other political groupings as a means to advance the needs of women (as well as broader compromises that may not be politically exclusive). Such initiatives, like those pursued by the Northern Ireland Women's Coalition in the late 1990s, are often framed as being in the general interest and broadly favouring the enhancement of human rights, rather than simply in terms of advancing women's interest per se (Fearon, 1999). Some examples of how these structural biases to negotiations play out in the practices of transition are now set out.

Institutional transformation and under-enforcement

For many transitional societies, institutional transformation is critical. Legal and political institutions may have been corrupt or involved in serious and systematic human rights' violations. Enforcement of the law may have been sullied, and belief in the neutrality of law may be degraded or compromised. As a result, the transformation of institutions is central to transitional agreements, including reform of the police, the courts, the military, and the administrative bodies of the state. The question of how the transformation of legal institutions is conducted, and who participates in this process, is of fundamental importance to the restructuring of relationships within any new legal dispensation. Such institutional transformation enables the redistribution of state or regime power and benefit within a future rights and equality framework.[24] While transitional justice discourse emphasizes accountability as a benchmark of enforcement, institutional reform is rarely viewed as a measure by which the success of a transitional process can be gauged. As the scope of the transitional justice frame expands to encompass legal reform and restructuring of political and legal institutions (as forward looking measures to address the legacies of the past) (Bell et al., 2007), it is important that these dimensions be seen as enforcement related, and that their success be bench-marked to include gains for women.

The modalities of institutional reform are complex in transitioning societies, and are often bound up with the issues of differential community confidence alluded to above. They may involve reform of the police, the military, the civil service, the courts, the judiciary, and the legislature, offices that deal with criminal prosecutions within the state, and a variety of other micro locales of political and legal power. Change in any of these institutions is politically fraught, and contains the ingredients of re-hashing the political agreements that prefigure them. Compromise is inevitable. Such compromises ultimately involve striking a balance of compromise between elite men already in power and their willingness to share such power and benefit with men seeking it.

An important aspect of deal making already noted is the fracturing of the reform process from the negotiation and agreement context into the transitional phase. Institutional reform, although pre-figured in peace and other agreements (Bell, 2009a), is rarely detailed within broad framework agreements. Framework agreements may signal significant review in these arenas, but their precise formulations are often left to the implementation phase of negotiation processes. As a result, women, if poorly or marginally represented at the negotiation process, may have limited ability to frame legal reform in terms of a women's agenda.[25] Following from the discussion above, even if, as mandated by United Nations Security Council Resolution 1325, women are appropriately represented in the relevant agreement phase, they are often cut out of key conversations in highly gendered ways. For example, as explored in the context of security sector reform, while security is central to the change process in post-conflict or post-repressive environments, women, by virtue of their historic absence from military, police, and paramilitary forces are rarely involved in, or have the capacity to be centralized in, these conversations (Ní Aoláin, 2009). As a result, security sector reform, including such important sites as Demobilization, Demilitarization, and Reintegration (DDR), reform of the police and military, the framing of new legal standards for accountability, and lustration rarely involve women. Their absence is allied with structural biases that make invisible women's needs and harms, whether by the reintegration of combatants without recognizing the shift from public to privatized violence that follows, police reform without addressing the cultures of masculinity that pervade policing-military cultures, accountability with minimal regard to sexual violence, or lustration without reference to gendered crimes. These examples illustrate how certain 'core' transitional issues, that are central to women's lived lives, frequently involve women being left out of the picture. There is a consistency of practice across state, non-state, and international actors in facilitating these outcomes (Ní Aoláin and O'Rourke, 2010).

Importantly, issues such as security become construed as key issues, whether actual or rhetorical, are specifically mapped by enforcement targets, and are invariably the subject of direct specified actions in many agreements. In this context, states and non-state actors will view a lack of progress in such designated arenas as evidence of bad faith and as a failure of enforcement, whereas women's rights protections are not similarly situated – neither in the rhetoric nor the actuality of their implementation.

Crucially, the neutral character of liberal equality norms introduced by transitional justice mechanisms raises critical questions about the representativeness of the architects of institutional transformation. The presence or absence of women, and what they do or do not gain, may be core to the potential for institutional transformation to deliver benefits to women, but are not part of the negotiation itself. Here representation takes on a dual importance, both in signifying the relationship of presence to outcomes, but also affirming the relationship between negotiation outcomes and enforcement in practice.

Despite the lofty goals outlined for the transitional moment, institutional change remains contested territory in the post-conflict context. It remains even more deeply contested and elusive for women. Meaningful transformation entails starting a more sophisticated conversation that enables us to see the genuine pitfalls that exist in transitional societies. This conversation requires deeper understanding of how institutional resistance encompasses gendered, social class and other 'identity securing' systems of privilege.[26] As a starting point, if we were simply to pay due attention to the outcomes of under-enforcement, we might more acutely see what is at stake, and why transitional societies sometimes 'fail' to move forward positively. This view illuminates the point that the presumed benefits of transition do not apply equally to all. The paradox remains that transitions may result in a re-ordering and transforming in the public space, and a retrenchment and instilled patriarchy being reasserted in private. This reality creates the context in which under-enforcement thrives and gives space for the core political agreements to be undermined by an ongoing process of contestation and retrenchment.

Part three: the effects of entrenched under-enforcement

What are the consequences for strategic under-enforcement of agreed positions in transitional societies in general, and for women in particular? In answering this question, reflection is required on the differing substantive elements involved. The classification of a society in transition, as represented through a peace agreement or other mechanism, frequently symbolizes the sum of an intricate and delicate negotiation between opposing parties (usually male dominated military entities). It has often been the means to stem the horror of serious communal violence within a territory. Such agreements stand as the immediate basis upon which parties to a conflict have agreed to an end in hostilities. In this context, every compromise is raw, and under-enforcement has the potential to unravel the 'deal' agreed. If the transitional framework is to aid a society to deal with the trauma of the past and create transformed institutions, then political and social inequality also have to be part of the conversation needed to create a future in which all parties are included on an equal basis. However, the elements of the agreed deal that most frequently fail to be implemented, fall short of implementation, or simply fail to be enforced at all, are those that most acutely affect women. In this view, the consequences of under-enforcement may have significant and underestimated gender differentiation. Consequences are not only a lack of acknowledgement for the experiences of the past (during conflict or repression), that may be significantly disabling for women, but also include the failure to ensure a transformative future for women. That impacts on the woman as citizen and equal rights bearer in any new dispensation as well as in access to substantive equality for women in the distribution of social and economic goods.

If transitional processes are intended to lead to both private and public transformations, thereby enabling the possibility of women participating as political and legal equals benefiting from the redistribution of state power in transition, commitments made to women's equality in the rhetoric of peace treaties need to be applied, where possible, with legal force. The narrative that emerges in many post-conflict societies is that the compact concerning equality is frequently excluded from the negotiation table, or, when included, is at the 'soft' and not 'hard' end of legal enforcement. Women get principles and aspirations, former combatants receive clear legal mandates to disarm, be compensated, and revert to civilian life. The consequences that follow are also that women have few avenues to challenge the distribution of political and social goods. The lack of formal enforcement, contrasted with the privilege that attaches to certain parts of the transitional agreement, operates not only as a form of exclusion, but as a means to entrench the status quo.

Despite a lack of all-encompassing statistical information, women are easily identifiable as victims in the context of repression and conflict. They are more likely to be refugees, more likely to be internally displaced, more likely to have care responsibilities, more like to experience sexual and penetrative violence (Vlachova and Biason, 2005). Placing the economic and social status of women squarely in the frame of analysis is critical to understanding why transition often fails to deliver for women. Generally speaking, equality, economic redistribution, and social justice are off the table for the purposes of transition.[27] Commitments to economic and social transformation are generally articulated as vague principles, not as binding rules to which consequences for lack of enforcement attach. No transitional agreement benchmarks progress on discrimination, health, education, housing, and food security as central to its articulation of the transformation necessary to lead to a peaceful or more politically liberal polity. This leads to a clear enforcement gap which cuts across both genders, but is, for the reasons outlined above, acutely felt by women. In practice the social and political dimensions of inequality and discrimination, through which different groups are constituted in the transitional society, are generally left to the vicissitudes of the enforcement struggle to translate what was gained by parties representing these groups in negotiations to meaningful policy on the ground. These post-agreement arenas are the sites in which under-enforcement plays out practically, and where women are even less likely to be present and have the political capital to enforce the principles and commitments made in general terms as concrete outcomes that benefit them in concrete terms.

This process of societal change triggered by transitional agreements may also represent what Thomson alludes to in other contexts as a time 'open to challenge' in the mainly male competition to reassert hegemonic gender power (Thomson, 2008). This is tandem with pre-existing structural and social exclusions that have a deeply gendered hue meaning that transition may not constitute transformative social change for women and may instead be a critical moment of backsliding.[28]

Part four: conclusion

The invisibility of women in conflict discourse, and the absence of gender awareness in the transitional context, is core to understanding how women's day-to-day lives get left out of consideration and result in exclusion. From exclusion, or under-inclusion, comes under-enforcement of equality and gender-sensitive commitments resulting from transitional negotiations. The precarious role of women in transitional discourse maintains the invisibility of gender regimes operating within these contexts. This insecure role sustains the normative fiction that conflicts and repressions have gender-free impact. Women's invisibility in these narratives conceals how gender regimes frame what is in view for analysis. Yet, positively, gender as an organizing principle could restructure the discursive 'frame for understanding',[29] making the transitional moment potentially transformative.

The academic and policy spotlight centres on violence, human rights abusers and their male perpetrators, and victims in transitional contexts. Negotiations are often premised on the imperative of ending intra-male public violence (with an evident lack of regard for the continuance of private sexualized violence). Arguably transitional discourse with an almost exclusive focus on male actors sees only half, albeit the most apparent and visible half, of what is going on. In reality women (and their dependent children) figure disproportionately as victims of conflict and repression, and are amongst the most marginalized people with the least resources who are most in need of enforcement of rights-based liberal norms of equality and autonomy.

A translation gap between agreement and enforcement is testament to a wider problem experienced in many transitional societies. There are many reasons for this under-enforcement, including the regrouping of political opposition to key reform elements of the political settlement, and the resistance to reform on the ground. There is a need to demand a much broader conception of transitional justice than one that focuses solely on 'dealing with the past' in terms of human rights abuses. Transitional justice requires transformation not merely transition, and the measurement of transition requires paying close attention to the lived experiences of women, and placing those firmly in the 'fix' offered in negotiated transitions. The 'fix' should be allied to hard law enforcement, with clear benchmarking and consequences for the parties to political processes, when issues affecting women are not addressed.

A broader notion of redistributive justice in transition, which encompasses recognition of structural inequalities and exclusions and their intersectional impacts on women's potential to participate as equals in the transitional society, is a key aspect to addressing under-enforcement. In articulating this broader notion of transition, we begin to really see how the totality of reform is part of the transitional justice paradigm and, thus, we recognize that meaningful change in a transitional society constitutes a wide and not a narrow class of issues. However, once we start to see this expanded notion of transition we must also understand the pitfalls that accompany it, in particular the danger that under-enforcement poses to many transitioning societies. We should not under-estimate the capacity of elite actors and institutions to regroup and resist the changes that have been landscaped by a peace negotiation process, and the process of transformation itself to be subverted. For women, greater attention to the cost of under-enforcement politically, socially, and economically should be allied to a more coherent internalization of the costs to the process of making peace, or securing the political space when women are effectively excluded.

Notes

Thanks to Sean Burk for research assistance.

1. Developing specific themes from wider analysis on the concept of under enforcement as applied to transitional societies (Ní Aoláin, 2005; Ní Aoláin and Rooney, 2008).
2. See, for example, Fineman's exploration of the legal effects of the differences between men and women and among different women and Conaghan's attempt to explain the tendency for legal scholars to divorce gendered legal perspectives from the goal of reducing the disadvantaged status of women. (Fineman, 1992; Conaghan, 2000).
3. For a critical analysis of such presumptions, see Mani's detailed arguments outlining four basic dilemmas that 'underscore and confound" the nexus between transitional justice and development. (Mani, 2008).
4. Sager's concern is the extent to which Courts may fail to enforce the (US) Constitution to its full conceptual boundaries. He identifies a number of key policy and jurisprudential consequences for such failure. They include firstly the assumption following pragmatic under-enforcement that the conception in the public domain in fact represents the fullness of a particular constitutional provision. In consequence there is the potential failure by government to fill the gap and/or take seriously the potential universe of claims which may exist. Secondly, the view that government officials have a legal obligation to obey an under-enforced constitutional norm which

extends beyond its interpretation by the federal judiciary 'to the full dimensions of the concept which the norm embodies' (Sager, 1978, 1226–27).

5. Bell also notes the complexity of peace agreements, and also questioning whether peace agreements constitute legal documents (Bell, 2009a).
6. Including as a starting point the form of transition whether one from authoritarianism to a more liberal democracy, from war to peace and/ or involving economic transition.
7. In the context of security during transition, international and local actors often focus on discrete instances of violence without taking into account the security threats posed by large-scale economic deprivation (Ní Aoláin, 2009).
8. So, for example in the Palestinian/ Israeli context the Oslo, Cairo, Wye River, and the U.S. backed 'Roadmap" negotiations did not include women. Two Israeli women participated in the non-state sanctioned Geneva Accord of 2003.
9. For example, in the Northern Ireland context, the 1993 Joint Declaration on Peace (Downing Street Declaration), which was the political precursor to military ceasefires by domestic paramilitary organizations and predated the broad framework agreement, outlined of a series of principled positions agreed by the Republic of Ireland and the United Kingdom governments (Major and Reynolds, 1993).
10. Examples of these classic framework agreements include, for example, the Burundi Peace Agreements, the Belfast Agreement, the Lóme Accords in Sierra Leone, and the South African Interim Constitution (Bell, 2009).
11. Various commentators have documented the limited outcomes of Security Resolution 1325 (O'Rourke, 2008; Neuwirth, 2002; Puechguirbal, 2010).
12. The resolution requests that UN-assisted justice, security sector reform (SSR), and disarmament, demobilization and reintegration (DDR) initiatives consult with women and women-led organizations in order to develop effective mechanisms for providing protection from violence including sexual violence. It calls on UN member states to end impunity for sexual violence and to ensure that all victims of sexual violence have equal protection under the law and equal access to justice. Finally, it urges countries contributing troops to take appropriate preventative action on sexual exploitation and abuse and to deploy a higher percentage of women peacekeepers and police (UN Security Council, 2008).
13. Cogent examples of implementation agreements include the Israeli/ Palestinian Interim Agreement (Oslo II) intended to take forward and implement parts of the Oslo I Agreement, as well as the more successful South African Final Constitution.
14. As was the case in Bosnia and Herzegovina with portions of the Dayton Framework Agreement for Peace, particularly those provisions devoted to property repossession and the facilitation of return (Moratti, 2008; Philpott and Williams, 2008).
15. A separate Constitutional Convention might be called to advance the specific work of agreement on legal principles and values. The success of such bespoke approaches for advancing women's interests and needs remains open. Nonetheless, results and success for women have been mixed, as we discuss infra below.

16. Various researchers have examined the scope of protections for women under customary law and various negatives of such protections. Such examinations have looked at countries such as Liberia (Isser, Lubkemann and N'Tow, 2009), and Namibia (Ubink and Van Rooij, 2010); and areas of basic rights such as land and property ownership and access (Benschop, 2004).
17. The need for such reform stems from the institutional bias of international male elites as they engage with post-conflict or post-repressive societies (Ní Aoláin, 2009).
18. Five weeks after the invasion of Afghanistan, First Lady Laura Bush claimed, 'The fight against terrorism is also a fight for the rights and dignity of women' (Rawi, 2004).
19. Some women in Afghanistan attempted to influence political action prior to the war. The Revolutionary Association of Women of Afghanistan (Rawa) gave footage of the execution of its leader, Zarmeens, to the BBC and CNN, only to be told that it was too shocking to broadcast. After September 11 2001 the footage was aired repeatedly. Rawa's photographs documenting Taliban abuses of women were used without the organization's permission. The photos were reproduced as flyers and dropped by US warplanes as they flew over Afghanistan (Rawi, 2004).
20. Unassailable until a feminist and human rights literature emerges to challenge the rhetoric, as has happened in the US and from Afghanistan in the wake of the war. See Amy Zalman's review of the competing perspectives from the war (Zalman, 2003).
21. The needs differ based on the varied experiences of violence and marginalization during the conflict and post-conflict transition (Ní Aoláin and Cahn, 2009). Marín highlights the different needs of women when assessing the various ways in which reparations help victims cope with the effects of violations. These include different needs and expectations in the realms of material restitution, rehabilitation and reintegration, symbolic recognition, and guarantees of non-repetition. (Marín, 2009).
22. Note that Dianne Otto makes a parallel point in her analysis of the success and/or failure of UN Security Council Resolution 1325 as she notes the lack of Chapter VII status for the provision (Otto, 2009).
23. Whether the transition is compacted or ruptured is a key issue in this regard.
24. In this case, law is seen as a complex set of practices with material and political effects. Conaghan observes such an example in describing the British Government's Women's Unit (Conaghan, 2000).
25. There are exceptions of course, for example in the context of reproductive rights reform in South Africa the women's movement was highly successful in its influence on including reproductive rights within the contours of the constitutional reforms. However, as Rachel Rebouché has demonstrated, it is not entirely clear in practice whether the reform agenda has delivered substantially better outcomes for women on the ground (Rebouché, 2009).
26. Other works have focused on a deeper analysis of the fundamental relationship between intersectionality, inequality and under-enforcement (Ní Aoláin and Rooney, 2008). Seeing these relationships is the start of probing the benefits of intersectional analysis as a tool for analysing the problems of under-enforcement particularly as they negatively impact upon those

women and children who constitute the group most seriously affected by armed conflict and repression. In this view, under-enforcement and inequality are structurally linked.

27. Various scholars and human rights leaders have indentified reasons for this limited development and marshalled arguments for a stronger focus on economic and social rights in transitional justice movements (Muvingi, 2009; Pasipanodya, 2008; Arbour, 2006).
28. I argue (with Hamilton) specifically that the re-establishing and formalizing of rule of law structures after a period of transition may ironically entrench prior exclusion of women and overturn certain opportunities for women only present while the state was in flux (Hamilton and Ní Aoláin, 2008).
29. Butler argues that a particular 'frame for understanding violence emerges in tandem with the experience, and that the frame works both to preclude certain kinds of questions, certain kinds of historical inquiries, and to function as a moral justification for retaliation' (Butler, 2002: 179).

References

L. Arbour (2006) 'Economic and Social Justice for Societies in Transition', *Transitional Justice Lecture Presented at New York University School of Law*, available at http://www.chrgj.org/docs/Arbour_25_October_2006.pdf (accessed 3 Aug 2010).

K. D. Askin (2009) *2009 Gender Report Card on the International Criminal Court* (The Hague: The Women's Initiative for Gender Justice).

C. Bell (2009a) *On the Law of Peace: Peace Agreements and the Lex Pacificatoria* (New York: Oxford University Press).

C. Bell (2009b) 'Transitional Justice, Interdisciplinarity and the State of the "Field" or "Non-Field"', *International Journal of Transitional Justice*, Vol. 3, 11–12.

C. Bell (2004) 'Women Address the Problems of Peace Agreements' in R. Coomaraswamy and D. Fonseka (eds) *Peace Work: Women, Armed Conflict and Negotiation* (New Delhi: Women Unlimited).

C. Bell and K. Cavanaugh (1999) 'Constructive Ambiguity or Internal Self-Determination? Self-Determination, Group Accommodation and the Belfast Agreement', *Fordham International Law Journal*, Vol. 22, 1356.

C. Bell, C. Campbell and F. Ní Aoláin (2007) 'Foreword Transitional Justice: (re) conceptualising the field', *International Journal of Law in Context*, Vol. 3, 81–88.

C. Bell, C. Campbell and F. Ní Aoláin (2004) 'Justice Discourses in Transition', *Social and Legal Studies*, Vol. 13, 306–28.

C. Bell and C. O'Rourke (2010) 'Peace Agreements or Pieces of Paper? The Impact of UNSC Resolution 1325 on Peace Processes and their Agreements', *International and Comparative Law Quarterly*, Vol. 59 (forthcoming).

C. Bell and C. O'Rourke (2007) 'Does Feminism Need a Theory of Transitional Justice? An Introductory Essay', *International Journal of Transitional Justice*, Vol. 1, 23–44.

M. Benschop (2004) 'Women's Rights to Land and Property', *Commission on Sustainable Development*, available at http://www.unhabitat.org/downloads/docs/1556_72513_CSDWomen.pdf (accessed 31 July 2010).

V. Brittain (2003) 'The Impact of War on Women', *Race and Class*, Vol. 44, 4–51.
J. Butler (2002) 'Explanation and Exoneration, or What We Can Hear', *Social Text*, Vol. 20, 177–88.
C. Chinkin (2009) 'Rape and Sexual Abuse of Women in International Law', *European Journal of International Law*, Vol. 5, 326–41.
C. Chinkin (2008) 'The Protection of Economic, Social and Cultural Rights Post Conflict', *Office of the High Commissioner for Human Rights*, Vol. 4, 7–9.
C. Chinkin and K. Paradine (2001) 'Vision and Reality; Democracy and Citizenship of Women in the Dayton Peace Accords', *Yale Journal of International* Law, Vol. 26, 103–78.
C. Collins (2009) 'Human Rights Trials in Chile during and after the "Pinochet Years"', *International Journal of Transitional Justice*, Vol. 4, 67–86.
J. Conaghan (2000) 'Reassessing the Feminist Theoretical Project', *Journal of Law in Society*, Vol. 27, 351–85.
K. Engle (2005) 'International Human Rights and Feminisms: When Discourses Keep Meeting' in D. Buss and A. S. Manji (eds) *International Law: Modern Feminist Approaches* (Oxford: Hart Publishing).
K. Fearon (1999) *Women's Work: The Story of the Northern Ireland Women's Coalition* (Belfast: Blackstaff Press).
M. Fineman (1992) 'Feminist Theory in Law: The Difference It Makes', *Columbia Journal of Gender & Law*, Vol. 1, 13–23.
B. Hamber (1998) 'Remembering to Forget: Issues to Consider when Establishing Structures for Dealing with the Past' in id. (ed.) *Past Imperfect: Dealing with the Past in Northern Ireland and Societies in Transition* (Derry/Londonderry: INCORE/UU).
M. Hamilton and F. Ní Aoláin (2008) 'Gender and the Rule of Law in Transitional Societies', *Minnesota Journal of International Law*, Vol. 18, 380–402.
D. Isser, S. Lubkemann and S. N'Tow (2009) *Looking for Justice: Liberian Experiences and Perceptions of Local Justice Options* (Washington DC: United States Institute for Peace).
J. Major and A. Reynolds (1993) 'Joint Declaration on Peace: The Downing Street Declaration', available at http://cain.ulst.ac.uk/events/peace/docs/dsd151293.htm.
R. Mani (2008) 'Editorial Dilemmas of Expanding Transitional Justice, or Forging the Nexus between Transitional Justice and Development', *International Journal of Transitional Justice*, Vol. 2, 253–65.
R. Rubio-Marín (2009) 'The Gender of Reparation in Transitional Societies' in id. (ed.) *The Gender of Reparations* (Cambridge and New York: Cambridge University Press).
M. Moratti (2008) 'Tackling Obstruction to Property' in D. F. Haynes (ed.) *Deconstructing the Reconstruction: Human Rights and the Rule of Law in Post War Bosnia and Herzegovina* (Hampshire and Burlington: Ashgate).
I. Muvingi (2009) 'Sitting on Powder Kegs: Socioeconomic Rights in Transitional Societies', *International Journal of Transitional Justice*, Vol. 2, 163–82.
V. Nesiah (2006) *Truth Commissions and Gender: Principles, Policies and Procedures* (New York: International Center for Transitional Justice).
J. Neuwirth (2002) 'Women and Peace and Security: The Implementation of UN Security Council Resolution 1325', *Duke Journal of Gender Law & Policy*, Vol. 9, 253–60.

F. Ní Aoláin (2009) 'Women, Security, and the Patriarchy of Internationalized Transitional Justice', *Human Rights Quarterly*, Vol. 31, 1055–58.

F. Ní Aoláin (2006) 'Political Violence and Gender During Times of Transition', *Columbia Journal of Gender and Law*, Vol. 15, 829–49.

F. Ní Aoláin (2005) 'Transition and Under-Enforcement', *Chair Lecture at Queens University Belfast* (on file with author).

F. Ní Aoláin (2000) 'Sex-Based Violence and the Holocaust – A Reevaluation of Harms and Rights in International Law', *Yale Journal of Law & Feminism*, Vol. 12, 65–83.

F. Ní Aoláin and N. Cahn (2009) 'Hirsch Lecture: Gender, Masculinities and Transition in Conflicted Societies', *New England Law Review*, Vol. 44, 2–9.

F. Ní Aoláin and E. Rooney (2008) 'Underenforcement and Intersectionality: Gendered Aspects of Transition for Women', *International Journal of Transitional Justice*, Vol. 1, 338–54.

F. Ní Aoláin and C. O'Rourke (2010) 'Gendered Justice and the Non-State Actors', in M. Reed and A. Lyons (eds) *Contested Transitions: Dilemmas of Transitional Justice in Colombia and Comparative Experience* (Routledge).

F. Ní Aoláin and C. Turner (2007) 'Gender Truth and Transition', *UCLA Women's Law Journal*, Vol. 16, 229–79.

A. Orford (2006) 'Commissioning the Truth', *Columbia Journal of Gender and Law*, Vol. 3, 851–83.

C. O'Rourke (2008) 'Feminism v. Feminism: What is a Feminist Approach to Transnational Criminal Law', *Remarks at ASIL Proceedings*, 274–78.

D. Otto (2009) 'The Exile of Inclusion: Reflections on Gender Issues in International Law over the Last Decade', *Melbourne Journal of International Law*, Vol. 10, 11–26.

T. Pasipanodya (2008) 'A Deeper Justice: Economic and Social Justice as Transitional Justice in Nepal', *International Journal of Transitional Justice*, Vol. 2, 378–97.

C. Philpott and R. C. Williams (2008) 'The Dayton Dialectic' in D. F. Haynes (ed.) *Deconstructing the Reconstruction: Human Rights and the Rule of Law in Post War Bosnia and Herzegovina* (Hampshire and Burlington: Ashgate).

N. Puechguirbal (2010) 'Discourses on Gender, Patriarchy and Resolution 1325: A Textual Analysis of UN Documents', *International Peacekeeping*, Vol. 17, 172–87.

M. Rawi (2004) 'The Rule of the Rapists', *The Guardian*, 12 February 2004, available at http://www.guardian.co.uk/world/2004/feb/12/afghanistan.gender (accessed on 2 Aug 2010).

R. Rebouché (2009) 'An Anti-Model for Reproductive Rights Reform: The South African Example', (working paper on file with author), 13–21.

L. Sager (1978) 'Fair Measure: the Legal Status of Underenforced Constitutional Norms', *Harvard Law Review*, Vol. 91, 1212–64.

A. Smith (2004) 'The Drafting Process of a Bill of Rights for Northern Ireland Public Law', *Public Law*, Autumn, 526, 535–36.

M. Thomson (2008) *Endowed: Regulating the Male Sexed Body* (New York: Routledge).

J. Ubink and B. Van Rooij (2010) 'Towards Customary Legal Empowerment', *International Development Law Organization* (Concept Note).

UN Security Council (2008) 'Security Council Resolution 1820 on Women Peace and Security', UN Doc. S/RES/1820.

UN Security Council (2000) 'Security Council Resolution on Women, Peace and Security', UN Soc. S/RES/1325.

UN Security Council (1999) 'Security Council Resolution 1272 on the Situation in East Timor', UN Doc. S/RES/1272.

M. Vlachova and L. Biason (eds) (2005) *Women in an Insecure World Violence against Women Facts, Figures and Analysis* (Geneva: Geneva Centre for the Democratic Control of Armed Forces).

A. Zalman (2003) 'Out of the Rubble: Competing Perspectives on the Lives of Afghan Women', *Women's Review of Books: A Feminist Guide to Good Reading*, available at http://www.wellesley.edu/womensreview/archive/2003/04/highlt.html (accessed 3 August 2010).

3

Neglected Crimes: The Challenge of Raising Sexual and Gender-Based Crimes before the Extraordinary Chambers in the Courts of Cambodia

Silke Studzinsky

Sexual and gender-based crimes have only recently begun to be treated as serious crimes in international law, and there are still many obstacles to their successful prosecution. This is especially true in the case of Cambodia, where trials against leading members of the Khmer Rouge are taking place before the special hybrid court set up for this purpose, the Extraordinary Chambers in the Courts of Cambodia (ECCC). The difficulties facing those who attempt to hold the perpetrators of sexual and gender-based crimes under the Khmer Rouge regime accountable for their acts are formidable. First, in view of the sheer scope and magnitude of the Khmer Rouge's violations of human rights, sexual and gender-based crimes are viewed by many in Cambodia as being of secondary importance; moreover, there is a widespread perception that the regime was highly moralistic and did not tolerate such crimes. Secondly, the jurisdiction of the ECCC has been interpreted in a restrictive way, posing problems for the prosecution of sexual and gender-based crimes. Thirdly, the most widespread form of such crimes under the Khmer Rouge was the practice of forced marriage, which has not yet been codified as a crime under international law, which raises additional problems for the prosecution.

This chapter analyses the challenge of raising sexual and gender-based crimes before the ECCC. In the following section, the Khmer Rouge regime is briefly described with special attention given to the perpetration of sexual and gender-based crimes, including the widespread practice of forced marriage. There follows an analysis of the structure and jurisdiction of the ECCC, and a discussion of recent attempts to define the crime of forced marriage, before turning to the treatment of sexual and gender-based crimes before the ECCC.

Historical background

From 17 April 1975 to 6 January 1979, the Communist Party of Democratic Kampuchea (CPK), also known as the Khmer Rouge, ruled Cambodia and attempted to rapidly transform the nation into an efficient and productive agricultural society under the leadership of the peasant class. To establish a communist country, the Khmer Rouge aimed to destroy the previous social order by dividing the society into two different classes. City dwellers who previously resided in Phnom Penh were deported to the countryside and classified as 'new people', while the peasantry became the nascent ruling class. The peasantry were classified as 'old' or 'base people' and given more privileges than the new people. Citizens were subjected to forced labour, which entailed working in rice plantations, salt fields, and building irrigation systems and dams, in order to fulfil production targets set by the government. They were organized in mobile units that were grouped by sex and age, families were separated, and personal relationships were either banned or closely regulated. Countless people died of starvation, overwork, and a lack of medical treatment. Some victims were used for medical experimentation. LeVine (2007; 2010) uncovered abuse of pregnant women by regime members for medical training purposes. The Khmer Rouge closed all businesses, confiscated private property, forbade the use of money, banned religion, halted education, eliminated health care, and revoked any notions of parental authority. The regime also abolished the judicial system. Individual rights were non-existent; everyone was controlled by a Khmer Rouge cadre who assigned them work, controlled the amount of food consumed each day, and greatly interfered in their personal lives.

The Communist Party, and in particular its Standing Committee, was referred to as 'Angkar' or 'Organization'. It gained full control of everyone and every aspect of Cambodian society. Angkar was often compared to a pineapple, in the sense that both had hundreds of 'eyes'. Those whom Angkar considered to be enemies of the revolution were sent to re-education centres or security centres (prisons), which were established throughout the country. At these centres, Khmer Rouge cadres treated the victims inhumanely, often resorting to torture in an attempt to induce confessions regarding their alleged betrayals of Angkar. Subsequently, the victims were taken to be executed at killing fields located all over the country. Increasing numbers of 'enemies' were later identified within the ranks of the Khmer Rouge themselves, and the resulting internal purges encompassed workers in government ministries, members of the military, and the Communist Party. Approximately 1.7 million people died during the Democratic Kampuchea (DK) period (Becker, 1998; Kiernan, 2002; Chandler, 1999).

During the Khmer Rouge era, there was evidence of sexual and gender-based crimes. Although Vietnamese troops entered Cambodia and brought an end to the period of Democratic Kampuchea on 6 January 1979, some Khmer Rouge practices continued in remote regions, including organized weddings (LeVine, 2007; 2010).

In order to achieve its agricultural production targets, the Khmer Rouge ordered the strict separation of men and women with only minor regional variations in the uniformity with which the policy was enforced (McGrew, 1999). Harbouring any special feelings towards others was strictly prohibited as it could distract the people from their revolutionary work. Rules stipulated that the need to love, serve, and sacrifice was a duty intended to benefit Angkar and the collective as a whole, which excluded the possibility of maintaining individual and private relationships, except insofar as these were subordinated to the overall goals of the government. In 'The Twelve Codes of Conduct of the Combatants' the Khmer Rouge listed the rules that combatants had to abide by, and that were also expected to be followed by the civilian population. These included the obligation to respect, love, and serve people, workers, and farmers; the obligation to devote one's life to the people, and the obligation to struggle and fight bravely against enemies and to be prepared to sacrifice one's life (Documentation Center of Cambodia, 1999a).

Marston (2002: 109) has concluded that 'instead of an emphasis on individual women and men in interaction with each other we have the image of women as a class interacting with men as a class'.

The Khmer Rouge attempted to establish a 'gender-neutral' state where women contributed equally to the development of the new country and had to work as hard as their male counterparts. Haircuts were required to be uniform and any feminine behaviour was considered 'anti-revolutionary' and was forbidden. Essentially, the state regulated private life in its entirety (Jacobson, 2008: 222). Sexual relationships with the opposite sex were forbidden before matrimony and, even within marriage, the consent of Angkar was required for meetings between spouses, with slight regional variations in practice. Violations of these rules were considered a moral offence. Tan (2004–2005) has found that there existed no prohibition of relationships between members of the same sex, and that the strict separation of male and females actually fostered such relationships.

There is evidence of rape and sexual assault committed during the DK period. The victims were very unlikely to report or complain about the incident since, if such crimes were revealed, both the perpetrators *and* the victims would be harshly punished or executed (Nakagawa, 2008: 16). Evidence also suggests that the perpetrators of sexual crimes were sometimes allowed to go unpunished if they were regarded as committed and reliable revolutionaries. For example, a request was sent to the chief of a prison that a certain prisoner, charged with rape, be released because he was considered to be an 'honest' person (Documentation Center of Cambodia, 1999b). In a separate case, the chairman of another prison was charged with rape. After an investigation determined that he was committed to the revolution, he was neither punished nor dismissed.[1]

Despite evidence of sexual and gender-based crimes, the first trial against Ieng Sary and Pol Pot, held in August 1979 before the People's Revolutionary Tribunal, included no investigation into gender crimes – no doubt due to the overwhelming sense of shock that followed the discovery of the numerous killing sites and mass graves.[2] Even today, the common perception of the crimes committed by the Khmer Rouge is that this was a puritanical regime where sexual crimes did not occur or, if they did, were severely punished. Nakagawa (2008: 15) has reported that when she began to research sexual violence during the DK period, she was told that she would not succeed in interviewing survivors because all the victims were killed. However, she found nearly 100 victims or eyewitnesses of sexual violence in her first study, and a further 24 cases that are documented in her second edition (2008).

The rules requiring the separation of the sexes and harsh punishment for 'moral offences' purported to protect women from being sexually assaulted (Vickery, 1984: 187); indeed Vickery has even asserted that because of these policies, women during the DK period were less in danger of sexual violations than before. Contrary to this argument, several studies show that under the Khmer Rouge sexual crimes were committed, against both men and women, that survivors exist, and that a number of involuntary same-sex relationships developed – in part as a consequence of the forced separation of sexes (Jacobson, 2008; Tan, 2008; Nakagawa, 2008; LeVine, 2010).

The range of crimes committed during the DK period includes, but is not limited to: the mutilation of sexual organs as gendered punishment (Jacobson, 2008: 228); the exchange of sex for food, by starving victims and under general coercive circumstances (Frieson, 2001); rape before executions in prisons and re-education camps by Khmer Rouge officials, and among Khmer Rouge soldiers (Nakagawa, 2008); rape of male victims (Tan, 2005); sexual assaults, forced nudity, and sexual enslavement (Documentation Center of Cambodia, 1999a); foetuses taken from pregnant women, sometimes when these women were still alive (Locard, 2004: 258); and virginity controls.[3]

The policy of group marriages during the DK period is unique. It differs from other instances of forced marriages, such as those performed in Sierra Leone, whereby girls and women were abducted, forcibly married to militia members, and became so-called 'bush wives' who were required inter alia to provide sexual services to their new husbands. Forced marriages under the DK regime were conducted in a widespread and systematic manner in accordance with the Khmer Rouge policy to establish a strong and massive work unit by replacing familial and individual ties with loyalty to Angkar. Vickery (1984: 186), has suggested, '[t]hat policy was to encourage the formation or maintenance of at least nuclear family units of husband, wife, and children'. This is contradicted, however, by the widespread policy of separating the couples after some nights, and sending the spouses to different work sites. Children were also separated from their mothers.

Since the Khmer Rouge had destroyed the traditional family structure, Angkar replaced the family and selected appropriate spouses who were married in pre-organized group weddings of up to 300 couples. Generally, it was impermissible to refuse to be married and those who refused were punished. Usually, the new couples had never met each other before participating in the organized mass weddings.[4] The ages of those subject to forced marriage varied according to whether the intended spouse was a soldier or civilian. The age requirement for female soldiers was 20–25 and for male soldiers 25–30 years (Mam, 2000: 54). A consequence of the strong demand for soldiers was that these were married at later ages than civilians. For the latter, no strict age policy is known to have been applied, but among those now seeking justice before the Extraordinary Chambers, are survivors who were forcibly married between the ages of 14–17.

In stark contrast to the Cambodian tradition where a wedding lasts several days and is accompanied by various ceremonial rituals, mass weddings were brief events and were often held after sunset, presumably in order not to disrupt the working day. They denied the individuals' cultural rights by including no traditional rituals, and usually excluded the participation of family members. The forced marriages were combined with political meetings during which the couples were reminded of their duty to follow the orders of Angkar and had to swear to remain in marriage as determined by Angkar.

LeVine (2007; 2010) has ascertained that, in many cases, sexual intercourse was directly prescribed, but these orders were only addressed to the males. Of 88 males among a total of 192 interviewees, 76 (more than 86 per cent) received the order to engage in sexual intercourse. Haing Ngor (1987: 293) states that women subjected to forced marriage were expressly directed to remain quiet if their husbands were to 'become angry' – a phrase used in Khmer to refer to male sexual arousal.

The fact that, after 1978, huts were sometimes prepared for the newlywed couples prior to the ceremonies suggests that these mass weddings became highly organized affairs. Some new couples had to spend the first night(s) together under the real or assumed control of Khmer Rouge soldiers. KR soldiers remained under the huts (the structures of which varied according to region and resources) to monitor and report if there was any disagreement between the couple. Evidently, men were also forced into marriages, and thus were victims of this practice; however, there are also cases of men taking advantage of forced marriage to abuse and exploit their partners (Nakagawa, 2008: 21–2).

LeVine (2007; 2010) has established that forced marriages were a widespread practice and has also identified a general pattern in the conduct of marriages occurring across the country. This leads to the conclusion that the imposition of mass weddings was ordered by the Standing Committee of the Communist Party, which was the only group with the power to orchestrate such nationwide practices. LeVine (2007; 2010) holds that the mass weddings were gradually institutionalized over time and place and were implemented nationally by 1978. Evidence shows that, as early as the end of 1975, groups of up to 20 Khmer Rouge cadres were gathered and a decree was read aloud declaring that Angkar directed everybody to marry for the sake of increasing the revolutionary population.[5] Furthermore, women were put under pressure to take handicapped soldiers as husbands to reward the latters' revolutionary achievements.[6]

Although researchers and scholars have repeatedly discussed the existence of such mass weddings during the DK period, they have done so without specifically acknowledging the coercive component of such marriages (Short, 2005; Chandler, 2000, 1999; Kiernan, 2002). For this reason, these forced marriages were not initially considered to be serious crimes.

The ECCC: structure and jurisdiction

In early 1997, the UN initiated its efforts to establish an international criminal tribunal to try the Khmer Rouge leaders for the most serious human rights violations that occurred under their rule. In June of that year, the Cambodian government formally requested UN assistance to establish such a tribunal. In 2006, after nearly ten years of negotiations regarding the structure of the Court, its international and national character, and the balance between both sides, the Court was finally established as a national court, Extraordinary Chambers in the Courts of Cambodia, supported by the UN. Proceedings before the ECCC started in June 2007, when core judicial personnel began working at the Court in Phnom Penh.

The ECCC is a unique type of hybrid court, which differs in structure significantly from the other internationalized or international tribunals. It was formed according to the provisions of the ECCC Law 2001, as amended in 2004 (ECCC, 2004). Essentially, the ECCC Law of 2004 is the implementing legislation of the Agreement of 27 October 2004 between the UN and the Royal Government of Cambodia (RGC) (UN and RGC, 2003). Nevertheless, the ECCC is a Cambodian – not an international – institution, which is a consequence of its establishment under domestic law (Acquaviva, 2008).

According to both the Agreement and the ECCC Law of 2004, the governing procedural law is the domestic Cambodian code of criminal procedure, which has been in force since August 2007 and is very similar to the French Criminal Procedure Code. Thus, the procedure reflects the civil law tradition and is inquisitorial rather than adversarial. International procedural law guides in cases of a lacuna; however, there is still uncertainty on the interpretation or application of Cambodian law in cases where this appears inconsistent with relevant international standards (ECCC, 2004: arts. 20 *new*, 23 *new*, 33 *new*). In addition, the Court adopted the *Internal Rules* in June 2007, which, according to their preamble, consolidate Cambodian procedural law (ECCC, 2010b). This is not in accordance with the ECCC Law, which does not envisage any authority establishing internal rules binding on the judicial officers of the ECCC.[7]

The ECCC Law lists the crimes over which the Court has jurisdiction, including domestic crimes enumerated in the Cambodian Penal Code of

1956, such as homicide, torture, and religious persecution. Additionally, the ECCC Law confers jurisdiction over crimes under international law, including genocide, crimes against humanity, and war crimes where these amount to grave breaches of the Geneva Conventions of 1949, destruction of cultural property in armed conflict, and crimes against internationally protected persons.

The Court's temporal jurisdiction is limited to the Democratic Kampuchea period from 17 April 1975 until 6 January 1979, while its personal jurisdiction is limited to the prosecution of senior leaders and those most responsible for the worst atrocities under the regime.

The staff in all sections of the Court is composed of international and national personnel. As a result of the RGC-UN negotiations, the Pre-Trial and Trial Chambers are composed of three national and two international judges, and the Supreme Court Chamber has four national and three international judges. However, all decisions must be made by a qualified majority and every decision must have the support of at least one international judge.

Foreign lawyers can only act in cooperation with a Cambodian counterpart, and they are only permitted to speak after the Cambodian counterpart has requested his or her recognition (this request must be made separately before each judicial body of the Court where the foreign lawyer wishes to represent his or her client).

The investigations are initiated by the Office of the Co-Prosecutors (OCP) and conducted by the Office of the Co-Investigating Judges (OCIJ). In addition, the parties to the proceedings (the prosecution, civil parties, and defence) may request investigative actions intended to develop a broad and comprehensive portrayal of the historical facts as part of the truth-building process.

As a court that deals with mass atrocities, the ECCC is unique because it established the right of victims to become civil parties who are allowed to support the prosecution; to participate in the proceedings; and to request moral and collective reparations (ECCC, 2010b: 23[1]). Further, the civil parties enjoy such rights as legal representation and, through their lawyers, access to the case file, and they also have the right to question the accused, the witnesses, and the experts; to summon witnesses and experts; and to appeal certain decisions (ECCC, 2010b, 23[1], 74[4], 77[4], 80[2], 90, 91[2]).

Although the ECCC was established upon carefully negotiated principles, it is beset with problems. Allegations of corruption and mismanagement have compromised the Court's reputation and threatened its funding (Open Society Justice Initiative, 2009). Moreover, as a unique tribunal, the Court is often forced to resolve complex legal, procedural, and evidentiary issues without being able to refer to any previous cases. In dealing with a high number of victims as civil parties in trials for mass crimes, the Court is also treading on new territory. These challenges will make it more difficult to achieve the ECCC's goals of justice and national reconciliation. Consequently, true justice may have to be achieved outside the courtroom through a more comprehensive process of national reconciliation and education (Assmann, 2010).

Despite various efforts undertaken by international and internationalized war crime tribunals to recognize and investigate sexual and gender-based crimes in international humanitarian law, it appears, both in theory and in practice, that the legal framework at the ECCC remains unable to address sexual and gender-based crimes, especially sexual crimes, appropriately. This failure is underscored by the limited number of crimes enumerated in the ECCC Law, which copied the language set forth in the Statute of the International Criminal Court for Rwanda (ICTR, 1994). Thus, the definition of crimes against humanity under the ECCC Law follows the ICTR Statute in requiring the element of discriminatory intent (on national, political, ethnic, racial, or religious grounds) for each crime. However, proving discriminatory intent on any of the specified grounds is extremely difficult in cases of sexual and gender-based crimes in the specific context of the Khmer Rouge regime.

The Agreement between the UN and the Royal Government of Cambodia, ratified on 4 October 2004, promulgated on 19 October 2004, and the ECCC Law of 2001 as amended in 2003, promulgated on 27 October 2004, are intended to be mutually consistent.[8] The Agreement defines crimes against humanity in Article 9 in accordance with the definition adopted by the Rome Statute of the International Criminal Court (ICC, 1998).[9] The definition of crimes against humanity in Article 7(1) (g) of the Rome Statute differs from that of the ICTR Statute in two important respects. First, it does not require the specific element of discriminatory intent, and, secondly, it enumerates a wider range of sexual and gender-based crimes, including not only rape (as in the ICTR Statute) but also sexual slavery, enforced prostitution, enforced pregnancy, enforced sterilization, or any other form of sexual violence of comparable gravity (ICC, 1998, art. 7[1](g)).

However, the ECCC Law falls far short of appropriately addressing sexual and gender-based crimes, referring only to rape (ECCC, 2004, art. 5), and it makes no reference to the Rome Statute that the Agreement, to which it is meant to give effect, explicitly takes as a model.[10] One way to deal with this lacuna in the legal frame of sexual crimes is by adhering to the terms set forth in the Agreement, which address a wider range of sexual and gender-based crimes. Since the ECCC Law of 2004 is an implementing law, that was intended to enact the provisions of the Agreement, the terms of the latter should prevail over the ECCC Law. This approach finds support in the Vienna Convention on the Law of Treaties, whose provisions would suggest that the Agreement take precedent over any inconsistent and contradicting norms set forth by the ECCC Law (Dyrchs, 2008: 120; UN and RGC, 2003: art. 2[2]). Moreover, when bearing in mind the historical origins of the ECCC Law that is derived from the Agreement, it seems clear that the discrepancies between them are the result of an oversight. Therefore, the definition of crimes against humanity codified in the Rome Statute, as referred to by the Agreement, should be used as a legal framework for investigating sexual crimes at the ECCC. In any event, despite the fact that specific sexual and gender-based crimes were not explicitly included in the jurisdiction of the ECCC by the ECCC Law, it can be argued that such crimes must fall within the scope of 'other inhumane acts' under the ECCC Law.

Forced marriage as a crime against humanity

The Rome Statute of the International Criminal Court does not enumerate a specific crime of forced marriage, despite the fact that this offence contains certain elements which are not comprised by the existing variety of sexual and gender-based crimes specified in the Rome Statute. While forced marriage could well be defined as constituting 'other inhumane acts' (ICC, 1998, art. 7[k]), a concise and universally valid definition of the crime of forced marriage is still lacking. Recent developments both in jurisprudence and academic writing have made important advances in this respect. However, we still lack a definition applicable to the circumstances of all cases.

Notable contributions have been made in this regard by the Special Court for Sierra Leone, established as an internationalized tribunal to prosecute the crimes perpetrated during Sierra Leone's civil war. After the Appeal Chamber of the Special Court for Sierra Leone (SCSL) recognized forced marriage as a new crime within the category of crimes against humanity, for the first time in an international(ized) tribunal (SCSL, 2008, paras. 175–202), the Trial Chamber of the SCSL found three leaders guilty of the count of forced marriage. This was cumulative with sexual enslavement and rape, and classified as an 'other inhumane act' within the category of crimes against humanity in the RUF (Revolutionary United Front) case (SCSL, 2009, paras. 164–9).

In that case, the Trial Chamber determined that 'the constitutive elements of the crime of other inhumane acts' are:

> (i) The occurrence of an act or omission that inflicts great suffering or serious injury to body, or to mental or physical health
> (ii) The act or omission is sufficiently similar in gravity to the acts referred to in Article 2(a) to Article 2(h) of the Statute [of the Special Court for Sierra Leone]
> (iii) The Accused was aware of the factual circumstances that established the character of the gravity of the act
> (iv) The Accused, at the time of the act or omission, had the intention to commit the inhumane act or acted in the knowledge that this would likely occur.
>
> (SCSL, 2009, para. 168)

The Trial Chamber was satisfied that these prerequisites were fulfilled. It also found that 'forced marriage' requires a forced conjugal association based on exclusivity between the perpetrator and the victim, which is a distinct element from those required to establish the crimes of rape and sexual slavery, and that this additional element is therefore not subsumed by sexual slavery or rape. The Chamber held it permissible to cumulatively convict a defendant of counts of rape, sexual slavery and forced marriage (SCSL, 2009, paras. 2306–7).[11]

Despite the importance of the recent judgments at the SCSL regarding the recognition of forced marriage as a crime against humanity, the circumstances and facts surrounding how girls and women were forced into marriages during the conflict in Sierra Leone differ significantly from other situations, such as the marriages imposed on couples in Cambodia during the DK period. Therefore, a fuller definition of forced marriage, that encompasses all of its aspects, is required; such a definition could increase the chances that such a crime be included in the investigations and jurisprudence of future cases.

Scharf and Mattler (2005: 22) have proposed a definition that recognizes certain key elements of the crime of forced marriage. However, it is tailored to the specific situation in Sierra Leone and focuses only upon women as victims.[12] To properly address the different circumstances under which forced marriages occur, and to ensure that the definition is generally applicable to both women and men as victims, the author suggests the following definition:

> Forced marriage as part of a widespread or systematic attack against the civilian population can be directed similarly against women and men. It contains the following elements:
>
> (i) the marriage was performed without obtaining the consent of both parties involved
>
> (ii) the marriage was performed by force, or by threat of force or coercion, such as that caused by fear of violence, duress, detention, psychological oppression or abuse of power, against such person or another person, or by taking advantage of a coercive environment or such persons' incapacity to give genuine consent. In addition, *one or more* of the following elements characterize a forced marriage:
>
> a. the intention to cause either or both of the parties to have sexual intercourse without their consent, or either or both of the parties to provide sexual services to the other party without consent
>
> b. to force the victim into an exclusive conjugal association, including short-term conjugal relationships as determined by the party exercising coercion.

The proposed definition aims to include all the elements that potentially make up the varieties of forced marriages. It attempts to explain that not all elements apply to all situations, as various combinations of these elements will apply to different forced marriages, depending on the circumstances. All statutes of international and internationalized courts currently omit forced marriage as a specific crime, and only allow subsuming the crime under 'other inhumane acts' which is not adequate. This current situation does not respond to the reality in which forced marriages are used as a weapon in combat and war in order to gain effective control over the civilian population and may be used, not only against women, but against men too, as the Cambodian example well demonstrates.

Taking the ruling of the SCSL into account, the Trial Chamber of the ECCC could both include other serious crimes not explicitly mentioned in the ECCC Laws of 2001 and 2004, nor in the Agreement between the UN and the RGC, within the category of 'other inhumane acts', and, also, charge these crimes cumulatively because they require different elements.

The ECCC and sexual and gender-based crimes

At the ECCC, sexual and gender-based crimes, in particular forced marriages throughout Democratic Kampuchea, came to light only recently, and only through the efforts of the legal representatives of civil parties. Although this development is to be welcomed in drawing attention to such crimes, the relatively short amount of time remaining for the ECCC to complete its work is not conducive to thorough investigations of sexual and gender-based crimes in the DK period.

There are various longstanding reasons for the continued failure to address such crimes appropriately. Despite a growing awareness of sexual and gender-based crimes in recent times, the imposition of forced marriages during the DK period has been mistakenly construed as amounting simply to a series of arranged marriages, a practice which occurs in Cambodia at present. Moreover, sexual and gender-based crimes are often disregarded and neglected in the aftermath of mass atrocities that caused the deaths of thousands of people, or are taken less seriously than other crimes. In particular, sexual crimes have been considered as 'by-products' or 'collateral damage' that do not deserve priority attention. In addition, there is a lack of participants with a gender-sensitive perspective in key decision-making positions, both nationally and internationally. Consequently, people who are attuned to the seriousness of sexual and gender-based crimes have less influence on the common perception of historical and judicial facts, and thus on the planning and conduct of the prosecution of cases.

Due to the limited time and resources allocated to the ECCC, it is recognized that a strategic selection of cases, crimes, and crime sites is necessary if the Court is to function efficiently. Nevertheless, to ignore sexual and gender-based crimes until very near to the closing of the investigations, particularly the crime of forced marriage, which affected a substantial number of victims, is detrimental to the justice-seeking process. It also contradicts recent developments on the international level such as UN Security Council Resolutions 1325 (UN, 2000) and 1820 (UN, 2008) related to sexual and gender-based crimes. These resolutions have been influential in the struggle against all types of sexual violence, especially Resolution 1820 that recalled '... [t]he inclusion of a *range* of sexual violence offences in the Rome Statute of the International Criminal Court and the statutes of the ad hoc *international* criminal tribunals' (emphasis added).

Despite this, it is clear that the strategy of the ECCC's investigating bodies has excluded consideration of sexual and gender-based crimes.

Although several witnesses and/or victims mentioned such crimes in their testimony, they were asked no further questions on these issues, nor were any specific investigations conducted. This lack of interest on the part of investigators seems to reflect the (flawed) investigation strategy. As discussed below, the ECCC is now showing itself somewhat more receptive to this issue.

It is important to stress that a gender-sensitive approach is crucial in investigating sexual and gender-based crimes. Only appropriately trained investigators and interpreters, as well as prosecutors and judges with a gender-sensitive attitude and specific training, can ensure that such crimes are taken seriously, in a manner that enables victims and witnesses to speak of their experiences without severe discomfort, and takes their needs into account.

At the ECCC there are no members of staff trained to address gender-sensitive issues. Currently, all investigators, as well as the Cambodian interpreters, are male. When victims of sexual and gender-based crimes began submitting complaints, Co-Lawyers for civil parties requested that female investigators and interpreters with gender training be hired to guarantee that the further traumatization of victims of sexual violence would be avoided as far as possible. The request was ignored. When a second request was filed, the Office of the Co-Investigating Judges acknowledged '...[t]he need for gender-sensitive techniques in cases concerning sexual and gender-based violence testimony ...' but asserted that '... [a]lthough the current staffing of OCIJ does not include female investigators, all efforts are being made to ensure best practices are fully implemented' (ECCC, 2009b, para. 15). However, the OCIJ seems very far from best practice. A recent interview of a victim of gang rape by two male interrogators and one male interpreter led to the victim's psychological collapse. Since the OCIJ has begun to conduct investigations on forced marriages, the nature and choice of terms used by male investigators when interrogating female victims has consistently demonstrated a lack of background knowledge of the historical, cultural, and legal aspects of this and related crimes. In addition, investigators' use of euphemistic terms such as 'making love to someone' rather than referring to sexual intercourse during the first night of a non-voluntary marriage tends to obscure rather than clarify the fact-finding necessary for evaluating the nature of the crime.

In February 2009, Civil Party Co-Lawyers requested that the Office of the Co-Prosecutors provide a Supplementary Submission in Case 1 against Kaing Guek Eav, alias 'Duch'. In particular, the Civil Party Lawyers requested the investigation of at least one case involving a group wedding among the staff and medical personnel of a re-education centre that was under the Accused's control. Despite the obligation of the OCP to determine the status of a complaint within 60 days, the request was ignored (ECCC, 2010b, rule 49).Six months later, the Office of Co-Prosecutors explained that the reason for not having dealt with the submission was their opinion that the request was belated after the indictment was issued.[13]

It certainly would have been possible to investigate this case in a timely fashion and include the results of such investigations in an additional closing order,[14] which could have been joined with the existing indictment.

On several occasions, the Trial Chamber rejected Civil Party Co-Lawyers' attempts to raise the issue of a mass wedding that occurred in the re-education centre at Prey Sar which was ordered by the accused Kaing Guek Eav, alias 'Duch', deeming the issue 'irrelevant'.[15] The judges offered no clear reason for refusing to consider the crime.

In addition, the ECCC's *Internal Rules* fail to address both how to present evidence in cases involving sexual violence, and how to provide adequate procedural protections for victims giving evidence. Hence, no safeguards for the testifying victim exist. One consequence of this lack of safeguards is that the victims' prior sexual conduct is often raised in a manner that is insensitive to any victim of sexual violence (ICC, 2002, rule 70).

The existing situation cannot encourage survivors of sexual and gender-based crimes to come forward to tell their stories. Without the opportunity to have their grievances appropriately addressed by the ECCC, they will be in the same situation as they would be if they appeared before the domestic courts and investigative bodies. Therefore, the conditions at the ECCC mirror the situation in Cambodian society, where the victim suffers discrimination and moral guilt is ascribed to him/her. This is, therefore, inconsistent with the ECCC's purpose to serve as a model Court in providing justice, especially to the victims.

The ECCC has, however, taken a step forward in its dealing with sexual and gender-based crimes since the submission by Civil Party Co-Lawyers of a case concerning the multiple rapes of a transgender individual, who was also forced to marry a woman, as well as four more cases of forced marriage affecting both sexes (ECCC, 2008a). These cases were part of the investigations in Case 002 against Nuon Chea, Ieng Sary, Ieng Thirith, and Khieu Samphan, the alleged senior leaders of the Khmer Rouge. The investigation was closed in early 2010.

The transgendered victim was forced to behave like a man, to cut her hair, to destroy her chosen sexual identity, and to assume an unwanted male identity. When the Khmer Rouge took power, she was assigned to a group of 20 transgendered people, of whom all except herself were eventually killed or forcibly disappeared. During this time, she directly witnessed the rape of one of her friends. She has provided evidence that addresses how sexual minorities were treated during the DK period, indicating that sexual violence was one of the means used to punish what was regarded as deviant behaviour. At a well-attended press conference held in Phnom Penh on 3 September 2008, she announced her intention to testify before the Court.[16] Gay communities and other sexual minority groups in Asia strongly welcomed her attempt to receive public acknowledgement of the sexual and gender-based crimes committed against her, and recognized the filing of her complaint as a milestone in the struggle to address gender-based violence committed against sexual minorities because of their sexual orientation.[17] This show of solidarity encouraged her to participate in the proceedings and to seek justice by revealing the truth. However, enormous barriers remain, as became apparent when this victim/survivor was required to complete the Civil Party application form necessary for a victim to participate as a civil party before the ECCC. This form requires detailed accounts of all the individual incidents survivors experienced during the Khmer Rouge regime, often an intensely traumatic experience. In cases of this kind, the problem is compounded by the fact that the interview is conducted by male investigators, and the *Internal Rules* exclude the civil party's lawyers from being present during such an interview. All attempts to amend this Rule had failed. Again, this demonstrates that the Court lacks a gender-sensitive approach to vulnerable victims of sexual and gender-based violence. Moreover, the investigators lack the time, patience and willingness necessary to create circumstances in which such survivors can speak comfortably. Yet, being effectively deprived of a voice in this way would exclude such survivors from being acknowledged as a persecuted sexual minority and interfere with the healing process that the Court holds out to such people. In October 2008, three women and one man filed the first applications as civil parties related to forced marriages, in which they described in detail the circumstances of their group weddings (Seiha, 2009). In one case, 24 couples were married in one ceremony, in which each couple was required to spend the first night together in small cubicles separated from each other by palm leaves. These four civil parties are from the same village; one of them, already marginalized in her community for choosing to live alone, has faced unpleasant encounters with her neighbours after applying to testify about the practice of forced marriage. Nevertheless, such survivors draw strength from the solidarity among the civil parties, and derive support from other victims of forced marriages who have spoken about their own compulsory wedding ceremonies under the KR. The process is closely accompanied by the Transcultural Psycho-Social Organization (TPO) which provides socio-psychological support to victims and witnesses before the Court. However, the services are not financed by the Court, which does not offer any mental health services to victims and witnesses, even to highly vulnerable victims of sexual violence.

Regrettably, the current situation shows that Cambodian officials of the ECCC still harbour doubts regarding the possibility of a man being raped, do not think it worthwhile to investigate the imposition of forced marriages as a crime, and are of the opinion that the fact that couples remain together invalidates the crime.

Despite such obstacles, these cases represent the first steps in the efforts necessary to establish the truth regarding the history of gender-based rights violations, which may encourage other victims to file complaints. More importantly, the investigation of these cases can draw society's attention to past and present sexual and gender-based violence in order to prevent their recurrence.

In April 2009, the Office of the Co-Investigating Judges forwarded the above mentioned cases of forced marriages, and the similar accounts of three other victims, to the Office of the Co-Prosecutors, which has the ability to make a Supplementary Submission addressing the crimes in order to determine the scope of OCIJ investigations. Not surprisingly, the Office of the Co-Prosecutors responded to the OCIJ by issuing a very limited Supplementary Submission, that requested and authorized the judges to investigate *only* those five cases in which extensive details regarding forced marriage had been provided in the application for recognition as a Civil Party, excluding other cases that referred to forced marriage from further investigations.

The Office of the Co-Prosecutors understanding of what crimes constitute a 'forced marriage' is limited to only 'forced sexual relations' without taking into account other elements such as being forced into a conjugal relationship. Three additional victims of forced marriages have never been asked to provide further details about their experiences during the investigation thus far. The ECCC's failure to properly investigate is consistent with the experience that gender-based crimes, and in particular sexual crimes, are sensitive and rarely revealed without being asked for.

Nevertheless, in November 2009 the Co-Investigating Judges made public that they included forced marriages throughout Democratic Kampuchea into the current investigations.

Although sexual and gender-based violence, including forced marriage, is mentioned in numerous witness statements on the case file, these statements provide little or no information about the surrounding circumstances, and are not sufficiently detailed for inclusion in the indictment without further examination. In July and December 2009 Civil Party Co-Lawyers therefore submitted two investigative requests to the Office of the Co-Investigating Judges calling for a total of 86 people, who were either victims of sexual and gender-based violence or direct witnesses of such incidents, to be identified and interviewed again with a view to gaining additional information. Both requests were rejected, with the exception of one requested interview, and upheld by the Pre-Trial Chamber on appeal.

Because one of the main obstacles to the recognition of the existence of sexual and gender-based violence was, and is, a lack of focus on identifying victims of sexual and gender-based violence, a support project called 'Cambodian Defenders Project – Gender-Based Violence Project' (CDP-GBV Project) was created by the German Development Service ('DED') in conjunction with CDP, a Cambodian legal NGO. It started its work in March 2009.[18] Its primary focus is assisting and supporting victims of sexual and gender-based crimes during the DK period, and providing them with the information necessary to enable them to participate in the ECCC proceedings. This project concerns primarily sexual violence directed against both sexes, supports the Court's contribution to transitional justice, and works closely together with existing projects in the field. The CDP-GBV Project encourages awareness of the specific gender-based crimes committed during the DK period that wrought the complete transformation of Cambodian society, among them sexually related crimes, the separation of families, and the destruction of culture and traditions.

One challenge faced by this project is that survivors do not always perceive themselves as 'victims' of forced marriage, nor does society, because they did not protest the order received from Angkar before being married. Furthermore, some couples who were forced to marry, but have stayed together beyond the DK regime, likewise do not identify themselves as victims of forced marriage.

Moreover, LeVine (2007; 2010) established in over 1000 interviews, of which 192 were formally recorded, that fears and anxiety actually decreased among some victims following forced marriage. This was because they were able to live a more communal life as a result of being placed in post-wedding communal work sites, while having access to more food and rest as well as traditional systems such as protective amulets and so on. However, it is very likely that this relatively positive assessment of forced marriage is attributable to its status relative to the other gross atrocities and heinous crimes that people suffered throughout the DK period.

Therefore, it is a huge challenge for the CDP-GBV Project to raise awareness among the Cambodian people that genuine consent was impossible to obtain under the generally coercive circumstances that surrounded all facets of life during the DK period, as well as arguing the fact that because couples choose to remain together does not invalidate the original crime. One of the ways to face this challenge is to train field workers in relevant ECCC matters, along with outreach officers, to develop a gender-sensitive approach towards survivors. This can be conducted through the existing structures and channels established by other NGOs that are capable of facilitating the process.

In the light of the narrow investigative strategy adopted by the ECCC, and the lack of appropriate and sensitive mechanisms for dealing with victims, this project has become very important to ensure that complaints or Civil Party applications intended for submission are sufficiently detailed and provide precise descriptions of the crimes experienced. The project will also contribute to the truth-finding process, and this is necessary to ensure that sexual and gender-based crimes are included in the closing order. As previously discussed, these sexual and gender-based crimes remain omitted from the common perception of crimes committed during the DK period. Given the fact that investigations were closed with the issuing of the closing order in September 2010, the project needed to move as quickly as possible. By July 2010, 211 victims of sexual and gender-based violence, both men and women, had been interviewed within this project and their forms submitted to the ECCC. Recent experience has demonstrated that those victims who came forward to submit their stories to the Court encouraged other victims to follow them.

In the closing order (indictment), issued on 16 September 2010, the Co-Investigating Judges charged the defendants with having implemented a countrywide policy of forced marriages, and subsumed this under rape and other inhumane acts. But rape outside of the context of forced marriages is excluded as a charge because it was not the common purpose of the accused persons, according to the judges. The CIJs consider that 'the official CPK policy regarding rape was to prevent its occurrence and to punish the perpetrators. Despite the fact that this policy did not manage to prevent rape, it cannot be considered that rape was one of the crimes used by the CPK leaders to implement the common purpose' (ECCC, 2010a, para. 1429). In contrast, the Co-Prosecutors requested in their final submission to also indict the accused for rape cases at several security centres.

The challenge for Case 2 will be to include these rape cases as part of the systematic and widespread attack against the civilian population.

Conclusion

Ensuring that victims have access to justice, and conducting appropriate investigations into sexual and gender-based crimes, are core elements of any transitional justice proceedings intended to promote the rule of law, faith in the judicial system, and the reconstruction of society. These elements cannot be neglected or ignored by war crimes courts and tribunals. The intrusive DK policies of forced marriage, separation of families, and abolishing cultural traditions has had, and continues to have, an enormous impact on Cambodian society, reflected in recurring tendencies of domestic violence, gender discrimination, violence against sex workers and homosexuals, and widespread sexual abuse of children of both sexes. It is important to note that investigations into sexual and gender-based crimes differ significantly from investigations into other types of crimes. The specific forms of stigma, trauma, harm, and suffering endured by victims of crimes targeting gender, and the overarching societal impact, must be taken into account when gender-based violence is investigated. Especially in countries engaged in transition, raising awareness of such crimes, and prosecuting them appropriately, not only contributes to the justice process itself, but is a necessary tool to further gender equality and to ensure access to the justice system for precisely these vulnerable victims. Neglecting sexual and gender-based crimes for the sake of supposedly strategic plans to limit the scope of criminal investigations, means leaving the wounds of the victims unhealed, and tarnishing the legacy of the transitional justice process. Moreover, the truth-building process will be deficient if such crimes are not energetically prosecuted, creating a negative impact on the post-conflict society as a whole.

As this chapter has shown, both in terms of its limited jurisdiction, and the lack of gender-sensitive procedures, the ECCC remains far behind recent developments in transitional justice with regard to sexual and gender-based violence. At the same time, however, its inclusion of survivors and witnesses as civil parties represents an innovative feature which has been utilized by such survivors and witnesses, with support from their legal representatives, to highlight crimes to which the ECCC itself has attached low priority; in particular sexual and gender-based crimes.

Although it is too soon to be able to determine the overarching impact on today's society in Cambodia of making the sexual and gender-based violence committed by the Khmer Rouge visible, at least small steps have been taken to encourage people to speak out about their experiences, to find their individual sexual autonomy, and to exercise their right to sexual self-determination.

Notes

Invaluable help was provided by Fitria Chairani, LLM graduate (2010) National University of Singapore in conducting the research for this article, Alison Yewdell, JD Candidate (2010) Washington University School of Law and Katrina Gordon, BA English Literature (1996) and Dip Law, University of Sydney, Australia (2009) in editing the use of English.

1. The related witness statement is on the case file and still confidential.
2. Comment of Thun Saray, President of the Human Rights NGO ADHOC, who was heavily involved in the work of the trial preparations in 1979, to the author on 17 December 2008. The People's Revolutionary Tribunal at Phnom Penh was constituted in Cambodia in 1979 by Decree law to try the Ex- Prime Minister, Pol Pot, and Ex-Deputy Prime Minister for foreign affairs, Ieng Sary. The hearing was held from 15 to 19 August 1979. Pol Pot and Ieng Sary were sentenced to death in absentia for genocide. The process was never recognized internationally and was criticized for political bias. In 1996 Ieng Sary received an amnesty from the King and his troops joined the government's military.
3. This latter practice was mentioned by a Cambodian individual participating in the ongoing trials before the ECCC, in interview with the author on 15 September 2008.
4. Of course there were some exceptions to this general principle as it also occurred that somebody could ask permission to marry a certain person.
5. This information is based on the testimony of a civil party.
6. Author's interview of a female civil party on 3 July 2009.
7. In their August 2008 Decision on Nuon Chea's Appeal Against Order Refusing Request for Annulment, the Pre-Trial Chamber ruled that the Internal Rules are self-contained procedural law and a primary source, thus superseding Cambodian and international procedure, and that Cambodian Criminal Procedure applies only when a question unaddressed by the Internal Rules arises (ECCC, 2008b). However, it is highly debatable whether judges in a civil system are entitled to approve regulations that, although created in good faith, violate conventional legal interpretation (Studzinsky, 2009; Worden, 2005).

8. The first ECCC Law of 2001 was a law which the UN has not accepted. The purpose of the Agreement (signed 6 June 2003 and ratified 19 October 2004) was to amend the existing ECCC Law of 2001. But the amended ECCC Law dated 27 October 2004 did not fully harmonize the changes required by the Agreement and included inter alia the definition of crimes against humanity as adopted by the Statute of the International Criminal Court for Rwanda instead of referring to the definition in the Rome Statute as the Agreement did (Etcheson, 2006; Worden, 2005).
9. Article 9 of the Agreement states that: '[t]he subject-matter jurisdiction of the Extraordinary Chambers shall be ... crimes against humanity as defined in the 1998 Rome Statute of the International Criminal Court and grave breaches of the 1949 Geneva Conventions and such other crimes as defined in Chapter II of the Law on the Establishment of the Extraordinary Chambers as promulgated on 10 August 2001.' (UN, 2003).
10. The parliamentary debate on the ECCC Law does not elaborate on this discrepancy and gives no further indication for the limitation of crimes against humanity.
11. To understand the recent development, see the comprehensive summary by N. Jain (2008: 1017–22), of the Trial Chamber's decision in the AFRC case through the dissenting opinion of Justice Doherty and the Separate Opinion of Justice Sebutinde until the Appeal Judgment in which finally 'forced marriage' has been recognized for the first time as a distinct and proper crime. It appears to be continued by the Trial Chamber in the RUF case.
12. The following is the definition suggested by Scharf and Mattler (2005):
    1. The perpetrator attached the right of marriage to one or more persons without the individual's consent by threat of force or coercion, such as that caused by fear of violence, duress, detention, psychological oppression or abuse of power, against such person or persons or another person, or by taking advantage of a coercive environment or such person's or persons' incapacity to give genuine consent;
    2. The perpetrator caused such person or persons to engage in one or more acts of a sexual nature, and/or forced domestic labor, child bearing, or child rearing;
    3. The perpetrator makes it so that the individual is unable to dissolve the marriage;
    4. The conduct was committed as part of a widespread or systematic attack directed against a civilian population; and
    5. The perpetrator knew that the conduct was part of or intended the conduct to be part of a widespread or systematic attack directed against a civilian population.
13. The notification of this fact was by simple e-mail.
14. Closing order is the term for indictment according to the Cambodian law and the Internal Rules of the ECCC.
15. Kaing Guek Eav stands trial for charges of war crimes and crimes against humanity. He was the chairman of the prison S-21 where more than 12,000 prisoners were tortured and killed. The trial started on 16 February 2009 and the hearings concluded on 17 September 2009 (ECCC, 2009a).
16. See press conference under 'Highlights of the ECCC' http://www.eccc.gov.kh/English/news.list.aspx?attribute=&selector=&page=14.

17. See for example gender-related networks like Gender Dynamix under http://www.genderdynamix.org/content/view/357/204/; http://www.genderdynamix.org/images/stories/articles/2008–09pressrelease%201st%20civil%20party%20on%20gender%20based%20violence.pdf and breakthrough in LGBTI rights advocacy. 'It will be our victory if gender based violence in general and discrimination and abuses to sexual minorities (LGBTI) in particular, be considered a crime against humanity.' Or, http://birdofparadox.wordpress.com/ or, http://www.martinforeman.com/world/borsorbo.html (accessed 1 June 2009).
18. The CDP-GBV Project (Cambodian Defenders Project–Gender-Based-Violence Project) is financed by the German Development Service DED (Deutscher Entwicklungsdienst) in the framework of the Civil Peace Service.

References

G. Acquaviva (2008) 'New Paths in International Criminal Justice? The Internal Rules of the Cambodian Extraordinary Chambers', *Journal of International Criminal Justice*, Vol. 6, 129–51.

K. D. Askin (1997) *War Crimes against Women* (The Hague: Kluwer Law International).

J. Aßmann (2010) 'The Challenges of Genocide Trials: "The Cambodian Situation"' in C. J. M. Safferling and E.-A. Conze (eds) *The Genocide Convention Sixty Years after its Adoption* (The Hague: T. M. C. Asser Press).

E. Becker (1998) *When the war was over: Cambodia and the Khmer Rouge revolution* (New York: Public Affairs).

D. P. Chandler (2000) *A History of Cambodia* (Boulder: Westview Press).

D. P. Chandler (1999) *Brother Number One. A Political Biography of Pol Pot* (Boulder: Westview Press).

H. J. De Nike, J. Quigley and K. J. Robinson (2000) *Genocide in Cambodia, Documents from the Trial of Pol Pot and Ieng Sary* (Philadelphia: University of Pennsylvania Press).

Documentation Center of Cambodia (1999a) *Sexual Abuse Cases under the Democratic Kampuchea (the Khmer Rouge) Regime*, translated Tieng SopheakVichea, (Phnom Penh: DC-Cam).

Documentation Center of Cambodia (1999b) *Activity story of Tauch Sitha, People (CIA)*, TSL 4289 (Phnom Penh: DC-Cam).

S. Dyrchs (2008) *Das hybride Khmer Rouge-Tribunal – Entstehung, Entwicklung und rechtliche Grundlagen* (Frankfurt am Main: Peter Lang).

ECCC (2010a) *Closing Order*, Case File No: 002/19-09-2007-ECCC-OCIJ, 15 September 2010, D427, available at http://www.eccc.gov.kh/english/cabinet/courtDoc/740/D427Eng.pdf (accessed 13 November 2010).

ECCC (2010b) *ECCC Internal Rules*, as revised 17 September 2010, available at http://www.eccc.gov.kh/english/cabinet/fileUpload/121/IRv6-EN.pdf (accessed 14 December 2010).

ECCC (2009a) *Civil Parties' Co-Lawyers' Request for Supplementary Preliminary Investigations*, Case File No: 001/18-07-2007-ECCC/TC, 9 February 2009, E11, available at http://www.eccc.gov.kh/french/cabinet/courtDoc/250/E11_EN.pdf (accessed 30 May 2009).

ECCC (2009b) *Order on Request for Investigative Action Concerning Forced Marriages and Forced Sexual Relations*, Case File No: 002/19-09-2007-ECCC/OCIJ, 18 December 2009, D268/2, available at http://www.eccc.gov.kh/english/cabinet/courtDoc/491/D268_2_EN.pdf (accessed 14 December 2010).

ECCC (2008a) *First Civil Party Application before the Extraordinary Chambers in the Courts of Cambodia (ECCC) on Gender-Based Violence under the Khmer Rouge Regime*, Press Statement by Civil Parties Lawyer Silke Studzinsky, available at http://www.eccc.gov.kh/english/cabinet/press/73/PressRelease_1st_civil_party_on_Gender_Based_Violence.pdf (accessed 1 June 2009).

ECCC (2008b) *Decision on Nuon Chea's Appeal against Order Refusing Request for Annulment*, Case File No: 002/19-09-2007-ECCC/OCIJ (PTC06), 26 August 2008, D55/I/8, available at http://www.eccc.gov.kh/english/cabinet/courtDoc/123/D55_I_8_EN.pdf (accessed 2 June 2009).

ECCC (2004) *Law on the Establishment of the Extraordinary Chambers in the Courts of Cambodia for the Prosecution of Crimes Committed during the Period of Democratic Kampuchea*, amended pursuant to the Agreement on 27 October 2004, NS/RKM/1004/006, available at http://www.eccc.gov.kh/english/cabinet/law/4/KR_Law_as_amended_27_Oct_2004_Eng.pdf. (accessed 1 June 2009).

C. Etcheson (2006) *A 'Fair and Public Trial': A Political History of the Extraordinary Chambers, Justice Initiative*, available at http://www.justiceinitiative.org/db/resource2?res_id=103182, (accessed 21 January 2009).

K. Frieson (2001) 'In the Shadows: Women, Power and Politics in Cambodia', *Occasional Paper Series*, No. 26 (Victoria: Center for Asia-Pacific Initiatives).

ICC (2002) *Rules of Procedure and Evidence*, available at http://www.icc-cpi.int/Menus/ICC/Legal+Texts+and+Tools/Official+Journal/Rules+of+Procedure+and+Evidence.htm (accessed 21 December 2010).

ICC (1998) *Rome Statute of the International Criminal Court*, available at http://untreaty.un.org/cod/icc/statute/romefra.htm (accessed 1 December 2010).

ICTR (2004) *Statute of the International Criminal Tribunal for Rwanda*, available at http://www.un.org/ictr/statute.html (accessed 1 June 2009).

T. Jacobson (2008) *Lost Goddesses: the denial of female power in Cambodia* (Copenhagen: NIAS Press).

N. Jain (2008) 'Forced Marriage as a Crime against Humanity', *Journal of International Criminal Justice*, Vol. 6, 101–32.

M. S. Kalra (2001) 'Forced Marriage: Rwanda's Secret Revealed', *UC Davis Journal of International Law and Policy*, Vol. 7, 198–222.

B. Kiernan (2005) *The Pol Pot Regime: Race, Power and Genocide in Cambodia under the Khmer Rouge, 1975–79* (New Haven: Yale University Press).

P. LeVine (2010) *Love and Dread in Cambodia. Weddings, Births and Ritual Harm under the Khmer Rouge* (Singapore: National University of Singapore Press).

P. LeVine (2007) *A Contextual Study into the Marriages Under the Khmer Rouge: The Ritual Revolution*, unpublished PhD Thesis, Asian Studies/Anthropology (Australia: Monash University).

H. Locard (2004) *Pol Pot's little red book. The sayings of Angkar* (Chiang Mai: Silkworm Books).

K. Mam (2000) *Democratic Kampuchea (1975–1979): Women as Instruments for Social Changes* (Phnom Penh: Documentation Center of Cambodia).

J. Marston (2002) 'Khmer Rouge songs', *Crossroads: An Interdisciplinary Journal of Southeast Asian Studies*, Vol. 16 No. 1, 100–27.

L. McGrew (1999) 'Cambodian Women at Year Zero', *On the Record – Women of Southeast Asia Fight Violence*, Vol. 5, available at http://www.advocacynet.org/resource/530 (accessed 1 December 2010).

K. Nakagawa (2008) *Gender-Based Violence during the Khmer Rouge Regime, Stories of Survivors from the Democratic Kampuchea (1975–1979)*. (Phnom Penh: [publisher unknown]).

H. S. Ngor (1987) *A Cambodian odyssey* (New York: Macmillan).

Open Society Initiative (2009) *Recent Developments at the ECCC*, available at http://www.justiceinitiative.org/db/resource2?res_id=104249 (accessed 30 May 2009).

C. P. R. Romano, A. Nollkaemper and J. K. Kleffner (2004) *Internationalized Criminal Courts – Sierra Leone, East Timor, Kosovo, and Cambodia* (Oxford: Oxford University Press).

M. P. Scharf and S. Mattler (2005) 'Forced Marriage: Exploring the Viability of the Special Court for Sierra Leone's New Crime Against Humanity', *Case Research Paper Series in Legal Studies – Working Paper 05–35* (Cleveland: Case Western Reserve University).

T. Seiha (2009) 'Press Release: Co-Lawyers for Civil Parties requesting investigations for the crime of Forced Marriage under the control of Duch', *KHMERnews.com*, 13 February 2009, available at http://www.khmernews.com/view/press-release/2538/ (accessed 28 May 2009).

P. Short (2005) *Pol Pot: Anatomy of a Nightmare* (New York: Henry Holt and Co.).

SCSL (2009) *Prosecutor vs. Issa Hassan Sesay, Morris Kallon and Augustine Gbao*, (SCLS-04-15-T), Trial Chamber I, 2 March 2009, available at http://www.sc-sl.org/LinkClick.aspx?fileticket=D5HojR8FZS4%3d&tabid=215 (accessed 15 December 2010).

SCSL (2008) *Prosecutor vs. Alex Tamba Brima, Ibrahim Bazzy Kamara and Santigie Borbor Kanu*, (SCSL-04-16-A), Appeals Chamber, 22 February 2008, available at http://www.sc-sl.org/CASES/ProsecutorvsBrimaKamaraandKanuAFRCCase/AppealJudgment/tabid/216/Default.aspx (accessed 15 December 2010).

S. Studzinsky (2009) 'Nebenklage vor den Extraordinary Chambers of the Courts of Cambodia (ECCC) – Herausforderung und Chance oder mission impossible?', *Zeitschrift für Internationale Strafrechtsdogmatik*, Vol. 4 No. 1, 44–50.

UN (2008) *United Nations Security Council Resolution 1820*, S/RES/1820.

UN (2000) *United Nations Security Council Resolution 1325*, S/RES/1325.

UN and RGC (2003) *Agreement between the United Nations and the Royal Government of Cambodia concerning the Prosecution under Cambodian Law of Crimes committed during the Period of Democratic*, signed in Phnom Penh on 6 June 2003, available at http://www.eccc.gov.kh/english/cabinet/agreement/5/Agreement_between_UN_and_RGC.pdf (accessed 14 December 2010).

M. Vickery (1984) *Cambodia 1975–1982* (Boston, MA: South End Press).

S. Worden (2005) 'An Anatomy of the Extraordinary Chambers' in J. Ramji and B. van Schaack (eds) *Bringing the Khmer Rouge to Justice: Prosecuting Mass Violence before the Cambodian Courts* (Lewiston: The Edwin Mellen Press).

Part II

Transitional Justice and Social Change

4

Continuities of Violence against Women and the Limitations of Transitional Justice: The Case of South Africa

Romi Sigsworth and Nahla Valji

> The civil war is over, but the new war is rape...During the war we had peacekeepers to prevent further violence...but women do not have peacekeepers to stop rape.
>
> Tupee Kiadi (Monrovia resident)[1]

Over the past two decades increased attention has been paid to the experiences of women and girls during conflict and the need for comprehensive redress for crimes committed against this group, in particular sexual violence crimes.[2] Sexual and gender-based violence (SGBV),[3] however, does not begin with conflict or political instability and end with a transition to peace or democracy, nor are women's experiences of violence and human rights violations limited to crimes of a sexual nature.[4]

Comparatively little has been said of the experiences of women in the period after political conflict formally ceases or, more specifically, on the rising levels of social and criminal violence that seem to accompany the majority of transitions or 'post-conflict' periods.[5] In countries as diverse as South Africa, Guatemala and Liberia, violence against women has continued at levels akin to, or surpassing, those experienced during the conflict. This violence is informed by pre-conflict power relations, but is directly rooted in the legacy and consequences of the conflict (Pankhurst, 2000; 2007b; Meintjes et al., 2001). As such, violence against women continues to be a crime that, whilst it may have differing motivations in different contexts, has the same net effect – to reinforce women's subordinate and unequal role in society. It is also the crime most likely to be met with silence, shame, and impunity.

To date, the mechanisms of redress intended to secure justice and ensure non-repetition of violence, namely transitional justice mechanisms, have responded inadequately to these crimes. For this reason, this chapter highlights that, for many women, 'peace' does not usher in security or justice, but simply the continuation of violence in new guises. Furthermore, there are very real limitations to transitional justice mechanisms for a specific group of victims in seeking redress – limitations that raise a challenge to existing transitional justice mechanisms and norms around a truly gendered approach to justice.

Drawing on the case of South Africa, a country whose experience is generally portrayed as a successful 'model' of transitional justice, this chapter looks at the high levels of criminal and social violence, in particular violence against women, that has accompanied the post-apartheid period. To give just a few of the grim statistics:

- in 2008–09 71,500 sexual offences were reported to the South African Police Service (SAPS)[6]
- it is estimated that a woman is killed by her intimate partner every six hours, making it the highest femicide rate that has ever been recorded anywhere in the world[7]
- in 2007–08, 167,347 protection orders were applied for under the terms of the Domestic Violence Act. (South African Police Service, 2007; Centre for the Study of Violence and Reconciliation, 2008)

While such statistics can give us an indication of levels of SGBV in South Africa, the reality is, in fact, much worse. Many acts of sexual violence go unreported, both to the State and NGOs as well as to the victim's family and friends, as such evidence suggests that the number of rapes in South Africa may be up to nine times that of the reported statistics (Jewkes and Abrahams, 2002).

These endemic levels of sexual and domestic violence mean that the levels of violence against women in South Africa are arguably some of the highest of any country 'at peace' in the world. By making the argument that the causes of this violence are rooted in the past, and the nature of the transition itself, the authors examine how the limitations of transitional justice mechanisms, through their gendered definitions of 'violation', 'political' and 'transition', fail to address the ways in which political violence can shift form through a transition period. This shifting undermines the gains of peace and perpetuates insecurity for large sections of the population. The continuing violence poses challenges to the goals of non-repetition, human security, and democratization;

highlighting the weaknesses of an exclusively backward looking discourse in transitional justice which is blind to current violations. The authors conclude by adding their voice to the growing call to revisit existing mechanisms of redress, acknowledgement, and prevention.

Violence against women: continuities and continuums

> [W]ars don't simply end. And wars don't end simply.[8]

There is now growing recognition that SGBV does not begin with the onset of conflict and cease the moment that conflict ends. There are multiple and intersecting theories as to why violence against women continues, and may escalate, in post-conflict settings. Pre-existing gendered hierarchies and patriarchal norms, which inform the dominant forms of masculinity in pre-conflict settings, can run up against shifting gender roles and identities during the conflict, as well as new values of gender equality introduced during the transition. In this context, where the conflict has left a legacy of normalized violence, ongoing trauma, and a proliferation of small arms, feelings of threat, insecurity, and loss of status may play out in acts of violence against marginalized or less powerful groupings.[9]

Violence against women can therefore be seen as, fundamentally, an assertion of power. Or, as Caroline Moser argues, violence against women is motivated by a desire to get or keep power. The distinction between types of violence – political, economic, or social – is defined by the type of power that is under threat or in need of reinforcement. As gender is 'embedded in relations of power/powerlessness' (Moser, 2001: 37), each of these forms of violence can be, and are, profoundly gendered. Distinguishing between forms of violence and their concomitant underpinnings of power highlights the interlinkages between violence perpetrated against women in pre-conflict contexts as well as during conflict and post-conflict.[10] This analysis resonates with Charlotte Bunch's view of violence against women as a form of domination that 'results from the structural relationships of power, domination, and privilege between men and women in society' (Bunch, 1991). In any post-conflict setting, these power relations between genders are destabilized and in flux, leading to the need by some men to regain or reassert power, often manifested in violent forms.

Recognizing the continuities of gendered power relations helps to unveil the pre- and post-conflict continuities in violence against women. Jelke Boesten, drawing on extensive research in Peru, notes the importance of considering violence against women as a continuum. She argues for a recognition of the 'continuity and affinity in the use of violence rather than rupture and exceptionality' (Boesten, 2010). The advantage of this approach lies in the fact that it compels us to not only look at and distinguish between the forms of violence through different contexts, but also, and arguably more importantly, to analyse such violence in terms of the 'underpinning norms, values and institutional structures that normalize certain violence and exceptionalize others' (Boesten, 2010).

Kimberly Theidon, reflecting on the often-present post-conflict surge in violence against women (a phenomenon she refers to as the 'domestication of violence'), argues that the causes can be found in the:

> enduring impact of the militarization of daily life and the forging of militarized masculinities ... [which results in] an increase in domestic violence; a phenomenon noted in many post-conflict settings. (Theidon, 2009)

Others researching the rise in domestic violence in the aftermath of war have found that the violence perpetrated by soldiers and ex-combatants against their own spouses or partners further blurs the distinction between war and peace, and public and private (Nikolic-Ristanovic, 2000; Pankhurst, 2007a; Meintjes et al., 2001). The continuities and commonalities in both motivation and cause that underline violence against women also belie the standard bifurcation of war/peace, conflict/post-conflict, and political/personal as false and meaningless. Conceptualizing violence against women in terms of these unnatural binaries serves not only to obscure violence against women perpetrated before and after conflict, but also conceals forms of SGBV committed during conflict that do not 'fit the accepted rape script in which victim and perpetrator abide by the logic of two opposing warring camps and their strategic needs' (Boesten, 2007).

Where rape is seen in terms of the above binaries, women must 'fit' their experiences of sexual violence into the accepted boundaries in order to have their violations recognized. For example, in examining the claims of Guatemalan women requesting political asylum in the US, Julie Hastings found that women used an almost 'scripted' narrative of state-perpetrated rape in order to fit the authorities' definition of rape as a political act (Hastings, 2002). In the context of sexual violence in conflict, Boesten notes that, paradoxically, 'the thesis that rape is a weapon of war can also obscure practices of war-time sexual violence that do not fit the thesis' clear cut definition. It can exclude many acts of gendered violence during and after war that emerge from processes of reconciliation, reconstruction and truth seeking' (Boesten, 2010: 111).

Transitional justice, and the international laws on which it is premised, posits war-time rape – perpetrated by publicly recognized political actors – as somehow lying outside of the continuum of violence against women in which it is inherently embedded, singling it out alone for the possibility for redress. In doing so, it casts the one as 'extraordinary', the rest as inherently 'ordinary'. Consequently, the current framework depoliticizes and renders invisible many crimes, to the extent that 'a majority of victims are neglected and unrecognized by society at large, as well as by the mechanisms of redress it establishes' (Boesten, 2010: 113).[11]

The gendered limitations of transitional justice

The costs of SGBV, both during and after conflict, are wide-ranging. Personal costs to survivors include the impact on mental and physical health, reproductive health complications, and the increased risks of contracting HIV or other sexually transmitted infections (Sigsworth, 2008). On a societal level, the costs can be seen in the impact on development, social services, and human security. Continuing and even increasing levels of violence against women in post-conflict contexts 'hinders [women's] full participation in society' and 'limits their ability to pursue options in almost every area of life' (Carrillo, 2005). Violence not only impedes women's access to their rights and the agency to fulfil their human capability,[12] it impedes women's participation in broader development initiatives, or the ability to earn an income at precisely the moment when the country's skills and resources are most needed. Moreover, insecurity and violence decreases women's ability to be productive, organize, or mobilize (including in relation to post-conflict justice needs), move about freely, take public transport, find trusted caregivers for their children, or carry out other activities of daily life – in other words, to be full citizens of the new democracy.[13] The continued threat of insecurity to large sections of the population undermines the transitional justice goal and established right to non-repetition.[14] It also leaves the largest structural injustice in any society untouched.

How post-conflict societies deal with gendered violence, and in particular with rape and rape victims, directly affects the gender regimes (re)established in post-conflict societies (Pankhurst, 2007a). Recognizing the continuities as well as the shared roots of violence against women during conflict has obvious implications for mechanisms of redress in post-conflict contexts, and is likely to be one reason that false dichotomies are perpetuated or left as they are. Questioning pre-conflict gendered power relations in order to interrogate the gendered premise of existing laws, conceive of gender-sensitive and equitable mechanisms of redress, and develop gendered post-conflict policy may seem daunting. It is easier to simply address surface issues, those that fit the gendered paradigm that existed pre-conflict.

Until relatively recently, international law related to conflict and post-conflict issues was distinctly un-gendered in that it paid no attention to women's different positioning to men during and in the aftermath of conflict. Instead, it adopted as its starting point men's experiences of conflict in the public sphere (Ní Aoláin, 2009a). As pressure grew to recognize the importance of a 'gendered' perspective, the tendency to 'add women' to existing legislation dominated. The limitations of this reform have been that it has failed to reflect women's experiences during and after conflict and, as a result, their needs for redress.

An example of progressive but limited reform can be seen in the developments in the area of international 'soft' law, in particular the adoption of UN Security Council (UNSC) resolutions 1325, 1820, 1888, and 1889. All four of these resolutions have signalled a positive evolution in terms of international standards and have substantially increased awareness of sexual violence in conflict as a peace and security issue. The three more recent UNSC resolutions all give mention to 'sexual violence in conflict and post-conflict situations'. While this is seminal progress, there remains an absence of a conceptualization of the continuum of gendered violence through conflict to a post-conflict setting, which would assist in informing a comprehensive response. As a result, while these resolutions collectively contribute to furthering efforts for redress for sexual violence in conflict, they also risk reinforcing existing understandings of violence against women during conflict as something distinct from pre- or post-conflict violence, and address only those forms of violence that 'fit' the limited paradigm. As such, they do little to address the continuing and often increased levels of violence experienced by women 'after the conflict' (Pankhurst, 2000; Ní Aoláin, 2009b).[15]

Fionnuala Ní Aoláin explains the limitations of international law in relation to the differential harms suffered by women, noting that:

> while the growth of international criminal law is in many ways welcome for women, its role is not entirely gender neutral. The delineation of the acts it considers to be 'international crimes' reveals

> ingrained and troubling gender bias. It also demonstrates a troubling lack of 'capture' for the harms experienced by women despite being praised for its advances in encouraging gender-sensitive legal accountability. (Ní Aoláin, 2009a)[16]

The recognition of sexual violence as an 'international peace and security' issue is a step forward and should be lauded as such. However, it should also be recognized that one consequence of placing sexual violence firmly in the political sphere and linking it to broader peace and security implications is that it reinforces or entrenches the divide between political and personal, extraordinary and ordinary violence. It accepts the pre-existing terrain as legitimate – that is, enduring levels of violence against women in post-conflict contexts are no longer a regional or international peace and security issue, but rather one of individual security and domestic legislation and, as such, fall outside the ambit of the gains that have been made in the international legal framework.

The post-conflict backlash of violence against women in South Africa

The following section draws on South Africa as an illustrative case study to highlight the experience of post-conflict continuities of violence and the limitations of current transitional justice approaches, as well as to explore some of the reasons for ongoing violence against women in a specific post-conflict context. An analysis of why South Africa continues to suffer from such high levels of violence against women, 16 years after the transition to democracy, reveals a number of complex and inter-related factors. Many of these are rooted in, or exacerbated by, the former authoritarian state, the history of institutional and everyday violence of apartheid, as well as the militarized violence of the liberation conflict itself. None of these factors can be viewed in isolation, and all work together to inform the perpetration and perpetuation of SGBV in current day South Africa.

South Africa's struggle against apartheid was simultaneously a struggle against both racism and sexism. Gender issues were part of the overall political agenda – even if accorded a place secondary to racial emancipation – with women playing a crucial role in all areas of the anti-apartheid movement. In the new democracy, women's groups have worked extremely hard to ensure that, at least in terms of legislation and policy, women and women's rights are afforded maximum protection.

The South African constitution is one of the most progressive in the world in guaranteeing the rights of women. Women constitute 30 per cent of the national legislature, affirmative action legislation includes women as intended beneficiaries; and the Domestic Violence Act (1998) and Sexual Offences Act (2007), along with their associated policies, provide a sound legislative framework for dealing with SGBV.

Despite these formal measures, the backlash experienced by women and the price paid for their increased demands for equality have been severe. The construction of damaged and violent masculinities over years of political and interpersonal violence (and on the back of a culture of deep-rooted patriarchy), which have become deeply entrenched and are now destabilized or threatened in a new democratic order, is one of the fault lines for continued and increased violence against women in post-apartheid South Africa. Patriarchy requires that men hold more power and control than women and, as a result, 'masculine power is often defined through men's capacity to effect their will' (Sigsworth, 2009). Sexual and domestic violence are both ways in which men can assert their power. Violence against women can, therefore, be seen as an indicator to other men, and to women, of position, status and masculinity, thereby making violence a means to 'achieve a masculine dominant ideal, and as such ... a means of self-communication by men about their own powerfulness' (Sigsworth, 2009). In the post-conflict context of South Africa, masculinity has therefore become about:

> the need for control and power, often manifested in the violent subordination of more vulnerable groups, most likely to be represented by women and children. This phenomenon is keenly illustrated by a comment made by a self-confessed but un-incarcerated rapist who acknowledged that after committing the act of sexual violence he felt, 'I was the best, I had put her down ... [also] it made me feel even better ... to know I am a man because a woman is bowing down to you'. (Vogelman, 1990)

Political equality for women, and an equal-rights based constitution, mean little in this context of deeply ingrained patriarchy. Helen Moffett observes that ordinary men, from politicians to the 'man on the street', may espouse formal equality between men and women but insist that 'democracy stops at my door'. Moffett believes that 'a devils' bargain' has been struck whereby women are widely accepted as having equal political status, even within structures like parliament, as long as they remain subordinate in the private and domestic realms, and that SGBV 'covertly performs the function of policing this fault-line' (Moffett, 2006). As such, 'women (instead of black people) have become the potentially powerful, unstable subclass that must be kept in their place' (Moffett, 2006: 143). The following story illustrates this point eloquently:

> A taxi-driver openly described how he and his friends would cruise around at weekends, looking for a likely victim to abduct and 'gang-bang'. His story was unselfconscious and undefended: he showed no awareness that he was describing rape, much less criminal behaviour. When the interviewer pointed out that his actions constituted rape, he was visibly astonished. What was most striking was his spontaneous and indignant response: 'But these women, they force us to rape them!' He followed this astonishing disavowal of male agency by explaining that he and his friends picked only those women who 'asked for it'. When asked to define what he meant, he said, 'It's the cheeky ones – the ones that walk around like they own the place, and look you in the eye.' (Moffett, 2006: 138)

One particular manifestation of the male need to force women to conform to gendered stereotypes in South Africa is 'corrective rape', whereby lesbian women – 'perceived as representing a direct and specific threat to the status quo' (Martin et al., 2009: 5) – are punished and 'cured' of their sexual orientation through the violent act of rape. A study conducted by ActionAid found that the verbal abuse before and during the corrective rape focused on being 'taught a lesson' and being 'shown how to be a real woman and what a real man tasted like'. Women who choose not to identify as heterosexual are being victimized 'for daring to step outside the boundaries of what their families, communities and wider society prescribe for them' (Martin et al., 2009).

South Africa, therefore, provides a wealth of evidence to support the theory of a 'backlash'. This is a phenomenon experienced in countries where the conflict and transition may have led to new roles and status for women, which is then met with a shutting down of these spaces and roles, either formally through policy shifts, or through the use of other means, including violence, to reassert traditional gender hierarchies (Meintjes et al., 2001).

Liz Walker describes the backlash as emanating in response to feelings of threat which have arisen as traditional notions and expressions of masculinity have been destabilized through the transition. The response by some men to this perceived threat has been 'violent, ruthless, and reactionary' (Walker, 2005). In her research with former perpetrators of violence against women in the Alexandra Township, Walker found that men expressed feeling threatened by women's new rights and the perception of equality. In the words of one interviewee,

> I know women who are providing for themselves now, and that threat is actually what may be evoking a lot of violence... It is that threat of knowing that I can no longer hold onto the same position I held... I suppose you could say I feel weaker. I'm not saying the rape is a new thing but it's playing itself out in why men are being more violent. (Walker, 2005)

Violence can, therefore, be the expression of a perceived loss of masculine power, whereby 'many... young men experience the social upheaval of the apartheid and post-apartheid eras, and the associated feelings of powerlessness and marginalization, as emasculation' (Simpson and Kraak, 1998). For such young men, violence becomes a way of 'symbolically reasserting their masculine identity' and is enacted through any number of violently criminal acts. Violence against women remains 'a relatively simple [and accessible] but violent performance of masculinity that can achieve a feeling of ascendancy over both women and other men' (Sigsworth, 2009).

Brandon Hamber's research on shifting masculinities in post-apartheid South Africa concluded, similarly to Walker, that violence was used by men who were feeling disempowered as a means of reasserting their masculinity (Hamber, 2006). Many of the men interviewed by Hamber and his team perceived the post 1994 South Africa as a place where women had attained dramatic gains, despite clear evidence to the contrary. In reality, women continue to be impoverished, unemployed, and insecure in relation to men overall.[17] These men, however, perceived reality differently, and believed that women were using the excessive gains they secured through the transition to 'persecute men'. Hamber also found that the link between women's advancement and the increase in violence against women was mentioned repeatedly in focus groups of both men and women. One male in a focus group made this direct association between men's feeling of being 'threatened' by women's gains and the use of sexual violence:

> So I think that's the reason why you'd find that incidents of violence against women... not that they were not there in the past but they were administered within the family environment. But right now

> they are so in the open because it's the only weakness that you can now use against women. You can't use financial resources against them because now they are pretty much earning more than us. So we can't use that, whereas in the past we've had that leverage of saying I am working alone, I don't need your money, but right now you can't say that. So then people start using – they are looking for another weakness within a woman. And that weakness right now is sexual weakness. That we can always rape you, we can physically show you our strength. (Hamber, 2006)

An analysis of this sense of 'emasculation' in the new South Africa, or perceived loss of status and power, and consequent violence, was provided by Graeme Simpson and Gerald Kraak early on in the transition, and is worth quoting in full:

> The sources of men's sense of emasculation and its relation to violence are deep-rooted and complex. Given the enduring tradition and history of patriarchal society, in which men have been accustomed to political and economic power, and the more recent realities of political and social change, in which they feel a loss of power and control, violence has become an important vehicle for re-asserting their masculine identity and influence. This is as true of family killings in white middle-class Afrikaner[18] society – where political and social changes have eroded the traditional power bases of Afrikaner men – as it is in black working class society – where unemployment may be experienced in exactly the same way. Economic and political changes are fundamentally undermining the identities conferred upon men by patriarchy. Formidable obligations and a sense of responsibility are interpreted in male-specific terms: men as breadwinners, men as guardians, men as protectors. As men fail to earn the bread and fail to act as guardians – whether in a political or economic context – they fail in their responsibility as protector. They must seek alternative vehicles for sustaining a sense of self and identity. And violence is such a vehicle. (Simpson and Kraak, 1998)

In short, the compounded impact of high levels of unemployment common to most post-conflict societies, shifting gender identities, and the inability to play the traditional role of provider, appear to have all contributed to feelings of emasculation.

Yet, while feelings of threat and perceived loss of status may explain a sense of anger or frustration, they do not explain why such frustration manifests itself in violence. In South Africa, as with many post-conflict contexts, much of the reason lies in the country's violent and repressive history. During apartheid, laws and services were available to, and benefitted, only particular sectors of society, resulting in the current ambivalence towards, and lack of adherence to, basic laws relating to daily life across much of the population. The significant social change over the transition to democracy in the way that people live, family structures and codes of behaviour has impacted on child rearing and socialization. In addition, the ever-widening gap between rich and poor has further entrenched already high levels of inequality in society; themselves a form of brutal structural violence and dehumanization that has pervaded all aspects of society and social relations. Simpson and Kraak argue that 'the historical consequences of marginalization and impoverishment that were translated into overtly political violence in the past, are now manifesting in other forms of social conflict and violence outside of the formal political arena' (Simpson and Kraak, 1998).

This 'introversion' of political violence has led to high levels of violence generally in South Africa. Within this context, the perpetration of SGBV has become particularly normalized. Recent studies have shown that the perpetration of sexual violence is widespread among all sectors of society. A study conducted in three districts of the Eastern Cape and Kwa-Zulu Natal, across 1738 households, found that the rape of a woman or girl had been perpetrated by 27.6 per cent of the men interviewed (Jewkes et al., 2009). A study on sexual violence among men and women in Cape Town found that more than one in five men openly admitted to having perpetrated sexual assault against women (Kalichman et al., 2005). There is also a clearly intergenerational transmission of violent norms, in that 'children experience, internalize and then replicate the use of force and violence in the home, community, by police, at school and so on' (Sigsworth, 2009). Recent statistics from Childline South Africa revealed that 43 per cent of all cases of sexual assault reported to Childline nationally were committed by children under 18 (Redpath, 2003). Moreover, a study conducted on a sample of 283,500 learners (14 years of age and up) to map the extent of sexual violence among the youth in South Africa found that, nationally, approximately 9 per cent of all respondents said they had been forced to have sex in the past year. The proportion of males who admitted forcing sex on someone ranged between 6 per cent in the lower age groups to 25 per cent in the older age groups (CIETAfrica, 2000).

Differentiating between this 'ordinary' and normalized violence against women perpetrated in a post-conflict context, and the 'extraordinary' violence perpetrated against women during conflict, misses the way in which violence against women itself becomes the response to transition, destabilization and the reinforcement of traditional norms. One submission to the South African Truth and Reconciliation Commission highlights the links and continuities between violence against women pre, during and post-conflict: '[a] political rape has no different consequences. It has exactly the same reason behind it – a violent act against a woman ... In fact the women [are] being punished as women' (Gender and Truth and Reconciliation Commission, 1996).

Towards a gender-equitable peace

To break the continuum of violence against women post-conflict, and ensure that violence against women does not increase once 'peace' has been re-established, will necessitate doing more than what has been the usual approach to societies in transition to date. This approach has largely focused on the violence perpetrated during the conflict itself without a more nuanced understanding of gendered power relations and how they shift during and after conflict. There is a need to reconceptualize transitional justice from the point of view of women's lived experiences, so that transitional justice mechanisms accurately reflect the intended goals for all of the population, not only one part of the population.

In transitional societies there is a need to be not simply backward looking, but to redefine the legacy of the conflict to encompass those factors which lead to increased levels of violence against women post-conflict, such as women's position relative to men pre-conflict, as well as the breakdown in communities, families, and social relations during conflict. Part of this is the need to revisit the violations that transitional justice seeks to redress, which at present are informed by a male experience of conflict. It is important that a fundamental rethink of the field of transitional justice as a whole be conducted in terms of when it is employed, what violations it covers, how redress is sought, and so on. If this does not happen, there is a risk that institutions and mechanisms of transitional justice actually serve to entrench old fault lines of marginalization through their reinforcement of falsely constructed notions of political /personal, conflict/ post-conflict. As such, perhaps the first step needs to be targeted research on, and a radical rethink of, the relationship between transitional justice and gender justice in order to explore the extent to which transitional justice mechanisms have engaged with gender justice and the actual impacts of transitional justice mechanisms on the lived realities of women (and men) in post-conflict contexts.

The strengthening of criminal justice systems must be a priority in post-conflict contexts. Justice reform must include an agenda to prioritize SGBV crimes and women's access to justice, in order to mitigate against impunity and the continued rise in crimes of SGBV. However, as crucial as using prosecutions as a transitional justice mechanism and strengthening the criminal justice system are to ensure there is no impunity for the perpetrators of SGBV in a post-conflict setting, it is important that

> [a]ccountability for crimes against women ... means more than punishing perpetrators: it should involve establishing the rule of law as the cornerstone of peace-building and restoring public trust, as well as ensuring that women have full access to the rule of law and that they play a key role in constitutional, legislative and judicial processes. (Sigsworth, 2008: 15)

This necessitates an approach that moves beyond a solely punitive approach to SGBV to one which better tries to understand the causes of SGBV and treats this as part of the strategy for stabilization and democratization post-conflict. That is, not as a personal issue, but very much as a threat to the security of individual citizens and the success of the transition in general. As Ní Aoláin notes:

> gender centrality has often focused almost exclusively on holding war crimes perpetrators accountable for sexual violence. We cannot, however, evaluate the credibility and value of such accountability mechanisms without an eye to the broader transitional and gendered dynamic of the society in question. Moreover, we cannot hope to dislodge practices of violence to women (before, during and after conflict) unless we are prepared for a hard interface with the social embeddings of violence in the individual identities and social practices of men. (Ní Aoláin, 2009b)

Security is also a precondition for development, reconciliation, and recovery.[19] A coordinated response is required across all programming, which in turn needs to be informed by women's lived experiences. For example, if domestic violence rises in the aftermath of conflict as a response to the transition and its resulting instability, then programming – including immediate emergency relief and humanitarian assistance – must keep this issue at the centre of its designs. It must ensure that they are addressing violence against women through preventative measures, but equally that they are not aggravating it unintentionally in the delivery of assistance. All post-conflict programming – from agriculture, to health and housing, property restitution to peace-building, DDR and institutional reform – must conduct gender assessments as a starting point to inform their policies and implementation, and should understand the local gendered relations and context in which they operate.

The prevention of violence post-conflict also means moving beyond a focus solely on women. Addressing only one side of the equation cannot lead to the needed solution. Men and boys experience conflict and are brutalized by violence in different ways. Post-conflict reconstruction, healing, and reconciliation must focus on reconstructing these identities and focusing on the relationship between men and women, not just on one side of the equation. More research needs to be conducted into the concept of 'masculinities' and the experiences and impacts of conflict on men, in order to better understand their attitudes and behaviour post-conflict. As gender activists, we can sometimes use the term 'masculinities' too easily and loosely with inadequate attention paid to the construction, shifts and power relations within masculinities. We need to better understand how gendered norms fuel violence more generally – not just sexual violence – and what the use of SGBV against men and boys in conflict tells us about the motivations of perpetrators of sexual violence more generally (Okello, 2008). Understanding the social norms and social context of SGBV – that is, its intended meaning for those who perpetrate it, whether during conflict or after – could reveal much about an effective prevention and intervention agenda. Research seems to show that the prevention of violence, against women in particular, can be successful where men and boys are encouraged to build empathy. Programmes with men and boys including deliberate discussions of gender and masculinity, as well as clear efforts to transform such gender norms rather than merely acknowledging or mentioning gender norms and roles, bring success (Barker et al., 2007). There is a need to have transitional justice responses that consider the shift of identities in post-conflict contexts and, in particular, engage with masculinities in transition.

Ultimately, one of the most fundamental goals of transitional justice in post-conflict contexts must be that of a gender-just peace.

Notes

The views expressed in this chapter are those of the authors and not of their respective institutions.

1. 'LIBERIA: "The new war is rape"' 19 November 2009, *IRIN: Humanitarian news and analysis*.
2. Advances in laying the foundations for securing justice for women's experiences of sexual violence in conflict include:
   - the four UN Security Council Resolutions on Women, Peace and Security (1325, 1820, 1888 and 1889);
   - seminal judgements such as that of the *Akayesu* case before the International Criminal Tribunal for Rwanda, which recognized rape as an instrument of genocide and a crime against humanity;
   - the *RUF* judgment before the Sierra Leone Special Court which marked the first conviction on a charge of 'forced marriage'; and
   - increased attention paid to the acknowledgement of women's experiences of conflict and needs for redress in truth commission and reparation programme mandates.
3. In this chapter, we use the term 'gender-based violence' to refer to violence against women perpetrated against their bodies because they are women. Apart from sexual violence, gender-based violence also includes wife battery and other forms of physical and psychological abuse. We use the term 'rape' to refer to penetration of the body under coercion, and 'sexual violence' to refer to a broader range of sexual acts and mutilations. Rape is sexual violence, while sexual violence is not necessarily rape.
4. Whilst this chapter does address the issue of SGBV, it does not seek to reinforce this victim identity, nor does it imply that women's experiences of conflict are solely that of victimhood devoid of agency.
5. We use the term 'post-conflict' here and elsewhere in this chapter fully aware that for women, 'post-conflict' and 'peace' are ill-fitting descriptions of this period given the high levels of ongoing violence against women.
6. Available at http://www.saps.gov.za/statistics/reports/crimestats/2009/categories/total_sexual_offences.pdf.
7. The rate is 8.8 per 100,000 female population of 14 years and older (Mathews et al., 2004).
8. Enloe, 2004: 193.
9. Though the Eastern DRC cannot be characterized as 'post-conflict', recent research in the region shows that between 2004 and 2008, the number of civilian rapes increased by an astounding 1733 per cent or 17-fold, while the number of rapes by armed combatants decreased by 77 per cent. These findings imply a normalization of rape and the breakdown of social norms generally. Much of this shift is likely due to the fact that many of these civilians were former members of fighting forces now integrated into communities causing a displacement of violence generally into the community and home, illustrating the factors at play in the continuation of violence and the indistinct boundaries between 'war' and 'peace'. Harvard Humanitarian Initiative with support from Oxfam America, *'Now, The World Is Without Me' An investigation of sexual violence in Eastern Democratic Republic of Congo* (April 2010).

10. While violence in conflict has its own motivations unique to the conflict context – for example the humiliation of the male 'other'; the intended impact on family and community; genocidal intentions – these forms and motivations are facilitated and informed by women's unequal positions and ascribed roles in all contexts.
11. The Peruvian Truth and Reconciliation Commission encountered multiple difficulties in defining sexual violence and applying this definition. In practice, Commission interviewers sometimes rigidly applied the rules. For a particularly striking case of diverging interpretations between interviewer and interviewee of what constitutes sexual violence see Boesten, 2007.
12. In developing Amartya Sens' 'capabilities approach' – a theory for evaluating justice, freedom, and quality of life – feminist scholar Martha Nussbaum lists 'bodily integrity' (the ability to move about freely and secure from the threat of violence, in particular domestic and sexual violence) as one of the core elements inherent in this approach and therefore foundational to the overall goal of 'justice'. See Nussbaum, 2003.
13. For example, research conducted in metropolitan South Africa in 1999, five years after the democracy, found that 80 per cent of women reported feeling unsafe or very unsafe walking around their own neighbourhood at night. Focus groups conducted by one of the authors found that women in informal settlements reported not being able to leave their girl children alone with even close family members or neighbours for fear of violence and abuse (Bollen and Artz, 1999).
14. The guarantee of non-repetition should not be defined so narrowly as to suggest that it covers only the re-establishment of conflict in the same form and guise as the past. New, or continued, forms of violence which remain after the meta-conflict, and which are directly rooted in the legacy of that conflict, must equally be included in this guarantee. However new research positing a direct relationship between gender inequality and state-level political conflict may suggest the need to establish gender justice as a guarantee of non-repetition in the more conventional sense as well. See Caprioli, 2003.
15. Ní Aoláin notes that there is statistical evidence to suggest that post-conflict societies experience higher levels of domestic and intimate violence.
16. The notion of differential harms has stark implications for transitional justice mechanisms and efforts at redress. In particular, the differential ways in which trauma manifests in women and men, coupled with the contexts of both patriarchal and localized culture, mean that women experience harm differently from men, which in turn has implications for what needs redress and how that redress is achieved. Ní Aoláin argues for the need to rethink the conceptualization of 'harms' in law and, by extension, in transitional justice. The starting point needs to take into consideration the pre-existing and compounding effect of the normalized 'hidden injuries' inherent in all gender-oriented societies – 'that lived internalized experience of lower gender status as personal failure' (Howe quoted in Ní Aoláin, 2009a) – in order to give meaning to the harm experienced by women, and take this harm into consideration when creating institutions of redress.
17. The most recent statistics show the rate of unemployment in South Africa to be around 30 per cent for men and 47 per cent for women (see: http://www.growthcommission.org/storage/cgdev/documents/LaborMarkets/Bhorat.

pdf). See also Kehler, 2001. Available at: http://www.bridgew.edu/Soas/jiws/fall01/kehler.pdf

18. The word 'Afrikaner' refers to the white, Afrikaans speaking ethnic group in South Africa.
19. As noted in the UN Secretary General's report on 'Peacebuilding in the Immediate Aftermath of Conflict' (A163/881-S2009/304), 11 June 2009: 'persistent violence, intimidation and discrimination are obstacles to women's participation and full involvement in post-conflict public life, which can have a serious negative impact on durable peace, security and reconciliation, including post-conflict peacebuilding'.

References

G. Barker and C. Ricardo (2008) *Men, Masculinities, Sexual Exploitation and Sexual Violence: A Literature Review and Call for Action* (Rio de Janeiro; Promundo and Men Engage).

J. Boesten (2010) 'Analyzing Rape Regimes at the Interface of War and Peace in Peru', *International Journal of Transitional Justice*, Vol. 4 No. 1, 110–29.

J. Boesten (2007) 'Marrying the Man Who Raped You: Domesticating War Crimes in Ayacucho, Peru' in D. Pankhurst (ed.) *Gendered Peace: Women's Search for Post-War Justice and Reconciliation* (New York: Routledge).

S. Bollen and L. Artz (1999) *Violence against Women in Metropolitan South Africa: A Study on Impact and Service Delivery*, ISS Monograph 41 (Pretoria: Institute for Security Studies).

C. Bunch (1990) 'Women's Rights as Human Rights: Toward a Re-Vision of Human Rights', *Human Rights Quarterly*, Vol. 12, 486–98.

M. Caprioli (2003) *Gender Equality and Civil Wars*, CPR Working Papers, Paper No. 8 (Conflict Prevention and Reconstruction Unit).

R. Carrillo (2005) *Violence Against Women: An Obstacle to Development* (Colombo: Social Scientists' Association).

Centre for the Study of Violence and Reconciliation (2008) *The South African Domestic Violence Act: Lessons from a Decade of Legislation and Implementation* (Johannesburg: CSVR).

CIETafrica (2000) *Executive Report, Beyond Victims and Villains: South Johannesburg, 1997–2000*. Summary Report, available at http://www.ciet.org/en/documents/projects_library_docs/2006224131250.pdf.

C. Cockburn (2004) 'The Continuum of Violence: A Gender Perspective on War and Peace' in W. Giles and J. Hyndman (eds) *Sites of Violence: Gender and Conflict Zones* (Berkeley, CA: University of California Press).

J. El-Bushra (2003) 'Fused in combat: gender relations and armed conflict', *Development in Practice*, Vol. 13 No. 2–3, 252–65.

J. El-Bushra and I. M. G. Sahl (2005) *Cycles of Violence: Gender Relations and Armed Conflict* (Agency for Co-operation and Research in Development), available at http://www.acord.org.uk/cycles_of_violence.pdf.

C. Enloe (2004) *The Curious Feminist: Searching for Women in a New Age of Empire* (Berkeley and Los Angeles: University of California).

B. Goldblatt and S. Meintjes (1996) *Gender and the Truth and Reconciliation Commission A Submission to the Truth and Reconciliation Commission*, May 1996, available at http://www.justice.gov.za/trc//hrvtrans/submit/gender.htm.

P. Green and T. Ward (2009) 'The Transformation of Violence in Iraq', *British Journal of Criminology*, Vol. 49 No. 5, 609–27.

B. Hamber (2006) *'We Must be Careful How we Emancipate Our Women': Shifting Masculinities in Post-Apartheid South Africa*. Paper presented at the Re-Imagining Women's Security: a Comparative Study of South Africa, Northern Ireland and Lebanon Round Table, United Nations University, New York, 12–13 October 2006.

J. A. Hastings (2002) 'Silencing State-Sponsored Rape in and Beyond a Transnational Guatemalan Community', *Violence Against Women*, Vol. 8 No. 10, 1153–81.

IRIN Humanitarian news and analysis (2009) *LIBERIA: 'The new war is rape'*, 19 November 2009.

S. Jacobs, R. Jacobson and J. Marchbank (eds) (2000) *States of Conflict: Gender, Violence and Resistance* (London: Zed Books).

R. Jewkes and N. Abrahams (2002) 'The Epidemiology of Rape and Sexual Coercion in South Africa: an Overview', *Social Science & Medicine*, Vol. 55 No. 7, 1231–44.

R. Jewkes, Y. Sikweyiya, R. Morrell and K. Dunkle (June 2009) *Understanding Men's Health and Use of Violence: Interface of Rape and HIV in South Africa* (Pretoria: Medical Research Council).

S. Kalichman, L. Simbayi, M. Kaufman, D. Cain, C. Cherry, S. Jooste and V. Mathiti (2005) 'Gender Attitudes, Sexual Violence, and HIV/AIDS Risks among Men and Women in Cape Town, South Africa', *The Journal of Sex Research*, Vol. 42 No. 4, 299–305.

J. Kehler (2001) 'Women and Poverty: The South African Experience', *Journal of International Women's Studies*, Vol. 3 No. 1.

A. Martin, A. Kelly, L. Turquet and S. Ross (2009) *Hate Crimes: The Rise of Corrective Rape in South Africa* (London: ActionAid).

S. Mathews, N. Abrahams, L. J. Martin, L. Vetten, L. van der Merwe and J. Jewkes (2004) *'Every six hours a woman is killed by her intimate partner': A National Study of Female Homicide in South Africa,* MRC Policy Brief no. 5 (Pretoria: Medical Research Council).

S. Meintjes, A. Pillay and M. Turshen (eds) (2001) *The Aftermath: Women in Postconflict Transformation* (London: Zed Books).

H. Moffett (2006) '"These Women, They Force us to Rape them": Rape as Narrative of Social Control in Post-Apartheid South Africa', *Journal of Southern African Studies*, Vol. 32 No. 1, 129–44.

C. O. N. Moser (2001) 'The Gendered Continuum of Violence and Conflict: An Operational Framework' in C. O. N. Moser and F. C. Clark (eds) *Victims, Perpetrators or Actors: Gender, Armed Conflict and Political Violence* (New York: Palgrave Macmillan).

F. Ní Aoláin (2009a) *Exploring a Feminist Theory of Harm in the Context of Conflicted and Post-Conflict Societies*, Minnesota Legal Studies Research Paper No. 09–45 (University of Minnesota Law School; Transitional Justice Institute, University of Ulster).

F. Ní Aoláin (2009b) 'Gender, Masculinities and Transition in Conflicted Societies', *New England Law Review* (forthcoming), Minnesota Legal Studies Research Paper No. 09–49.

I. Niehaus (2005) 'Masculine Domination in Sexual Violence: Interpreting Accounts of Three Cases of Rape in the South African Lowveld' in G. Reid and L. Walker (eds) *Men Behaving Differently* (Cape Town: Double Storey Books).

V. Nikolic-Ristanovic (2000) *Women, Violence and War: Wartime Victimization of Refugees in the Balkans* (Central European University Press).

M. C. Nussbaum (2003). 'Capabilities as Fundamental Entitlements: Sen and Social Justice', *Feminist Economics,* Vol. 9 No. 2–3, 33–59.

M. Okello (2008) *Gender and Traditional Justice in Northern Uganda: Progressive or Conservative?* Presentation at the 'Gender and Transitional Justice in Africa: Progress and Prospects' Conference organised by the International Centre for Transitional Justice (ICTJ), 4 – 5 September 2008.

D. Pankhurst (2007a) 'Post-War Backlash Violence Against Women: What Can "Masculinity" Explain?' in D. Pankhurst (ed.) *Gendered Peace: Women's Search for Post-War Justice and Reconciliation* (New York: Routledge).

D. Pankhurst (2007b) *Gender Issues in Post-War Contexts: A Review of Analysis and Experience, and Implications for Policies,* Peace Studies Working Paper 9 (Bradford: University of Bradford).

D. Pankhurst (2003) 'The "Sex War" and Other Wars: Towards a Feminist Approach to Peace Building', *Development in Practice,* Vol. 13 No. 2–3, 154–77.

D. Pankhurst (2000) 'Post-War Backlash Violence against Women: What Can "Masculinity" Explain?' in D. Pankhurst (ed.) *Gendered Peace: Women's Search for Post-War Justice and Reconciliation* (New York: Routledge).

J. Redpath (2003) 'South Africa's Heart of Darkness', *SA Crime Quarterly,* Vol. 4, 17–24.

R. Sathiparsad (2005) '"It is Better to Beat Her": Male Youth in Rural Kwa-Zulu Natal Speak on Violence in Relationships', *Agenda,* Vol. 66, 79–88.

R. Sigsworth (2009) *'Anyone can be a rapist': an overview of sexual violence in South Africa.* (Johannesburg: Centre for the Study of Violence and Reconciliation).

R. Sigsworth (2008) *Gender-Based Violence in Transition* (Johannesburg: Centre for the Study of Violence and Reconciliation).

G. Simpson and G. Kraak (1998) 'The Illusions of Sanctuary and the Weight of the Past: Notes on violence and gender in South Africa', *Development Update,* Vol. 2 No. 2, 1–10.

South African Police Service (2007) *SAPS Domestic Violence Report 1 July – 31 December 2006,* available at http://www.pmg.org.za/docs/2007/070912saps.htm.

E. A. Stanko (2003) *The Meanings of Violence* (London: Routledge).

D. Steinberg (2009) *Beyond Victimhood: Protection and Participation of Women in the Pursuit of Peace,* International Crisis Group, available at http://foreign.senate.gov/imo/media/doc/SteinbergTestimony091001p1.pdf.

K. Theidon (2009) 'Reconstructing Masculinities: The Disarmament, Demobilization, and Reintegration of Former Combatants in Colombia', *Human Rights Quarterly,* Vol. 31 No. 1, 1–34.

K. Theidon (2007) 'Gender in Transition: Common Sense, Women, and War', *Journal of Human Rights,* Vol. 20 No. 60, 3–30.

N. Valji (2009) 'Gender Justice and Reconciliation' in K. Ambos, J. Large, and M. Wierda (eds) *Building a Future on Peace and Justice: Studies on Transitional Justice, Peace and Development The Nuremberg Declaration on Peace and Justice* (Berlin; Springer Publications).

L. Vetten, R. Jewkes, R. Sigsworth, N. Christofides, L. Loots and O. Dunseith (2008) *Tracking Justice: The Attrition of Rape Cases through the Criminal Justice System in Gauteng*. (Johannesburg: Tshwaranang Legal Advocacy Centre, Medical Research Council South Africa & Centre for the Study of Violence and Reconciliation).

L. Vogelman (1990) 'Violent Crime: Rape' in B. McKendrick and W. C. Hoffman (eds) *People and the Violence in South Africa* (Cape Town: Oxford University Press).

L. Walker (2005) 'Negotiating the Boundaries of Masculinity in Post-Apartheid South Africa' in G. Reid and L. Walker (eds). *Men Behaving Differently* (Cape Town: Double Storey Books).

5

Transitioning to What? Transitional Justice and Gendered Citizenship in Chile and Colombia

Catherine O'Rourke

As the field of transitional justice has burgeoned, the hegemony of the legal frame of analysis has been convincingly challenged by a range of disciplines, such as anthropology (Theidon, 2007; 2009), political science (Elster, 2004), psychology (Hamber, 2009), and others (see generally Bell, 2009). The inadequacy of the legal frame was most cogently revealed by two particular insights. The first insight emerged from the legal discipline itself, namely the peculiar political role for law in transition, 'that of effecting and assisting transition' (Bell et al., 2004: 307). In conflicted or authoritarian states, the coinage of law, legal institutions, and the rule of law is degraded. Hence, paradoxically, transitional justice involves the rehabilitation of law itself, to be achieved through specifically legal devices; most commonly amnesty, truth seeking, reparations, and reform to legal institutions. Law is both the object and subject of transition. It is now widely acknowledged that the peculiar political role for law in transition cannot be adequately captured or understood by exclusively doctrinal analysis (Bell et al., 2004). The second pertinent insight is derived from non-legal analysis of transitional justice. Transitional justice devices, although legally framed and nominally past-focused, have a range of important long-term and non-legal implications for societies emerging from conflict or repression. Transitional justice legal devices are now broadly linked to degrees of reconciliation (Hamber, 2009), economic development (Mani, 2002), security sector performance (United Nations Secretary General, 2004), and political equality (de Greiff, 2007) in post-conflict and post-authoritarian societies. In general, there is increasing awareness of the significance of law in transition in forging a new political and normative order in transitional states. Transitional justice devices, by naming certain forms of harm for particular rebuke and punishment, while remaining silent on other forms of harm, can strongly influence the social understanding of particular harms (see, for example, Ní Aoláin, 2000). Specifically legal and past-focused devices carry a range of non-legal and forward looking implications.

This chapter begins to probe the gender implications of the dual insights that, specifically legal devices have a range of non-legal implications, and that multi-disciplinary analysis is necessary to understand the full range of long-term consequences of nominally past-focused devices. More specifically, the chapter explores how transitional justice devices influence the incorporation of citizens into the political community of post-conflict and post-authoritarian states. Principally, the chapter contends that legal innovations around amnesty, truth seeking, and reparations implicitly privilege (recognize and validate) certain forms of political activity, and deny or devalue other forms of political activity. The selective validation of political activities of women and men work to differentially incorporate men and women into citizenship of transitional states. In this way, past-focused legal devices have longer-term implications for the political dispensation of a society emerging from conflict or repression. The chapter draws on feminist theories of citizenship, and applies them to the transitional justice devices utilized in Chile and Colombia in order to illustrate these dynamics.

Part one: gendered citizenship and transitional states

Feminist approaches to citizenship

Citizenship is a contested concept. The classic definition of citizenship offered by T. H. Marshall (1950), as membership of a political community and incorporating political, social, and economic dimensions, is enduring, but not undisputed. Citizenship is broadly linked to a set of symbolic and material benefits, including legal rights, economic benefits and state services, education, due process of law, and opportunities to participate in political decision-making. Citizenship also refers to the duties assumed with membership of the political community, and it has both legal and political understandings.[1] The legal definition of citizenship, derived from the liberal tradition, tends – though not necessarily – to have an exclusionary emphasis. The focus is on the legally prescribed barriers and obstacles (residency, place of birth, marriage, kinship) to membership of the political community. Within this understanding, the desirability of citizen status is apparent, and the rights and privileges of citizenship are jealously guarded.

The narrow and legalistic conception of citizenship offered by the liberal tradition has attracted feminist criticism for its reification of a gendered public/private divide. The rights and entitlements of citizenship, ostensibly afforded on a gender-neutral basis, address only the citizen's public existence and relationship of the citizen to the state. Citizenship is defined in a gender-neutral fashion, as a set of rights and duties accruing to both men and women on identical terms. However, as Anne Phillips observes, 'One of the most common tricks of the trade is to smuggle real live men into the seemingly abstract and innocent universals that nourish political thought' (Phillips, 1993: 77). Liberal rights ignore and neglect the citizen's existence within the private sphere of home and family – the sphere in which women, not coincidentally, live most of their lives. It is this neglect of the private sphere that works to deny women the benefits of citizenship.

By contrast, the political definition of citizenship, with which this chapter principally engages, offers more accommodating and inclusive potential. The political definition of citizenship, derived from the civic republican tradition, prioritizes the active citizen who earns the rights of citizenship through civic practices. Within this conception, citizenship is meant as an equalizing term, emphasizing the fundamental political (though not material) equality of all members of the polity. Each individual is thereby afforded a role in the collective decision-making of the polity.

Nevertheless, the civic republican conception of citizenship has been critiqued too for its 'universal pretensions' (ibid.: 77). In particular, feminist analysis has focused on the way in which traditionally masculine modes of political activity have been privileged within the civic republican conception of citizenship. In the classical social contract, the only political activity recognized as such was military activity, the soldier-citizen (see generally Snyder, 1999). The state provided its protection to citizens in return for the individual citizen's willingness to defend the state. As a paradigmatically male activity, making full citizenship contingent on military service necessarily precluded women from the material and symbolic benefits of citizenship. Over time, as notions of political activity have broadened and evolved, active participation in the polis (committees, assemblies, democratic fora) has been emphasized. However, to be an active member of the polis requires free time and autonomy to pursue formal political activity. Both free time and autonomy tend to be in short supply for the majority of women, who manage the responsibilities of home and family, increasingly in addition to work in the formal world of employment. Feminist analysis reveals the male coding of these sites (assemblies, parliaments, committees) and modes (confrontational, oppositional) of political participation (see generally Jones, 1990; Lister, 1997).

Transitional legal devices and political citizenship

Gender analysis focuses on the differential terms under which men and women have been incorporated into citizenship, both historically and in contemporary times. These insights acquire particular resonance when considering the transitional state. In transitional justice, law may be the subject and object of transition, but the state is the site of transition. The state, in the foundational transitional justice scholarship of Teitel (2000) onwards, is to be rehabilitated and re-grounded by transition. Within this narrative, transition marks a rupture, a 'clean break', with the legal, political, and normative order of the past conflicted or repressive state. Transition, it is argued, constitutes a renewed moment for the incorporation of citizens into the state.

Adopting the civic republican understanding of citizenship, this chapter contends that transitional justice devices can expand the repertoire of activities recognized as 'political' and, in so doing, expand the repertoire of activities that form the basis of citizenship in transitional states. Changes to legal norms and institutions can positively affirm a broad spectrum of women's and men's mobilization and political activity. Conversely, transitional legal devices can reaffirm and perpetuate traditional gendered and limited norms of political participation. Principally, the chapter contends that legal innovations around amnesty, truth seeking, and reparations implicitly privilege certain forms of political activity, and deny or devalue other forms of political activity. By establishing gendered categories of 'good' and 'bad' political activity, transitional justice devices substantially influence the terms of citizenship for men and women in societies emerging from conflict or repression. In particular, the chapter explores the relationship of transitional justice devices to historically dominant forms of gendered citizenship, namely the citizen-mother and the citizen-soldier.

Political motherhood and the citizen-mother

Feminist critiques of the civic republican tradition have given rise to efforts to revise citizenship in a way that recognizes and validates women's daily activities as political. Empirically, it is noted that in periods of political repression, women's political activity is often defined by their maternal identity. Mobilization tends to occur as the politicization of the woman's private maternal role (Alvarez, 1990; Chuchryk, 1989; Schirmer, 1988). Feminist interventions into citizenship have divided dramatically on the political relevance of motherhood. Positively, such activism can be seen as challenging traditional, and harmful, divisions between the public and the private that operate to exclude women from citizenship. So-called private experiences of motherhood are recognized for their political nature, and the public is thereby transformed to include and value the quotidian experiences of women. This political practice converges interestingly with a prominent strand of feminist citizenship theory. 'Maternal feminists' have suggested that citizenship be re-ordered to privilege the presumed maternal values of caring and selflessness. Most notably, the work of Sara Ruddick (1980) and Jean Elshtain (1981) has advocated a 'social feminism' and maternal citizenship, whereby the caring and selflessness of the maternal relationship would be privileged, and located at the centre of the political organization of the state. Contrary to traditional liberal commitments of autonomy and rationality, social feminism advocates caring, compassion, and relational values as the cornerstone of citizenship.

Others, however, are more circumspect about the location of motherhood at the centre of women's claims to equal citizenship. Feminists such as Carole Pateman (1988) note that, in the classical social contract, motherhood and the (re)production of citizens was the exclusive basis upon which women were incorporated into citizenship. Despite the noted valorization of maternity that accompanies political motherhood, such valorization rarely translates into equal political power of men and women in practice (Lister, 1997: 149). Furthermore, there is an easy slippage from political motherhood to compulsory maternity that can effectively undermine any claim to equal citizenship. Despite the noted shortcomings of prevailing liberal and civic republican conceptions of citizenship, citizenship is premised on a commitment to fundamental political equality. Every citizen is entitled to participate in the public sphere on a basis of equality. By contrast, the mother–child relationship, while caring, is uneven and unequal. Furthermore, maternal feminism rests on a flawed assumption of women's superiority as (potential) mothers, a notion that also undermines any commitment to political equality. Women perform a variety of public and private roles, and to collapse women's political consciousness into motherhood neglects and undermines a range of women's political activities.

These observations on the potential of political motherhood as the basis of citizenship frame the discussion of gender dynamics driving transitional justice in Chile. As Part two sets out, the installation, maintenance, and, ultimately, the demise of the Chilean military dictatorship were intimately connected to the prevailing construction of political motherhood in the country. State-led initiatives around truth telling and reparations determined the extent to which this prevailing construction of women's citizenship persisted into the new democratic polity.

Militarized masculinity and the citizen-soldier

The classic construction of citizenship depended on military service. The civic republican tradition that emerged from ancient Greece was explicit in its association of military service and civic participation through the foundational ideal of the Citizen-Soldier (Snyder, 1999: 1). The link between citizenship and military service, and the correlation of civic virtue and martial activity inaugurated in the ancient Greek conception of civic republicanism, is largely regarded as dismantled within the contemporary liberal democratic state (Yuval-Davis, 1997). In particular, the emergence of the welfare state is credited with widening the terms and benefits of citizenship from civil and political concerns to social rights also (Marshall, 1950). The lingering resonance of this definition of military activity and citizenship has been exposed, however, in an analysis of the contemporary correlation of military service and citizenship privileges in Israel (Schachar, 1999). Similar dynamics have been identified in the material and symbolic benefits afforded to surviving US soldiers of the Vietnam war and ongoing wars in Iraq and Afghanistan (Snyder, 1999). These contemporary examples suggest that the equation of citizenship and military service is not an historical oddity, but is an equation that continues to be exploited by belligerent states today. Through legal and economic incentives, the citizen-solider becomes re-privileged in the political organization of states confronting international or internal military threat.

These observations on the enduring relationship of citizenship and military service frame the discussion of the gender dynamics of the contemporary process of transitional justice in Colombia. Part three interrogates whether the transitional justice process has reignited and reinscribed the relationship of citizenship status to military activity in the country.

Part two: transitional justice and the citizen-mother: political motherhood in Chile

Political motherhood in Pinochet's Chile

On 11 September 1973, the Chilean military carried out a military coup deposing the democratically elected socialist President Salvador Allende thus ending his attempted 'peaceful road to socialism'. From 1973 until the return of democracy in 1990, a particularly pernicious military dictatorship operated in Chile, led by army General Augusto Pinochet. The Chilean Congress was closed and then dissolved as soon as the military took power. Left wing political activists and trade unionists were rounded up, detained, and many were tortured and 'disappeared' by the regime. Thus, the '[t]raditional institutional channels of political power were systematically dismantled' (Chuchryk, 1989: 73). Within this context of highly restricted political expression, the military regime sought to marshal women's political activity, in their maternal role, behind the regime. Immediately after the coup, General Pinochet set about reorganizing the national network of 30,000 Mothers Centres (*Centros de Madres, CEMAs*) established in the 1950s by Church and charity groups to train women in crafts in order to earn extra family income. General Pinochet appointed his wife as Director of the centres.

The state's promotion of political motherhood was also reflected in the adoption of pro-natalist policies. Advances made under the Allende government in public health planning programmes and reducing the number of backstreet abortions, were immediately and dramatically reversed with the installation of the military regime (Casas, 2004). Therapeutic abortion was not formally criminalized by the military regime until 1989. However, the medical practice of therapeutic abortion was effectively ended with the military's usurpation of power in 1973 (*Red Chilena contra la Violencia Doméstica y Sexual*, 2008). Thus, compulsory maternity, and the obliteration of women's autonomy in reproductive matters in Chile, was entrenched in the early days of the military regime.

Side-by-side with the regime's politicization of maternity, and the institution of compulsory maternity in the country, political motherhood was also deployed in opposition to the military regime. Female relatives of the tortured and 'disappeared' organized on the basis of their maternal identity to challenge the state's repressive tactics.

Women were prominent in the early opposition to the military regime, principally through the Association of the Families of the Detained-Disappeared (*Agrupación de Familiares de Detenidos-Desaparecidos*, AFDD). The traditional sites of political participation had been dismantled by the military regime, and these were classically male spaces. Conversely, women's forms of political activity, within communities and on the basis of a common maternal identity, were actively fostered by the military regime's valorization of maternity and expansion of the Mothers' Centres. Sexist assumptions about the inherently 'apolitical' character of women's organizing initially insulated the AFDD from the worst extremes of state oppression. Regarded as 'apolitical', the organization's activity could pose no credible threat to the military regime. AFDD organizing, on the basis of a common maternal identity, but to *resist* the state, thus marked 'the subversion of an ideology' (Chuchryk, 1989).

Although the AFDD's organizing has proven to be the most celebrated form of women's organizing under the dictatorship, women were also involved in large numbers in subsistence organizing of popular kitchens (*ollas comunes*) to sustain the popular sector during the harsh economic times engendered by the dramatic liberalization of markets in Chile under the military regime. Further, although to a lesser extent, feminist organizations emerged under the dictatorship, engaging in consciousness-raising among women and campaigning on issues such as domestic violence and reproductive rights. Both these subsistence and feminist organizations were to play a substantial role in the popular social mobilization that eventually brought the military regime to an end.

Truth telling and political motherhood

The Chilean National Truth and Reconciliation Commission (TRC) was established by presidential decree in 1990. The Statute provided for the TRC to 'clarify in a comprehensive manner the truth about the most serious human rights violations'. 'Serious violations' were defined as 'persons who disappeared after arrest, who were executed, or who were tortured to death'. While the range of violations to be considered was drawn relatively narrowly, the Commission was also tasked to investigate the 'antecedents and circumstances' of those violations.

In its work, the Commission drew heavily on the records and accounts of the established human rights and victims' non-governmental organizations,[2] including the AFDD. In doing so, the veracity and worth of the work of these organizations was deservedly acknowledged. However, it is only women's activism on the basis of a maternal identity that is recognized. Women's subsistence and feminist organizing is not acknowledged in the TRC Report as operating in the defence of human rights, nor were women recognized as organized 'victims' of the regime. Substantial gendered lacunae, and a highly partial account of women's political subjectivity, can thus be identified in the official 'truth' to emerge from the TRC.

Further, the narrow mandate underpinning the TRC obscured from view most of women's gender-specific experiences of the dictatorship, as women were not generally the 'direct victims' who lost their lives to the military regime. Uniquely within the Report, the section on disruption to family life notes that the repression had a gender-specific impact on broader society. This acknowledgement is under the heading 'Change of Roles':

> The imprisonment, disappearance, or death of a family member, usually the head of the house or a son, leads to a change in the usual roles within the family: women have to look for the missing person, flee, or get paying jobs with long hours in order to maintain the home; children have to leave school and go to work; the older daughters, closest relatives, and neighbours replace the mothers in taking care of the younger brothers and sisters. (Report of the Chilean National Truth and Reconciliation Commission, 1993, Part 3.4.E.2)

However, the TRC Report betrays little understanding of this challenge to traditional gender roles as one of the potentially emancipatory outcomes of the awfulness of violent conflict and political repression. In feminist accounts of the military regime, it is this loosening of societal gender norms that presented one of the rare beneficial consequences of the repression (Chuchryk, 1994; Fisher, 1993). The Report's account betrays a wide gap between official and feminist understandings of these dynamics.

Within political science analysis of democratization, the Chilean case is typically designated a 'pacted' transition (see, for example, Waylen, 2000: 32). The protracted nature of the Chilean transition from dictatorship, in which the military junta was removed from power by means of a plebiscite of its own design, meant that Chile's post-authoritarian democracy was unusually constrained by the constitutional, political, and legal structures put in place by the predecessor regime. The arrest of General Pinochet in London in 1998, followed by the election of socialist President Ricardo Lagos in 2003, formed the backdrop to a flurry of renewed activity to deal with Chile's authoritarian past. With his election, President Lagos embarked upon a range of initiatives to render further official accounting of the past. Principal among these initiatives was the appointment of a Commission to investigate torture and political detention perpetrated by the military regime, the Chilean National Commission on Political Imprisonment and Torture (*Comisión Nacional sobre Prisión Política y Tortura*, 2005). The Commission is more popularly known as the Valech Commission.

The Valech Commission played a crucial role in finally bringing to light the extent of sexual violence perpetrated against female dissidents under the military regime. It marked the first detailed official account of women's victimization under the regime (O'Rourke, 2009). Indeed, before the Valech Commission – initiated 13 years after the return to democracy – there is little evidence of any distinctively feminist articulation of harms experienced under the military regime. Nevertheless, the broad diffusion of the TRC Report must be contrasted with the limited reach of the Valech Commission Report. While the TRC Report was published in full as an insert to a Chilean national daily paper, the report of the Valech Commission was only made available on the internet. 'It's had a reduced impact. It has not yet become part of the historical legacy', concludes prominent Chilean feminist, Lorena Fries (interview with author, 2008, author's translation).

Further, the Valech Commission Report was not universally welcomed by Chilean feminists or women victims. In response to the official publication of the Report, a declaration was made by women ex-prisoners under the dictatorship (*Agrupación de Mujeres ex Prisioneras Políticas*, 2004). The Declaration was heavily critical of the reparations proposed in the Valech Commission Report. In particular, the absence of provision for palliative care for victims of sexual violence was regarded as discriminatory. In addition, there was an angry response to the decision to make reduced reparations payments to torture victims who had already been beneficiaries of the previous reparations programme. The women were determined to assert their direct political involvement in the opposition to the dictatorship, and that their torture was for this reason:

> The militant women and opposition do not accept being treated in our new political dispensation as 'the mothers or wives of...'. We suffered the torture independently of being single or married to militants, therefore, there cannot be confused or subtracted from the reparation [already received] for the assassination or disappearance of a spouse, the reparation to be awarded for having been an individual

> victim of torture. (*Agrupación de Mujeres ex Prisioneras Políticas*, 2004, author's translation)

The women directly affected by the recommendations of the Valech Commission thus sought to contest the re-privileging of the maternal role, and the denial of broader political subjectivity of female dissidents.

On the whole, there is little evidence of an effort to validate multiple diverse forms of women's political subjectivity through official truth seeking initiatives in Chile. Instead, the traditional maternal role is formally recognized and privileged. Efforts to value the existence and work of women within the private sphere are valuable. However, in Chile such efforts operated perversely to obscure and devalue the multiple other roles of women and their participation within the formal public sphere. Furthermore, these lacunae in the official narrative of the past were not harmless. To further quote Lorena Fries:

> I believe that [feminist engagement with the past] is very important – important because it has also to do with what is made visible in the past ... It touches another theme, which is: to what extent are women political subjects? If you don't recognize women as political subjects in the past, historically, they will not be recognized in the present. (author's translation)

The very limited recognition of women's political subjectivity in official accounts of the past must be understood within the broader political context of post-authoritarian Chile, in which women's formal political activity was reduced (indeed, the number of female municipal heads in the country actually diminished with the return to democracy [Craske, 1999: 4]). Further, the period immediately after the return to democracy witnessed the dramatic demobilization of women's social movements in the country (Fitzsimmons, 2000). Rather than challenging the worrying retreat of women from the Chilean public sphere by affirming women's political subjectivity in its multiple forms, the narrow and prescriptive valorization of women's maternal role in official Chilean truth seeking reinforced the retreat of women into the private sphere of post-authoritarian Chile.

Reparations and compulsory maternity

The broad acceptance of the 1991 Report of the Truth and Reconciliation Commission marked an auspicious start to the process of reconciliation in post-authoritarian Chile. However, the expectation that the Commission's Report would lead to prosecutions of the responsible state agents was disappointed. Instead, the 1978 amnesty law cast a long shadow over the courts, as an unreformed judiciary continued to construe the amnesty law as prohibiting even the investigation of the military's human rights violations. The continued broad jurisdiction of the military courts bolstered this impunity. In this context, state efforts to deal with the past shifted to a focus on reparations. The National Corporation of Reparations and Reconciliation (*Corporación Nacional de Reparación y Reconciliación*, CNRR) was established in 1992. As a means of acknowledging and compensating for damages caused by the state, the Corporation established a monetary allowance to be given to family members of the detained-disappeared, and of those who had been executed for political reasons. The Reparations Law also provided for medical benefits, including psychological counselling for the families. The health benefits extended to families of the detained and tortured, as well as returning exiles. Finally, the law provided a subsidy for high school and college education, and waived tuition fees at public institutions of higher education for the children of the victims.

Pablo de Greiff has advanced a political and normative understanding of reparations in transitional justice, contending that as well as their important material implications, reparations provide an opportunity to 'enhance civic trust' between citizens and states emerging from periods of mass violence and political repression (2007: 156). De Greiff argues that reparations can offer the basis for a new social contract in transitional societies, founded on solidarity, mutual recognition, and respect. Fair and effective delivery of reparations can be an important milestone in establishing the legitimacy of states emerging from mass violence and political repression. The values underpinning the reparations programme can advance the values that, it is hoped, will found the newly (re)formed state. Drawing on de Greiff's work, it is submitted, reparations programmes can selectively acknowledge and validate certain forms of political activity, while ignoring and negating others. In this manner also, reparations payments are closely linked to the incorporation of citizens in transitional states.

The decision to include only those disappeared or executed by the dictatorship (and, controversially, the human rights violations perpetrated by the left wing resistance) within the mandate of the Truth and Reconciliation Commission resulted in a heavy gender imbalance in those recognized as 'direct victims' of the regime. However, the decision to award reparations to the families of victims meant that beneficiaries were largely surviving female relatives. The Chilean reparations programme is widely celebrated (see, for example, Kritz, 2009). However, consistent with the enduring valorization of the family under the dictatorship and in the TRC, surviving female relatives of victims were obliged to conform to 'conventional' family forms in order to qualify for reparations. Mothers of victims who were born outside of marriage were not entitled to pensions awarded under the reparations programme. The mothers of victims who were born within marriages that were subsequently annulled were similarly excluded.[3]

Further, a theme of unexpected prominence in the final report of the Reparations Corporation was how to deal with the 'interruption of intrauterine life' (*Corporación Nacional de Reparación y Reconciliación*, 1996: 40–1, author's translation). It was decided that state-perpetrated violence against women, which resulted in the loss of pregnancy, amounted to a violation of the right to life of the foetus within the Chilean legal order, in which the right to life begins at conception. On this basis, women who lost pregnancies were entitled to monetary reparation. The loss of the pregnancies was no doubt a devastating loss for the women involved. The Corporation's decision to include lost pregnancies involved the recognition of new 'victims' of the regime, and new female beneficiaries of the reparations programme. Nevertheless, there are two particularly worrying aspects of the Corporation's reasoning and decision in this aspect of the reparations programme. Firstly, as already noted, due to the restrictive mandate of the TRC and the reparations programme, the abuse and violence suffered by these women on their own bodies, independent of their pregnant condition, is given no recognition in this formulation of the 'interruption of intrauterine life'. These women exist in the reparations programme's monetary allowance only as vessels for the 'unborn child',[4] and the harm that these women experienced is only recognized as vicarious through the ending of the pregnancy. Perversely, the privileging of the foetus as the political actor obliterates the individual political subjectivity of each of the dissident women subjected to torture. Rather, the pregnancy is the basis of their political subjectivity. This particular aspect of the reparations programme constitutes the only occasion on which legal creativity was used to actually *expand* the number of women to benefit from the monetary allowance, and is to be contrasted with the exclusion of surviving female relatives who did not conform to 'conventional' family forms.

Further, strikingly similar gender dynamics can be observed in the reparations payments emerging from the much later Valech Commission. The Commission devised a new reparations programme for victims of torture and political imprisonment, and their families. In terms of the reparations programme designed by the Commission, the Report deals at some length with the definitions of 'victimhood'. A decision was made not to design a reparations programme based on a ranking of types of torture suffered, or length of time spent in detention. Rather, all those determined to be 'victims' would share the same entitlements. The Commission determined that children, who were detained along with their parents and because of their parents' political activity, would be entitled to a half-share of reparations. Similarly, those born in prison were also awarded a half-share of reparations payments. In the Valech Commission Report, as in the 1996 Report of the Reparations Corporation, the issue of 'intrauterine life' features prominently:

> The Commission also received testimonies from individuals who were in gestation when their mothers were being tortured, as well as individuals who were the product of rape committed while their mothers were in detention, which also constitutes a form of torture. In all of these cases, the mothers gave birth after their release from detention. The Commission is of the conviction that these individuals must also be considered victims. Whoever was in gestation when their mothers suffered torture are included in the same category as children born in prison and of children detained together with their parents [that is entitled to half-reparations]. Those who were born as a result of rape are considered direct victims [and therefore entitled to full reparations]. (ibid.: 74–5; author's translation)

The Valech Commission grounded its work in international law, invoking the statutes and jurisprudence of the International Criminal Tribunals for the former Yugoslavia and Rwanda, and the International Criminal Court. Thus, past human rights violations were determined with reference to contemporary international law. However, in its treatment of pregnancies resulting from rape in detention, the Valech Commission largely departed from established international legal categories. The vicarious torture of a foetus through the torture of a pregnant woman has no precedent in international law, yet this was the basis on which children subsequently born outside of detention to women tortured during their detention were awarded equal symbolic and material recognition of reparations as those children who were themselves detained. By contrast, the established offence of enforced pregnancy, codified in the Rome Statute, does not feature anywhere in the Commission's Report. The harm of compulsory maternity is invisible in both the account of the past, and the subsequent reparations.

The valorization of motherhood in transitional justice in Chile must be understood within the context of the social and legal reality of compulsory maternity in the country. The privileging of the foetus in official truth seeking and reparations reinforces a prevailing Chilean legal narrative of foetal rights. A blanket ban on abortion (Center for Reproductive Law and Policy, 1998) and the highly fraught and restricted distribution of emergency contraception (Casas, 2008), mark the practical outworkings of a punitive valorization of maternity in Chile.

Part three: transitional justice and the citizen-soldier: militarized masculinity in Colombia

Forging citizenship in a fractured state: re-arming the citizen-soldier in Colombia

Six decades of multi-actor and multi-causal violence in Colombia sets the backdrop to the contemporary process of transitional justice in the country. Multiple competing actors with both military capacity and political power, operating in parallel or opposition to the state, have undermined any claim by the state to the monopoly on legitimate coercion in the country. Strong regional variations in terms of wealth, ethnic profile, state presence, and conflict density, further erode Colombian claims to statehood.

Conflict violence has reinforced popular disenfranchisement from the state. Left wing guerrilla groups emerged in the 1960s as part of a surge in the revolutionary armed left in Latin America. The Colombian state's fostering of 'self-defence' groups among civilians to resist guerrillas in rural areas where the state's presence was weak or absent, further undermined the state's claims to the monopoly of coercion, the rule of law, or popular legitimacy. Since the 1980s, the enormous profits generated by the drug industry have allowed a range of violent actors sufficient resources to institute localized systems of patronage and clientelism throughout large regions of the country. Therefore, popular disenfranchisement from the state was reinforced and extended through material incentives of employment, land, and income; all secured through cooperation with the dominant violent actor in any particular area. Clientelist networks have become central to the political organization of the country, as high levels of voter abstentionism in guerrilla and paramilitary dominated zones demonstrate that political rights are ceded in return for material survival. By the end of the 1990s, the country was teetering on the brink of failed statehood. The state's fragility has undermined the centrality of citizenship as the key organizing concept of the Colombian polity; instead, localized systems of clientelism have been dominant.

Against this backdrop, more recent security initiatives adopted in Colombia have endeavoured to make the state relevant once again. The policy of 'Democratic Security' inaugurated by President Alvaro Uribe upon his election in 2003 sought to reassert Colombian statehood and re-establish citizenship in the country (*Presidencia de la República Ministerio de Defensa Nacional República de Colombia*, 2003). According to the policy, the state's assertion of its military presence in regions of the country in which the state was traditionally absent was central. In order to reassert Colombian statehood, the Democratic Security policy emphasized the need for all Colombians to collaborate to this end. Hence, one of the three pillars of 'Democratic Security' is the solidarity and cooperation of all citizens in defence of democratic values (ibid.: 12). The policy noted that there is a tendency to assume that there are only two paths in Colombia, either that of peace, pursued by the political leadership, or the path of war, pursued by the armed forces. Instead, Democratic Security emphasized the responsibility of civil society leaders, and society in general, to pursue the campaign for order and stability.

In practical terms, full citizen involvement in Colombia's pursuit of security and order has taken the form, firstly, of 'rural peasant armies'. These are mobile army brigades, operating high in the mountains, composed of rural peasants who perform their military service in their places of residence (ibid.: 10). Secondly, there are a 'network of informants'. This network consists of civilians with links to illegal armed organizations, who provide information relating to the prevention and prosecution of criminal activities in return for financial compensation (ibid.: 61). The financial compensation is an incentive for former members of illegal armed groups to return to those groups in order to obtain intelligence on their activities. With this policy of Democratic Security, Colombian citizenship has been explicitly and repeatedly linked to (largely clandestine) military activity.

In addition to the 'democratization' of the Colombian conflict, through the widespread induction of Colombian civilians into army forces to combat guerrilla groups, the Democratic Security policy has also sought the demobilization of one set of non-state armed actors, namely the paramilitary groups. Through a series of presidential decrees, individual and group demobilization has been facilitated by legal incentives such as pardons and immunity from future prosecution, and economic incentives including food, shelter, and employment opportunities. The process sets the political and legal context for the reintegration of armed illegal actors into the Colombian political community. Dedicated zones have been established in Colombia to facilitate the demobilization process.

As noted above, transitions from conflict or political repression, as ruptures with the former political order, constitute a renewed opportunity for the incorporation of citizens into the polity. Transitional justice devices, in turn, impact the terms of incorporation of citizens. Amnesties or reduced penalties for violence have been a mainstay of the transitional justice landscape (see generally Mallinder, 2008). Processes of disarmament, demobilization, and reintegration (DDR) of combatants are increasingly central to efforts to build sustainable peace in the aftermath of violent conflict (UN DPKO, 1999). Without diminishing the presence of women in combatant forces, or the prominence of men in civilian populations, there is nevertheless an often unspoken gender profile of DDR: namely, that the process involves the reintegration of a largely male (former) combatant group into a disproportionately female civilian population. The gender differential between returning and receiving communities means that, although DDR is officially concerned with ensuring the conditions which enable former combatants to cease violence and return to their communities of origin, the terms of DDR can have enormous impact on the gender relationships within returning communities, and hence on the renewed political community of the transitional state. In the Colombian context, women's organizations have undertaken extensive monitoring and reporting of the violence that penetrates these zones dedicated to the demobilization of paramilitaries, linking them to a generalized 'insecurity' and the 'growing militarization of civilian life' (Mujer y Conflicto Armado, 2005). There is extensive evidence of the targeting of female civil society leaders for violent assassination by illegal armed groups. The continuance of this violence in parallel with the transitional justice process signals the extent to which women's political subjectivity is being undermined through transitional justice in Colombia. Moreover, it has been found that the reinsertion process was imposing further limitations on the rights of free associations and expression of women as a consequence of the hegemony of paramilitarism in the zone (Corporación Humanas, 2005). Further, increases in prostitution, sexually transmitted diseases, and adolescent pregnancies point to the coercive dynamics of sexual relations that prevail in the demilitarization process. The penetration of violence in these demilitarization zones, and the range of threats to the physical security and political organization of women living therein, graphically demonstrates the basis for 'renewed citizenship' of illegal armed actors within the Colombian transitional justice process.

Joshua Goldstein's (2001) seminal work on gender and conflict has exposed the cross-cultural moulding of men into warriors – war does not come naturally to men from biology, so they must be socialized into fighting. In this formulation, masculinity is not automatic; it must be constantly earned and re-earned through the performance of violent military activity. Through this process of socialization, masculinity and military activity become fused. In turn, citizenship and military masculinity are fused. As R. Claire Snyder observes:

> [T]he Citizen-Soldier functions as a prescriptive ideal that calls for male individuals to engage in the civic and martial practices that constitute them as masculine republican citizens. At the same time, the masculine character of the ideal undermines the participation of female individuals in civic and martial practices because these practices constitute not just citizenship but also masculinity. (1999: 2)

There is much evidence to suggest that, through the Democratic Security policy, the Colombian state is actively pursuing the militarization and masculinization of citizenship in Colombia. The next section now turns to truth and reparations initiatives within the contemporary transitional justice process in Colombia to consider their implications for gendered citizenship in the country.

Reparations

The Justice and Peace Law of 2005 established a residual and *sui generis* process of accountability for leaders of paramilitary groups: 'alternative penalties', namely the deprivation of liberty for between five and eight years, are imposed on demobilized combatants, provided that the former combatant admits responsibility for each of his/her criminal acts in a quasi-judicial process of disclosure. The obligation to make reparation is a liability, not of the state, but of the confessed human rights' violators. In the Colombian case, it is estimated that there are around 3.5 million potential beneficiaries of reparations for the conflict, of whom about 80,000 have sought reparations under the Justice and Peace Law (Barraza and Guzmán, 2008: 117). To date, 80 per cent of these applicants are women. Thus, the process by which reparations are awarded by largely male perpetrators to largely female beneficiaries has important implications for the citizenship claims of both men and women in Colombia.

The Justice and Peace Law establishes a judicial procedure for the pursuit of reparations claims by individual victims against individual perpetrators, who are being demobilized within the terms of the law. Awarding reparations is the final stage in the Justice and Peace process before sentencing. The award of reparations is considered only in the case of an express petition by the victim. (The prosecutor also has discretion to make a petition for reparations on behalf of an individual victim, although the law provides little clarity as to the circumstances in which this discretion should be exercised). The law imposes a considerable burden on victims. As well as having to bring the petition, the victim must indicate the reparation that he/she claims, and provide evidence that supports this quantification of the harm. The victim is then expected to agree the amount of the reparations with the perpetrator through a process of conciliation. If an agreement cannot be reached, the court can make this determination.

Criticisms have centred on the requirement that the victim requests that the offence be considered for reparations. The difficulties for victims are to satisfy the evidential requirements in order to be awarded reparations, and, in particular, the fear of victims to participate in the process of conciliation with the perpetrators of the violence they experienced (Grupo de Trabajo, 2008: 64–5). The conciliation requirement is a disincentive for victims to make a petition for reparations, due to the fear of facing perpetrators. The relationship between victim and perpetrator is highly unequal, and the law establishes no procedural protections to mitigate this inequality. The law has been heavily criticized by feminists for too great a reliance on conciliation between the perpetrator and victim. Conciliation or mediation has been roundly resisted by feminist lawyers and women's organizations in cases of gendered violence. Procedural and other safeguards provided by the adversarial process to the victim, or less capable party, are critical (Howe and McIsaac, 2008). Laura Nader (1992) argues that, through conciliation for family disputes, justice is being replaced by 'harmony'; in particular, that broader societal harmony dependent on minimizing disruption to gender relations as the basic organizing unit of society. As Colombian feminist Julieta Lemaitre (2002) argues, this focus on the resolution of conflict neglects the inequalities of power between the parties, and the urgency of the victim to reach a solution no matter what the price. Although this scholarship emerges from feminist analysis of conciliation in cases of domestic violence, concerns about gendered inequalities of power between the parties are surely all the more acute in the case of a perpetrator who belongs to a paramilitary organization. Contrary to aspirations for the effective use of reparations to advance equal citizenship, making reparations payments contingent on the outcome of a conciliation process between the perpetrator and the victim risks perpetuating the violence and inequality of power relations between these two actors.

Truth telling

The judicial process established by the Justice and Peace Law was intended to satisfy victims' rights to truth, by requiring former combatants participating in the Justice and Peace process to provide a comprehensive and truthful account of their illegal activities (identified in the law as '*versión libre*'). In Colombia, however, manifold problems have been identified in the quality of truth emerging from the contemporary transitional justice process. Practical obstacles, such as the insufficient number of prosecutors and lack of resources, mean that the paramilitaries, and not the state nor victims, are directing the *versiones libres*.[5] The process is providing a forum for paramilitaries to justify and defend their activities either as defending the community against guerrillas, or as the 'social cleansing' of prostitutes, rapists, and drug dealers. Women's organizations have noted that sexual violence barely appears in the *versiones libres*, and, to the small extent that it does feature, the practice is presented as rare and isolated rather than widespread and systematic (La Ruta Pacifica et al., 2009). Further, the focus on isolated offences is contributing nothing to the clarification of the relationship between the paramilitaries and state forces, economic interests, or political parties.

The 'truth' of paramilitary activities emerging from this process thus appears to be isolated acts of criminality, justified by 'social cleansing' objectives of the perpetrators, and without any gender-specific impact. This narrative allows the paramilitaries to valorize their criminal activities as both political and benign, suggesting a deeply troubling basis for the 'renewed' membership of these former paramilitaries within the Colombian political community. Military activity has been privileged as the primary civic activity in Colombia. The equation of masculinity, military activity, and citizenship is particularly troubling in a country attempting to exit conflict. It is a construction of citizenship that is highly gendered, highly partial, and ultimately highly antithetical to even the most modest claims of transition.

Conclusion: disrupting gendered citizenship in transitional justice

The discussion of citizenship in this chapter raises legitimate questions about the value of citizenship as a theoretical and political tool in feminist engagement with transitional justice. As apparently inherently gendered and exclusionary, premised on the control of women's bodies, and the re-privileging of masculine violence, might the pursuit of equal citizenship best be abandoned in favour of more transformative political goals in transitional justice? In particular, with its focus on liberal legal rights and narrowly-defined political activity, does citizenship simply work to re-establish a damaging and exploitative division of public and private in transitional societies? As a unique conjuncture of public and private, and of law and politics, transitions constitute rare moments for the re-drawing of the public/private divide. Yet feminist theorists have critiqued dominant forms of citizenship for their reification of the traditional and exploitative distinction between the public and private.

The Chilean experience, in which transition was accompanied by the large-scale retreat of women from formal political activity, was not unique to that case. In particular, feminist political science analysis of democratization transitions repeatedly draws attention to the under-representation of women in new democratic institutions, and the tendency for transitions to be accompanied by the large-scale retreat of women from the public sphere of protest and politics to the retrenched (though reorganized) private sphere of domesticity and capitalist development (see, for example, Fitzsimmons, 2000). This chapter modestly proposes that, by valuing the multiple political subjectivities of women, beyond a singular focus on women's maternal role, transitional justice devices might act as a bulwark against the retreat of women from public life in transition. Ultimately, the focus on citizenship turns us away from the traditional feminine spheres of the kitchen and the nursery, and back to the traditional 'public sphere' (the polis, assembly, civil society, and social movements). However, the reinstatement of the specifically political in transition should not be understood as bad for women or limiting for men. For example, for women's movements seeking to make gains through the transitional state, the overall project of rehabilitating the public sphere is helpful. The state can thereby become a legitimate site of feminist activity and feminist gains. Further, the value of a private sphere, free of state interference, resonates all the more in cases of transition. For prior regimes, characterized by the perpetration of violence in the 'private' sphere such as in house searches or strip searching prisoners, establishing a private sphere, free of interference from a state of still dubious legitimacy, is an understandable priority.

In Colombia, efforts to re-establish security and order are defined by the militarization of everyday life and the re-privileging of violent actors in the political organization of the country. A particularly combative form of armed masculinity has been forged in Colombia, and has been reinscribed through transitional justice devices in the country. Contrary to this process of militarizing and masculinizing all forms of political activity, however, Kimberly Theidon (2009) has cogently argued that – in addition to relieving former combatants of their guns and bullets – demilitarization processes must also attend to disarming the hegemonic form of masculinity that privileges and sustains violence in the conduct of social relations. Transitional justice devices can contribute to disarming militarized and masculinized forms of citizenship by reinvigorating and valuing non-military forms of citizenship, such as civil society mobilization for peace, justice, and human rights. Transitional justice devices have a role to play in disarming the citizen-soldier.

As past-focused legal devices, transitional justice mechanisms are not the primary site for (re)establishing the public sphere and political community of transitional societies. Nevertheless, as the case studies demonstrate, transitional justice initiatives can valorize or negate different forms of political activity of men and women. Transitional justice devices therefore influence the incorporation of citizens into the transitional state, either on limiting and gendered terms, or – potentially – on an inclusive basis of political equality.

Notes

The author gratefully acknowledges Carmel Roulston and the volume editors for valuable assistance in writing the chapter.

1. There is a third 'identity' dimension often attributed to citizenship (Kymlicka, 1995). This dimension is not explored in the chapter.
2. The *Vicaría de la Solidaridad* was established in 1976 to conduct human rights work under the auspices of the Catholic Church in Chile. This work was supplemented by the (non-Catholic) Christian Churches Foundation for Social Assistance (*Fundación de Ayuda Social de las Iglesias Cristianas*, FASIC). The Chilean Human Rights Commission was established in 1978 to draw attention to the regime's use of torture, and the Corporation for the Promotion and Defense of People's Rights (*Corporación de Promoción y Defensa de los Derechos del Pueblo*, CODEPU) emerged in 1980. All of these organizations were extensively consulted and referenced in the formulation of the Chilean Truth and Reconciliation Commission Report.
3. This was finally changed in 2003 during the Presidency of Ricardo Lagos; see further Lira (2006).
4. 'Hijo neonata' is the language used in Report when detailing each individual pregnancy in the list of victims appended to the report, (*Corporación Nacional de Reparación y Reconciliación*, 1996: 852–4).

5. For a detailed account of the operation of the Justice and Peace Law, and its noncompliance with international human rights standards, see International Federation for Human Rights (2007).

References

Agrupación de Mujeres ex Prisioneras Políticas Sobrevivientes de la Red de Centros de Tortura Clandestinos del Régimen Militar de Pinochet (2004) *Declaración de las Mujeres ex Presas Políticas bajo la Dictadura* (Santiago de Chile: Centro Estudios 'Miguel Enríquez).

S. Alvarez (1990) *Engendering Democracy in Brazil: Women's Movements in Transition Politics* (Princeton: Princeton University Press).

C. Barraza Morelle and D. E. Guzmán (2008). 'Proceso de reparación para las mujeres víctimas de violencia en el marco del conflicto armado colombiano', *Sin Tregua: Políticas de Reparación para Mujeres Víctimas de Violencia Sexual durante Dictaduras y Conflictos Armados. Santiago de Chile* (Santiago de Chile: Corporación Humanas).

C. Bell (2009) 'Transitional Justice, Interdisciplinarity and the State of the "Field" or "Non-Field"', *International Journal of Transitional Justice*, Vol. 3 No. 1, 5–27.

C. Bell, C. Campbell, and F. Ní Aoláin (2004) 'Justice Discourses in Transition', *Social and Legal Studies*, Vol. 13 No. 3, 306–28.

L. Casas Becerra (2004) 'Women and Reproduction: From Control to Autonomy? The Case of Chile', *American University Journal of Gender, Social Policy and the Law*, Vol. 12, 427–51.

L. Casas Becerra (2008) 'La Saga de la anticoncepción de emergencia en Chile: avances y desafíos', *Serie Documentos Electrónicos N°2, Noviembre, Programa Género y Equidad* (Santiago de Chile: FLACSO Chile & UNFPA).

Center for Reproductive Law and Policy and Open Forum on Reproductive Health and Rights (1998) *Women Behind Bars: Chile's Abortion Law, a Human Rights Analysis* (New York and Santiago: Center for Reproductive Law and Policy).

P. M. Chuchryk (1989) 'Subversive Mothers: the Women's Opposition to the Military Regime in Chile' in S. E. Charlton, J. Everett, and K. Staudt (eds) *Women, the State, and Development* (Albany: State University of New York Press).

P. M. Chuchryk (1994) 'From Dictatorship to Democracy: The Women's Movement in Chile' in J. Jaquette (ed) *The Women's Movement in Latin America: Participation and Democracy* (Boulder, San Francisco and Oxford: Westview Press).

Comisión Nacional sobre Prisión Política y Tortura (2005) *Informe de la Comisión Nacional sobre Prisión Política y Tortura* (Santiago: Ministerio del Interior, El Gobierno de Chile).

Corporación Humanas (2005) *Riesgos para la seguridad de las mujeres en procesos de reinserción de excombatiente – estudio sobre el impacto de la reinserción paramilitar en la vida y seguridad de las mujeres en los municipios de Montería y Tierralta departamento de Córdoba* (Bogotá: Corporación Humanas).

Corporación Nacional de Reparación y Reconciliación (1996) *Informe Final de la Corporación Nacional de Reparación y Reconciliación* (Santiago de Chile: La Corporación).

N. Craske (1999) *Women and Politics in Latin America* (Cambridge: Polity Press).

P. de Greiff (2007) 'Justice and Reparations' in J. Miller and R. Kumar (eds) *Reparations: Interdisciplinary Inquiries* (New York and Oxford: Oxford University Press).

M. Dietz (1985) 'Citizenship with a Feminist Face: The Problem of Maternal Thinking', *Political Theory*, Vol. 13 No. 1, 19–37.

J. B. Elshtain (1981) *Public Man, Private Woman: Women in Social and Political Thought* (Princeton and Chichester: Princeton University Press).

J. Elster (2004) *Closing the Books: Transitional Justice in Historical Perspective* (Cambridge: Cambridge University Press).

J. Fisher (1993) *Out of the Shadows* (London: Latin American Bureau).

T. Fitzsimmons (2000) *Beyond the Barricades: Women, Civil Society, and Participation after Democratization in Latin America* (New York and London: Garland Publishing).

J. Goldstein (2001) *War and Gender* (Cambridge: Cambridge University Press).

Grupo de Trabajo: Mujer y Género, por la Verdad, la Justicia y la Reconciliación (2008) *Recomendaciones para Garantizar los Derechos a la Verdad, la Justicia y la Reparación de las Mujeres Víctimas del Conflicto Armado en Colombia* (Bogotá: Grupo de Trabajo).

B. Hamber (2009) *Transforming Societies after Political Violence: Truth, Reconciliation, and Mental Health* (New York: Springer).

W. J. Howe and H. McIsaac (2008) 'Domestic Violence and Mediation: A Dialogue', *Family Court Review*, Vol. 46, 592–4.

International Federation for Human Rights (2007) *Colombia: La Desmovilización Paramilitar, en los Caminos de la Corte Penal Internacional*.

K. B. Jones (1990) 'Citizenship in a Woman-Friendly Polity', *Signs*, Vol. 15 No. 4, 781–812.

W. Kymlicka (1995) *Multicultural Citizenship: A Liberal Theory of Minority Rights* (Oxford: Clarendon Press).

N. Kritz (2009) 'Policy Implications of Empirical Research on Transitional Justice' in H. van der Merwe, V. Baxter, and A. R. Chapman (eds) *Assessing the Impact of Transitional Justice: Challenges for Empirical Research* (Washington DC: United States Institute of Peace).

La Ruta Pacifica et al. (2009) *Declaración Final, Foro Internacional 'Verdad, Justicia y Reparación Integral: una deuda pendiente con las mujeres víctimas de las violencias'*, 25 June 2009 (Bogotá).

J. Lemaitre Ripoll (2002) 'Justicia Injusta: Una Crítica Feminista a La Conciliación En Violencia Conyugal', *Derecho Privado*, Vol. 16 No. 27, 73–98.

E. Lira (2006) 'The Reparations Policy for Human Rights Violations in Chile' in P. de Greiff (ed.) *The Handbook of Reparations* (Oxford and New York: Oxford University Press), pp. 55–101.

R. Lister (1997) *Citizenship: Feminist Perspectives* (Basingstoke and New York: Palgrave Macmillan).

L. Mallinder (2008) *Amnesties, Human Rights and Political Transitions: Bridging the Peace and Justice Divide* (Oxford: Hart Publishing).

R. Mani (2002) *Beyond Retribution: Seeking Justice in the Shadows of War* (Cambridge: Polity Press).

T. H. Marshall (1950) *Citizenship and Social Class* (Cambridge: Cambridge University Press).

Mujer y Conflicto Armado (2005) *Informe sobre Violencia Sociopolítica contra Mujeres, Jóvenes y Niñas en Colombia*, Quinto Informe, Junio 2004 – Junio 2005 (Bogotá).
L. Nader (1992) 'From Legal Process to Mind Processing', *Family and Conciliation Courts Review*, Vol. 30, 486.
F. Ní Aoláin (2000) 'Sex-based Violence and the Holocaust – A Re-evaluation of Harms and Rights in International Law', *Yale Journal of Law and Feminism*, Vol. 12, 43–84.
C. O'Rourke (2009) *The Law and Politics of Gender in Transition: A Feminist Exploration of Transitional Justice in Chile, Northern Ireland and Colombia*, D. Phil. thesis, Faculty of Law, University of Ulster.
C. Pateman (1988) *The Sexual Contract* (Cambridge: Polity Press).
A. Phillips (1993) *Democracy and Difference* (Oxford: Polity Press).
Presidencia de la República Ministerio de Defensa Nacional República de Colombia (2003) *Política de Defensa y Seguridad Democrática* (Bogotá).
Red Chilena contra la Violencia Doméstica y Sexual (2008) *Violencia Sexual y Aborto: Conexiones Necesarias. Gloria Maira Vargas, Paula Santana Nazarit, Siomara Molina Sáez* (Santiago de Chile).
Report of the Chilean National Truth and Reconciliation Commission (1993) (translated by Phillip E. Berryman) (Notre Dame: University of Notre Dame Press)
S. Ruddick (1980) 'Maternal Thinking', *Feminist Studies*, Vol. 6 No. 2, 342–67.
A. Schachar (1999) 'Whose Republic?: Citizenship and Membership in the Israeli Polity', *Georgetown Immigration Law Journal*, Vol. 13, 233–72.
J. G. Schirmer (1988) ' "Those Who Die for Life Cannot be Called Dead:" Women and Human Rights Protest in Latin America', *Harvard Human Rights Yearbook*, Vol. 1, 41–76.
R. C. Snyder (1999) *Citizen-Soldiers and Manly Warriors: Military Service and Gender in the Civic Republican Tradition* (Lanham, MD and Oxford: Rowman & Littlefield Publishers).
R. Teitel (2000) *Transitional Justice* (New York: Oxford University Press).
K. Theidon (2007) 'Transitional Subjects: The Disarmament, Demobilization and Reintegration of Former Combatants in Colombia', *International Journal of Transitional Justice*, Vol. 1, 66–90.
K. Theidon (2009) 'Reconstructing Masculinities: The Disarmament, Demobilization, and Reintegration of Former Combatants in Colombia', *Human Rights Quarterly*, Vol. 31, 1–34.
United Nations Department of Peacekeeping Operations (1999) *Disarmament, Demobilization and Reintegration of Ex-Combatants in a Peacekeeping Environment: Principles and Guidelines* (New York: United Nations).
United Nations Secretary General (2004) *The Rule of Law and Transitional Justice in Conflict and Post-conflict Societies* (New York: United Nations).
G. Waylen (2000). 'Gender and Democratic Politics: A Comparative Analysis of Consolidation in Argentina and Chile', *Journal of Latin American Studies*, Vol. 32, 765–793.
N. Yuval-Davis (1997) *Gender and Nation* (Thousand Oaks and New Delhi: Sage Publications).

Part III

Potentials and Limits of Agency

6
Asserting Their Presence! Women's Quest for Transitional Justice in Post-Genocide Rwanda

Rirhandu Mageza-Barthel

Following the Rwandan genocide, which took place between April and July 1994, the country hosted a wide range of transitional justice mechanisms to deal with the atrocities including judicial measures such as national trials, and the *gacaca* tribunals which sought to render justice on a local level. The genocide claimed between 500,000 and 1 million lives of Tutsi and moderate Hutu, and it was highly gendered with 250,000 women raped, 60 per cent widowed, and many more displaced (Twagiramariya and Turshen, 1998: 102). Dealing with its aftermath remains a serious challenge on all levels.

Much has been written on transitional justice in Rwanda. This chapter will redirect the focus of analysis away from a punitive (or restorative) understanding of transitional justice, towards an area which is equally important in dealing with the legacy of large-scale human rights violations such as those experienced during genocide, the lobbying of interest groups – here women – regarding the legal reforms which affect transitional and gender justice. In this sense, the concern of this chapter is to provide an example of women *asserting their presence* through their agency as policy shapers, rather than as victims of a period of violence which must rank amongst the most systematically conducted incidences of sexual violence against women during wartime.

Having experienced mass violence, countries face the challenge of how to reconcile the tension between retrospective accountability and future needs. In this context, national legislation takes on a particularly important role in plotting the country's future social and political order. Against this backdrop, this chapter analyses women's political agenda-setting in Rwanda by looking at the processes leading up to the engendering of the Organic Law on Prosecuting Crimes of Genocide or Crimes against Humanity (1996) as well as the Matrimonial Regimes Law (1999).[1] In so doing, the author will argue that these two interventions in the country's transitional period represent a turning point in gender relations, which has laid the foundation for further gender equitable changes. These laws are so far reaching because, together, they have significantly altered the rights of Rwandan women. They take gender-specific experiences into account when seeking to redress past genocide-related atrocities and when aiming to secure women's equality by ensuring their (property) ownership within Rwandan society in the future. In drawing on semi-structured interviews[2] with women who have been active in shaping Rwanda's gender politics, this chapter explores women as agents of post-conflict transformation who take on international standards of transitional justice when voicing, and mobilizing around, their national experiences. Nevertheless, despite their successes, both areas, gender-based violence and women's access to property, have yielded ambivalent material results, remain contested, and continue to be major issues for Rwanda's women's movement today.[3]

Many accounts of Rwanda's genocide consider ethnic rivalries between the majority Hutu and the minority Tutsi as the central dynamic culminating in the events of 1994. This chapter will question this argument by emphasizing that ethnic belonging is socially constructed and thus fluid (Ottaway, 1999; Straus, 2007: 123–4); and that, in the case of Rwanda, ethnicity has been subject to manipulation, polarization, and instrumentalization before, during, and after the genocide. Significantly, ethnic belonging transcends the transitional period (1994–2003) and continues to impact on efforts to consolidate political power and to control the historically strong Rwandan state (Twagiramariya and Turshen, 1998: 103; Straus, 2007: 124; see also Longman, 2006). This chapter refrains, from discussing issues pertaining to ethnic relations, and focuses on gender relations instead. In recognition of the fact that these social determinants cannot easily be separated, the author concentrates on gender since *all* women were affected by the gender discriminatory laws in the period preceding the genocide as well as in the ensuing transitional period (albeit to different extents depending on their ethnic and political membership).

To pursue the argument, the discussion begins with the gender dynamics of the Rwandan genocide, and then critically appraises approaches related to the domestication of international gender norms, putting forth the idea that women's political participation represents a significant factor which has contributed to shaping a gender-responsive post-genocide legal framework in Rwanda. This argument is then exemplified by tracing two processes of women's agenda-setting – the Genocide Law and the Matrimonial Regimes Law – in order to, lastly, review the utility of gender norms as tools for both social and political transformation in post-conflict societies such as Rwanda. This will be achieved by weighing the normative impact against Rwandan women's material – lived conditions – to selectively outline where further interventions would be necessary to secure the gains reached between 1994 and the end of Rwanda's initial transitional phase in 1999.[4]

Engendering the Rwandan genocide

The Rwandan genocide can be counted amongst the most horrific crimes of the twentieth century. Even though the scope of the violence seems beyond comprehension, René Lemarchand and Maurice Niwese (2007) argue that genocides need to be understood in their own specific context. In Rwanda, a long history of ethnic manipulation, as well as local and national political power struggles for control of the Rwandan state, have ensued since decolonization (Straus, 2007). Discrimination and political persecution took place at various points during the first decades of the Republic (1959–73),[5] leading to the flight of many Tutsi abroad, who then formed an influential diaspora. The power struggles eventually reached a peak at the onset of democratization efforts when exiles under the leadership of the Rwandan Patriotic Front (RPF) staged military attacks against the then regime, leading to a civil war (1990–93) and was followed by the genocide in 1994.

The Rwandan genocide drew international attention to the gendered nature of genocides. In this context, women's roles varied greatly. While some were targets of genocidal violence, others belonged to its masterminds, perpetrators, and supporters or showed bravery in hiding victims (African Rights, 1995). Even though women were similarly implicated in the genocide like men, men were killed for belonging to a specific ethnic group or the political opposition, while women, on account of their gender, were subjected to different experiences, in particular sexual violence. Not least since the wars in the former Yugoslavia and Rwanda, has sexual violence against women turned into a distinctive feature of ethnopolitical violent conflict where rape is employed strategically as a weapon of war. Since ethnic identity is commonly transferred patrilineally, it is a means to procreate one's own community whilst erasing the other, simultaneously stigmatizing the violated women as well as infecting them with HIV/AIDS so that they die gradually (Twagiramariya and

Turshen, 1998: 104). Furthermore, rape and sexual violence are carried out with the aim of humiliating the other community for not being able to protect its women. These strategies illustrate how women are targeted both physically and socially during conflicts.

In Rwanda, as a consequence of the massacres, women made up 70 per cent of Rwanda's total population in the genocide's immediate aftermath.[6] They lived in dismal conditions, with their homes destroyed and their loved ones either dead, imprisoned, or fugitive on account of alleged participation in the genocide. Because of these dynamics, as Sheila Meintjes et al. (2001) illustrate more generally, there can be no aftermath for women. Since a conflict has an immediate bearing on the post-conflict context, it leads to shifts in gender relations so that subtly, and out of necessity, gender demarcations are renegotiated. This was the case in post-genocide Rwanda where the challenging of restrictive gender roles tied in with processes that had started before 1994 (Jefrevomas, 1991; Taylor, 2001), but was amplified as a result of the post-genocide situation. The social shift took place parallel to the general political change of power in Kigali after 1994, which was expected to bring with it an overhaul of national policies and institutional settings. The military victory of the RPF had put an end to the genocide and ushered in a transitional period under a RPF-led Government of National Unity (GNU). This arrangement lasted until the first national elections in September 2003 in which the RPF emerged as the strongest party. It is against this backdrop that women intervened in the processes of transitional justice. They endeavoured to seek recognition for their genocide-related experiences, to institutionalize their newfound freedoms, and to secure their continued existence.

Domesticating international gender norms

This section discusses the utility of international norms as tools for gender equitable reforms, since the impetus towards more gender equality resulted from women's activism at the international level that peaked in the 1990s (Ruppert, 1998: 27–8; Ruppert, 2000: 54–7). A further important reason for focusing on international norms lies in the fact that they demarcate acceptable from unacceptable standards of behaviour within the international community and thus constitute the benchmark by which transitional justice is measured nationally (Finnemore and Sikkink, 1998: 891; Risse, 1999: 529). The author regards the United Nation's (UN) gender norms, specifically the Convention on the Elimination of All Forms of Discrimination against Women (CEDAW), as well as the Beijing Declaration and its Platform for Action (PFA), as a set of instruments which complement each other and, as such, present women with a range of tools for their political activism. These instruments need to be discussed in more detail in this chapter since they have been critiqued widely by feminist legal and political scholars for being difficult to enforce. In contrast to the UN's security norms, for example, the UN's gender norms are regarded as less binding or 'soft'. The reasons for this are manifold, including, for instance, that they bear on the private sphere, remain unregulated by national laws, or are insufficiently codified internationally to be binding (Charlesworth and Chinkin, 2000: 72–7; see Benedek et al., 2002). Offering a snapshot of the UN norms shows which tools were available to Rwandan women in their reconstruction effort whilst criticizing the top-down application of these norms.[7]

Before analysing CEDAW and the PFA, which were later employed in Rwanda, a brief outline of their content and implementation mechanisms is necessary. Interestingly, during the period under discussion, we find a pertinent double-omission in universal women's human rights and conflict norms. Until the PFA arising from the Fourth World Women's Conference held in Beijing in September 1995, UN gender norms were conflict-blind, and conflict norms, as in international humanitarian law, contained a notable gender bias.[8] The Beijing Conference is credited with reviving the UN's and its member states' commitments to gender equality for three reasons. Firstly, the high participation rate can be regarded as an indicator for the conference's success. At Beijing, 189 states were represented and more than 30,000 women attended the parallel NGO Forum in which diverse social groups debated crucial topics, including women's political representation and their wartime experiences. Secondly, in comparison to previous decades, feminist and women's organizing had come to a climax at the local, national, and international political levels with a united transnational women's movement coming to the fore (West, 1999: 184). Thirdly, the PFA stands out since it formally defines women's rights as human rights with states reaffirming their commitment to CEDAW (under further discussion later). A particular novelty is that the PFA specifies particular areas for action, the 12 Critical Areas of Concern, whose worldwide implementation would lead to greater gender equality. Review conferences have been planned in five year intervals as a mechanism to monitor implementation levels across the globe with states being encouraged to continue their regular reporting on CEDAW. Crucially, for the first time, a gender norm has contained a conflict dimension.

Critical Area E on 'Women and Armed Conflict' – according to which states are obliged to protect women during armed conflict as well as to reduce the incidence of human rights abuse in conflict situations, to promote women's participation in conflict resolution, to reduce excessive military spending, and to protect women refugees and internally displaced persons (United Nations, 1995).

Although the PFA marks a shift in the conflict-blindness of gender norms, a central critique of the UN's gender norms holds true; gender norms differ from other human rights norms because they remain contested, even at the international level. CEDAW is a case in point. As the UN's first norm dedicated to women's equality it was passed in 1979, during the UN's Women's Decade (1975–85). It identifies discrimination against women as the common source of gender inequality, and lays out what constitutes discrimination against women widely.[9] Amongst other areas, it highlights women's discrimination in both the private (for example in households and marriage) and the public spheres (for example in national legislation, politics, and the workplace). When acceding to CEDAW, states take on the obligation to abolish all visible forms of discrimination against women and to include its provisions in their national legislation as well as their constitutions. CEDAW initiated a review committee, to which states regularly submit progress reports in order to monitor state implementation. Similar to the PFA, CEDAW does not envisage sanctions for non-complying states. Instead, they are regulated by an *informal* mechanism to pressure states to comply with its provisions, in which non-governmental organizations publish shadow reports, showing gaps or omissions in state implementation, and official state reports.

As of October 2010, 186 states have ratified CEDAW (United Nations, 2010). According to international law, CEDAW as a treaty would be most binding on states parties, but the plethora of reservations entered have considerably limited the convention's reach. Numerous state parties retain reservations against the core principles contained in Articles 1 and 2, which respectively define discrimination against women as well as the mechanisms for its abolishment (United Nations, 2010). By its very nature non-treaty international law, such as the PFA, is not nearly as binding on states as CEDAW. The Beijing review conferences in 2000 and 2005 were not able to extend the boundaries of gender equality further, as many gender activists had hoped. Instead, resistance by an alliance of conservative states that included the United States, Iran, and the Holy See led to a mere consolidation of states' commitments to the PFA. This alliance was first established during the Beijing Conference, grew significantly stronger during the follow-up process, and continued to challenge the liberal provisions reached in 1995 (West, 1999: 188–90; Wichterich, 2000: 18–32).

Rwanda has been party to both UN gender norms from the earliest stages, and ratified CEDAW in March 1981 (United Nations, 1981: 13). At the Beijing Conference in 1995, a Rwandan delegation composed of approximately 40 men and women from government and from Rwanda's larger women's organizations actively participated in the proceedings. It was headed by the then Minister for Gender, Family and Social Affairs, Aloysia Inyumba, who is now a Senator in the Parliament of Rwanda. For the Rwandan delegates, the conference outcomes provided a framework regarding gender norms at a time when, within Rwanda, most social and political norms had been shattered by the genocide. As shall be discussed later, the international norms provided an opportunity structure with which women could strengthen their domestic activism.[10]

Despite their limitations, the UN's gender norms have provided a backdrop against which gender relations have been renegotiated in Rwanda, and they raise conceptual questions about how international norms can serve as tools for enforcing transitional justice processes for women at the national level. Constructivist approaches within the discipline of International Relations have dealt with the domestication of human rights norms and prove to be useful for the ensuing discussion. Although belonging to the extensive family of human rights norms, gender norms do not encounter the same international acceptance as other human rights norms. This is the point of departure for an analysis which explores the domestication of human rights norms in the global South (Risse, Ropp and Sikkink, 1999). The following section elaborates their approach by focusing on key categories of norm domestication; the quality of norms, their salience, and their contextuality.

The quality of norms

As alluded to above, the quality of human rights norms is a factor which strongly affects their domestication. In this regard, the mechanisms envisaged to ensure compliance need to be well established, which is why the question of a norm's codification and the degree to which it is *legally* binding have been raised. Although related, attention must be drawn to adjacent aspects which are *politically* important when speaking of a norm's domestication at this stage, namely its significance and its practicability.

With regard to the first aspect, states are most compelled to adhere to the prohibition of genocide or the anti-torture imperative, for instance, because they are perceived as embodying one of the core human rights, the right to life and bodily integrity (see Risse and Sikkink, 1999: 2; Liese, 2006). Norms may even be significant, as Martha Finnemore and Kathryn Sikkink maintain (1998: 894), when states particularly resist them as in the case of women's right to vote or the laws of war. In light of this characteristic, these two issue areas are placed next to each other as if they were qualitatively similar. However, if one differentiates between the 'softness' of gender norms and the strong war and security norms, it becomes apparent that a norm's enforceability is also conditioned by how far it is contested internationally (Askin cited in Rehn and Sirleaf-Johnson, 2002: 89).

This brings us to the aspect of practicability. Despite highlighting these differences, three traits suggested by Finnemore and Sikkink (1998: 906–8) can also contribute to the domestication of a norm. Firstly, they argue that states might be motivated by seeking international legitimation. Secondly, they indicate that the clearer a norm is, and the more detailed its provisions are, the more one can expect it to be followed. This idea implies that states are willing to sign up to norms once they can anticipate their duties. Finally, they propose that previous state commitments to equality regimes enable new equality claims to take hold nationally. The last two features are particularly relevant for women's rights, as Sonja Wölte demonstrates in the Kenyan case, because states' prior accession reinforces proponents' demands so that they are able to hold states accountable to already existing obligations (Wölte, 2008: 159–61 and 172–9). To recap the reasoning on the quality of norms so far, next to norms' significance, it is both the question of enforceability (in respect of the mechanisms to ensure implementation) and also the norms' practicability (in terms of detailing issue areas and strategies within norms as well as the linking of new norms to previous norms) that determine their domestication norms.

Norms and their salience

Having introduced the quality of norms as a factor which influences their domestication, we should now turn to their salience. When considering the domestication of an international norm, it is important to note that states and their societies already adhere to several different normative frameworks so that other political, social, religious, and even cultural norms need to be taken into account. As elaborated below, these existing frameworks and structures influence the extent to which new policy principles can take hold. It is therefore significant to problematize the interaction of international and domestic norms (Finnemore and Sikkink, 1998: 894). In an environment of both complementary and competing norms, certain norms will carry more weight and be more visible than others, particularly as some norms may be explicitly formulated and others might manifest themselves in the form of social expectations. The salience of an international norm – its legitimacy and its validity – is subject to it being congruent with domestic norms. For

> when the international norm conflicts with understandings, beliefs, or obligations established in the domestic sphere, domestic actors may then find appeals to the international norm to be ineffective in garnering support for a particular policy. (Cortell and Davis, 2000: 74)

This implies that international norms will take hold to varying degrees under different conditions in different contexts.

In order to become effective in substance rather than merely being adopted in a formal sense, international norms need local advocates that mobilize support for their acceptance. These advocates, however, are not necessarily positioned across the governmental/non-governmental divide; rather interest groups mobilize according to who stands to gain or lose if the norm were implemented. Thus, it is important to also problematize relations within state boundaries as the implementation of a norm may take place in an uneven manner within a state, with its acceptance varying along established social cleavages. Moreover, opposition to a norm can emerge on account of unequal power relations in historical international relations, as in the situations where communities in the global South were exploited by states from the global North. Opponents can thus snub normative interventions by referring to them as a continuity between former and current relations of dominance.

The contextuality of norms

The argument regarding the salience of norms requires us to carefully consider the socio-political relations within a country as well as the interaction of the international and the domestic political spheres, because, for international norms to be domesticated, they must be negotiated between domestic actors. For such a process of negotiations to take place, domestic norm proponents and their opponents need to be equal, which is frequently not the case (Risse, 1999: 534–7). At this stage, it is important to pose the question of power in form of the actors' access to the public sphere and the control of the state. Acknowledging power asymmetries requires addressing how power is distributed, who is excluded from or included in power, and who determines the topics of negotiation (Fraser, 1996). This does not necessarily run along the main cleavages such as ethnicity. For instance, commentators on Rwandan politics have argued that, since decolonization, several struggles over the Rwandan state have taken place between the aforementioned ethnic groups, but also between Northerners and Southerners, between extremists and moderates, and between RPF supporters and their opponents. Moreover, dissenters – including women – have been excluded from power and their claims stifled (see Newbury and Baldwin, 2001; Taylor, 2001; Longman, 2006; Burnet, 2008).

So how were international gender norms translated into Rwandan politics and legislation? An analysis of the first phase of Rwanda's transition will show that women's equality was a by-product of the post-genocide context. It was born out of necessity in a time and space in which women were a key resource for post-conflict reconstruction. They had to organize resourcefully, so as to influence the Rwandan state to enact gender-responsive provisions. With this argument in mind, outlined below is the context of Rwandan women's political activism in order to evaluate the norm's impact in Rwanda's post-genocide setting.

Women's participation and representation in post-genocide Rwanda

After the genocide, and based on their horrific experiences, Rwanda's women took it upon themselves to organize in various forms and at different political levels to challenge the status quo. Parallel to the reconstruction of state structures some non-governmental organizations, which had already existed before the genocide, needed to be revived. In the context of post-conflict Rwanda, however, a distinction between governmental and non-governmental organizations appears artificial (Burnet, 2008: 375), because – as a result of the utter destruction of political and social institutions, scarce resources and limited levels of expertise – an interdependent relationship developed between these two sectors. These structures and the distribution of political power are important to understanding how women were able to intervene in the two bills under discussion in this chapter. But let us first consider the relevant organizations more closely.

To date, the biggest and most viable women's organizations belong to the umbrella organization, *Pro-Femmes Twese Hamwe*, which was established prior to the genocide and has since tripled its membership. Before 1994, it functioned as a counter-weight to *Urunana rw'Abanyarwandakazi mu Majyambere* (URAMA) which, similar to other countries under one-party rule, was simultaneously the ruling party's women's wing as well as part of the state structure. URAMA was meant to represent all of Rwanda's women, but was not seriously consulted on policy matters or governmental decisions (CEDAW Committee, 1994). In contrast, Pro-Femmes, whose key members can be traced back to the 1985 Third World Women's Conference held in Nairobi, has always been politically active. Amongst its members, *Réseau des Femmes Oeuvrant pour le Développement Rural* seeks to advance women's stake in rural development, *Haguruka* promotes women's and children's rights and *Duterimbere* aims to strengthen women's economic participation. After the genocide, these organizations took up their work alongside new organizations focused on dealing with the repercussions of the violence. In addition, groups representing genocide survivors have established themselves as prominent political actors, with many starting off as self-help organizations, such as *SEVOTA*, a local support group for genocide widows and orphans. *AVEGA-Agahozo,* an organization of genocide widows which offers counselling and embarks on advocacy and lobbying on behalf of its members, has advanced to one of the strongest national women's organizations. The Rwandan Women's Network, a network of grassroots initiatives, grew out of the US-based Church World Service, and provides women who have experienced sexual violence during the conflict with access to health facilities and shelter through its programme Polyclinic of Hope. Since the genocide mainly targeted Tutsi, many women's organizations tend to principally address their material losses and trauma, although it might not be their aim to reproduce ethnic cleavages.[11]

On the governmental side, the Ministry of Gender, Family and Social Affairs (*MIGEFASO*),[12] led until 1999 by Aloysia Inyumba, is mandated to mainstream gender issues into governmental policies and legislation as well as to conduct gender trainings. Inyumba's residency was critical in defining the ministry's direction immediately after the genocide. As a respected leader within the governing RPF her own political position lent her efforts much force. Thus, the ministry was not just another gender ministry without clout, but one which could successfully seek dialogue and influence other ministries. This influence has to be considered against the backdrop of the Rwandan political system where the

Executive still takes on a prominent role in shaping national politics. Even though the parliament is supposed to propose and pass legislation, it relies heavily on the former's directive role, technical expertise, and financial resources so that decision-making remains firmly in government hands. Furthermore, the Rwandan government perceives non-governmental organizations not as independent agents, but as its extended arm, with Inyumba exemplarily referring to the government as 'policy-initiators' and to NGOs as 'policy-implementers'.[13] This nonetheless has not prevented women's organizations from drawing on government to achieve their objectives regarding gender equality guarantees (Burnet, 2008: 376–7).

After 1994, the RPF government engaged in a widespread institution-building process. Various new state structures were created with the aim of increasing participation, although they have often been influenced by actual and alleged security concerns. The principle of free choice, for example, was restricted in the 1998 electoral processes of the women's councils,[14] whose candidates were vetted for political compliance and who were thereafter not chosen by secret ballot but by public queuing behind delegates' favoured candidates (Burnet, 2008: 365–8). Nonetheless, because women form the bulk of the population, their participation is pivotal for the legitimacy of any larger political undertaking. In parliament in 1996, women formed the Rwandan Women Parliamentarian Forum *(Forum des Femmes Rwandaises Parlementaires, FFRP),* a cross-party caucus for *all* female members of parliament, with the objective of exchanging views and influencing legislation on behalf of women by revising discriminatory legislation and introducing gender provisions in newly proposed bills. Between the end of the genocide and the first elections in 2003 the RPF was the only party to allot half of its seats in the unicameral Transitional National Assembly to women, although the critical 30 per cent level was not reached until after the transition.[15] In this respect, it is often named by its representatives as the motor in Rwanda's parliament promoting women's rights. Today women constitute 56 per cent of Rwanda's parliament, a level no other country has ever secured.

Seeking justice for genocidal rape and sexual violence

In order to deal with the legacy of the genocide, the government created a number of transitional justice provisions in which the prosecution of sexual violence took on a dynamic role. Most importantly, it developed a law to judge perpetrators; the 1996 Genocide Law. That was the first, and perhaps the most significant, law in which women intervened on account of their gender-specific experiences during the genocide. The law initially created four categories into which people who committed genocide-related crimes were divided. This classification decided in which of the punitive transitional justice systems suspects were tried, how they were to be punished, and how long their respective sentences were to be. Accordingly, in the initial version, the first category was reserved for the most prominent génocidaires, such as those who planned, instigated, or participated overly zealously in massacres. They were tried by the national justice system or the International Criminal Tribunal for Rwanda (ICTR), an ad hoc UN tribunal based in Arusha, Tanzania. The second category was for 'perpetrators, conspirators or accomplices' (Article 2), the third for persons who seriously assaulted others, and the fourth for those who committed property offences. Suspects of these categories could be tried by the national justice system or the semi-traditional *gacaca* tribunals, which are modifications of local village courts. The 2004 Gacaca Law merged the previous Categories 2 and 3, with only three categories remaining (Schabas, 2008: 224–5). Based on a crime's gravity, punishment could be as severe as the death penalty (until it was abolished) in the first category. In the latter categories, punishment ranged from life imprisonment to civil damages claims or community work.[16]

In its final version, the 1996 Genocide Law places 'persons who committed acts [of] sexual torture' in the first category (Article 2, Category 1 (d)). However, when the draft bill was originally presented for public consultation, it had placed sexual violence into Category 4 alongside property and other serious assault forms. Looking at the international precedents and the significance – or the lack thereof – given to gender norms globally, as discussed above, this is hardly surprising. For women who were survivors of genocidal rape and other forms of sexual violence this was, however, not acceptable and they pooled their resources to change the categorization.

So, how did Rwandan women manage to engender this law? Despite being stakeholders in the transitional justice process, women's groups were neither consulted nor were they provided with the opportunity to discuss the matter prior to the bill being tabled. In an interview, an activist, who counselled women genocide survivors at the time, recalled that she heard about the law's provisions over the radio. Consequently, after hearing about the bill, she put it up for discussion in her counselling session and so gathered women's opinions on it. In essence, they felt that sexual violence was not being considered as a strategic weapon of genocide, and that their numerous experiences were not understood as instrumental to the genocide, but rather regarded as singular or even marginal assaults. During the interview, she reflected on the implicit value of their experiences in the bill. Genocidal rape survivors were placed alongside their non-human property, and alleged perpetrators were not prosecuted as criminals within the criminal justice system, but merely subjected to civil claims. In her words,

> because in the third category [as redefined in 2004], there were truly mundane things, such as the goats which we lost, the tools which were taken, and things like this... In the [recent] third category, they were not punished criminally...if they were in the first category they had to be punished criminally like others who were in the first category![17]

In her recollection, such a classification was only possible because policy-makers lacked the analytical tools to realize that men and women experience conflicts differently, even though women's experiences were constitutive for the genocide as a whole. She argued that Rwandan women neither conventionally occupied the public arena nor expressed their concerns in public, particularly regarding sexual violence and genocidal rape, because of the associated stigma, shame, and embarrassment. Her criticism of the neglect of these women's perspectives is shared by an activist from AVEGA, who has pointed out that women, as survivors, should not have to be the sole advocates for gender equitable laws, but that it was also the government's responsibility to seek justice on their behalf. In this sense, she views survivors as involuntary parties to the conflict:

> And [we were] saying, *it should not be only our responsibility*! It is the responsibility of the state, the government. It is the responsibility of the international community! [We were saying] 'So help us, it is your duty!' [Emphasis by interviewee][18]

Before turning to the government to lobby for their concerns, women survivors needed to garner support from other women's organizations to increase their influence, particularly since it is often difficult for African women to turn to their governments for redress (Rai and Lievesley, 1996). In order to make sure that they received sufficient support, the women's survivor organizations turned to their fellow, more experienced organizations, which were better resourced to approach as sensitive and as crucial a topic (see Burnet, 2008: 377; Newbury and Baldwin, 2001: 105–13). To their advantage, the then Coordinator of *Pro-Femmes* was also the President of *Réseau des Femmes* and a Beijing Delegate, so she was able to use her position to put the issue on the top of the organizations' agenda. The diversity of *Pro-Femmes'* members, who organize around their professional or social interests, has also brought bundled expertise. As media experts for example, the Rwandan Association of Media Women (ARFEM) provided much-needed coverage on the issue. Moreover, it proved to be very beneficial that the lobbying activities became subsumed under *Pro-Femmes'* programme Campaign Action for Peace, launched in 1996, which has been widely cited as being central to the achievements of the women's movement in Rwanda (Baines, 2005; Powley, 2003). By contributing to peace-building efforts in post-genocide Rwanda, the programme could link itself to the dominant discourses in the country, which encouraged post-conflict reconstruction and cross-ethnic nation building.[19] Furthermore, it has streamlined the activities of women's organizations, since all *Pro-Femmes* members have to align their activities with the programme. In addition, it has allowed women to participate in the public sphere, and created a culture of dialogue as well as collaboration amongst women by enabling them to air their views publicly and to take on responsibilities not traditionally ascribed to women (Baines, 2005: 226; Newbury and Baldwin, 2001: 104–5). Based on the renegotiation of gender relations in the social sphere in which women have been the carriers of reconstruction efforts (as discussed below), they have been able to enter the political domain (Mageza-Barthel, 2008).

After women's organizations had mobilized each other, the parliamentary women's group FFRP was invited to take part in the advocacy campaign. A meeting was held in which women testified on what impact the sexual violence experienced during the genocide had made on their daily lives. After hearing these testimonies, and the concerns of the women's organizations, FFRP members joined a support march and, soon thereafter, took their views to parliament to lobby their male colleagues within the various political parties. It was now the turn of the women's organizations to support the FFRP by providing it with analysis, research, and material on women's experiences during the genocide. This task sharing between governmental and non-governmental women turned into a model which is being used to the present day. With the combined involvement of these organizations, the problem which was national in scale, but had been dealt with under the guise of a parochial, even personal problem, crossed from the local to the national political level. Because of extensive lobbying rooted in women's genocide and post-genocide experiences, perpetrators of rape and sexual violence could now be tried under Category 1 – a resounding success for the Rwandan women's movement, asserting women's rights with respect to the genocide's violations.

Revising the matrimonial regimes

In post-genocide Rwanda, a further challenge to gender relations arose from the high competition for resources between survivors, the Internally Displaced People (IDP), and returning refugees. With roughly 2.7 million refugees[20] relocating to Rwanda between 1994 and 1997, and a further 1 to 2 million IDPs gradually leaving the camps in the years to follow, questions around property ownership became increasingly pressing (Prunier, 1995: 63 and 312; Twagiramariya and Turshen, 1998: 101). It is estimated that 34–50 per cent of all households in 1996 were headed by women and girls, who risked being displaced and left in abject poverty (Burnet and RISD, 2003: 184–200; Nowrojee, 1996: 2). Moreover, women in general had no legally guaranteed rights to the resources they depended on, including the bank accounts they managed, and the properties they lived on, which were often held in their fathers' or husbands' names. Despite the fact that they were granted equal rights in certain statutes (such as the 1991 Constitution), other pieces of legislation reduced them again. With respect to business transactions, women were relegated to the legal status of minors. According to Rwandan customary law, men, as household heads, have had control over their family's property. Whilst women were not overtly prohibited from owning property, it was because of contradictory provisions in civil law that many women were disadvantaged and patriarchal norms reinforced. Referring to the continued impact of a law dating back to 1913 Villia Jefrevomas (1991: 382) notes,

> they can vote, but their husbands' consent is required for them to engage in commerce, register a business, buy land, act as a witness, or undertake court action. Women can open bank accounts, but husbands have the right to withdraw money from their wives' accounts without permission.

This weighed most heavily on their access to, and ownership of, land so that women, irrespective of their marital status, were dependent on the nuclear family unit. In the event that they had any influence over property, it was only temporary in nature (Longman, 2006: 137). Since many women are subsistence farmers and traditionally responsible for reproductive work, not having direct land rights has been detrimental, in particular because many men, who mediated women's access to ownership, were not present after the genocide for, in most cases, they were fugitive, imprisoned, or deceased. Even under these circumstances women found ways to circumvent their discrimination. As an activist working with *Pro-Femmes* recounts, one form of protest prior to the legal revisions was that women increasingly opened bank accounts and ran businesses under the names of their spouses or brothers – fully aware of the risk this carried.[21]

Lawmakers, too, stood before several challenges. At the time, the shaky newly-found peace and local co-existence (Buckley-Zistel, 2006) was seriously threatened by land and property disputes, and the absence of men in society proved to be an additional burden. So, inheritance rights needed to be reformed to respond to the property situation. One activist closely links the need for a new property regime to the dominant goal of the newly installed government to foster economic growth and reconstruction, 'We fought for women's economic rights, because otherwise the transformation, which was taking place, would be useless'.[22] In this sense, as an activist from AVEGA highlights, this period was characterized by enormous political change.

In post-genocide Rwanda, people who were previously discriminated against could now speak out.[23] This was particularly relevant for women from the minority Tutsi group, who, in the pre-genocide period, were discriminated against on account of their gender as well as their ethnic designation. 'Prior to this, women from Tutsi families, and even Tutsis in general, could not protest against anything let alone struggle against their discrimination. They had to keep quiet. Living day by day.'[24] On a social level, the changes were stipulated by the role women played in the post-genocide reconstruction process. The necessities of providing shelter and nurturing remaining family members forced women to either break existing social taboos or face problems of daily subsistence. Countrywide, they began forming self-help associations, building houses, and milking cows – all tasks previously ascribed to men (Powley, 2003: 15; Mageza-Barthel, 2008: 175–7). Under the existing provisions, however, women remained vulnerable, even if development funds were established to reconstruct the country at the local level with the expectation that women would benefit.

Realizing this problem, MIGEFASO, the FFRP, rural women, and women entrepreneurs embarked on a campaign of lobbying the Justice

Ministry to address this inequality. Once again, the responsibilities were distributed according to the scheme employed during the process to engender the 1996 Genocide Law. MIGEFASO provided the Executive's support and technical know-how, while women's organizations took on various roles. They contributed crucial data about how many women were widowed or had a husband in prison, and they visibly supported the passage of the law by attending the parliamentary debates, cheering for their position from the visitor's gallery,[25] and later raising awareness around it, so that women could claim their rights. In this period, women's voices also became increasingly more audible, with many more women's organizations existing than before the genocide; whether as smaller associations or as national groups. Amongst the larger group of returnees, women who had lived in exile for a considerable time injected their ideas and experiences gained in their different host countries, enriching the campaign tremendously. As the AVEGA activist recalls,

> because there were women from Burundi, women from the Congo, women from Uganda, women from Tanzania, who had different *ideas*. And you could see that all had to be together, because all of them were *Rwandese* and from our experience of genocide, they tried to involve every woman *here*. Not saying 'You are a Tutsi, you are a Hutu, you came from here or there'. [Emphasis by interviewee][26]

Nevertheless, under general conditions of mistrust and social fragmentation, organizing around a common agenda was a considerable challenge, yet government and donors exercised financial and political pressure on women's organizations to organize across the ethnic divide.[27]

In contrast to the revision of the 1996 Genocide Law as illustrated above, the impetus for a codified solution for inheritance rights came from the government. By now, the Gender Ministry had taken up its work and defined a role for itself within the governmental machinery where it had begun conducting training on gender issues in 1999, targeting both ministries and the population at large (Powley, 2003: 19). Because local women's councils had been elected in the previous year, the Ministry was able to channel resources from pursuing matters associated with daily survival at the local level, to dealing with national, strategic issues. In this context, MIGEFASO, in partnership with women's organizations, was able to push for a new law by initiating processes and bringing more partners on board. Once again this model of state-societal relations in the post-genocide period typifies African experiences (Rai and Lievesley, 1996). In the words of the AVEGA activist, 'they [women's organizations] also got the chance *to be involved by the government* in political issues' [emphasis added].[28] To the present day, MIGEPROFE's support for women's political agenda-setting has proven to be crucial in a political system in which the Executive sets the tone.

As a result of women's concerted effort, the Matrimonial Regimes Law was passed in 1999. Although the Law also establishes three matrimonial regimes for civil marriages, it is generally referred to as the Inheritance Law, as its most significant reforms are regulating women's succession, enabling them to control their property, and allowing for boys and girls to inherit equally. It also indirectly addresses the land issue by defining land as property, while leaving its precise regulation to a land law, which was eventually passed in 2005.

Reviewing norms as tools for gender equity

To summarize, overall the normative changes were a resounding success for the Rwandan women's movement, even though the processes depicted here seem far smoother than they actually were. The selected cases illustrate that the immediate post-genocide period was one in which various urgent needs had to be met and competing positions – including from women with various backgrounds – needed to be negotiated on how to shape Rwanda's future socio-political structures.

Regarding the implementation of gender norms, contestations within the women's movement echo the critique discussed above. Does one implement universal documents word for word (as one activist insisted), or can political declarations generally be seen as irrelevant in providing women with any measure of security (as another highlighted)? It is surprising that neither CEDAW nor the PFA were *explicitly* used as tools for women's agenda setting in the processes under discussion. Instead, as shown, women had to devise strategies with which they could bring the UN's gender norms to bear on the Rwandan context. As such, one would assume that this had to do with the norms' quality. Indeed, one of the key challenges women faced in setting the political agenda can be seen in the tools they employed. Although the PFA appeared to be of sufficient formal quality by being detailed, succinct, and linked to CEDAW and other human rights norms, Rwandan women were *not* able to openly refer to the UN's gender norms. Neither the 1996 Genocide Law nor the 1999 Matrimonial Regimes Law explicitly refers to CEDAW or the Beijing documents, even though Rwandan policy-makers repeatedly asserted that within the Rwandan context, these laws were closely related to the commitments made at Beijing. They often attribute this omission to their lack of technical know-how at the time, as well as to the urgency of other domestic problems as a legacy of the genocide, rather than their rejection of the norms as such. In fact, in order to emphasize the significance attributed to the gender norms, interviewees stressed the participation of the large, mixed Rwandan delegation at the Beijing Conference, who had an impact on the content of the PFA by invoking women's experiences in armed conflicts (Layika, 1995), and who subsequently 'brought Beijing home'. This implied domestication corroborates the norms' potential salience, and, by creating formal structures with which to record the norms implementation, their quality was amplified in Rwanda. Initially, with the UN's support, members of the delegation established the Beijing Follow-Up Secretariat to ensure conference commitments were met. The then Gender Minister, Inyumba, in particular, sought budgetary guarantees with which to secure the documents' implementation. And yet, she first experienced resistance from her peers:

> Inyumba was the Minister at the time. In Cabinet, her colleagues were laughing at her, because they didn't understand. The one thing she fought for was for a budget item for the implementation of Beijing.[29]

This mockery could either be based on the perception that there were seemingly more urgent matters, which needed to be addressed, or it could be interpreted as the gender norms' lacking salience in the Rwandan context. Still, there was a further prominent reason why referring to UN gender norms was difficult in Rwanda at the time. During the genocide, the UN – and the international community more generally – failed to intervene to stop the genocide, leading to its rather negative perception in the country, despite its efforts to reconstruct the country beyond the transitional period. Against the backdrop of such a controversial history, using a UN document to appeal for more gender equality did not seem like a good strategy.

And yet, if these categories for *explicit* norm referral were absent, how could the UN's gender norms still *implicitly* serve as tools for women engaging in the transitional justice processes? Here, the author's conclusions go beyond the framework elaborated above. Since, after the genocide, gender issues were not a national priority, women had to increase their prominence by placing them at the top of their agenda and appearing as a unified group across social divides. They constantly had to prove that they were capable of taking on crucial post-conflict reconstruction tasks so that they could use their achievements to draw attention to themselves as a significant social group worthy of political support. To counter images of women as the 'weaker' sex, *Pro-Femmes* initiated a programme called Women Can Do It.

The women's organizations saw the norms' key contribution in strengthening their ability to analyse the national context, as such contouring their demands. They could fall back on, amongst others, *Haguruka's* legal expertise on women's rights and latch onto the previous government's ascension to CEDAW, whose implementation was, at best, scanty. In particular, this attribute relating to the norms' quality created opportunity structures, which opened the window for the Rwandan women's movement to assert itself in holding its government accountable to meeting these obligations (see Wölte, 2008). Furthermore, women opted for a strategy in the form of arguments that could be related to locally. For instance, invoking the much-lauded family to argue for greater equality was highly effective. Women would lobby male parliamentarians by addressing them as their kin and employing 'motherist' terms (Burnet, 2008: 377). They would bring the problem closer to home by asking them, for instance, whether in the case of their death they would have wanted their daughters or wives to be dispossessed by a distant uncle.

Nevertheless, some Rwandans rejected anything associated with Beijing, suggesting that these ideas were foreign to the country. Key governmental actors, such as Inyumba, pre-empt this critique by pointing to the Beijing Conference's African preparatory process which mitigated the continental focus.[30] Moreover, the gender norms' (lack of) salience, and their contextual-specificity, point towards the conclusion that the resistance women encountered in pursuing the revision of the two laws can be traced back to the direct interests of those who stood to lose out should the changes become effective. Giving up their patrilineally acquired privilege was not in some people's interests – who were scattered across Rwandan society *and* the gender divide. So that the process,

> ... was most difficult, because as women we faced resistance from men and women in society and at Parliament. Because it is the mother or the brother of the man who dies who profit ...[31]

This mirrors the experience of other countries, such as Uganda, where women not only faced resistance in the rural areas where customary law dominates, but also amongst legislators who suggested that women might gain twice, by inheriting their parental as well as spousal property (Kawamara-Mishambi and Oronji-Odida, 2003: 176–80).

As a result, penetrating the distribution of power was crucial to advocating for the Matrimonial Regimes Law, which set a precedent for further women's campaigns. In a political system with a top-down political culture, the Executive's dominant political role had to be taken into account. If majority support for an initiative could not automatically be assumed, then strategic action encompassed ensuring the support of the person or the party pushing the political agenda. Assuming that influential men could influence other men more easily, Rwandan women sought out men as conduits to further women's interests. And so, close working relationships were maintained with those whom the FFRP felt shared their goals.

Transitional justice and gender justice?

In closing, having established the role of gender norms in the struggle of Rwandan women against impunity for perpetrators of sexual violence and gender discrimination in the genocide's 'aftermath', it is now essential to consider the long-term effects of these significant legal changes. The question arises if and how they have had an impact on a wider conception of gender justice.

If gender is taken seriously as an analytical tool of intersecting social determinants, then one has to recognize that women are not a homogenous group and that they have experienced the genocide and the post-genocide period differently. To embark on a course of substantive equality, lobbying and advocating for women's interests would need to acknowledge this, even in the face of national unity, and even if women's experiences might mirror each other (Twagiramariya and Turshen, 1998; Taylor, 2001; Baines, 2003). Within the group of 'women', the 1996 law predominantly seeks justice for genocide survivors, whereas the 1999 law speaks to this group specifically *as well as* others who were disadvantaged by the existing property regime. In this sense, a legal framework has been established to address gender-specific experiences of conflict and discrimination. The question of accountability towards women, which makes the negotiation of difference within women's structures increasingly topical, cannot be overemphasized (Goetz and Hassim, 2003; Wölte, 2008). Problematizing women's socio-economic position today should illustrate the challenges in gender relations.

Rwanda is the only country in the world to surpass gender parity in its parliament. This is a remarkable benchmark from which women could potentially stake their claims politically. Without a doubt, such levels of representation were only possible because women had proven themselves as socially and politically active members of society. Yet absolute poverty still haunts large parts of its society. According to a Beijing Follow-Up Secretariat report, close to 57 per cent of Rwandans live on less than FRW 250 a day (approx. €0,36[32]). In this context, women's vulnerability is far higher than that of men. For each widower in Rwanda, you will find eight widows. Of these, more than two thirds are illiterate and close to 90 per cent live in rural areas or rely on the informal sector to cover their basic needs (Beijing Secretariat Rwanda, 2007: 21–2). Widows require special consideration since many still encounter social discrimination for lack of a husband. Moreover, some genocide widows, who also fall under this category, were intentionally infected with HIV/AIDS so that they would 'die of sadness' after hostilities ceased (Nowrojee, 1996: 1). More so, the urban-rural divide has a decisive impact on the situation of Rwandan women since material, educational, and social resources can be better accessed in urban areas. As a result, women's mediated access to resources has hardly changed. Interestingly, divorcees and women who live in separation from their husbands are slightly more at risk of being poor than widows, confirming the protection accorded by the Inheritance Law, and underscoring the decisive benefit derived by double-income households.

These concluding observations beg several questions. Do the current matrimonial regimes work for women if women fall into a poverty trap at the end of the spousal relationship? What have been the effects of a large genocide-related male prison population dependent on women's reproductive labour? Lastly, how arduous is the process of enforcing legal norms, if they are to effectively compensate the inequalities left by social norms? Under these conditions, the overarching question now becomes how can women continue to assert their presence in their quest for equity beyond the transitional period?

Despite these remaining challenges the case illustrated in this chapter is of major significance for the field of transitional justice. Much literature on transitional justice focuses on women as victims of sexual violence and abuse, as well as on mechanisms and strategies to assure their representation and the enforcement of existing legislation. The merit of this analysis notwithstanding, this chapter has sought to illustrate that women as *survivors* of gender-specific violence (during the 1994 genocide) have become active agents in times of transition where future gender equality is in the process of (re)negotiation. In this regard, the achievement of the women of Rwanda is a considerable success.

Notes

My sincere appreciation goes to Prof. Dr. Uta Ruppert (Frankfurt), my *Doktormutter,* and Prof. Sheila Meintjes (Witwatersrand), my co-supervisor, for their invaluable input to my dissertation from which this text draws. I would also like to thank the volume editors – their insightful feedback has contributed to the chapter in its current form.

1. Officially: Organic Law No. 08/96 of August 30, 1996 on the Organization of Prosecutions for Offences Constituting the Crime of Genocide or Crimes against Humanity Committed since October 1, 1990 (hereinafter Genocide Law) as well as Law No. 22/99 of 12/11/1999 to Supplement Book I of the Civil Code and to Institute Part Five regarding Matrimonial Regimes, Liberalities and Successions (hereinafter Matrimonial Regimes Law).
2. Interviews were mainly conducted in Kigali, Rwanda, between July and October 2008, the names of interviewees have been anonymized.
3. The Rwandan gender activists' goal of seeking to further women's rights by consulting the United Nation's gender norms places them within an understanding of transnational women's movements (Wölte, 2008: 28–35; Ruppert, 1998: 54–5).
4. Rwanda's transitional period was extended in 1998 with a second period taking place between 1999 and 2003 (Burnet, 2008: 365).
5. A first wave of political violence took place 1959–64, followed by a second wave 1972–73 (Prunier, 1995: 61).
6. This statistic is now called into question by the very people who used it, yet it still bears witness that women were, and are, the majority of the Rwandan population (Beijing Secretariat, 2008: 1; Twagiramariya and Turshen, 1998: 102).
7. Since then, however, the UN's gender norms have changed significantly, and with the two, more recent, UN Security Council Resolutions on Women, Peace and Security – UNSCR 1325 (2000) and UNSCR 1820 (2008) – they have grown increasingly more conflict-specific.
8. By primarily protecting women's 'honour' the Geneva Conventions replicate stereotypical views on women in armed conflicts in essence by regarding women either as dependent and vulnerable, or as objects of male conquest (Gardam and Charlesworth, 2000: 159; Charlesworth, 2000: 213).
9. In Article 1, discrimination is identified as the source of women's worldwide inequality and is broadly defined as having various forms. It reads: 'For the purposes of the present Convention, the term "discrimination against women" shall mean any distinction, exclusion or restriction made on the basis of sex which has the effect or purpose of impairing or nullifying the recognition, enjoyment or exercise by women, irrespective of their marital status, on a basis of equality of men and women, of human rights and fundamental freedoms in the political, economic, social, cultural, civil or any other field'.
10. For a more detailed discussion on opportunity structures and agency, please refer to Chapter 7 by Angelika von Wahl in this volume.

11. Interview with AVEGA activist, 22 July 2008.
12. MIGEFASO was renamed Ministry for Gender and Women in Development (MIGEPROFE) in 1999 (Burnet, 2008: 367); it is currently led by Dr Jean d'Arc Mujawamariya.
13. Interview with Aloysia Inyumba, 21 October 2008.
14. Women's councils are an instrument to channel women's political participation through women-only elections, and were created in 1998 (Burnet, 2008: 368). However, because they were founded towards the end of the political process discussed in this chapter, and mostly active at the local level, they are not described here further.
15. In 1994 women totalled 14 per cent and were just over 25 per cent in 1999 (Longman, 2006: 144)
16. The death penalty was abolished in 2007, with the last sentence being handed down in 2003 (Amnesty International, 2007).
17. Interview with gender activist, 22 September 2008.
18. Interview with AVEGA activist, 22 July 2008.
19. How far women's organizations in post-conflict contexts can be autonomous is an important question, which unfortunately exceeds the scope of this chapter. Instead, to address this question, reference is made to the interwoven nature of Rwanda's political society.
20. Once again, the cited numbers are controversially debated. Returnees include those who fled Rwanda during the first and second waves of political violence (see endnote 5), their offspring, as well as those (both survivors and potential suspects) who had fled Rwanda during the genocide and its immediate aftermath.
21. Interview with *Pro-Femmes* activist, 10 October 2008.
22. Ibid.
23. Despite efforts at nation-building prohibiting political mobilization and organization along ethnic lines, a recent Constitutional Amendment defines the 1994 Genocide as having been orchestrated against the Tutsi people, enabling Tutsi survivors to identify as such (see Musoni, 2008).
24. Interview with AVEGA activist, 8 October 2008.
25. During repeated visits to Parliament, the visitor's gallery was eerily empty – underlining how exceptional this non-governmental participation was.
26. Interview with AVEGA activist, 8 October 2008.
27. Interview with AVEGA activist, 22 July 2008.
28. Interview with AVEGA activist, 8 October 2008.
29. Interview with *Pro-Femmes* activist, 10 October 2008.
30. Interview with Aloysia Inyumba, 21 October 2008.
31. Interview with *Pro-Femmes* activist, 10 October 2008.
32. Currency Converter, available at: http://finance.yahoo.com/currency-converter

References

Amnesty International (2007) 'Rwanda abolishes death penalty', 2 August, available at http://www.amnesty.org/en/news-and-updates/good-news/rwanda-abolishes-death-penalty-20070802.

African Rights (1995) *Rwanda: Not so innocent. When Women Become Killers* (Kigali and London: African Rights Publication).

E. K. Baines (2005) 'Les femmes aux mille bras: Building Peace in Rwanda' in D. Mazurana, A. Raven-Roberts and J. Parpart (eds) *Gender, Conflict and Peacekeeping* (Oxford: Rowman & Littlefield Publishers).

E. K. Baines (2003) 'Body Politics and the Rwandan Crisis', *Third World Quarterly*, Vol. 24 No. 3, 479–93.

W. Benedek, E. M. Kisaakye and G. Oberleitner (2002) *The Human Rights of Women: International Instruments and African Experiences* (London and New York: Zed Books).

S. Buckley-Zistel (2006) 'Remembering to Forget: Chosen Amnesia as a Strategy for Local Co-Existence in Post-Genocide Rwanda', *Africa*, Vol. 76 No. 2, 131–50.

J. E. Burnet (2008) 'Gender Balance and the Meanings of Women in Governance in Post-Genocide Rwanda', *African Affairs*, Vol. 107, 361–86.

J. E. Burnet and RISD (2003) 'Culture, Practice and Law: Women's Access to Land in Rwanda' in L. M. Wanyeki (ed.) *Women and Land in Africa: Culture, Religion and Realizing Women's Rights* (Cape Town and London: David Philips and Zed Books).

CEDAW Committee (1994) *Concluding Observations: Rwanda 1993* (CEDAW/C/RWA/3), available at http://www1.umn.edu/humanrts/cedaw/rwanda1993.html.

H. Charlesworth (1999) 'Feminist Methods in International Law', *The American Journal of International Law*, Vol. 93 No. 2, 379–94.

H. Charlesworth and C. Chinkin (2000) *The Boundaries of International Law: A Feminist Analysis* (Manchester: Manchester University Press).

A. P. Cortell and J. W. Davis, Jr (2000) 'Understanding the Domestic Impact of International Norms: A Research Agenda', *International Studies Review*, Vol. 2 No. 1, 65–87.

M. Finnemore and K. Sikkink (1998) 'International Norm Dynamics and Political Change', *International Organisation*, Vol. 52, 887–917.

N. Fraser (1996) *Justice Interruptus: Critical Reflections on the Postsocialist Condition* (London: Routledge).

A. M. Goetz and S. Hassim (2003) *No Shortcuts to Power: African Women in Politics and Policy-Making* (London and New York: Zed Books).

J. Gardam and H. Charlesworth (2000) 'Protection of Women in Armed Conflict', *Human Rights Quarterly*, Vol. 22 No. 1, 148–66.

V. Jefrevomas (1991) 'Loose Women, Virtuous Wives, and Timid Virgins: Gender and the Control of Resources in Rwanda', *Canadian Journal of African Studies*, Vol. 25 No. 3, 378–95.

S. Kawamara-Mishambi and I. Oronji-Odida (2003) 'The "Lost Clause": The Campaign to Advance Women's Property Rights in the Ugandan 1998 Land Act' in A. M. Goetz and S. Hassim (eds) *No Shortcuts to Power: African Women in Politics and Policy-Making* (London and New York: Zed Books).

F. U. Layika (1995) *Témoignage Présenté Devant le Tribunal de Beijing le 1er Septembre 1995* (unpublished conference paper).

R. Lemarchand and M. Niwese (2007) 'Mass Murder, the Politics of Memory and Post-Genocide Reconstruction: The Cases of Rwanda and Burundi' in B. Pouligny, S. Chesterman and A. Schnabel (eds) *After Mass Crime: Rebuilding States and Communities* (Tokyo: United Nations University Press).

A. Liese (2006) *Staaten am Pranger: Zur Wirkung internationaler Regime auf innerstaatliche Menschenrechtspolitik* (Wiesbaden: VS Verlag).

T. Longman (2006) 'Rwanda: Achieving Equality or Serving an Authoritarian State' in G. Bauer and H. E. Britton (eds) *Women in African Parliaments* (Boulder and London: Lynne Rienner).

R. Mageza-Barthel (2008) 'International Norms: An Entry Ticket to Women's National Representation?' in C. Camus, A. Hornung and F. Imlinger (eds) *Im Zeichen des Geschlechts: Repräsentationen – Konstruktionen – Interventionen* (Königstein/Taunus: Helmer Verlag).

S. Meintjes, M. Turshen and A. Pillay (eds) (2001) *The Aftermath, Women in Post-Conflict Transformation* (London and New York: Zed Books).

E. Musoni (2008) 'Parliament Amends Constitution', *The New Times*, 25 June.

C. Newbury and H. Baldwin (2001) 'Confronting the Aftermath of Conflict: Women's Organizations in postgenocide Rwanda' in K. Kumar (ed.) *Women and Civil War. Impact, organizations, and action* (Boulder and London: Lynne Rienner).

B. Nowrojee (1996) *Shattered Lives: Sexual Violence during the Rwandan Genocide and Its Aftermath* (New York and London: Human Rights Watch).

M. Ottaway (1999) 'Ethnic Politics in Africa: Change and Continuity' in R. A. Joseph (ed.) *State, Conflict, and Democracy in Africa* (Boulder: Lynne Rienner).

Permanent Executive Secretariat for the Follow-Up of the Beijing Conference (2007) *Poverty Reduction and Socio-Economic Promotion for the Rwandan Woman* (Unpublished).

E. Powley (2003) *Strengthening Governance: The Role of Women in Rwanda's Transition* (Hunt Alternatives Fund).

G. Prunier (1995) *The Rwanda Crisis: History of a Genocide,* 2nd repr. (New York: Columbia University Press).

S. Rai and G. Lievesley (eds) (1996) *Women and the State: International Perspectives* (London: Taylor & Francis).

E. Rehn and E. Sirleaf-Johnson (2002) *Women, War and Peace. The Independent Experts' Assessment on the Impact of Armed Conflict on Women and Women's Role in Peacebuilding* (New York: United Nations).

T. Risse (1999) 'International Norms and Domestic Change: Arguing and Communicative Behavior in the Human Rights Area', *Politics & Society,* Vol. 27, 529–59.

T. Risse, S. C. Ropp and K. Sikkink (eds) (1999) *The power of human rights: International norms and domestic change* (Cambridge: Cambridge University Press.)

T. Risse and K. Sikkink (1999) 'The Socialization of International Human Rights Norms into Domestic Practices. Introduction' in T. Risse, S. C. Ropp and K. Sikkink (eds) *The power of human rights: International norms and domestic change* (Cambridge: Cambridge University Press.)

U. Ruppert (2000) 'Material, relational, global: Feministische Theorie und Praxis internationaler Politik', *Femina Politica*, Vol. 1, 25–37.

U. Ruppert (1998) 'Global Governance: Das Ende der Illusionen oder ein neues Ideal internationaler Frauenpolitik?' in B. Holland-Cunz and U. Ruppert (eds) *Frauenpolitische Chancen globaler Politik: Verhandlungserfahrungen im internationalen Kontext* (Opladen: Leske+Budrich).

W. A. Schabas (2008) 'Post-Genocide Justice in Rwanda: A Spectrum of Options' in P. Clark and Z. D. Kaufman (eds) *After Genocide: Transitional Justice, Post-Conflict Reconstruction and Reconciliation in Rwanda and Beyond* (London: Hurst & Company).

S. Straus (2007) 'Origins and Aftermaths: The Dynamics of Genocide in Rwanda and their post-genocide Implications' in B. Pouligny, S. Chesterman and A. Schnabel (eds) *After Mass Crime: Rebuilding States and Communities* (Tokyo: United Nations University Press).

C. C. Taylor (2001) *Sacrifice as terror. The Rwandan genocide of 1994* (New York: Berg).

C. Twagiramariya and M. Turshen (1998) '"Favours to Give" and "Consenting Victims": The Sexual Politics of Survival in Rwanda' in M. Turshen and C. Twagiramariya (eds) *What Women Do In Wartime: Gender and Conflict in Africa* (London: Zed Books)

United Nations (2010) *United Nations Treaty Collection*, available at http://treaties.un.org/Pages/ViewDetails.aspx?src=TREATY&mtdsg_no=IV-8&chapter=4&lang=en.

United Nations (1995) *Beijing Declaration and Platform of Action, adopted at the Fourth World Conference on Women*, available at http://www.unhcr.org/refworld/docid/3dde04324.html.

United Nations (1981) *Convention on the Elimination of All Forms of Discrimination Against Women*, 18 December 1979, UNTS Vol. 1249, available at http://treaties.un.org/doc/Treaties/1981/09/19810903%2005-18%20AM/Ch_IV_8p.pdf.

L. A. West (1999) 'The United Nations Conferences and Feminist Politics' in M. K. Meyer and E. Prügl (eds) *Gender Politics in Global Governance* (Oxford: Rowman & Littlefield Publishers).

C. Wichterich (2000) *Wir wollen unsere Rechte Jetzt – Und Zwar mit Zinsen: Fünf Jahre nach der 4. Weltfrauenkonferenz in Peking: Bilanzen, Positionen, Perspektiven* (Studien & Berichte der Heinrich-Böll-Stiftung, Nr. 5).

S. Wölte (2008) *International – National – Lokal: FrauenMenschenrechte und Frauenbewegung in Kenia* (Königstein/Taunus: Helmer Verlag).

7
How Sexuality Changes Agency: Gay Men, Jews, and Transitional Justice

Angelika von Wahl

For the Homosexuals the Third Reich has not yet ended.

Historian Hans-Joachim Schoeps,
West Germany 1962

Research on transitional justice looks at how newly established democracies come to terms with their authoritarian or totalitarian pasts, and the often severe human rights abuses of such regimes. This chapter focuses on the ineffectual mobilization of homosexual men after National Socialism (NS), and contrasts their case with that of the Jewish community. While the rest of this volume concentrates on the question of transitional justice and gender, this chapter specifically investigates some of the issues around transitional justice and *sexuality* (although gender remains a factor as well). Gender issues have only recently emerged as an area in transitional justice studies; sexuality is a very new subject in the field. However, by paying attention to sexuality-related issues, we usefully expand the boundaries of traditional transition studies, adding important new insights.

The goal of the this chapter is to better understand the specific political, social, and legal situation of gay men as victims of human rights abuses, and to shed light on how the question of transitional justice changes when we talk about *sexuality* and *sexual identity*. Under what circumstances do gay men become victims of state sponsored crime? Do they achieve justice – in the forms of public apologies, restitution, or reparations – once the oppressive regime or its laws have been dismantled and, if so, how? What particular political, social, and discursive hurdles and/or opportunities exist for this minority, and under what circumstances can obstacles be overcome? To begin the investigation of an area that is rather under-researched this chapter will analyse the transitional justice process through *social movement research*, utilizing concepts such as political opportunity structures, social mobilization, and framing to demonstrate why the struggle for symbolic and material reparations for gay men *failed*, while it succeeded (respectively speaking) for the Jewish community. What can we learn from feminist research in trying to understand the political and social situation of gay men in post-war Germany?

Analysing claims for reparations

This study applies social movement research to the study of transitional justice, specifically to the struggle for symbolic and material reparations such as governmental apologies and restitution. More precisely, it will compare governmental attempts to provide *symbolic and material reparations* for cases of severe human rights abuse. While many states have participated at some time in the infliction of injustice and atrocities – be it during war with neighbouring states, the colonization of other countries, or violent acts within their own territory – it seems that relatively few cases of human rights abuse have produced reparations. Some states have publicly apologized, paid compensations, or returned lost property, while other states quite literally 'got away with murder'. In a time of continued human rights abuse and attendant global restitution claims, it becomes increasingly important to ask what factors lead governments to grant reparations, and to examine what kind of specific reparations are made and to whom. Why do some categories of victims seem more likely to gain necessary legal and/or organizational resources and receive at least some kind of reparation? Why do other groups fail? And, what role does gender, sexuality, and sexual identity play in the process of transitional justice?

The focus lies in the question of how and why the *same* state – in this case Germany – has treated claimants *differently*. Using this comparative intra-state framework, social movement theory will be applied to the articulation and development of reparations claims in two cases: German Jews and homosexual men in post-war West Germany. As Dieter Rucht has shown, *situational* circumstances can produce *different* opportunities for *different* social movements in the *same* state (Rucht, 1998). This finding goes a long way towards emphasizing the most relevant factors in intra-state comparisons of mobilization for transitional justice issues. This chapter will argue that the *organization of claimants*, the *framing of demands* by claimants, and the *specific political opportunity structure* each group faces, explains the profoundly different outcomes.

Regarding the cases discussed here, it should be stated explicitly from the start that the human rights violations during World War II against Jews and homosexuals were different in scope and extent. On the one hand, the Nazis aimed at the complete annihilation of millions of Jewish people, men, women, and children, through industrial style killings, while a much smaller group of homosexual men was severely persecuted, imprisoned, tortured, or killed in concentration camps. Thus the extent and nature of the atrocities must be taken into account to explain the willingness of governments to recognize and attempt to rectify human rights abuse. However, even when these differences are taken into account, both cases constitute severe human rights violations at the exact *same* historic time and by the *same* state. It is the sameness of place and time that is of particular interest to this discussion. While one side has received broad symbolic and material reparations and become a focus of the political culture, the other side was first criminalized and then became what has been described as 'forgotten victims' (Grau, 1995; Lautmann, 1977). Given the contextual similarities, what factors explain the radical differences in terms of outcomes? Why has the democratically elected government of West Germany responded so differently to the past human rights abuses of these two groups? And what does this tell us about transitional justice and *sexuality*?

Gender, sexuality and the problem of agency

One of the main problems for homosexuals in modern history has been organizing politically and developing effective agency. This is where we can fruitfully utilize some of the insights of feminist theory. Simone de Beauvoir offers a seminal explanation to help understand women's lack of agency. As Beauvoir has famously shown, historically women do not form a common identity based on their gender *as women*, but rather understand themselves as members of the different religious, ethnic, and social groups to which they belong (Beauvoir, 1952). Identification with various social categories and classes keeps women separated from each other, even if they suffer the same gender-based oppressions, and share similar interests in protecting themselves and/or seeking equality, liberty, or justice. This fact has a myriad of effects on their ability to identify socially with each other and organize politically. Women, by themselves, have not formed regional, or national, and politically relevant communities like ethnic or religious groups (and, notably, neither have men). Because those regional or national communities have been dominated by masculine values, interests, and structures women have often had difficulties forming associations and cooperating outside of traditional family ties, or autonomously of state prescribed functions and interests. Only with the extension of citizenship to women in the late nineteenth and early twentieth centuries has their ability to organize for their interests become attainable. As a result, women's movements have emerged in nearly all industrializing and democratizing states.

In terms of large-scale human rights violations like expulsions, massacres, and genocides, women have been victims *as part* of their religious or ethnic groups. However, women have also been victims *as women*, through molestation, rape, mutilation, sterilization, forced pregnancy, and infanticide (Peters and Wolper 1995; Rubio-Marin, 2006; Duggan and Abusharaf, 2006). The author's earlier research on the reparations claims by Korean sex slaves (or so-called Comfort Women) has shown that the hurdles to mobilization were initially extremely high for women. The claims for reparations by Korean women were mostly ineffective until the modern women's movement in the 1980s galvanized new identities and enabled social agency. Guilt, shame, and trauma are factors often influencing victims of sexual violence – and not the perpetrators – so that survivors are effectively silenced. A part of the problem for Korean women was their invisibility and erasure as individual victims and a recognizable social group. As a result, female claimants were neither addressed on an individual nor on a community level in transitional justice measures (von Wahl, 2008).

This chapter argues that *homosexual* men (and lesbians) have historically faced similar challenges to heterosexual women in terms of the lack of a unified group identity and subsequent problems in mobilizing after human rights abuses. However, obvious differences between the experiences of women and gay men also exist. Prominent among these are the issues of *visibility* (women do not 'come out' and cannot hide their identity as readily), and the continued *criminalization* of gay sex. Men, regardless of their own sexual orientation, are still benefiting from the privileges of masculinity and patriarchy, and might support social ideas that are otherwise at odds with their sexuality. At the same time, they can also become the victims of a variety of homophobic policies and sexual assault. In short, while there are differences between the mobilization and organization of interests on the grounds of gender and sexuality, gay men and women have sometimes both been disadvantaged through the multiple and sometimes contradictory social identities to which they belong.

Before we turn to the next section, there needs to be some clarification on the terminology and time-specific relevance of the central factors at work here; that is sexuality and sexual identity. As Foucault demonstrated, same-sex behaviour does not historically imply a gay male identity (Foucault, 1978). Only in the nineteenth and twentieth centuries did a modern gay identity arise that became politically relevant. Thus, it is important to delineate the differences and overlaps between the categories of sexuality and sexual identity as they develop over time and for the group under consideration. This chapter focuses on the persecution and lack of exoneration of men on grounds of their sexuality, here defined as sexual *behaviour*. However, with the formation of the modern *gay identity* after World War II, particularly after 1968 and the end of outright criminalization, identity politics became an increasingly important and useful factor in demanding equality or justice (Pretzel, 2002; Jensen, 2002). It is after the solidification of the modern gay rights movement in Germany that gay *identity* and *behaviour* overlap much more closely, resulting in a more successful push for some forms of reparations.

The basis of the argument is that reparations are the outcome of 'politics'; that is, the distribution of power between claimants and the state. The formulation of identities, interests, strategies, and the usage of political pressure are crucial in receiving governmental recognition and reparations. Governments do not act on the issue of transitional justice without being prompted, because what is morally and politically just is contested after human rights abuses have stopped. The focus of the analysis here is on the conditions and form of *agency*, in particular on the organization of the interests and identities of survivors through social mobilization in West Germany. The analysis shows that claimants are neither universally able to make their experience and demands heard, nor able to develop a resonating and salient 'injustice frame' (Gamson et al., 1982). Thus a patterned hierarchy among similarly situated claimants emerges.

This chapter assesses the responsiveness of the West German government towards two claimant groups. Of particular interest are timing (when the government began to respond), the number/proportion of the people affected by reparations, and the quality and extent of the state concessions (material and/or symbolic). What factors have an effect on the level and timing of governmental response? Three concepts lie at the centre of the analysis:

1. Existing or emerging political opportunity structures,
2. The identity and social mobilization of claimants,
3. The framing of reparation demands.

Social movement theory and reparations

Social movement theory has developed a number of useful concepts and tools for the analysis of agency in a political context. We can also apply these concepts to the description and analysis of agency in general, and to the investigation of mobilization for reparations after severe human rights abuses specifically. There are three levels that help us differentiate among reparations.

The political opportunity structure

The first social movement concept, that can facilitate an analysis of agency to understand claims making for restorative justice, is called Political Opportunity Structures (POS). Social scientists have developed the concept of POS especially to understand the *differences* in movement mobilization and their structural origins. Instead of focusing on the resources and the ideology of the movement itself, this approach shifts perspective to the *external* and contextual factors, such as political and economic structures, institutions, opponents, potential allies, and mass media. These contextual, or institutional, factors can have an effect on the strategies of social movements, in particular the *channels of access* to political power that they use (Della Porta and Diani, 1999; Pierson, 1994).

The majority of comparative studies applying the POS approach in the study of social movements are cross-national or diachronic (Kitschelt, 1986; Rucht, 1998). In contrast, this chapter compares two groups in the *same* state and in the *same* time period, in West Germany 1945–2008. Both of the groups analysed were earlier victims of the Nazi regime, and some survived concentration camps or incarceration, although the level of harm directed at the Jewish population was more systemic and designed for mass killing. Nevertheless, we would assume that many of the demands put forward after 1945 by claimants, the political channels they used, and the strategies they developed would be very similar because such individuals (and their supporters) *both* faced the same West German state, the same democratic institutions, the same laws, and the same public – or so it would seem.

Theoretically, this chapter demonstrates that an intra-state comparison of social movements illuminates the different forms the POS can take *even* when approached by relatively similarly situated social actors in the same polity. Empirically, this shifts our attention to the more subtle political, legal, cultural, and social differences *among victims* of the Nazi regime in their negotiations with the Federal Republic of

Germany. It also demonstrates their ability or inability to secure symbolic or material reparations for past suffering, loss of property, health, and life. Theoretically, it cautions us against relying too heavily on the idea of *national* POS as explanatory variables as they are displayed in the comparative literature (open/closed, centralized/decentralized, two-party/multi-party). Instead the present study shows that the POS can be quite different for groups even if they share substantially overlapping claims and operate in the state.

Important here is the influence of culture, about which social movement research on POS has been relatively limited. The neglect of culture – of the social movement itself and the larger society – is particularly problematic in an analysis of struggles for recognition and reparations. Fortunately recent research has begun to include cultural dimensions into the debate (Rucht, 1998; Duyvendak et al., 1997; Ferree et al., 2002; Hobson, 2003; Polletta, 2008). Because of the limitations of structural approaches this chapter adds two concepts that focus on how culture constrains demands or sometimes challenges the status quo: identity formation and issue framing.

Social mobilization

The second approach utilized in social movement research deals with the issue and intricacies of actual mobilization of political actors. Canonical social movement theory reveals an important bundle of factors relating to the mobilization of people. Within this body of literature two related concepts are relevant; one being *identity formation* and the other *organization and resources.*

The definition and analysis of 'identity' is vast and can, of course, not be discussed here in detail, but post-modernism has contributed much to identity studies and asserts that it is fragmented and situated (Foucault, 1978; Young 1990). Postmodern approaches have criticized the false universalism of liberalism that has excluded the experiences and needs of marginal groups. It allows for, and predicts, the emergence of new identities as discourses change and old centres of powers, weaken. Charles Taylor was one of the first in 1992 to speak about struggles over recognition as opposed to older struggles over redistribution (Taylor, 1992; Honneth and Fraser, 2003). Recognition implies the public acknowledgement of historic devaluation and discrimination of individuals or groups and can be a sign of respect, citizenship, membership, or atonement. Both state recognition as political victims (or the denial of this status), and self-recognition by survivors themselves are important aspects of counteracting social stigma and building a collective identity on which claims can be formulated. A minimal degree of collective identity constitutes a *precondition* in order to utilize robust political agency as a social movement for restorative justice. The resources available to the movement and its participants influence the degree of mobilization as well (McAdam et al., 1996). Specifically, one should ask what organizational, legal, and material resources were available to claimants, and in what context were demands made? Do prior social bonds and networks exist which could be utilized in mobilization efforts?

Framing the debate

Thirdly, the struggle for reparations also occurs in the realm of culture and *symbolic* politics; that is, the ways in which a debate is framed. Symbolic politics rests on the transportation of compelling ideas, subsequent transformation of discourse, and governmental response to changes in public opinion. The way social movement organizers frame their demands to the public allows them to attribute to events a specific meaning that, in return, can mobilize affected individuals or groups, thereby changing the identity of those affected as a result (Snow and Benford, 1988). Characteristics of the human rights abuse suffered by a group, and how those characteristics are presented to the public, strongly influences the chance of success for groups seeking reparations (Howard-Hassmann and Lombardo, 2007).

It is important that the development of an injustice frame supports the compelling conclusion that the government violated shared moral standards. A crucial hurdle that social movements need to jump, if they want to mobilize successfully, is constructing a community through building social bonds that can transport ideational and mobilizing potential, thus articulating a compelling frame of interpretation for reparations demands. These interpretative frames not only enable communities of claimants, as well as supporters, to strengthen the group itself, but also help facilitate and steer interactions with the state, the media, and the public.

Differentiating the levels of reparations

To grasp the shades of empowerment and agency achieved by claimants, the author has developed the distinction between *categorical, individual*, and *collective reparations* (von Wahl, 2008). This differentiation helps us to come to grips with the specific outcomes of mobilization for restorative justice and is particularly useful for our analysis of sexuality and transitional justice.

Categorical reparations only involve the acknowledgement that victims exist or have existed. This is a form of minimal recognition since it only extends to an abstract category of victims. It is abstract because specific survivors are not known, and remain nameless and faceless. We know of their existence through historic record, but we do not know their individual stories. And, importantly, they do not know of each other in a way that would allow for communication, mobilization, and agency. When survivors are too intimidated to come forward, even though historical documentation demonstrates that these victims exist, then the public neither knows them as individuals nor as collectives. As a result, symbolic and material reparations are highly unlikely. This situation existed in the case of homosexuals after the end of National Socialism; they were only known as a category of victims. As we will see later, homosexuals were easily pushed into secrecy by continuing public taboos and institutionalized homophobia.

The next level of reparations is constituted through *individual* restitution, rehabilitation, or apologies to survivors. Here, individual claimants are publicly known and have asserted their civil, political, and/or social rights. The instance of individual reparations entails material reparations (through restitution and so on), and/or symbolic reparations (through public apologies and so on) to individual victims.

The final and most comprehensive level is *collective* reparation. These reparations view claimants as members of social groups, who may have lost collective goods such as community property (churches, libraries, meeting places, etc), common land, as well as businesses that belonged or catered to a recognizable community. In the case of collective reparations, a community would receive reparations for the destruction of these collectively held entities.

The relationship among these three levels is important to understand. Whereas individual and collective reparations acknowledge the victim, categorical reparations are highly static as claimants do not exist. It is basically a situation of victimization without claimants and thus not sufficient as a meaningful form of reparation. Individual reparations are a step into the light of recognition, but they require the willingness to disclose one's identity. In addition, some claimants are perceived as having a 'community' and others not. A combination of apologies and material reparations holds the most promise for the claimants in the cases presented here.

Two case studies on agency and transitional justice

This section lays out two historic cases that occurred at the same time and in the same state. It describes and compares the cases according to the previously identified factors (political opportunity structures, identity and social mobilization, and framing). The goal is to advance our understanding of why claimants' demands for reparations succeed or fail.

German Jewish victims and the West German state

Nazi anti-Semitic policies took effect immediately in Germany after the National Socialists gained power in 1933.[1] These policies were aimed at removing Jews from their professions, seizing their property, drastically cutting civil, political, and social rights, and threatening and ending lives and livelihoods in an unprecedented and systematic way. Anti-Semitic politics peaked with the planned extermination and following mass slaughter of European Jewry in concentration camps (the so-called 'Final Solution'), resulting in the murder of about six million Jews. What kind of restitution and reparations did Jews receive after the defeat of Germany by Allied Forces? What role did the social mobilization of the Jewish community and individual claimants play in this process? And what was the articulation of specific injustice-frames?

During World War II, German Jewish refugees were already in contact with international and American Jewish groups, working on the formulation of restitution claims (Goschler, 1992). At the pan-American conference of the Jewish World Congress, in Baltimore in 1941, three basic arguments about future restitution were put forward:

1. Jewish claims should have priority over all demands towards Germany
2. Not only German, but also European Jews should have access to redress
3. Jewish demands for restitution were part of the larger reparations issue.

(Goschler, 1992: 40)

It was clear to these Jewish organizations that these questions could not be solved through law alone, and that political means were crucial. However, since the full extent of the Holocaust was not yet publicly known, these early claims seemed premature to many (Barkan, 2000: 4).

In addition, at the time intra-state religious, ethnic, and/or cultural groups were not part of an international politics so that claims by Jews, such as restitution, were a novelty. In 1943, the former Viennese lawyer, Ernest Munz, wrote that the collective attack on European Jews necessitated a collective reaction (Munz, 1943; Goschler, 1992: 41) The development of these claims was also helped forward by one branch of Judaism, Zionism, which argued for a new Jewish homeland with the goal of establishing a nation state. Elazar Barkan argues that '[t]his formulation constructed a fundamental connection between all Jews and Zionist ideology, thereby creating a modern identity that had not existed previously' (ibid: 5). The active connection of a religious/ethnic identity to an emerging national identity powerfully and effectively advanced Jewish claims for reparations.

In the 1940s, Jewish campaigning was at best recognized as pressure from a sub-national group; a group that, so far, had little legal standing in international politics and law. Hence, it is not surprising that Jewish representatives were not even invited to the Paris Reparations conference in 1945. However, since material restitution is an established aspect of international law, the military governments occupying Germany supported the claims and quickly enacted legislation to return or, if that was impossible, give identifiable property to victims of Nazi persecution; a policy that went against the desires of the emerging German regional governments (or *Länder*) in a federal structure. The dominant American occupying forces in the West designated the Jewish Restitution Successor Organization (JRSO) as the legal successor to heirless property. After these initial steps, Jewish efforts regarding broader forms of reparations intensified. The emerging official definition of a Nazi victim mirrored the Nuremberg Laws of 1935 and embraced persons persecuted because of race, religion, or political beliefs (so-called 'Opfer des Faschismus', OdF, or Victims of Fascism). Non-German victims, and groups outside the particular definition of race, religion, or political beliefs, such as homosexual men, were excluded.

An important turn of events occurred in 1949 when Jewish groups united in the fight for reparations, despite deep ideological disagreement and political fragmentation, and formed an organization comprising 22 Jewish organizations called the Conference of Jewish Material Claims (later known as the Claims Conference) (Zweig, 1987). The founding of the Claims Conference indicates the emergence of three features mirrored in social movement theory as explored above:

1. The formation of a social movement organization for reparations
2. The articulation of a unified Jewish identity that could speak with one voice during negotiations with West Germany and,
3. The emergence of a political and discursive strategy in response to the political opportunity structures, in particular, the legal requirements of international negotiations.

Through agreements with the West German government, signed in 1952 in the Netherlands, the Treaty of Wassenaar contained reparations in the form of assistance provided to the newly established state of Israel, and to Jewish communities throughout the world. In 1956 these reparations payments comprised over 80 per cent of the budget of the new state of Israel. The Federal Restitution Law of 1957 limited total payments to Jewish survivors to 1.5 billion German Marks, along with the provision that all claims were to be satisfied up to at least 50 per cent of the damage. Reparations were to go to individual survivors or, when none existed, to the Jewish community and to the new Jewish state. The 1964 amendment raised the required damage payments to 100 per cent and provided a hardship fund of 800 million German Marks for those survivors who had not filed their application in time.

The Federal Republic of Germany (FRG) agreed to pay Israel compensation of 3 billion German Marks to assist in the integration of uprooted and destitute refugees from Germany and lands formerly under German rule. (Schwerin, 1972; Kritz, 1995) The FRG also paid 450 million German Marks to the Claims Conference for the resettlement of Jewish victims living outside of Israel. By July 1971, the combined total payments from the Federal Law for Compensation of the Victims of National Socialist Persecution (BEG), the Federal Restitution Law (AKG), the Luxembourg Agreement with Israel, and other global agreements amounted to 40.91 billion German Marks. In October 1980, after a number of lobbying attempts from victim's organizations, 400 million German Marks were transferred to the Claims Conference, and, in 1981, 100 million German Marks were earmarked for non-Jewish victims of persecution (Pross, 1998). Although Christian Pross points out that many claims were stymied by the German bureaucracy and dragged on for years, the total of reparations in the late 1990s was about 115 billion German Marks (about 70 billion US dollars). The payments will continue, as the German state pays monthly pensions to about 120,000 Holocaust survivors around the world.

Interestingly, the FRG moved more slowly on the level of symbolic reparations. The climate towards reparations for Jews was unquestionably hostile in the first 10 years after 1945. Germans saw themselves as victims of the war, especially of the Soviet Union, and were reluctant to pay reparations to the Jewish community or to admit guilt for genocide (Moeller, 1995; Goschler, 1992). Nevertheless, after the founding of the Federal Republic of Germany, the first Chancellor, Konrad Adenauer – leader of the newly established conservative Christian Democratic

Party (CDU) – became an important ally for the demands by the Jewish community (Schrafstetter, 2003).

In contrast, even though the German population showed much sympathy for expellees, refuges, and POW's – a sentiment that was widely upheld by the government, academia and the media – it had little to say about its own involvement in the past humiliations of daily life, or even 'Kristallnacht' of 1938. As the poet and songwriter, Wolf Biermann, put it ironically, 'the Germans will never forgive the Jews for the fact that they murdered them' (in Kugelmann, 1989: 136). The debate about the involvement and the guilt of the 'average' German regarding the persecution of Jewish Germans and other victims of National Socialism began at last in the 1960s. As a result of the Auschwitz trials in 1964, and the social and generational changes of '1968', public perception in the Federal Republic shifted towards a more sympathetic view of Nazi victims. Since then, the idea and contested process of 'Vergangenheitsbewältigung', or 'coming to terms with the past', has produced a political culture of atonement in Germany that is reflected in repeated apologies by public leaders, such as Chancellors and Presidents, in school textbooks, the media, in the spread of Holocaust memorials, and a more open and self-critical public discourse.

As this case study sketches out, the attainment of symbolic and economic reparations was largely the outcome of the successful organization and mobilization of Jewish interests through the Jewish Claims Conference, supported by the American policies on restitution, and the German Chancellor's need to find an acceptable compromise. Importantly, this is coupled with the construction of a new *national* identity – in the form of Israel – that fit into the traditional framework of international negotiation, and rendered their campaign for reparations so effective. In a sense, the individual identity of Jews in Europe (and elsewhere) expanded through Zionism from a religious identity to include a recognizable and common national identity. The construction of this new identity, and the framing of the issue in national terms, had a tremendous impact on the perception of reparations. The Jewish community became visible and relevant as both an ethnicity/religion *and* a nation, which, in turn, gave reparation claims a much stronger political standing.

From the onset, the Claims Conference and the newly established Federal Republic of Germany employed a two-pronged approach to reparations. Individuals and the community (Jewish communities in Germany and Israel) have both been recipients of reparations. Not only was it understood that Jewish communities existed and suffered, but a new kind of community, a nation state, was established and became a recipient as well.

Although the destruction of individual lives, families, and communities can never be undone, Kurt Schwerin claims that the West German record in terms of accepting legal and financial responsibility (restoring properties, and indemnification for material damage) for the Holocaust and human rights abuses 'is a favourable one', especially when compared to East Germany and Austria (Schwerin, 1972: 47; Kim, 1999). Ariel Colonomos and Andrea Armstrong characterize it as the most comprehensive reparations programme ever instituted (Colonomos and Armstrong, 2006), whereas others are more critical of the German reparations process (Pross, 1998). The general perception of relative comprehensive reparations needs to be questioned when analysing the case of other Nazi victims, in particular homosexual men.

Male homosexuals and the German state

The Nazis condemned homosexuals as 'socially aberrant' and, soon after taking over, banned all male homosexual and lesbian associations, clubs, and publishing houses. They ransacked Magnus Hirschfeld's progressive Institute for Sexual Science, burning thousands of books from that institute's library as part of a larger book burning in Berlin in 1933. Since the founding of the Second German Reich in 1871, anti-homosexual laws existed in the Criminal Code as Paragraph 175, and the Nazis amended Paragraph 175 in 1935, very broadly criminalizing 'lewd and lascivious' behaviour. In addition, Nazi leader Heinrich Himmler created the 'Reich Central Office for Combating Homosexuality and Abortion', a sub-department of the Gestapo (Mosse, 1985). The police stepped up raids on homosexual meeting places, seized address books, and created networks of informers. Between 1933 and 1945, an estimated 100,000 men were arrested as homosexuals, and some 37,490 were officially defined as homosexuals and sentenced. Most of them spent time in regular prison, but between 5000 and 15,000 were incarcerated in concentration camps.[2] In the camps some became victims of medical experiments, sterilization, and castration (Deutscher Bundestag, 14/2619, 27 January 2000). About 60 per cent of these concentration camp inmates died, although exact numbers are difficult to come by. Paragraph 175 had always been directed at male homosexuals, and lesbians were not persecuted in the same way (Schoppmann, 1991; 1998). Nevertheless, some lesbians were probably incarcerated under the Nazi regime as 'asocials' or 'prostitutes', but their numbers were extremely low (Schoppmann,1998; Schikorra, 1998).

Research on homosexual victims and their situation after the war began relatively late, and there is only very limited information. Most of the studies focus on the larger cities or certain regions, and consist of historical micro-studies of individual cases collected in local archives. The goal of these studies is to understand the individual situation of survivors in the larger political and legal context of the regions and the Federal Republic (Pretzel and Roßbach, 2000; Müller and Sternweiler, 2000; Pretzel, 2002; Rosenkranz and Lorenz, 2005; zur Nieden, 2009).

Continuation of anti-homosexual policies in West Germany (1945–69)

One would expect that, after the war ended, political opportunity structures for all citizens (that is access to parties and organizations, and restoration of civil, political, and social rights and privileges) would open up again and that the state would recognize all victims of Nazi persecution as such. However, under Allied Military Government, Germany retained Paragraph 175 in its identical form as under National Socialism. This particular legal continuity was permitted and enforced, even though the Allies did not otherwise allow the retention of laws that had drastically increased in severity under the Nazis. Some homosexuals were even forced to serve out their terms of imprisonment set under the Nazi regime.

After 1949 the Christian Democratic government of the newly founded Federal Republic of Germany also defended the continued use of Paragraph 175, and the severe criminalization of homosexual activity and relationships. Their arguments centred on the 'biological differences of the sexes' and the 'natural order of life', and were supported by conservative rulings of the Federal Constitutional Court in 1957 (Moeller, 1994). Between 1950 and 1969, in the continually homophobic climate of West Germany, over 100,000 legal investigations were opened, and 59,316 gay men were again sentenced. Neither homosexual individuals nor the vibrant gay community that existed during the Weimar Republic were recognized as 'persecuted' by the Nazi regime in the legal sense, because they did not belong to 'political, racial, or religious groups' designated by the Nuremberg Laws (Hoffschildt, 2000; zur Nieden, 1999; Gerlach 2002). Because of the continued criminalization, lack of recognition, and lack of political support, homosexuals were not included in the aforementioned West German BEG (Bundesentschädigungsgesetz) which regulated (among other things) the restitution and reparation claims of former victims of the Nazi regime. In the repressive political and social climate, homosexuals, who were theoretically included in the 1957 Federal Restitution Law (*Allgemeines Kriegsfolgengesetz*, or AKG), did not dare to apply for compensation in order to avoid the risk of attracting further stigmatization or persecution.

Failed social mobilization and resignation (1946–60)

Who can successfully represent the interests of homosexual claimants? This question lies at the core of this chapter. The domestic victims of National Socialist policies were defined officially as only those persecuted for religious, political, or racist reasons. In 1945 a group of concentration camp survivors in Berlin organized under the Soviet military administration, formally bringing together, under one umbrella, the 'Victims of Fascism' (or OdF). This group became part of the city's social administration, representing claimants, and deciding who qualified as a recognized victim and was thus eligible for the coveted OdF-identification card. The survivors who could demonstrate that they had suffered in concentration camps, and belonged to the aforementioned groups, could receive an OdF-identification card, which enabled them to gain access to much needed food, housing, and jobs, as well as a certain social recognition. A committee of other former Nazi victims, which included lawyers and prominent individuals, assessed the validity of the applications. By 1946 the organization included about 9000 people, excluding Jews, Sinti, and Roma, whose cases were represented by a division dealing with victims of the Nuremberg Laws. However, homosexuals, 'Asocials', criminals, victims of euthanasia or forced sterilization, displaced persons, and other groups were not eligible.

The territorial and legal division of Germany amongst the Allies also split the association of the Victims of Fascism. In 1948, the 'Association of the Persecuted of the Nazi Regime' (Vereinigung der Verfolgten des Naziregimes, VVN) was founded in West Berlin. This association stated that *anti-fascist activity* as the cause for incarceration was a precondition for membership, and that the mere fact of prosecution for homosexual behaviour was insufficient (zur Nieden, 2009). While some courageous individuals, like the medical doctor Rudolf Klimmer, petitioned the VVN to recognize homosexual victims and allow for compensation, there was no broader level of mobilization for the inclusion of homosexuals. Some individual legal cases were brought forward, and a few cautious scientific studies emerged stating that homosexuality was not aberrant or dangerous, but more was not possible, thus frustrating survivors and silencing further efforts.

This absence of mobilization contrasts profoundly with the range of negative consequences that homosexual men experienced under Nazi rule, and which continued to have a devastating effect in post-war and democratic West Germany. Among the most important long-term effects for gay men were registration with the police, and loss of employment and educational degrees. Additional consequences included convictions and sentencing, health problems, financial penalties, and responsibility for court and prison costs. If convicted under Paragraph 175, homosexual men faced a variety of post-release restrictions, such as loss of passports or restriction to a specific locality. Sentencing for Paragraph 175 often led to individual social decline via exclusion from professional organizations, the university, and political and social organizations, even after 1945 (Roßbach, 2002).

Failed denazification and exoneration through continued criminalization, discouraged claimants from coming forward, blocking paths back to a more normal existence. Because of continued censorship of gay media, communication among a larger group of individuals, and the development of a common identity, was severely hampered. Social groups that formed were afraid of police surveillance, public shaming, and loss of jobs. Homosexuals met only in small private circles where some of these issues were discussed; however, even these dwindled by the 1950s. By the general compensation deadline of 31 December 1959, only 14 gay men dared to disclose both their past incarceration and their sexual orientation, and to petition the government.[3] The few existing organizations for gay rights disbanded in 1959 and 1960 – defeated and unheard – with what must have been a sense of deep frustration (Pretzel, 2002). The *invisibility* and *continued criminalization* of homosexuality in post-war West Germany contributed to the inability of survivors to organize effectively, and claim eligibility for reparations.

Compared to the state's general willingness to pay for a number of Jewish abuses during the Holocaust, the invisibility of homosexual victims, the absence of corresponding social pressure, the difficulties in organizing legally, and the impossibility of articulating a convincing injustice frame during the conservative and sexually repressive Adenauer era, comprise the many obstacles faced by homosexual men. Allied forces did nothing to support claims by homosexuals, and the new republic even got away with the continued use of the identical Nazi law. Social mobilization and framing of demands by homosexuals in West Germany were stuck in a dead end without allies among political leaders, the parties, the courts, police, bureaucracy, or the media. Neither was there solidarity with the other victims of National

Socialism organized by the VVN. Gay men found all aspects of the political opportunity structure closed to them.

The gay liberation movement and the beginning of reform (late 1960s–70s)

In the late 1960s and early 1970s, when a modern gay liberation movement emerged in Germany (as in other Western states) along with student and women's movements, the continued silencing, criminalization, and prosecution of gay citizens finally came under censure. Indeed the whole Nazi period, and the complicity and involvement of parents and authority figures, was condemned by members of these new social movements. The more radical gay liberation movement emerged in West Berlin and was politicized through publications, demonstrations, and films (such as those by the director Rosa von Praunheim). Activists formed the group *'Homosexuelle Aktion Westberlin'* (HAW), which demanded an end to societal and governmental oppression. In 1969, when the Social Democratic Party came to power in an alliance with the Liberals, Paragraph 175 was at last reformed (and reformed again in 1973), to introduce the quasi-legality (*Straflosigkeit*) of homosexual acts between men over the age of 18.

Regarding Nazi crimes, however, no act of apology or broad reparation was connected with that legal reform. Four gay men received regular money from the Federal Restitution Law (AKG) out of a special hardship fund, and 16 survivors received a one-time payment of 5000 German Marks. No homosexuals received funds from the more generous fund for victims of the National Socialist regime (BEG). While a general liberalization began during the 1970s, the police continued to keep so-called 'pink lists', with the names and meeting places of homosexuals, for various uses.

Into the 1980s, the dominant legal position was that, while homosexuals were indeed political enemies of Nazi Germany and sent to concentration camps, this was done for reasons of 'order' and 'security' (Giessler, 1981: 13–14). In his famous 1985 speech, the German President, Richard von Weizsäcker, broke ranks with this argument and became the first highly ranked government representative to name homosexuals as victims of National Socialism during the commemoration of the fortieth anniversary of the end of World War II. However, official apologies from then-CDU Chancellor, Helmut Kohl, were not offered. Moreover, in 1986, the West German parliament reaffirmed the Federal Constitutional Court's view that that prosecution for violations of Paragraph 175 did not constitute 'National Socialist injustice' (Moeller, 1994). Only with increased pressure towards the end of the 1980s from the gay liberation movement and the new Green party, were homosexuals included among the category of the 'forgotten victims'. However, material compensation or reparations were severely limited. Out of nine homosexual men who applied for compensation, only one case was approved (Schoppmann as cited in Moeller, 1994: 427).

In 1994 and 1996, the conservative CDU government still maintained a position that the incarceration of gay men was neither typical Nazi injustice nor *'rechtsstaatswidrig'*, that is 'against the law'. However, following German unification and changing public views, Paragraph 175 was at last abolished. When the left wing Social Democratic-Green coalition formed a more progressive government in 1998, it was a watershed moment for gay men. On 7 December 2000, the Federal Parliament of Germany officially apologized to the homosexual victims of the Nazi regime, and, importantly, annulled their former criminal sentences.[4] This also included an apology for the fact that the laws of the Federal Republic of Germany supported continued harassment and ongoing criminalization of homosexuals until 1969.

Despite these changes, gay men sentenced under the Nazi regime have not received financial compensation as Nazi victims. The reason given is that, at the time, prosecution of homosexuals was legal under criminal law, the dominant discursive legal frame. Also, the eradication of homosexual and lesbian publishing houses, stores, restaurants, and infrastructure, as well as the destruction of the Institute for Sexual Science in Berlin, and the ownership of the centrally located land on which it stood, has not been adequately addressed. The founder of the institute, Hans Magnus Hirschfeld, had stipulated in his will that, in the event of dissolution, all assets should be handed over to the Humboldt University Berlin. However, West German courts ruled that the dissolution and Nazi take-over in 1934 was legal; and handing over the property to the Humboldt University, then the flagship university of East Germany, must also have been unpalatable. As a result, restitution or compensation to the gay community for the destroyed cultural and scientific institute has been denied. For the West German courts, collective compensation was not an issue since the existence of a gay 'community' was not recognized. The failure to decriminalize male homosexuality generated further individual and community related losses. In recent years gay activism in the unified Berlin has returned to the demand for compensation and funding for a new institute of Sexual Science.

Symbolic reparations: the Berlin memorial for gays persecuted by the Nazis (1993–2008)

Over the last decade, especially beginning with the coalition of left wing Social Democrats and Greens in Germany (1998–2005), important, but sometimes ambiguous, reforms have occurred in terms of symbolic reparations. The political opportunity structure has opened up for gay interests and rights, public opinion has become more tolerant, and there is more goodwill in the representation of homosexual distress under the Nazi regime. During its administration, the Social Democratic-Green coalition expanded the scope of gay/lesbian rights (for instance, the introduction of same-sex civil unions), and discussed the recognition, and possible reparation, of homosexual victims in parliament. The government also supported the long-standing demand by parts of the gay rights movement to build a memorial for homosexual victims of the Nazi regime.

With the establishment of a strong culture of atonement in Germany in recent decades, gay and lesbian groups in a variety of larger cities had begun to establish a mixture of small local memorials, such as plaques, statues, and '*Stolpersteine*', small pavement memorial stones. The politics of memory culminated on 27 May 2008, when a public monument (*Gedenkort*) for homosexuals persecuted under the Nazis was opened in Berlin. This memorial was the result of a long process of political mobilization from the German Lesbian and Gay Association, which began an initiative for building a memorial for the homosexual victims of the NS regime in 1993. On 12 December 2003, during a deliberation on a major memorial for the Jewish Holocaust, the German Parliament agreed to also build a small site for gay victims across the street. The purpose of the memorial was to remember the oppression of homosexuals during the Nazi and post-war period, and educate the public. Unfortunately, the memorial came into the crosshairs of identity politics and the competing interests of various groups of Nazi victims, or supposed victims. Trying to simultaneously address both the past and the present, that is the Nazi persecution *and* the continued discrimination of gays and lesbians in the Federal Republic, was complicated. High and diverse expectations led to a series of conflicts among constituents and supporters.

As a brief outline, firstly, the actual design of the monument to the memory homosexual victims (*Denkmal für die im Nationalisozialismus Verfolgten Homosexuellen*), a single, hollow, grey block of concrete, very similar to one of the 2711 concrete stelae of the Holocaust memorial, produced heated debate because of its local proximity to the latter.

Israel Gutman, the former head of the Jad-Vashem Holocaust museum in Israel, stated that the placement of a new memorial so close to the Holocaust memorial was a 'scandal', and declared that many Nazis were themselves homosexuals (Israel Gutman, 29 May 2008). This prejudice is not uncommonly held, but it offended gay activists profoundly as it lumped together Nazis and homosexual victims.

Secondly, the memorial divided its supporters too. A small, but vocal, group of feminists associated with the German feminist magazine *EMMA*, and its figurehead, Alice Schwarzer, argued that lesbians should also be represented in the memorial (EMMA, 2006). Historical records appear to be clear, however, that lesbians were *not* persecuted in any comparable fashion to men under the Nazis or after 1945 (Schoppmann,1991; Kokula, 1987). Thus they are historically not part of the targeted group. If, however, the memorial was intended to educate the public about the post-war bigotry against homosexuals more generally, then lesbians are another group to include. To the chagrin of many male supporters, the protest by the small group of influential feminists was able to successfully remove the perceived gender-specific *'exclusion'* from the memorial. In the eyes of identity politics, exclusion is the cardinal sin of traditional politics, and 'inclusion' a useful political tool in framing the debate. As a result of this rather ahistorical rally, the artistic video shown inside the memorial was changed to include images of women for the same amount of time as images of men.

To sum up, while the construction of the Berlin memorial with the support of the German Parliament (and numerous other smaller local monuments) is a success of symbolic recognition for the persecuted gay community, the debate illustrates the long legacy of failed denazification, and some of the intense competition among claimants. It also demonstrates the opportunities and dangers of identity politics in transitional justice debates at the intersection of gender and sexuality.

Sexuality, agency, and transitional justice

In conclusion we should return to the frame of analysis based on political opportunity structures, social mobilization, and framing as introduced earlier in this chapter. One factor explaining the differential outcomes in the politics of reparations is the ability of claimants' to organize interests, vis-à-vis *political opportunity structures*. As illustrated, after the end of National Socialism, homosexual victims did not enjoy political support by the Allies, the West and East German governments, the courts, mass media, or society. Continued criminalization of male homosexuality through Paragraph 175, the resulting inability to legally organize, and the censorship of gay newsletters and communication until 1969, severely undermined the ability to organize for material or symbolic reparations.

Theoretically, this chapter shows that we have to caution against the overemphasis of a *national* political opportunity structure as explanatory variable for movement failure or success. Instead, different societal groups experience different opportunities in transitional justice, even if they share some similar experiences in the same state and at the same time. The unequal access reflects, as Constantin Goschler has argued that there has never been an all-comprising identity of Nazi victims (Goschler, 1992). In addition to structural explanations for movement failure or success, the cultural aspects of social movements need to be taken into account when analysing claims related to reparations. On the one hand, claims coming from individuals or groups who are seen as 'morally degraded', 'aberrant' or 'criminal' by the vast majority of the population, and by core state institutions, face an uphill battle to find legal avenues, strong political allies, or resonant media to even enter the political system. The dominant culture puts up multiple hurdles against recognition of such demands. On the other hand, the case of homosexual men in post-war Germany also indicates that a 'new culture' informs a new identity, and can profoundly challenge the legal and political status quo in the long haul.

Social mobilization was severely restricted until 1969, and, as a result, limited public claims making for reparations by homosexuals in fundamental ways. The ability to share experiences and stories, pool resources, organize, and self-identify as homosexual individuals vis-à-vis social services, bureaucracies, and the courts was lacking. Under these circumstances, social mobilization and the development of a cohesive *identity* were hampered. As a result, the maintenance of invisibility and secrecy, that functioned to protect homosexuals from continued state repression, also made reparation claims impossible.

The mobilization of the modern gay and lesbian movement in the 1970s, the slow erosion of stigmatizing laws, and the highly dynamic, complex, and interactive 'identity politics' of the following decades, have enabled homosexual men to describe their victimization during the Nazi regime and build a bridge between current gay aspirations and the past. The symbolic politics regarding the Berlin memorial show that the representations of a collective 'homosexual' identity is difficult to maintain, and can pit different groups against each other in a competition. The social mobilization of the last decades has led to symbolic reparations, whilst material reparations have basically been a failure.

The reason for this failure is partly found in the inability to organize an effective movement in time.

As stated earlier, movements for reparations are in need of the invention of an effective and culturally resonant injustice frame. Here one could imagine frames that would benefit *both* groups of Nazi victims – Jews and homosexuals. Instead, one interpretative frame – the Holocaust – has become the global reference point for all kinds of groups. Framing the persecution of homosexuals for a short time as a 'Homocaust' shows the strategic appeal of the dominant injustice frame 'Holocaust', but it does not capture the historical reality of the Shoa. While the gay community has only partially been able to utilize the specific injustice frame of the Holocaust, it has nevertheless become slowly accepted as another victim of the Nazi ideology and state oppression.

Concluding comments are directed at two issues, firstly the problems of mobilizing for reparations on the grounds of sexuality in comparison to gender, religion, or ethnicity and, secondly, the issue of intersectionality already raised by Simone de Beauvoir. First, the comparison of the two cases of victims of Nazi crimes shows that, if claims based on ethnic and religious identity can be powerfully framed in terms of the assumed characteristics of the *national* identity, or attached to a national project, they are likely to be more successful – success being defined as having a higher likelihood, earlier acknowledgment of crime, and governmental willingness to consider material and symbolic reparations. It is worthwhile to note how the ethnic/national framing of the reparations issue has played out. Many of the Jewish survivors became part of a new nation state – Israel – others left for the USA, Canada, or other states. In the instance of the majority of the surviving Jewish population, a profound *separation* between perpetrators and victims has taken place, while homosexual men have continued living in Germany under a cloud of *secrecy* for several more decades, trying to fit in. Under the described circumstances, gay men in post-war Germany fell into the 'empty' class of categorical victims. Individual claims overwhelmingly failed, and the question of a 'community', which is culturally constructed, has historically disadvantaged homosexuals.

Second, intersectionality complicates the status and identity of victimhood, survivors, and claimants. Some homosexuals were Jewish – where does this leave these individuals? The vast majority of homosexuals were non-Jewish, did not become victims of direct Nazi persecution and continued their – albeit secretive – lives during and after Fascism. Many of them fought in the war, and possibly supported the policies and ideology of the Nazi government. Nevertheless, scholars have argued that the situation of Jews and homosexuals, and sometimes their historic circumstances, has been similar; when one group was persecuted, the other also did badly (Jensen, 2002). Historically then, Jews and homosexuals might both have been targets of conservative and Fascist ideologies, even though their fate has been different in many ways. This difference includes the respective success of demands for reparations by the Jewish community, and the failure by homosexual men to garner restitution and recognition. This failure illuminates the larger role of politics and sexuality in transitional justice.

Notes

1. This section includes extracts from Angelika von Wahl, 'Reparations, Gender, and Ethnicity: Why, When, and How Democratic Governments Get Involved' in Manfred Berg and Bernd Schaeffer (eds), *Historical Justice in International Perspective, How Societies are Trying to Right the Wrongs of the Past*, (Cambridge University Press, 2008). Reprinted with kind permission from Cambridge University Press.
2. The assessment on how many homosexuals died because of Nazi persecution varies dramatically. The numbers of 5000 to 15,000 are considered reliable (Lautmann, 1977). James Steakley (2002) gives a self-critical assessment about the inflated numbers (between 200,000 and 300,000) that were picked up from unsubstantiated press releases, and then circulated in the gay and mainstream press in the US. The American gay movement also picked up the use of the pink triangle as symbol of the movement and often equated the fate of homosexuals under National Socialism to the Jews.
3. Antrag auf Unrechtserklärung der nationalsozialistischen Paragraphen 175 und 175a Nr. 4 Reichsstrafgesetzbuch sowie Rehabilitierung und Entschädigung für die schwulen und lesbischen Opfer des NS-Regimes, Deutscher Bundestag, 14/2619, 27 January 2000, 1–7.
4. A debate over other forms of symbolic reparations, such as memorials commemorating the persecution of homosexuals, has been ongoing since the 1980s. An excellent introduction and overview of this debate can be found in Heinrich-Böll Stiftung (ed.) (1999) *Der homosexuellen NS-Opfer gedenken* (Berlin: Heinrich-Böll Stiftung).

References

E. Barkan (2000) *The Guilt of Nations: Restitution and Negotiating Historical Injustices* (New York: Norton).

S. de Beauvoir (1949) *The Second Sex*, translated by H.M. Parshley (1972) (New York: Penguin).

I. Buruma (1994) *The Wages of Guilt, Memories of War in Germany and Japan*, (New York: Farrar Straus Giroux).

A. Colonomos and A. Armstrong (2006) 'German Reparations to the Jews after World War II, A Turning Point in the History of Reparations' in P. de Greiff (ed.) *Handbook of Reparations* (Oxford: Oxford University Press), pp.390–419.

D. Della Porta and M. Diani (1999) *Social Movements: An Introduction* (Blackwell: Oxord).

Deutscher Bundestag, 14. Wahlperiode, Drucksache 14/2619, *Unrechtserklaerung der nationalsozialistischen Paragraphen 175 und 175a Nr. 4 Reichsstrafgesetzbuch sowie Rehabilitierung und Entschaedigung fuer die schwulen und lesbischen Opfer des NS-Regimes,* 27 January 2000.

C. Duggan and A. M. Abusharaf (2006) 'Reparations of Sexual Violence in Democratic Transitions: The Search for Gender Justice' in P. de Greiff (ed.) *The Handbook of Reparations* (Oxford: Oxford University Press), pp.622–49.

J. Duyvendak, M. Giugni, R. Koopmans and H. Kriesi (1997) *New Social Movements in Western Europe: A Comparative Analysis* (London: UCL Press).

M. Ferree, W. Gamson, J. Gerhards and D. Rucht (2002) *Shaping Abortion Discourse: Democracy and the Public Sphere in Germany and the United States* (Cambridge: Cambridge University Press).

N. Fraser and A. Honneth (2003) *Redistribution or Recognition: A political-philosophical exchange* (London: Verso).

N. Frei, J. Brunner and C. Goschler (eds) (2009) *Die Praxis der Wiedergutmachung, Geschichte, Erfahrung und Wirkung in Deutschland und Israel* (Munchen: Oldenbourg Verlag).

M. Foucault (1978) *History of Sexuality, Vol 1.* (New York: Random House).

W. A. Gamson, B. Fireman and S. Rytina (1982) *Encounters with Unjust Authority* (Homewood, IL: Dorsey Press).

C. Gerlach (2002) 'Anträge auf Anerkennung als "Opfer des Faschismus" (OdF) und "Politisch, rassisch, oder religiös Verfolgter" (PrV)' in A. Pretzel (ed.) *NS-Opfer unter Vorbehalt* (Lit Verlag), pp. 193–221.

H. Giessler (1981) 'Die Grundsatzbestimmungen des Entschädigungsrechts' in Bundesminister der Finanzen in Zusammenarbeit mit W. Schwarz (ed.) *Das Bundesentschädigungsgesetz, Teil 1, (Die Wiedergutmachung nationalsozialistischen Unrechts durch die Bundesrepublik Deutschland, Bd. 4)* (München: Beck Verlag), pp. 1–116.

C. Goschler (2008) 'Disputed Victims: The West German Discourse on Restitution for the Victims of Nazism' in M. Berg and B. Schaeffer (eds) *Historical Justice in International Perspective. How Societies Are Trying to Right the Wrongs of the Past* (Washington: Cambridge University Press), pp 93–110.

C. Goschler (1992) *Wiedergutmachung, Westdeutschland und die Verfolgten des Nationalsozialismus (1945–1954)* (München: Oldenbourg Verlag).

G. Grau (ed.) (1995) *Hidden Holocaust? Gay and Lesbian Persecution in Germany 1933–45* (Chicago, London: Fitzroy Dearborn).

I. Gutman (2008) *Holocaust Scholar Pans Monument to Nazi's Gay Victims* (Deutsche Welle, http://www.dw-world.de/dw/article/0,,3368183,00.html) 29 May 2008.

B. Hobson (ed.) (2003) *Recognition Struggles and Social Movements, Contested Identities, Agency and Power* (Cambridge: Cambridge University Press).

R. Hoffschildt (2000) 'Nach der Befreiung wieder in Haft, Der bündische Widerstandskämpfer Paul Hahn' in J. Müller and A. Sternweiler (eds) *Homosexuelle Männer im KZ Sachsenhausen* (Berlin: Verlag Rosa Winkel), pp. 354–8.

R. Howard-Hassmann and A. Lombardo (2007) 'Framing Reparations Claims: Differences between the African and Jewish Social Movements for Reparations', *African Studies Review*, Vol. 50 No. 1, 27–48.

E. N. Jensen (2002) 'The Pink Triangle and political Consciousness: Gays, Lesbians, and the Memory of Nazi Persecution', *Journal of the History of Sexuality*, Vol. 11 No. 1–2, 319–49.

B. Jellonek and R. Lautmann (eds) (2002) *Nationalsozialistischer Terror gegen Homosexuelle, Verdrängt und ungesühnt* (Paderborn: Schöningh).

H. Kim (1999) 'German Reparations: Institutionalized Insufficiency' in R. L. Brooks (ed.) *When Sorry isn't Enough: The Controversy Over Apologies and Reparations for Human Injustice* (New York: New York University Press), pp. 77–80.

H. Kitschelt (1986) 'Political Opportunity Structures and Political Protest: Anti-Nuclear Movements in Four Democracies', *British Journal of Political Science*, Vol. 16, 57–85.

I. Kokula, (1987) 'Schriftliche Stellungnahme zur Anhörung des Innenausschusses des Deutschen Bundestages am 24. Juni 1987' in Deutscher Bundestag (ed.) *Wiedergutmachung und Entschädigung für nationalsozialistisches Unrecht* (Bonn).

C. Kugelmann (1989) '"Tell Them in America We are Still Alive" The Jewish Community in the Federal Republic', *New German Critique*, Vol. 46 (Winter), 129–40.

R. Lautmann (ed.) (1977) *Seminar Gesellschaft und Homosexualität* (Frankfurt a. M.: Suhrkamp).

D. McAdam, J. McCarthy and M. Zald (eds) (1996) *Comparative Perspectives on Social Movements, Political Opportunity Structures, Mobilizing Structures, and Cultural Framings* (Cambridge: Cambridge University Press).

R. Moeller (1996) 'War Stories: The Search for a Usable Past in the Federal Republic of Germany', *American Historical Review*, Vol. 101 No. 4, 1008–48.

R. Moeller (1994) 'The Homosexual Man is a "Man", the Homosexual Woman is a "Woman": Sex, Society, and the Law in Postwar West Germany', *Journal of the History of Sexuality*, Vol. 4 No. 3, 395–429.

G. Mosse (1985) *Nationalism and Sexuality, Respectability and Abnormal Sexuality in Modern Europe* (New York: Howard Fertig).

J. Müller and A. Sternweiler (eds) (2000) *Homosexuelle Männer im KZ Sachsenhausen*, (Berlin: Rosa Winkel)

E. Munz (1943) 'Restitution in Postwar Europe', *Contemporary Jewish Record*, Vol. VI No. 4, 373.

S. zur Nieden (2009) 'Die Aberkannten, Der Berliner Hauptauschuss "Opfer des Faschismus" und die verfolgten Homosexuellen', in N. Frei, J. Brunner and C. Goschler (eds) *Die Praxis der Wiedergutmachung, Geschichte, Erfahrung und Wirkung in Deutschland und Israel* (Munchen: Oldenbourg Verlag).

S. zur Nieden (1999) '"...als 'Opfer des Faschismus' nicht tragbar." Ausgrenzung verfolgter Homosexueller in Berlin 1945–1949' in KZ-Gedenkstätte Neuengamme (ed.) *Verfolgung Homosexueller im Nationalsozialismus: Beiträge zur Geschichte der nationalsozialistischen Verfolgung in Norddeutschland* (Bremen: Edition Temmen, Vol 5), pp. 93–103.

J. Peters and A. Wolper (eds) (1995) *Women's Right – Human Rights, International Feminist Perspectives* (New York and London: Routledge).

P. Pierson (1994) *Dismantling the Welfare State? Reagan, Thatcher and the Politics of Retrenchment* (New York: Cambridge University Press).

F. Polletta (2008) 'Culture and Movements', *The Annals of the American Academy of Political and Social Science*, Vol. 619, 78–96.

A. Pretzel (ed.) (2002) *NS-Opfer unter Vorbehalt, Homosexuelle Männer in Berlin nach 1945* (Münster: Lit Verlag).

A. Pretzel and G. Roßbach (eds) (2002) *Wegen der zu erwartenden hohen Strafe: Homosexuellenverfolgung in Berlin, 1933–1945* (Berlin: Rosa Winkel).

C. Pross (1998) *Paying for the Past, The Struggle over Reparations for Surviving Victims of the Nazi Terror* (Baltimore and London: John Hopkins University Press).

B. Rosenkranz and G. Lorenz (2005) *Hamburg auf anderen Wegen, Die Geschichte des schwulen Lebens in der Hansestadt* (Hamburg: Lambda).

G. Roßbach (2002) 'Auswirkungen der NS-Verfolgung' in A. Pretzel (ed.) (2002) *NS-Opfer unter Vorbehalt, Homosexuelle Männer in Berlin nach 1945* (Münster: Lit Verlag), 43–69.

R. Rubio-Marín (ed.) (2006) *What Happened to Women? Gender and Reparations for Human Rights Violations* (New York: Social Science Research Council).

D. Rucht (1998a) *Modernisierung und neue soziale Bewegungen. Deutschland, Frankreich und USA im Vergleich* (Frankfurt and New York: Campus).

D. Rucht (1998b) 'Komplexe Phänomene – komplexe Erklärungen, Die politischen Gelegenheitstrukturen der neuen sozialen Bewegungen in der Bundesrepublik', in K.-U. Hellmann and R. Koopmans (eds) *Paradigmen der Bewegungsforschung, Entstehung und Entwicklung von Neuen sozialen Bewegungen und Rechtsextremismus* (Opladen: Westdeutscher Verlag).

C. Schikorra (2001) *Kontinuitäten der Ausgrenzung. 'Asoziale' Häftlinge im Frauen-Konzentrationslager Ravensbrück* (Berlin: Metropol 2001).

H. Schissler (ed.) (2000) *The Miracle Years. A Cultural History of West Germany, 1949–1968* (Princeton: Princeton University Press).

C. Schoppmann (1998) *Zeit der Maskierung, Lebensgeschichten lesbischer Frauen im 'Dritten Reich'* (Frankfurt: Fischer).

C. Schoppmann (1991) *Nationalsoziolistische Sexualpolitik und weibliche Homosexualitat* (Pfaffenweiler: Centaurus).

S. Schrafstetter (2003) 'The Diplomacy of Wiedergutmachung: Memory, the Cold War, and the Western European Victims of Nazism, 1956–1964', *Holocaust and Genocide Studies*, Vol. 17 No. 3, 459–79.

K. Schwerin (1972) 'German Compensation for Victims of Nazi Persecution', *Northwestern University Law Review*, Vol. 67, 489–520, in N. Kritz (1995) *Transitional Justice*, Vol. II, Country Studies, pp. 47–60.

D. Snow and R. Benford (1988) 'Ideology, Frame Resonance, and Participant Mobilization' in B. Klandermans, H. Kriesi and S. Tarrow (eds) *From Structure to Action: Social Movement Participation Across Cultures* (Greenwich: Conn.: JAI Press), pp. 197–217.

J. Steakley (2002) 'Selbstkritische Gedanken zur Mythologisierung der Homosexuallenverfolgung im Dritten Reich' in B. Jellonek and R. Lautmann (eds) *Nationalsozialistischer Terror gegen Homosexuelle, Verdrängt und ungesühnt* (Paderborn: Schöningh), pp. 55–68.

Stiftung, Heinrich-Boll (ed.) (1999) *Der homosexuellen NS-Opfer gedenken* (Berlin: Heinrich-Böll Stiftung).

C. Taylor (1992) *Multiculturalism and The Politics of Recognition* (Princeton: Princeton University Press).

A. von Wahl (2008) 'The Politics of Reparations: Why, When and How Democratic Governments Get Involved' in M. Berg and B. Schäfer (eds) *Historical Justice in International Perspective* (Cambridge: Cambridge University Press), pp. 39–68.

Without author (2006) 'Mal wieder die Frauen vergessen!' *EMMA* (September/October).

I. M. Young (1990). *Justice and the Politics of Difference* (Princeton: Princeton University Press).

R. Zweig (1987) *German Reparations and the Jewish World: A History of the Claims Conference* (Boulder: Westview Press).

Part IV

Politics of Justice and Reconciliation

8

Gender-Inclusivity in Transitional Justice Strategies: Women in Timor-Leste

Elisabeth Porter

Timor-Leste is proclaimed as a United Nations' success story, an example of how gender concerns and women's equality can be incorporated into peace building measures. There were groundbreaking results with a Gender Affairs Unit (GAU) in the United Nations (UN) Mission that worked with local and international women's groups to conduct democracy-training workshops and encourage women's participation in public life. Timor-Leste provides an apt case study of the past, present, and future continuum that is intrinsic to transitional justice. After a brief overview of the historical roots of the Timorese conflict, and an outline of examples that show UN gender-inclusivity, this chapter concentrates on the final report of the East Timor Commission for Reception, Truth and Reconciliation (CAVR) (*Chega,* 2006).[1] The Commission developed a gender-sensitive approach to seeking the truth about human rights violations that occurred 1974–99. While the Commission did integrate a gender perspective into its work, the recommendations of the Commission have not translated practically. However, there are many positive signs of a commitment to the promotion of equality for women.[2] This chapter will also show why broad understandings of justice are needed for culturally sensitive, holistic, transitional strategies.

Most East Timorese women and men live in rural villages. In addition to the domestic tasks of caring for children, the elderly and ill, gathering firewood and water, and cooking, women work alongside men in the fields. Outside of Dili, the capital, subsistence farming is the norm, where crop failure intensifies hardships, particularly in female-headed households. Timor-Leste 'holds first place in the global natal stakes, each female of child-bearing age responsible for 7.8 births' (Cotton,

2007: 458). Maternal mortality is estimated to be 800 per 100,000 live births, among the highest in the world (AusAID, 2008: 191). The UN Population Fund confirms poor nutrition, with 44 per cent of children under five 'being underweight, and 12 per cent showing indicators of wasting' (Cotton, 2007: 460). Despite Indonesia's attempts at development, 'Timor-Leste now ranks as the "worst performer" in East Asia and the Pacific in terms of human development' (Wandita et al., 2006: 286).[3] The statistics are stark. 'Forty per cent of the people in Timor-Leste still live in poverty (earning less than $US 1 a day), standards of education are among the lowest in the world and health services remain inadequate – all of which affects women disparately' (Wandita et al., 2006: 286–7).[4] As the least developed country in Asia, the challenges for Timor-Leste affect men as well as women in living with remnants of colonialism, high levels of poverty, rapid population growth, widespread unemployment, low skills and educational levels, minimal capacity in the public sector including service delivery in health and education, poor infrastructure, and a weak justice system. However, there are particular cultural and patriarchal norms that affect women specifically, and these relate primarily to early marriages at 15 with subsequent early pregnancies, the cultural acceptance of violence including domestic violence as normal, dowries which give men's families full right to control women, and to the notion that women humiliate their husbands if they stand for public positions.

East Timor conflict

East Timor was a Portuguese colony for more than 400 years.[5] The fall of the regime in Portugal, in April 1974, gave Portuguese colonial territories opportunities to exercise their right to self-determination. In East Timor, this precipitated a struggle for power between the main political parties. On 11 August 1975 Indonesia launched an armed invasion hoping to remove the Portuguese and establish control of the territory. The left wing Timorese party, Fretilin, responded with an armed insurrection and a brief civil war followed. The Portuguese colonial administration fled. Indonesia launched a full-scale invasion on 7 December 1975. Four other East Timorese political parties yielded to pressure from the Indonesian military to sign the Balibo Declaration proclaiming Portuguese Timor's integration with Indonesia. Fretilin, and its armed wing Falintil, retreated to the interior with thousands of civilians. In July 1976, the Indonesian Parliament declared East Timor its 27th province.[6] Thus began the war that lasted for 24 years, with great suffering caused by violations against citizens committed primarily by state agents in a climate of impunity. The bombings and military advances forced people to move frequently, and many died from hunger and disease. The 1991 Santa Cruz Massacre of young people by Indonesian security forces in Dili was filmed by a foreign journalist and helped to renew international efforts to alleviate East Timor's plight.

When Indonesian President Soeharto fell from power in 1998, change became possible. From June to the end of September 1999, the UN Mission of Support in East Timor (UNAMET) organized a referendum, typically referred to as the Popular Consultation, and supervised the ballot on 30 August 1999. The people voted overwhelmingly for independence. It was Indonesia's responsibility to maintain peaceful security. Immediately after the referendum, heavily armed militia groups, who were sympathetic to the integration of East Timor into Indonesia, goaded by factions within the Armed Forces of Indonesia, conducted a 'scorched earth' campaign whereby entire towns and villages were burned and looted, and people were attacked, forcibly evacuated, kidnapped, raped, or killed. The destruction of property was enormous. This violence resulted in the internal displacement of more than 300,000 people, with an additional 250,000–300,000 who voluntarily fled, or were forcibly taken, to West Timor (CAVR, 2006, 9.1.2–7). Although the country's youth did not experience the 1975 invasion with its subsequent bloodshed and repression, 'virtually the entire population was directly affected by the violence, intimidation, and destruction' following the referendum (Pigou, 2003: ii). Widows, who had known long-term suffering like the loss of a father in 1975 and a husband in 1999, felt that 'everything we had was gone for the second time' (in Pigou, 2003: 20).

In the wake of the post-referendum violence, the establishment of the International Force for East Timor (INTERFET), an Australian-led multinational stabilization force, attempted to restore peace and security from September 1999 to February 2000. From October 1999 to May 2002, the UN Transitional Administration in East Timor (UNTAET) held a mandate to provide transitional administration of the territory, including legislative and executive authority, the administration of justice, and preparing it for independence. Extensive authority was bestowed on the Special Representative of the Secretary General, the (late) Sérgio Vieira de Mello.[7] From May 2002 to May 2005, the UN Mission for Support for East Timor (UNMISET) provided backing to Timor-Leste's attempt to attain self-sufficiency. In the first four years since Timor-Leste's independence as a sovereign state on 20 May 2002, all the major institutions of state were established. Yet major youth unemployment, the growth of gang membership, major fissures within the ranks of the political elite, and simmering violence signalled potential for mass unrest. The resurgence of violence in 2006, between defence forces and rebel militia groups, produced more than 135,000 displaced persons. Between April and June 2006, the system of government effectively disintegrated. This disorder led to the collapse of the Alkatiri government, and a crisis following the 2007 parliamentary elections. With concern over the fragility of democratic governance and public security, the UN Integrated Mission in Timor (UNMIT) has provided support from August 2006 and is led by Ameerah Haq, a Bangladeshi woman (the mission is still ongoing). In February 2008, there was an assassination attempt on President Ramos-Horta by rebels, with a contingency of army mutineers stirring trouble. Any inference of political stability post-independence appeared a mirage. State building, nation building, and peace building are long-term processes (Porter, 2007).

During the brutal military occupation, women, like men, were deprived of food, displaced, detained, tortured, disappeared, denied self-determination, and killed. Women suffered when they were incarcerated, harassed, ostracized, and left as sole breadwinners for being part of resistance movements (or attached to men who were activists); as well as being sexually assaulted, raped, or taken as sexual slaves as intimidation against those in the resistance movements, or having known partners in the movements, or simply for being women. Forced sexual slavery with soldiers was common, with threats to harm family members if women did not comply. Gang rape was used as a tool of war, trafficking of girls and women occurred in West Timor camps, some forced sterilization was undertaken, and often wives were required to bury husbands and children who were killed by Indonesian militia (UNIFEM, 2004: 3–5). Violent masculinities manifest themselves when '"manliness" is equated with the sanctioned use of aggression, force and violence', particularly with the 'warrior/protector concept embedded in local traditions' (Myrttinen, 2005: 237–8). After the referendum, 'domestic violence became the country's most prevalent crime, comprising 40 per cent of all reported criminal cases in the year 2000' (Fairlie, 2002–03: 1081). Contributing reasons include the return of men who had participated in guerrilla warfare, were accustomed to conflict, and felt emasculated at the loss of their identity; and high levels of unemployment, which left them with few options for work, so frustrations were taken out on women.[8] In February 2000, training in gender and peacekeeping was provided to the military and civilian personnel, yet 'participants repeatedly pointed out the endemic problem of wife beating as a gender issue that could not be touched because it was "part of the culture"' (MacKay, 2005: 271).[9] Frequently, 'violence against women is not seen as a crime, but rather as a family problem to be resolved at the family or village level' (Soriano Menezes, 2009: 1).[10] We will return to this issue later.

The role of the UN in furthering gender justice

Having offered a brief overview of the conflict, we examine the role of the UN in integrating gender issues throughout its transitional justice programmes. The original organization of UNTAET included a Gender Affairs Unit, but senior UNTAET administrators thought it unnecessary and so did not create a specific budget. Throughout April to July 2000, it was established gradually with limited resources. Gender Focal Points were appointed in 13 districts to work with the Unit. Sherill Whittington, who headed the Unit, signalled the key successful practice, that the 'GAU opened the door to the women of East Timor from the very outset', including employing East Timorese counterparts to the international staff in the GAU (2003: 49). The GAU consulted women's NGOs closely. The United Nation's Development Fund for Women (UNIFEM), regional trainers, and UNTAET trained women in political skills workshops aimed towards increasing informed decisions about running as electoral candidates. UNIFEM worked with the GAU to assist *Rede Feto* (Women's Network of East Timor) to implement activities that would increase women's voter participation. UNTAET used incentives, like the promise of transport for voters, and media access for candidates. The Unit conducted gender training in induction sessions for management, and international and national civilian police. The Unit advocated gender equality through capacity-building workshops, the development of training materials, and gender analysis of legislature, It maintained networks with local women, and sought to mainstream a gender perspective throughout UNTAET. It was the first functioning GAU in a Peacekeeping Mission. Vieira de Mello concluded, 'I did not think a Gender Unit would help rebuild institutions from the ashes of what the militia left. I was wrong' (in UNIFEM, 2004: 1).

Timor-Leste has a history whereby, in addition to some women being guerrilla fighters, women's activism grew under conditions of colonialism and war, and continued to adapt during each new conflict crisis. The strength of local women's organizations that arose during the years of resistance to Indonesian control was an important factor in ensuring a specific emphasis on gender in the transitional process. It is estimated that there are over 500 international and national NGOs operating in Timor-Leste with an increasing number committed to gender issues (Trembath and Grenfell, 2007: 41). In June 2000, the First Congress of Women of Timor, *Lorosae*, was supported by UNTAET and organized by *Rede Feto*, and brought together 500 women whose priorities included participation in decision-making, justice, reparations, education, literacy, health, bottom-up economic growth, and development of an inclusive constitution (UNIFEM, 2004: 5). A Platform for Action developed at this Congress, demanding programmes that support women's participation in decision-making. Participants recognized the need for reconciliation, a truth commission, a special court for women, and rehabilitation programmes for victims of violence (Wandita et al., 2006: 293). A group working on the constitution organized meetings with women's groups, which led to a Women's Charter of Rights in Timor-Leste. The recognition of women's rights is included in the constitution, an achievement that can be partially attributed to the effectiveness of strong women's advocacy.

In the August 2001 elections, 27 per cent of those elected to the Constituent Assembly to administer the territory were women, one of the highest representations in the Asia-Pacific region. The wife of the then President writes, 'many women Parliamentarians report that they feel ill-equipped, both technically and in terms of experience, to be effective as legislators and representatives of their constituencies. They also claim to face discrimination and prejudice, and struggle to combine public duties with motherhood and onerous family obligations' (Sword Gusmão, 2006: 20).[11] All major human rights treaties were ratified in December 2002, including the Convention on the Elimination of All Forms of Discrimination Against Women (CEDAW). Yet, in reporting on the gender responsiveness of the transitional process, Whittington (2003) deplored the lack of gender analysis or sex disaggregation in reports on education, health, development, or poverty. However, the concerted attempt to integrate gender concerns into all aspects of UN Missions paved the way for a commitment to a gender-inclusive truth commission.

Commission for Reception, Truth and Reconciliation

The remainder of this chapter examines the extent to which the Commission was gender-inclusive, and effective in its recommendations. It will be argued that it was inclusive, but only partially effective in applying its recommendations, for reasons that relate to the priority placed on reconciliation. Prior to the Commission, formal procedures to address human rights crimes committed in East Timor had established a UN Commission of Enquiry (1999), and a special Indonesian Investigative Commission (1999–2000). A Serious Crimes Unit (SCU) to investigate war crimes, crimes against humanity, torture, sexual offences, and murder was established by UNTAET, and cases ready for trial were transferred to a Special Panel for Serious Crimes (2000–05). Human rights activists sought complementary additional processes. In June 2000, members of civil society, the Catholic Church, community leaders, and international experts met to consider transitional justice mechanisms in a workshop supported by UNTAET's Human Rights Unit.[12] The Unit conducted consultations in the 13 districts, and found vast community support for a commission that included truth-seeking, justice, reconciliation, and victim support. For many Timorese women, like women in other poor, conflict-affected countries, local notions of justice are tied with exigencies of human security, and the urgency of meeting human needs including health, nutrition, and socioeconomic sustainability.[13] Additionally, Timorese local, informal, indigenous justice systems are strong, and there is slow acceptance by some, and ignorance by others, of international human rights law. Men dominate as village and neighbourhood heads in traditional justice systems to settle community disputes, including domestic violence.[14] The Commission for Reception, Truth and Reconciliation (CAVR) thus incorporated the community demand for a reconciliation that did not forget justice and was culturally sensitive to local practices of justice. CAVR's mandate was to establish the truth about human rights violations and 'less serious crimes' committed during the political conflicts from 25 April 1974 to 25 October 1999; to assist in the reintegration of those who had committed these crimes via a community-based reconciliation process; and to help restore the dignity of victims of human rights violations.[15] On 21 January 2002, five men and two women were sworn in as Commissioners. Women's groups were involved in the consultative process surrounding the appointment process. On 15 May 2002, 10 of the 29 Regional Commissioners sworn in were women. The Commission collected 7824 statements from 13 districts.

UN Regulation 2001/10 required a gender-sensitive approach to be integrated into all aspects of CAVR. The Commission explicitly encouraged work practices to maximize opportunities for women to contribute in diverse ways. Measures to enhance women's voices included:

- proactive outreach work to encourage women's participation
- liaising with grassroots women's NGO networks to connect with their constituencies

- having national thematic hearings on women which included female victims and experts on gendered human rights violations
- support given to women witnesses
- devoting almost 10 per cent of Community Profile Workshops to participation only by women, given the culture of silence that values virginity and where women can be blamed for experiencing sexual violence
- providing women with the option of in-camera testimony (although all women chose public testimony)
- inclusion of women in statement-taking teams and training statement-takers on gender issues
- the development of an oral history archive of 200 women's testimonies.

(Nesiah, 2006: 19)

Despite a commitment to fill quotas of 30 per cent of the Commission's positions for women, cultural patriarchal norms, particularly in rural areas where women have not been as exposed to ideas of gender equality and have feared intimidation if they stand for office, made it difficult to recruit the desired proportion of women into district teams. Also, staff members needed to live away from home during field activities, posing problems for women with family responsibilities. In striving to overcome these barriers, women adopted informal ways of meeting rural women and visited many in their homes or villages to hear their concerns. For example, for single women returnees from West Timor, daily survival was difficult. The women and children were in poor health caused by long-term malnourishment in refugee camps. On their return, many planted crops, but had to wait for the harvest to feed their families.

Three aspects of the Commission's findings are significant: the nature of gender-based abuse; the public hearings on women; and women's truth-telling. First, the Commission found that 'although women were the victims of the same range of human rights violations as men, almost all cases of sexual violence ... were committed against women' (CAVR, 2006, 7.7.1–1). The Commission documented 853 reported instances of sexual violations; 46.1 per cent of these were rapes, 27.1 per cent were sexual harassment and other acts of sexual violence, and 26.8 per cent involved sexual slavery, with 93.3 per cent of all violations attributed to Indonesian security forces and auxiliaries (CAVR, 2006, 7.7.1–7). It was a widely accepted practice that members of the security forces raped and sexually tortured women while on official duty. Galuh Wandita, Karen Campbell-Nelson, and Manuela Leong Pereira (2006)[16] write with insight on CAVR's findings on gender-based abuse, summarizing the reasons underlying the violence. One group of targeted women were directly involved in resisting the Indonesian occupation as combatants, members of clandestine groups, or in playing a key logistical role by providing food or medicines to resistance members. A second targeted group were women related to men involved in the resistance or suspected of collaboration with the opposition. Both groups were targeted as political activists. A third group, with no clear connection to the resistance, suffered in a military operation as women. In all three groups, girls and women were detained, tortured, or sexually abused (Wandita et al., 2006: 290).

Second, the Commission conducted eight national public hearings and care was taken to ensure balance in the witness selection, including testimonies from men and women from different districts talking about different periods of the conflict with different perpetrator groups. In April 2003, there was a public hearing on 'women in conflict' and, in March 2004, one on 'children and the conflict'. These public hearings were broadcast on live national radio and on television with deeply emotional, disturbing, and compelling first-hand testimonies as women relived terrible times, often pausing amidst tears to regain composure, and exhibiting great dignity and inner strength. Most of the victims were young women when violated, and many were middle-aged at the time of giving their evidence, having 'harboured their darkest memories in silence' (CAVR, 2006, 7.7.1–5). During the hearing on women in conflict, activists from diverse women's groups presented a substantial submission on behalf of the women of Timor-Leste, demanding social and psychological support, and gender equality understood as inclusive in decision-making processes.

Third, 'truth reports are designed to relate what survivors most commonly refer to as the unspeakable' (Daly, 2008: 26), but 'no truth commission report can explain in a convincing and satisfying way the mysteries of human nature, the banality of evil' (2008: 27). The Commissioners prided themselves on careful listening to those who suffered abuses, whose voices related terrible experiences. The stories reveal extremes of human dignity in the face of human degradation. Despite the Commission's attempts to encourage women's participation, 'at the close of field operations only 21.4 per cent of deponents who provided statements were women' (CAVR, 2006, 1.6–174); which was 1642 statements from a total of 7668 (CAVR, 2006, 7.7.1–21). As has happened in other commissions, women typically testify about what happened to their sons, husbands, brothers, or fathers during conflict.

Heavy cultural taboos and personal shame often prevent women from giving detailed accounts of their suffering. Victims of sexual violence are vulnerable to community isolation and discrimination, stigmatization of children born through rape, being abandoned by one's spouse, inability to find a man willing to marry, and an overwhelming sense of humiliation when known as 'military wives' because family or personal 'honour' is violated. The Commission was sensitive to these cultural barriers on talking about sexual violations, using women statement-takers and victim support staff, and involving women in community discussions. Surprisingly, 'women spoke openly of the sexual violence committed against them, challenging the widely-held view that East Timorese culture forbade discussion of this subject' (CAVR, 2006, 10.3.2–134).

As mentioned earlier, CAVR linked practices of reconciliation with indigenous notions of justice that were familiar to victims. CAVR instigated Community Reconciliation Procedures (CRP) for acts like theft, minor assault, arson, intimidation, killing of livestock, or the destruction of crops. The procedures drew on traditional justice practices that involved local leaders and spiritual practices of confession and forgiveness, as well as principles of arbitration and mediation. In traditional customs of *kasu sala,* a traditional mediator rolls out a mat to establish facts, identify the wronged and the wrong doer, and to see what compensation is owed to the wronged party. Victims' hearings were held in the 65 sub-districts. An estimated 40,000 community members attended these hearings and 1379 perpetrators completed CRP (CAVR, 2006, 1.5–126). The UN regulation to be gender-inclusive meant that at least one of the CRP panel members at each hearing was a woman. During CRP, victims could make a statement about the incident under enquiry, question the deponent, tell their story to the community, and confront the perpetrator about the harm they had suffered. A panel then brokered an agreement for the perpetrator to complete 'acts of reconciliation' such as a public apology, community service, or more explicit reparations which sought to compensate the victim for possessions lost, stolen, or destroyed, such as the donation of animals or money to the victims, in order to be reaccepted into the community. In rural hearings, victims were given ceremonial objects like hand-woven textiles, coral necklaces, or ornaments. Victims who had urgent needs identified during panels were referred to the victim support staff. In duplicating similar traditional practices, CAVR's assumption was, that 'the reconciliation procedures serve as an important counterpart to the general principle of strict criminal liability because they make the admission of wrongdoing and the expression of remorse in an act of reconciliation a viable form of rendering justice to victims' (Stahn, 2001: 963), challenging narrow western notions of justice and reconciliation. Patrick Burgess[17] reflects on the interim review conducted by CAVR in mid-2003 whereby victims who had been part of CRP stated 'they felt more respected within their communities and there had been a change of relationship with the perpetrator' (2006: 187).

In addition to CRP, six healing workshops (one for women only), which combined interactive discussions, group counselling, singing, and art were attended by 82 women and 74 men. Each participant received an Urgent Reparations grant (CAVR, 2006, 10.3.3–143). The Urgent Reparations scheme addressed immediate physical, psychological, and economic needs of victims. Short-term alleviation of suffering was provided for direct survivors of violations such as rape, imprisonment, and torture and those who had suffered indirectly through the abduction, disappearance, or killing of family members. 'The harms-based extension of the notion of victim has great potential for engendering reparations' (Rubio-Marín, 2006: 31). Emphasis on primary beneficiaries allows for widows, whose husbands have been executed or have disappeared, and mothers who bore children through rape to qualify for reparations. A dependent's suffering, anxiety, hopelessness, and despair is 'treated as a direct violation' (Goldblatt, 2006: 80) that requires attention. CAVR was struck by the humble requests of survivors, seeking perpetrator accountability and simple assistance to enable them and their children to participate meaningfully in the fledgling democracy. The types of reparations offered were small, such as $US 200, urgent medical or psycho-social care, equipment for the disabled, setting up of survivors' self-help groups, commemoration of an event, provision of tombstones, or contracts with churches or counselling groups who could provide sustained help. Typically, grant recipients used the money to purchase food, clothing, shelter, medical treatment, the education of children, or to start income-generating pursuits.

For its long-term recommendations, the Commission placed 'reparations in a human rights framework' specifically linked with 'truth, justice and reparations', in order to restore victim dignity and begin to repair damaged relationships (CAVR, 2006, part 11–12.2). Yet, when reparations are tied to participation in truth-telling mechanisms, those who have not participated are deprived of access; a concern in other commissions. Including direct and indirect suffering expands the pool of beneficiaries. Hence, the guiding principle adopted for the reparations programme was that 'at least 50 per cent of program resources should be directed to female beneficiaries' (CAVR, 2006, part 11–12.6).[18] This is a proactive effort to address gender inequities that may arise in the formulation and implementation of reparations policies, in recognizing that fewer women participated in the statement-taking process. Beneficiaries include victims of torture, people with disabilities due to gross human rights violations, victims of sexual violence, widows whose husbands disappeared or were killed, and single mothers who have become primary breadwinners through being affected by conflict. The promised programmes include scholarships for school-aged children until they turn 18 years. Widows and survivors of sexual violence have been promised social services incorporating rehabilitation, skills training, and access to micro-credit for livelihood activities. Given that 'virtually none of the reparations measures' recommended or approved in commissions are ever implemented, with exceptions of South Africa and genocide survivors in Rwanda, the 'urgent reparations scheme implemented in Timor-Leste', while modest, was important (Rubio-Marín, 2006: 26).

In developing its recommendations, the Commission sought ideas from different sectors, including civil society groups. Women's groups conducted parallel research projects in order to provide informative recommendations to be included in the final report. Despite the fact that gender equality sits uncomfortably with male-dominated community traditions, final recommendations encourage the implementation of policies 'that ensure that the fruits of development are enjoyed equitably' (CAVR, 2006, part 11–3.2.6). Thus 11 specific recommendations are directed toward developing a culture of equality under the category 'Women', acknowledging women's crucial role in the diaspora, in resistance movements, and in maintaining families. The recommendations seek to address:

- individual needs of women victims
- social needs to counter prejudice against victims of sexual violence and outlaw further violence
- security needs to ensure gender-sensitive practices in security sector reform
- support of women's initiatives in the prevention and resolution of conflicts and peace building
- 'mainstreaming gender equality and the full participation of women in the economic, social, cultural and political life of Timor-Leste'.

(CAVR, 2006, part 11: 4.1)[19]

During CAVR's processes, the 'multilayered emphasis on community participation, perpetrator reintegration, truth-telling, and the integration of local customs and spiritual values' (Freeman, 2006: 35), combined with broad ideas on justice, is a compelling model for societies in democratic transition. Herein lies a major problem. In November 2008, the Timor-Leste Parliament postponed a debate over CAVR's recommendations, seeking further discussions on ceasing prosecutions for human rights violations perpetrated during the Indonesian occupation. This has been delaying the application of reparations as a demonstration of justice. Some of the recommendations can be acted on by NGOs, church and community groups, and individuals within communities. However, the targeted reparations programme requires funding and government support.

Recommendations documented by CAVR from healing workshops and women's hearings in 2003 and 2004 found that almost 50 per cent of women requested practical government assistance for access to health services and adequate housing, assurances of a good price for agricultural products, and guarantees of peace (Wandita et al., 2006: 299). The demand for justice as criminal prosecution was the third most ranked. Yet when the International Centre for Transitional Justice conducted 12 focus groups with five women-only groups, justice was high on the agenda, but this is a justice tied also to broad notions of human security and the ability to meet everyday needs. Former female political prisoners in Dili, 'acknowledged the success of removing an oppressive occupying regime, but were virtually unanimous in their concerns that independence has yet to be realized for many, as living conditions in Timor-Leste have remained extremely difficult' (Pigou, 2003: 16). The women refer, specifically, to unemployment, high educational fees, the loss of principal breadwinners, and the continuation of political corruption, collusion, and nepotism. As one woman said, as a victim 'of colonization who lost family, home, and husband, I feel that the liberation hasn't brought any advantage to my life. When justice is upheld, then the independence, which is obtained by bloodshed, is a true liberation. So, justice is the answer to all sufferings' (in Pigou, 2003: 19). This concept of justice entails the meeting of everyday needs and support to overcome psychological trauma, and compensate for losses. Responding to broad understandings of justice are more likely to prompt locally meaningful transitional justice strategies.[20]

The relationship between justice and reconciliation is undoubtedly complex. It seems to be the case that 'East Timorese leaders have opted for reconciliation and restorative justice while seeking a healing process in advocating good governance and alleviating pressing socio-economic needs' (Kingston, 2006: 273).[21] Restorative justice seeks to rebuild broken relationships and communities. On the surface, it may appear to compromise liberal, legal requirements of accountability and formal justice. Instead, Christine Bell and Catherine O'Rourke (2007) suggest that restorative justice approaches may be more accessible to women, given their flexibility in process, inclusivity, and ability to address survivor needs; but they offer a caution that 'restorative' is akin to 'post-conflict reconstruction', which may mean asking women to go back to a set of relationships that return them to a situation of injustice. Potentially, reconciliation can transform antagonistic attitudes and practices fuelled by hatred into new relationships that emerge through forgiveness, generosity of spirit, and an embrace of difference. The realities are thorny. 'The Timor-Leste leadership has chosen to sacrifice the pursuit of criminal accountability. Caught between the government's mobilization efforts for reconciliation with Indonesia and sectors of civil society that opposed this position, the soft voices of victims asking for reparations are barely audible' (Wandita, 2006: 289).[22] The reasons for connecting restorative justice with reconciliation are nuanced.

Former President Xanana Gusmão, in an interview with Jeffrey Kingston, expressed concern that prosecutions of Indonesians would open old wounds and said, 'We also must respect the courage of the Indonesians in accepting our independence and not disrupt the progress toward democratization by demanding formal justice' (in Kingston, 2006: 282). This response is in the spirit of traditional practices where the suspect's family can meet with the victim's family to beg pardon and ask the family to withdraw the complaint so as not to jeopardize relationships between families. In this case, not insisting on prosecutions has not been because of expressions of forgiveness from Indonesians. Kingston maintains that Gusmão 'has made a political choice that trying perpetrators must be subordinated to improving living conditions, governance, healing, and social justice' (2006: 289). This is consistent with local women's priorities on human security as integral to gender justice. Certainly the provision of nutrition, clean water, decent housing with sanitation, basic education, medical care, and psycho-spiritual counsel are crucial components of social justice and inclusive citizenship, but when these are at the expense of justice as accountability, political stability is fragile. The emphasis of the current President, José Ramos-Horta, and the current Prime Minister, Xanana Gusmão, on reconciliation is not merely politically expedient in order to appease Indonesia, or to stay aligned with leading donors, but appears to be based on a deep desire to shape public expectations toward healing through peaceful and democratic development.[23] Yet material hardship continues for the majority of Timorese and impunity for crimes remains an obstacle to reconciliation.

Conclusion

The Constitution's recognition of the principles of gender equality as fundamental rights and citizenship (Article 17), and equal participation of women and men as fundamental to democracy (Article 62), has translated into significant progress. In the elections of 2007, women achieved 29.2 per cent representation in the national Parliament, 19 of a total of 65, including women heading key Ministries.[24] The Office for the Promotion of Equality, set up in 2001 to advance gender equality, is now the Office of the Secretary of State for the Promotion of Equality (SEPI) and has achieved positive outcomes, especially in forming laws on domestic violence and developing a network of services for survivors of the conflict. The traditional *adat* system of justice administered primarily by men continues to uphold traditional gendered values that favour men. Hence SEPI and women's groups are seeking 'to make *suco* (local government) councils and chiefs more proactive in reducing domestic violence and assisting beaten wives' (AusAID, 2008: 196), including passing a 2004 decree permitting women to be elected as *suco* or *aldeia* (village) chiefs. The Judicial System Monitoring Programme, an NGO founded in 2001 to monitor processes dealing with perpetrators of human rights abuses, has extended its remit to aid the fledgling judicial system. Its Women's Justice Unit undertakes training to improve the justice sectors' understanding of women's rights, and the Victim Support Service provides legal assistance to victims of gender-based violence. In March 2009, there was the enactment of the Penal Code which criminalizes sexual offences as a violation of women's integrity and security.

Currently, UNMIT's mandate includes the mainstreaming of gender and assisting in the development of gender equality and women's empowerment, and has demonstrated an impressive array of outputs that coordinate the furthering of gender justice. There is massive international donor presence, and support in strengthening security, civil society, and women's equality. The Second International Women for Peace Conference, held in March 2009, formulated a Dili Declaration on Women, Peace and Security 2009, as well as a Resolution on Gender Justice submitted to the Government of Timor-Leste. This seeks actions on prosecution for crimes committed in 1999, and reinforces a broad notion of gender justice to include victim/survivor reparations of legal and medical support, psycho-social support, social protection, education, livelihood skills development, and economic opportunities. In August 2009, Timor-Leste presented its first report on implementing CEDAW. The UN Committee commenting on this report acknowledges positive progress, but expresses concern:

- with small numbers of women in leadership positions
- that women's ability to access legal justice is limited by illiteracy, persistence of traditional justice systems, and lack of information about their rights
- with the persistence of trafficking
- with 'the prevalence of a patriarchal ideology in the State party'.

(CEDAW/C/TLS/CO/1)

A NGOs Alternative Report (2009) presents responses from more than 87 NGOs. Of particular relevance is their critique of a lack of access to justice because the laws are written in Portuguese, the language of the minority elite, there are only four district courts, and women are discouraged from pursuing a lawsuit to preserve family pride. The Report indicates that the state has not incorporated CEDAW provisions into national legislation, nor tackled the problems of human rights violations against women (2009: 23). The commitment of local activists, men and women, to both human rights and local culture indicates 'the scope for potentially constructive interaction between these different constructions of justice and appropriate behaviour' (Brown, 2009: 155). However, increasing numbers of activists, educated Timorese, and diasporic Timorese recognize that 'notions of human rights and of gender equality are perhaps the most contentious, confusing and challenging for customary approaches' in terms of differing interpretations and practices of justice (Brown, 2009: 154–5).

Gender justice has not been realized in Timor-Leste. Perpetrators who committed human rights crimes remain free. Poverty is endemic. Gender discrimination is common. The implementation of reparations is almost non-existent. However, Timor-Leste provides a genuine attempt to put gender concerns at the centre of transitional justice processes. There have been exemplary gender-inclusive processes in seeking the truth about the violations women experienced, and seeking to include women in decision-making processes. Some of the deficiencies of the process seem to indicate the overwhelming nature of the task of nation building, the struggle in learning new skills of democratic governance, and the need to prioritize public security and develop the institutional aspects of state building.

We have seen that, in Timor-Leste, gender justice entails both ideals of human rights law and legal accountability, as well as practical notions of compensation for trauma sufferers and assistance with ongoing material hardships. These measures of psychological wellbeing, self-confidence, socioeconomic security, and inclusion in all peace building processes are essential for Timorese women to subjectively experience justice. What we can learn from this case study is that this broadening of understandings of justice illuminates the need for holistic approaches to transitional justice strategies that also are culturally sensitive and attentive to people's needs. While the women's networks and grassroots groups remain as active as they currently are in responding to these approaches, they need to be adequately resourced by the Government of the Democratic Republic of Timor-Leste, and by the international donor community, in addition to being supported with ongoing capacity-building in core skills. There are enough grounds to be optimistic that the historic work begun by the UN Gender Affairs Unit is continuing.

Notes

1. *Chega* is the Portuguese for 'enough'. The acronym CAVR is derived from the Portuguese name, *Comissão de Acolhimento Verdade e Reconciliação de Timor-Leste*. The term *acolhimento* means more than the English 'reception', it 'includes notions of welcoming, accepting, offering hospitality and forgiveness' and confirms mutual respect which was directed particularly toward refugees returning from West Timor.
2. The author visited Timor-Leste in October 2009 on an Australian Government AusAID funded project on 'Women, Peace and Security in the Asia-Pacific region' and had in-depth interviews with key persons and groups who are working to further women's equality. She was impressed with the collaborative work that local women and men and the international community are undertaking to support gender inclusivity in all processes and address gender equality and justice.
3. This was derived from 2003 statistics from the UN Development Programme *Human Development Report* (in Wandita et al., 2006).
4. Literacy rates taken by the Human Development Report 1995–2005 indicate 52 per cent literacy for women and 65 per cent for men (AusAID, 2008: 82). Other reports indicate 'almost two-thirds of adult women are illiterate' (NGOs Working Group, 2009: 39).
5. East Timor and Timor-Leste are used interchangeably, but Timor-Leste is used for events occurring after independence.
6. This was not recognized by the UN, who, from 1960, listed East Timor as a non-self-governing territory.
7. Vieira de Mello was East Timor's Transitional Administrator from 1999–2002. When UN High Commissioner for Human Rights, he was killed by a bomb attack in Baghdad on 19 August 2003.

8. See Fairlie's (2002–03) account of how the Indonesian Criminal Code, which applied to East Timor, failed to prohibit acts of domestic violence or rape when the perpetrator had coerced the victim into marriage.
9. MacKay (2005: 276) explains that lessons learnt in this training include the need for differing materials on gender, culture and human rights for pre-deployment training and in-mission training.
10. Flora Soriano Menezes writes as a legal researcher in the Women's Justice Unit, monitoring the treatment of women in cases of sexual assault and domestic violence.
11. This need for capacity-building and skills training was mentioned repeatedly in interviews the author conducted in 2009 in Timor-Leste.
12. This development is unique in the UN's legal practice (Stahn, 2001: 956).
13. See Porter (2006) for an analysis of how attentiveness to people's needs is requisite to responding meaningfully, and with compassion, to those who suffer injustices.
14. The advantage of going through grassroots structures with village elders is speed of resolution, a practice encouraged by the police.
15. Freeman suggests that it is innovative in combining a truth commission 'in tandem with a hybrid criminal court' with distinctions between 'harmful acts' and 'serious criminal offences' (2006: 77).
16. Wandita worked with the Human Rights Unit of UNTAET and was a member of CAVR's Steering Committee, a Deputy Director of the Commission and Program Manager. See her compelling testimony (2007: 3) detailing her knowledge of more than one hundred victims of rape and sexual violence. Campbell-Nelson coordinated the women's research team at CAVR and helped to write parts of the final report. Leong Pereira was Executive Director of the NGO *Fokupers*.
17. Burgess was the Director of Human Rights in UNTAET and UNMISET (2000–03) and Principal Legal Counsel for CAVR.
18. See Nesiah (2006: 37) for a summary of ways that commissions have addressed gender equity in design and implementation of reparations programs.
19. 'Women and *Chega*: Making Recommendations Reality' is a useful document. See www.cavr-timorleste.org/en/dissemination.htm (accessed 20 February 2009).
20. The *gacaca* hearings in Rwanda also reflect the need for justice and reconciliation to be linked to cultural traditions.
21. In March 2005 a bilateral Commission of Truth and Friendship (CTF), the first CTF between two states with a mandate on restorative justice, was established. While the CTF accepts institutional responsibility of the pro-autonomy militias as direct perpetrators (CTF, 2008: 114), its terms of reference precluded prosecutions, hence the reprieve even for 'crimes against humanity and war crimes' (Hirst, 2008: 18). Similarly, the Indonesian ad hoc Human Rights Court for East Timor set up in 2003 proved 'ineffective in handing prosecutions' (Wandita et al., 2006: 326), there have been many acquittals and 'incredibly lenient sentences' (Reiger, 2006: 156).
22. In particular, this refers to the leadership of Ramos-Horta and Gusmão. Dissent is often silenced by a reluctance to speak against government members who include revered leaders of the resistance.
23. The author's view on this has been influenced by reading Kingston's (2006) article quoting Gusmão's open reflections to him.

24. In 2010, women hold Ministerial positions in portfolios of finance, justice, and social solidarity, as well as the positions of Prosecutor-General, Vice-Minister for Health, and the Secretary of State for the Promotion of Equality. A Parliamentary Women's Caucus seeks to mainstream gender.

References

AusAID (2008) *Violence Against Women in Melanesia and East Timor. Building on the Global and Regional Promising Approaches* (Canberra: AusAID, Australian Government).

C. Bell and C. O'Rourke (2007) 'Does Feminism Need a Theory of Transitional Justice? An Introductory Essay', *The International Journal of Transitional Justice,* Vol. 1, 23–44.

M. A. Brown (2009) 'Security, development and the nation-building agenda – East Timor', *Conflict, Security & Development,* Vol. 9 No. 2, 141–64.

P. Burgess (2006) 'A new approach to restorative justice – East Timor's Community Reconciliation Processes', in N. Roht-Arriaza and J. Mariezcurrena (eds) *Transitional Justice in the Twenty-First Century. Beyond Truth versus Justice* (Cambridge: Cambridge University Press), pp. 176–205.

Commission for Reception, Truth and Reconciliation (CAVR) (2006) *Chega! The Report of the Commission for Reception, Truth and Reconciliation in Timor Leste (CAVR),* available at www.cavr-timorleste.org/en/chegaReport.htm (accessed 13 January 2009).

Committee on the Elimination of Discrimination against Women (2009) *Concluding observations of the Committee on the Elimination of Discrimination against Women. Timor Leste,* CEDAW/C/TLS/CO/1, 7 August 2009.

J. Cotton (2007) 'Timor-Leste and the discourse of state failure', *Australian Journal of International Affairs,* Vol. 61 No. 4, 455–70.

E. Daly (2008) 'Truth Skepticism: An Inquiry into the Value of Truth in Times of Transition', *The International Journal of Transitional Justice,* Vol. 2, 23–41.

M. A. Fairlie (2002–03) 'Affirming Brahimi: East Timor makes the case for a model criminal code', *American University International Law Review,* Vol. 18, 1059–102.

M. Freeman (2006) *Truth Commissions and Procedural Fairness* (Cambridge: Cambridge University Press).

B. Goldblatt (2006) 'Evaluating the Gender Content of Reparations: Lessons from South Africa', in R. Rubio-Marín (ed.) *Whatever Happened to the Women? Gender and Reparations for Human Rights Violations* (New York: Social Science Research Council), pp. 48–91.

M. Hirst (2008) *Too Much Friendship, Too Little Truth: Monitoring Report on the Commission of Truth and Friendship in Indonesia and Timor-Leste* (Menteng-Jakarta Pusat: International Centre for Transitional Justice).

Indonesia – East Timor Commission of Truth and Friendship (CTF) (2008) *From Remembering Comes Hope: Final Report of The Commission of Truth and Friendship Indonesia – Timor-Leste* (Denpasar).

J. Kingston (2006) 'Balancing Justice and Reconciliation in East Timor', *Critical Asian Studies,* Vol. 38 No. 3, 271–302.

A. Mackay (2005) 'Mainstreaming Gender in United Nations Peacekeeping Training: Examples from East Timor, Ethiopia, and Eritrea', in D. Mazurana, A.

Raven-Roberts and J. Parpart (eds) *Gender, Conflict, and Peacekeeping* (Lanham, MD: Littlefield Publishers, Inc.), pp. 265–79.

F. S. Menezes (2009) 'Interaction between formal and traditional justice systems. Local justice and formal justice: can the two systems work together in Timor-Leste?', *Second International Conference: Women for Peace.* Dili, 5–6 March 2009.

H. Myrttinen (2005) 'Masculinities, Violence and Power in Timor Leste', *Revue Lusotopie,* Vol. 12 No. 1–2, 233–44.

V. Nesiah (2006) *Truth Commissions and Gender: Principles, Policies, and Procedures* (New York: International Centre for Transitional Justice).

NGOs Working Group (2009) *Implementation of CEDAW in Timor-Leste.*

P. Pigou (2003) *Crying Without Tears. In Pursuit of Justice and Reconciliation in Timor-Leste: Community Perspectives and Expectations* (New York: International Centre for Transitional Justice).

E. Porter (2007) *Peacebuilding: Women in international perspective* (London and New York: Routledge).

E. Porter (2006) 'Can Politics Practice Compassion', *Hypatia,* Vol. 21 No. 4: 97–123.

C. Reiger (2006) 'Hybrid attempts at accountability for serious crimes in Timor Leste', in N. Roht-Arriaza and J. Mariezcurrena (eds) *Transitional Justice in the Twenty-First Century. Beyond Truth versus Justice* (Cambridge: Cambridge University Press), pp. 143–70.

R. Rubio-Marín (2006) 'The Gender of Reparations: Setting the Agenda', in R. Rubio-Marín (ed.) *What Happened to the Women? Gender and Reparations for Human Rights Violations* (New York: Social Science Research Council), pp. 20–47.

C. Stahn (2001) 'Accommodating Individual Criminal Responsibility and National Reconciliation: UN Truth Commission for East Timor', *American Journal of International Law,* Vol. 95, 952–66.

K. Sword Gusmão (2006) 'Women and Children First', *The Sydney Morning Herald,* 11–12 November, p. 29.

A. Trembath and D. Grenfell (2007) *Mapping the Pursuit of Gender Equality. Non-Government and International Agency Activity in Timor-Leste* (Melbourne: Globalism Institute, RMIT University).

UNIFEM (2004) *Gender Profile of the Conflict in Timor-Leste,* available at www.womenwarpeace.org/webfm_send/749 (accessed 13 January 2009).

G. Wandita (2007) 'Rape and Sexual Violence in the context of the Popular Consultation in East Timor 1999', Statement given at the Truth and Friendship Commission public hearing Jakarta, 29 March 2007, available at www.ictj.org/static/Asia/Indonesia/Galuh.hearing.eng.pdf (accessed 22 December 2008).

G. Wandita, K. Campbell-Nelson and M. Pereira Leong (2006) 'Learning to Engender Reparations in Timor-Leste: Reaching Out to Female Victims', in R. Rubio-Marín (ed.) *What Happened to the Women? Gender and Reparations for Human Rights Violations* (New York: Social Science Research Council), pp. 284–334.

S. Whittington (2003) 'Experience and Lessons Learned in UN Transitional Administration for East Timor', in *Economic and Social Commission for Asia Pacific: Putting Gender Mainstreaming into Practice, ST/ESCAP/2254* (New York: United Nations), pp. 47–51.

9

Frau Mata Hari on Trial: Seduction, Espionage, and Gendered Abjection in Reunifying Germany

Magdalena Zolkos

'Gender turn' in the politics of reconciliation and transitional justice

Recently, the notion of gender has been employed as an epistemological and critical category in the study of transitional justice, reconciliation, and historical memory. Most of the relevant studies have been singular or comparative analyses of a predominantly empirical and/or socio-legal character.[1] Also, in that context, important feminist contributions to these debates have discussed doing justice for sexual violence in post-war and/or post-conflict settings, with particular regard to the (inadequate) recognition of sexual violence as a strategy of war, and as a war crime in the Balkans, Rwanda, Sierra Leone, and elsewhere.[2] At the same time, however, so far there have been few attempts at *theorizing* gender as a modality of reconciliation and/or transitional justice,[3] in contrast to, for instance, the 'gender turn' in the Holocaust studies.[4]

The current debates on gender in transitional justice might suggest that, all their merits notwithstanding, the interdisciplinary project of 'gendering' the politics of reconciliation and transitional justice remains not only under-theorized, but perhaps also insufficiently reflexive about its own normative and disciplinary presuppositions.[5] In an attempt to change that state of affairs, the *International Journal of Transitional Justice* published, in 2007, an important and long-awaited issue on gender and transitional justice. Most of its contributions, while different in scope and focus, mapped critical and normative patterns of advocacy of women's inclusion and empowerment in transitional contexts. Importantly, the processes and institutions of transitional justice and reconciliation were identified as insufficiently attentive to the gendered aspects of historical violence and injustice. The contributors critiqued the lack of institutional 'atunement' to the category of gender, and to gendered narratives and affects. They have advocated different ways of achieving women's inclusion and empowerment in transitional and reconciliatory situations so that it becomes epistemically and politically possible to address historical injustice and past violence as *gendered events*. For example, in their important study of underenforcement and intersectionality Fionnuala Ní Aoláin and Eilish Rooney (2007) have argued that the processes of addressing historical violence and injustice have not sufficiently recognized the complexity of gendered experiences of past victimization. Only through institutional, political, and discursive inclusion and empowerment of gendered subjects can (the effects of) the wartime victimization of women be put to an end. Women should be supported to play the role of decision-maker strategists in the development of peace accords, and in the subsequent processes of historical justice and reconciliation (see also Navanethem, 2007).

A particularly important motif in gendering transitional justice has been the 'silence' of women. Silence is equated in this context with the non-incorporation of women's voices, experiences, and perspectives on historical injustice in transitional and commemorative institutions; and, often violent, systemic suppression or pacification of political claims attached to these perspectives. For example, Michelle Kelsall and Shanee Stepakoff (2007) have convincingly argued that the Special Court for Sierra Leone, created for the purpose of prosecuting those who carried the *greatest responsibility* for the atrocities committed during the war, was substantially flawed because of its 'gender bias'. While the court's mandate to prosecute crimes of sexual violence followed (and in some aspects exceeded) the trajectories set by the ICTY and ICTR (Article 2(g), the Statute of the Special Court for Sierra Leone), its realization of that objective was highly problematic. The authors pointed to gendered practices of *silencing* the subjects (both witnesses and survivors) through decisions about evidence inadmissibility and/or of testimonial irrelevance, predominantly in those cases that depended on women 'speaking out'. The argument was that the effects of such silencing practices were (re)traumatizing for the individuals because they resulted in psychological grief, bitterness, humiliation, and shame. Also, the effects of silencing were socio-political, as these practices undermined the legitimacy of the courts and, in the longer term, brought about a sense of the failure of justice and of reconciliation.

Much of the feminist normative engagement with the topic of transitional justice and reconciliation seems to have followed a linear trajectory of a 'passage' or 'movement' *from* the victimized condition (with its emblematic associations of passivity and disempowerment) *to* women's successful embodiment of roles grounded in the constructs of activity, agency, and control. What is interesting about the notion of 'movement' between these two conditions is that it follows an idea that has been quite central to reconciliatory imaginary as a whole. It is, namely, that reconciling society proceeds along a progressive temporal axis *from* the violent and/or unjust past, understood as a locus of barbarous and catastrophic events, *into* a radically different future – defined in terms of the denunciation of past violence and injustice. Thus, in the mentioned feminist approaches to transitional justice, 'successful' reconciliation is depicted as a systemically and symbolically transformative process, in which the capacity to address the gendered dimensions of historical injustice and violence depends upon a professional-institutional inclusion of gender subjects in the transitional architecture. Also, as others have critically pointed out, it seems to equate gendered experiences of historical injustice and violence with (mostly sexual, but also other forms of) victimization – and 'gendered subjects' with 'women'. Adopting a somewhat speculative tone, this chapter asks *what if we imagine and use gender differently* in the debates on reconciliation and transitional justice. It is specifically interested in gender as a concept capable of doing *a work of critique*, and thus of questioning, or subverting, the settled presuppositions about what reconciliation *means* and *does* politically – and also, perhaps, whether it is capable of interrogating the proposition that gendered empowerment links and intersects with the project of doing justice for the past.

Pankhurst (2008: 12) has argued for a broader understanding of 'a gender aware truth process', which aims not only at narrating 'the particular sufferings of women, but also [at] integrating into the conflict narrative, their experiences as fighters, survivors of attack and torture, household managers, and community leaders'. Regarding the dichotomous categorization of 'victims' and 'agents', it envisions transitional justice as advancement from one gendered social condition to another, building upon the assumption that the reconciliatory progression is not only desirable and achievable, but that it also forms an exclusive modality of gender empowerment in transitional context. Finally, it conceptualizes transitional justice and reconciliation as a (currently inadequate but ultimately) productive framework of gender-oriented post-conflict societal transformation. This chapter suggests that, rather than being ideologically neutral and pragmatic, as well as ultimately constructive, transitional justice also carries a potential for subjective violence. Importantly, that violence is not (always) connected to gendered exclusions or to an inadequate gender accommodation. Rather, at play here is a hegemonic pursuit to *absorb* and *usurp* the categories of gender and sexuality, and in turn to organize, govern, and mobilize gendered subjectivities for the transitional performances of justice-doing, reconciliation, and commemoration.

Theorizing trauma and 'speaking out'

The recent 'gender turn' in the transitional justice literature centres upon multifaceted marginalizations and exclusions of gender. In consequence, it suggests that empowering female voices in judicial settings, narrating their experiences and perspectives, and ensuring their institutional representation and visibility will strengthen (and possibly re-orient) the processes of 'coming to terms with the past', which might also have far-reaching progressive societal implications. This conflation of the act of speaking out with emancipatory promise plays out both at a personal psychological level, as a release from personal trauma, and at a collective socio-political level, as a working towards a reconciled political community (Herman, 1997).

This discursive trajectory has been strengthened by 'therapeutic approaches' to reconciliation insofar as they encourage subjective and testimonial self-disclosure (Acorn, 2004; Brudholm, 2008). These approaches are linked to a particular adaptation of trauma theory to the study of reconciliation, where 'trauma' functions as shorthand for the psychological damage that requires political response of 'healing'. In *Narrating Our Healing. Perspectives on Working Through Trauma* (2007), which analyses the narrative and social complexities of post-apartheid trauma, Chris van der Merwe and Pumla Gobodo-Madikizela argue that, while trauma means '"undoing of the self", and [a] loss [...] of control, loss of one's identity, loss of the ability to remember, and a loss of language to describe the horrific events', one can come to repossess one's life through practice of self-narration (van der Merwe and Gobodo-Madikizela, 2007: vii). Trauma and narration function in a binary opposition: while trauma entails 'the shattering of life's narrative structure, about a loss of meaning', (trauma) narration makes it possible to regain 'structure, coherence and meaning in life' (ibid.: 6).

The therapeutic effects of self-narration are connected to its relational dimensions; 'in order for the trauma narrative to heal, one's trauma narrative has to be received by an empathetic listener'; a *co-traveller* in a journey in which 'we "re-find" ourselves and re-find the language we have lost' (ibid.: 27). For the authors of *Narrating Our Healing*, it is because of the silencing of the victims of trauma (meaning not only social disparagement of their stories, but also the lack of 'sympathetic listeners') that their trauma remains *unmanaged, active*, 'repeated and "acted out"' (ibid.: 32). Consequently '[t]he story of the past continues to be unfinished as long as it is not spoken out', and trauma remains re-enacted through the 'repetition of violence' (ibid.: 35).

The discourse of therapeutic self-narrative is based on a construction of a close relation between personal healing and communal rapprochement (ibid.: 36):

> The dialogue of narratives should bring us together so that we understand clearly that we are a new people, breaking with the past, committed to a different life, to forging new and different relationships with one another. We should not be people frozen in the past; we should be moving forward. That is the importance of the narratives of our traumas – that they should help us find a way of remembering that does not increase the divide but brings us together. That is a challenge that is always before us.

Consequently, the imperative to make 'public spaces [...] intimate' (ibid.: 47) is forged:

> [...] 'talking about the hurts' triggers something in the audience with which they identify, which they receive and respond to. So when you express your pain, you are expressing it in the name of all those others who find a place in your heart to connect to with your story. Your story becomes the story also of others present, so my reaction, and your reaction to my story is also *our* reaction. When we embrace the story, we are embracing it with mutual feeling of connectedness. The consequence of that embrace is the hope that we need so badly, so that we can move forward after all our traumas.

The dictate of the narrative self-disclosure testifies to the fact that the production of reconciliatory speech has become a highly normative socio-political practice. The reconciliatory speech gains an almost *magical* quality in how its therapeutic emancipatory effects are imagined.[6]

Speech externalizes (thus, turning into a manageable narrative object) the traumatic experience that has so far *immobilized* and *possessed* the subject. This is undone via the confessional-testimonial act. In the reconciliatory speech, traumatic memory is being 'transform[ed] through language' (ibid.: 25). Self-narration is a cathartic ritual, which promises to achieve a clear separation between the subject's constitution and 'her' trauma, or 'her' memory, or 'her' past. The grammar of the possessive case indicates regained subjective autonomy vis-à-vis the past experiences of harm.

According to the logic of the reconciliatory speech, it is precisely because the act of speaking out is imagined as emancipatory and therapeutic (and only as such political), that it is opposed to 'silence', which becomes synonymous with the repressive motion of 'being silenced', or with being discursively and institutionally non-existent (Herman, 1997). Consequently, what remains unexplored are:

(i) alternative possibilities of interpreting silence as potentially dissident, subversive, and political; and
(ii) alternative perspectives on the practices of speaking out and narrating, of 'making public spaces intimate', as not necessarily emancipative or empowering, but as a compliant response of the subject to the array of reconciliatory interpellations, and as her/his *capturing within* (and identifying with) the disciplining and regulatory discourses of reconciliation and transitional justice.

This critique of the reconciliatory speech in transitional justice literature builds further upon the work of Joan Scott (1992) and Wendy Brown (1998). Scott questions epistemic reliance on the category of 'experience' to the extent that it remains closely tied to the vernacular of 'authenticity'. Her concern is that the notion of 'authenticity' codes a utopian idea of accessing a space of personal and subjective experience that remains impervious to discursive articulations of hegemonic powers. The argument for the investigation of political and discursive framing of 'experience' suggests caution in one's endorsement of 'women's stories' and 'women's perspectives' if by this one means an unproblematized source of alternative knowledge. The foundational epistemological and political working of 'experience' is linked to its conceptualization as an 'evidence for a world of alternative values and practices whose existence gives the lie to hegemonic constructions of social worlds' (Scott, 1992: 24). The problem with embracing 'experience' as 'uncontestable evidence and an originary point of explanation', is that it conceals the truth of its own discursive production and its historical-linguistic conditions of emergence (ibid.: 24, 34). In the gender-focused literature on transitional justice, the foundational character of women's 'experience' means that successful reconciliatory politics depend on its inclusive accommodation of pre-existing experiences of women (ibid.: 31).

Similarly, Brown has criticized the way that feminism has fetishized the idea of 'breaking [the] silence' through the endorsement of 'authentic experience' and 'personal narrative' (Brown, 1998: 313–14). She has aimed at disrupting the 'implicit equation between speech and freedom' (ibid.: 314), and to explore the interpretative and political possibilities of silence. Brown suggests that the contemporary confessional practice of 'compulsory discursivity' produces gendered subjectivities that operate within homogenizing categories even if, at the surface, it acknowledges the plurality of their occurrences, experiences, and narratives. More specifically, she argues that the imperative of narrative self-disclosure 'reinstate[s] a unified discourse in which the story of the greatest suffering becomes the true story of woman' (ibid.: 320). In transitional contexts, gendered subjectivities are produced through a plethora of reconciliatory interpellations (for example, the self-disclosure as a victimized subject). As such, these transitional identifications become *conserved* precisely because of the political and discursive circumstances of their emergence in the traumatic speech. Thus, Brown argues for the recognition of the ambiguous and unpredictable working of interpellative and performative speech, which lures the gendered subject with emancipatory promises, but also, possibly, secures their subjugation. The traumatized gendered subject of the transitional and reconciliatory order comes into being through the re-working and 're-occupation [of the noxious signs of past violation] through the work of domestication, ritualization, and re-narration' (Das, 2000: 205).

This chapter hopes to move beyond the critique of the political project of reconciliation that focuses on its *insufficient inclusion and accommodation* of gender categories. It suggests instead that, rather than being declared 'invisible', gendered/sexed subjectivities should be recognized as often positioned at the heart of the reconciliatory imperative. It also suggests that the peculiar centrality of gender/sex renders reconciliation politically problematic to the extent it *operationalizes* and disciplines the gendered body into a terrain of reconciliatory performance. Transitional justice stages the moment of 'speaking out' and 'breaking the silence' as a performance of the subject's reconciliation with their own traumatized self, and of the transitional community's dealings with its own collective traumas. In this way, it gains the possibility to initiate its own re-founding; its own successful moment of reconciliation; of regaining 'compatibility and consistency with oneself' (Pankhurst, 1999).

This chapter will now explore the complex dynamics of gender subject's narrative self-disclosure and the community's project of reconciliation as a moment of symbolic violence. It focuses on the discourses of corrective justice and reconciliation in the trials of women (formerly West German citizens), who were accused of espionage activities conducted prior to the 1989 transition under the label of 'sexpionage'. They were accused of spying for East Germany under the circumstances of being either involved in sexual relationships with the agents of the East German secret police, or being subjects of sexual blackmail. While this case is admittedly marginal to the contemporary gender-oriented literature on transitional justice, its peripherality can be also its strength from the perspective of the feminist critique of transitional justice and reconciliation,[7] insofar as it illuminates the political and ideological underpinnings of the reconciliatory project.

In bed with the enemy

This section prepares the ground for the analysis of gender categories in the discourse on 'sexpionage' in the unified/unifying Germany of the 1990s. Steven Pfaff (2001) characterizes the post-totalitarian regime of the German Democratic Republic (GDR) as a 'panoptic system of discipline and regulation', which linked 'political repression with principles of social security and well-being'. In that post-totalitarian society, which was based on a peculiar mélange of self-policing, selective repression, consumptionism, and dissidence, the population was largely reduced to societal withdrawal into privatized spaces (the 'niche society,' *Nischengesellschaft*). The functions of the secret police of the East German Ministry of State Security (*Ministerium für Staatssicherheit, MfS*, or Stasi) included 'policing internal dissent, [...] foreign intelligence, [...] counter-espionage, [...] surveillance of administrative and economic institutions and [...] investigation of political and criminal offences' (Pfaff, 2001: 389). Mary Fulbrook (1995: 22) describes two dominant East German 'mentalities of power', namely 'paternalism' and 'paranoia'. Here, the feature of 'paternalism' points in the direction of the East German realization of one of the constitutive principles of the communist state: the extent to which it was founded upon 'the desire to make things better for the mass of the people, to improve living conditions to enhance opportunities for self-expression and self-realization for all, in a more just and egalitarian society'. All of its state institutions, and Stasi in particular, operated within the terrain of close, subduing, and almost 'intimate and smothering' relationships with the citizens (Fulbrook, 1995: 22; Pfaff, 2001: 395).

The terminology of 'unofficial helpers' or 'unofficial collaborators' (*Inoffizieller Mitarbeiter*) refers to a group of people, whose number was estimated at 174,000 in 1989, and who cooperated with Stasi without being its full-time employees. The Stasi Document Law from 1991 (*Stasi Unterlagen Gesetz*) defined them as 'unofficial staff members [of the state security service]', that is, those who 'have made themselves available for the delivery of information to the state security services', regardless of whether theirs was a regular or singular act of cooperation.[8] The Stasi Document Law emphasized secrecy and voluntarism as defining characteristics of the collaboration. Barbara Miller (1999) gives an extensive account of what the Stasi recruitment and collaboration looked like, particularly in respect of the gender and class differentiations of the collaborators. The Stasi was a patriarchal organization (for example, a woman had never held a senior officer position within the area of recruitment and cooperation with the collaborators). It had, nevertheless, attached particular importance to the categories of gender in profiling, selecting, and screening its potential and existing collaborators. This was most conspicuous in the interpretation and practice of the so-called 'Focusing Principle'. In contrast with 'orientalizing' narratives presented to the international audience in the movie *The Lives of Others*, documentary material shows that most of the collaborators were not violently coerced, but rather motivated by political convictions or socio-economic benefits.[9] Also, activities of the Stasi officers hardly ever lived up to the stereotype of an 'exotic, [...] secret and intriguing' espionage, but had all the qualities of a mundane, routine work, with the supply of trivial information and time-consuming meetings. The gendering of the collaboration was reflected in, for instance, a number of 'recruitment profiles' from 1970, which described as 'desirable collaborators' women who had demonstrated 'emotional disharmony' and 'vulnerability' in their private and professional lives (from the profile of 'Stephana'); or had experienced 'loneliness', 'psychological difficulties', and 'intense [emotional] dependence' (from the profile of Monika Haeger), (Miller, 1999: 31, 62–3). The gendering of collaboration also played out at a more mundane, almost 'decorative' level. A booklet including cooperation guidelines for Stasi officers from the 1950s, which describes the organization of space where the interview takes place ('clean and tidy'), and the welcoming behaviour of the officers (who should offer the collaborator a snack and something to drink), advises also that, 'one should not forget to offer female unofficial employees something sweet to eat' (ibid.: 46). Regarding the relations between the collaborators and 'their' Stasi officers, Miller emphasizes not only the carefully staged 'comfort, coziness of the meetings, relaxed and friendly atmosphere, [and] friendly congeniality', but also a plethora of roles performed by the officers (including that of comrade, accomplice, mentor, and therapist), which conditioned the effectiveness of their work, as well as constituted a close, intense and almost intimate setting of their conversations (ibid.: 60–5).

In 'sexpionage' (or espionage by the 'Romeo method'), Stasi officers ('Romeo agents' or 'love commandos') were trained to recruit West German women as collaborators. They aimed at those who had access to classified material because of their work as secretaries or interpreters at the governmental, diplomatic, or military institutions (Melton, 2002: 56–7; Dennis, 2003: 198). The idea of conducting espionage by means of seduction and sexual blackmail was developed by the KGB, and was allegedly initiated by Lavrentyi Beria in 1930s/1940s (Lewis, 1976: 23–32). The 'Romeo method' of espionage was adopted and perfected by the Stasi foreign intelligence division (*Hauptverwaltung Aufklärung*) during the leadership of Markus Wolf. In his autobiography, *Man without a Face: The Autobiography of Communism's Greatest Spymaster* (1997), Wolf described sexpionage at length. He wrote about the 'Romeos' that, they 'were not Don Juans, much less Adonises [*trained in ars amatoria*], [but] ordinary men, [who nevertheless] realized that a lot can be done with sex' (ibid.: 135, 149). He admitted that:

> [I]n several cases, the human cost was high [and resulted] in disrupted lives, broken hearts, and destroyed careers. [...] But it does irk me that Westerners adopt such a strident moral tone against me on the subject. As long as there is espionage, there will be Romeos seducing unsuspecting Juliets with access to secrets. After all, I was running an intelligence service, not a lonely-hearts club. (ibid.: 150)

In an article published by *The Guardian* on 18 November 2004, Linda Pressly reported that in the 1990s there were 40 trials organized for women who were accused of espionage on sexual grounds. The most publicized case was a trial of Gabriele Kliem, who, in the 1970s and 1980s, worked as a secretary at the Office of Defense Cooperation at the American embassy in Bonn (Quoirin, 1999: 39). In 1977 she met Frank Dietzel, an alleged physicist and peace activist, who was a 'Romeo', and who approached her after months of careful East German intelligence investigation into details of her professional and private life. On the BBC 4 programme 'Sleeping with the Enemy' Kliem provided the following narration of her encounter with Frank Dietzel: 'He looked like my dream man, and I thought, if I could ever meet such a man I would be so, so happy. I fell in love with him the minute he came towards me. [After he proposed a date], [m]y first reaction was that I should get up and walk away as fast as I could, because a relationship with a man that good-looking would be disastrous. But I didn't, I just didn't.' Gabriele Kliem was engaged to Dietzel for seven years, and during that period she provided him with secret documents obtained at the American embassy, without, as she maintained, any suspicion about his true identity or intentions. In 1984, Kliem ended the engagement with Dietzel. In 1991, she was arrested and tried for espionage against Germany; that is, for *endangering the security and integrity of her state* (Quoirin, 1999: 72–3).

One of the most extensive accounts of the sexpionage trials in Germany in the 1990s is Marianne Quoirin's *Agents For Love. Why Ladies Spied for the East* (*Agentinnen aus Liebe. Warum Frauen für den Osten spionierten,* 1999). It is based on stories told by the involved women. The next section of this chapter provides discourse analysis of the narrative self-disclosures of Gabriele Kliem. It shows that, rather than being silenced or marginalized, these gendered narratives became central to the German transitional project of national reconciliation and reunification. This is because the stories (and narrated bodies) of these ambiguous female figures (who were, at the same time, *the betraying* and *the betrayed*) provided a potent representation of one of the key trauma of Germany's recent history. The trauma of the national split as a condition of a damaged unity, or of a painful chasm signifies here a *wound within* (Kristeva's 'horror within', 1982: 53), rather than a neat separation between two self-sufficient state entities. This chapter argues that, through their narrative self-disclosure, and, consequently, through a particular discursive framing of their gendered/sexed bodies, the ambivalent heroines of the sexpionage scandal are projected as symbolic externalizations of that trauma. Just like their bodies are penetrated by the Janus-faced enemy – *the loving spy* – so is the West German state *entered into,* treacherously permeated, and exposed in its moment of vulnerability. Sexpionage therefore signifies a highly subversive action for the political community of the (West) German state because of its mobilization of the symbol of rape, in which the (protective and reliable) border, the external and the internal, collapses.

In what follows, this chapter hopes to move further than note the synecdochic relation between (i) persecuting the betrayed/betraying women, and (ii) completing the reunification and re-founding of the political community of the German state (*as if* the 'Romeos' were to their Juliets, as the Juliets were to the [West] German state). More importantly, the narratives and sexed bodily projections of these women were fitted into, organized, and disciplined by the politics of reconciliation and reunification because these women became, for the German community, figures of abjection, both attractive and repulsive. As abject figures, they not only facilitated a framework for the community's self-understanding of *'what we have gone through'* and *'what we have become'*, but also, in the current transitional moment, *made their bodies available* for the *political project of purification*. This chapter follows Kristeva's and Butler's critical and post-structuralist interpretations of Douglas' text on defilement and purification (2004), in order to demonstrate that it was through the practices of self-narration (and the constructions of their corporeality and sexuality as 'disordered') that these women had come to inhabit the territory of abjection. They became for the reunifying German state figures of the 'cast off' and 'unclean', the one who is not external to the community's law, but who, through her peripherality and her exclusion, makes it possible for the community to externalize its own ambiguity (its 'horror within') and to engage in the performance of corrective justice (as rituals of purification). The community is thus able to re-unify, that is to institute its *oneness* or *wholeness* through the repossession (redemption) of that polluted/purified female body. The remaining part of this chapter focuses on 'alterations with subjectivity and within the very symbolic competence, implied by the *confrontation with the feminine*', and the way in which the reconciling community of the German state has 'code[d] itself in order to accompany as far as possible the speaking subject on that journey' (paraphrase of Kristeva, 1982: 58).

Purity and danger

The task of critical and post-structuralist interpretations of Douglas's writing on pollution, taboo, and social crisis (and the imperative of purification as political re-founding), requires us to question her structuralist distinction between the imposed order of culture and the *never-completely-tamed* disorder of nature (as a distinction between form and formlessness), as well as problematizing the belief that corporeal materiality precedes its socio-cultural significations (Butler, 1993, 27–31). The reason for using Douglas' text is that it provides an innovative lens for reading the gendered discourse of sexpionage. Following Butler, we draw upon Douglas' connection between, on the one hand, vulnerability of the 'polluted' and peripheral bodies, and, on the other hand, the discursive inscriptions of their ambiguity. This ambiguity means that their subversive working on the community is accompanied by the potential for, and promise of, the communal re-founding that these bodies come to signify. Kristeva (1982: 6–8) re-articulates that peripherality as 'abjection'. Socially, abjection operates through exclusion, which means that those who become 'abject bodies' neither *belong* nor *not-belong*, but rather constitute the very meaning of not/belonging by forming (and, at the same time, subverting) boundaries of the communal. Here, Lechte (2003: 10–11) suggests a link between abjection and 'corruptive [social] activities', such as betrayal.

For Douglas (2004: 44) pollution 'is never a unique, isolated event, [but always part of] a symbolic system'. Embodied subjects that are (seen as) marked by pollution, become 'persons in a marginal state [...] vulnerable and dangerous' (Douglas, 2004: 43). Importantly, that peripheral placement combines significations of subjective precariousness and the creative possibilities of renewal, 'to have been in contact with danger, [is] to have been at the source of power. The whole repertoire of ideas concerning pollution and purification is used to mark the [...] power of ritual *to remake a man*' (ibid.: 118, 120; emphasis mine). Assuming, as Douglas does, that society is conceptualized through reference to figures of *form-ness*, the simultaneously subversive and re-creative possibilities of 'polluted bodies' mean that they signify the 'inarticulate area, margins, confused lines' of the given societal form (ibid.: 122). The transitional moment of the German reunification signifies such an 'ill articulated social system'. What this means, to put it in perhaps over-simplified terms, is that the socio-political frictions and antagonisms, which have surfaced with the end of GDR, have been projected upon selected figures of the Other (Douglas calls them 'people in marginal states'). These figures are consequently constructed as the 'source of disorder', and become vested 'with inarticulate [subversive] powers' (ibid.: 124).

Another reason for referring to *Purity and Danger* in interpreting Kliem's story is that Douglas explores the signification of gendered/sexed bodies as a synecdoche of political community. Her understanding of rituals that express anxiety with bodily orifices is that they both parallel, and spill into, fear of the disintegration and disunity of the body politic (ibid.: 153). For example, in her critique of Bettelheim's *Symbolic Wounds*, Douglas re-interprets the rituals of inflicting knife wounds on male genitals not (as Bettelheim) as acting out of vagina envy, but as a gesture towards the horizon of a symmetrical, integral, and 'harmonious' community. She says, '[w]hat is being carved in human flesh is an image of society' (ibid.: 143).[10] The point is, of course, that this desired community is both 'necessary and impossible', that is, *conditioned by its unachievability.* For Slavoj Žižek (2000: 112–13), such rites point towards a 'traumatic kernel, [...] imbalance in social relations that prevent[s] the community from stabilizing itself into a harmonious whole, [where the rituals that express the phantasm of unity are] endeavors to cope with this traumatic antagonism, to heal its wound via the imposition of a balanced symbolic structure'.

In the interpretation of the bodies of women involved in sexpionage, as synecdochal representations of the reunifying Germany, and thus as material/discursive territories of the 'purifying rites' of corrective justice, the focus is, first, on the nexus of female sexuality, pollution, and the communal endangerment. Douglas is interested in those cultural-symbolic systems where female sexuality signifies (i) a particular susceptibility to befoulment and (ii) carries a strong subversive potential for the community. Whereas male sexuality becomes associated with 'pores through which the precious stuff may ooze out and be lost', it is the female sexuality that comes to designate the possibility of bodily/communal boundary-intrusion, 'the entry by which the pure content may be adulterated' (Douglas, 2004: 156). Kliem narrates her sexpionage involvement as structured by her pathological sexuality; excessive, deleterious, and fatalistic. The elements which constitute that discursive frame, and make her sexpionage story *readable* and *self-coherent*, are the frequent adolescent infatuations with older and married men, which had not led to any stable relationship, but had resulted in her two (aborted) pregnancies; a suicide attempt; a mental breakdown; and psychiatric hospitalization at the age of 21 (Quoirin, 1999: 128). Kliem recounts that sequence of events labelled as her 'eternal search for the father', (whom she had never met, and for whom Dietzel becomes the perfect substitution), (ibid.: 31–44). After her residence in Northern America, she returned to 'the country of her trauma', and Dietzel was one of over 40 men who responded to her personal advertisment in a newspaper (ibid.: 39). She describes Dietzel as not only physically attractive ('gorgeous,' 'stunningly handsome', and 'sexually radiating'), but also emotionally attuned. She recalls, '[h]e was always very kind [and] *had a lot of patience with me.* He was always very concerned [about me]. I hoped I could [create] a home together with him, and find there rest and security' (ibid.: 39, 44; emphasis mine).

As her sexpionage involvement becomes a single plot story of pathological female sexuality (and her involvement with Dietzel described as oscillating between 'erotic attraction' and 'sexual bondage,' ibid.: 73), it is evident that its discursive logic is that of a female being 'subject to the exigency of [her] body' (Douglas, 2004: 201). Importantly, her sexed body is signified as such through the numerous allusions to the instability and permeability of its boundaries. These corporeal and sexual meanings are narrated by Kliem as *self-destructive*, as a 'disordered body', or, to paraphrase Douglas, as a body 'at war with itself' (ibid.: 173). This sexual self-destructiveness reaches its epitome in the meeting with Dietzel. In other words, her retrospective sequencing of events into a coherent progression envisions that affair as an unavoidable catastrophe, where Kliem's interconnected sexual and suicidal drives manifest themselves as her imperilment of the *motherland*. That is strengthened by the narrative centrality of Kliem's psychological breakdown (one of the nodal points of the sexpionage discourse in general).[11] That 'event' works as an interpretative prism. The sketch of Kliem's personality as emotionally imbalanced, hypersensitive, hysterical, delusional, irrational, and escapist allegedly *explains* (and makes *legible*) her sexpionage story. It also results in her discursive construction as an abject body (Quoirin, 1999: 74–5). She becomes firmly constituted as *exceptional* and *different*. Already here, through her abject construction, her story fuels restoration of the undermined communal trust and unity, as her neurotic, pathological, and sexualized figure makes it possible to project upon her the anxieties about subversive potential and destructive desires of the other community members. That abject construction of the female body as driven by its sexuality and neurosis, means here that she is *readable* for the transitional community as 'neither subject nor object', but rather as an excluded repository of the community's own precariousness and ambiguity, and, for Kristeva (1982: 1–2, 4, 13–14), as the 'receptacle of narcissism', which becomes the site of communal prohibition to the extent that it testifies to the 'fragility of [its] law'.

In addition to the narrative constitution of the materiality/signification of Kliem's body as abject (polluted, pathologized, excluded), another discursive construction sheds light on her placement within the community as a site of subversion, namely the nexus of pollution, betrayal, and innocence. There is an apparent contradiction between 'betrayal' and 'innocence' to the extent that betrayal implies a premeditated noxious action, and hence cancellation of innocence. At stake in Kliem's narrative self-disclosure is thus elimination of the previously noted ambiguity of the betraying/betrayed subject, which means that she becomes *the betrayed*, and thus is also exempted from the attributed intent to harm her community. Here, both the secondary commentaries on the sexpionage affairs, and the testimonies of the involved women, have centred upon their, primarily non-political and non-ideological reasons for cooperation with the Romeos and, secondly, their ignorance of the agents 'true motives'. Kliem has claimed that never during their relationship had she realized that Dietzel was a Stasi agent (Quoirin, 1999: 72). Instead, she has emphasized her own vulnerability and gullibility, the power of her lasting ('blinding') infatuation with Dietzel, and her loyalty to the (West) German state, manifest in her hatred of 'all things Eastern'.

Regarding the centrality of the notion 'betrayal' for the sexpionage discourse, Kliem's narrative reclaims and reconstitutes that notion by both self-identification as victim of the sexpionage plot, and, and more importantly, as a *transparent corporeal medium* of the attack on her community. The violence is enacted upon the community *through* her body, where her corporeality becomes the community's weak link, the wooden receptacle of the Trojan horse dispossessed of any intention of aggression or treachery. In her story, she reduces herself to a shell of a female body that has *emptied itself,* hosted an alien and hostile element *within* (her womb), which she, in her ignorance, has consequently smuggled into her maternal home (an image which has been explored in popular culture, in the movies *Alien3* and *Alien Resurrection*, where Sigourney Weaver's Ripley mothers the increasingly anthropomorphized alien).

In this context, Kliem's seemingly infantile self-description as 'das befleckte Lämmchen' (a 'tainted lamb' or 'blemished lamb') constitutes a pivotal point of her narrative (ibid.: 75).[12] With a gamut of connotations (of her innocence, ignorance, victimization, and passivity), that figure of speech captures pollution as a *momentary/temporal instance* (the occurrence of blemish) with all its grave consequences for the transitional society. Here, if defilement is constructed and experienced as *something that has happened to the community* via the sexed/gendered body ('the anomalous thing'), it inadvertently reinforces the belief that there has been a different polity *prior to* the defilement; a polity whose internal trust and coherence ('unity, integrity [...] and oneness') have been disrupted by the treacherous act (Douglas, 2004: 67). Within the reconciliatory 'regime of truth' about the broken communal oneness, the figure of the 'blemished lamb' (the self-narrating victim) occupies an important place. Through logic of defilement, she is invested with the prior status of purity that now, in the political moment of transition, can and should be regained. In other words, in order to make notions of 'pollution' systemically operative, one needs to have *already* envisioned (and embraced) purity, both bodily and communally. For Douglas (2004: 67), the ideas of 'purity' are fuelled by theological desires; the desire for 'holiness' is understood as the 'right order', 'rectitude' and 'straight-dealing'. To be 'holy means to be whole, to be one'.

Social and personal 'purity', therefore, do not imply the immunity to contamination, but, on the contrary, 'its [pollution's] dangers fall [...] on the head of [...] the innocent' (ibid.: 166). The enactment of the figure of the 'blemished lamb' provides a lens through which one reads the sexpionage narratives as stories about the destruction of 'holiness' (that is individual innocence and communal oneness). That enactment is not only interpretative, but also political. The image of the 'blemished lamb' *declares* the sexed/gendered body to be an available and desirable site for the performance of corrective justice as ritual(s) of purification. Kliem narrates her trial as an experience of infantalization. Rather than *punished*, she feels *reprimanded* (like a 'little girl put in the corner'). At the same time, she remains deeply attracted to the redemptive promise of her societal reintegration, of 'washing away her blemish' (Quoirin, 1999: 75) through her submission to the reconciliatory 'regime of truth'. This infantalization is a strategy of de-sexualizing the materiality/signification of her body, of pacifying or 'taming' its disquieting and perilous meanings, and of destroying its ambiguities. The power of that abject body is that, through the corrective performances of purification, it comes to substantiate the community's own successful leap from its divided and dreary past, the overcoming of a trauma into a *hopeful future* of a 'new society, [...] free, unbounded and without coercion and contradiction' (Douglas, 2004: 195). The symbol of the 'washing away of a blemish', that is the re-instalment of her virginity, *flirts* with the fantasies of bodily (and societal) perfection – its impermeability. The authoritarian past is symbolized by the 'Old Eve, [who] together with fears of sex pollution, belongs with the [bygone] social organization', whereas the moment of transition announces the reign of 'the Second Eve, a virgin source of redemption crushing evil underfoot, [...] a potent new symbol' of the reconciled community, a community *at peace with itself* (ibid.: 195).[13]

Conclusions: on silence, reconciliation and the wound within

Rather than being silenced and marginalized, women who had been involved in the sexpionage affairs were encouraged to narrate their experiences. Their testimonies and confessions not only blended in with their submission to corrective transitional justice, but played a central role in what this text has termed rituals of purification and reconciliation in an attempt to suture the 'wound within' of the asunder German community. Their narrative self-constructions, as abject bodies, confirm the formative powers of their testimonies for the nation on its way to reunification. By projecting upon these sexed/gendered bodies feelings of horror and revulsion (combined with an almost erotic fascination), that reunifying community articulates its theological desires (oneness, wholeness, purity), and pushes away its self-destructive propensities by attributing them to the peripheral and transgressive figures of these 'fallen' women.

The narrative self-disclosure (Rothfield's 'the citizen-survivor,' 2006: 25) does not necessarily testify to the moment of liberation of the subject(s), to the extent that the story-telling signifies submission to the reconciliatory 'regime of truth', and the fulfilment of the role of the self-narrating victim/perpetrator. For Rothfield (2006: 32), the question is what happens to those who have fulfilled their testimonial (and abject) functions with the reconciliatory performances, and she suggests that the 'potential side effect of the testimonial cure [is] the (re) traumatized, the unsatisfied, unreconciled' person. And indeed, this seems to be an adequate representation of Gabriele Kliem's post-trial life. She describes herself as an anti-social, disillusioned person with a 'hermitic' existence (Quoirin, 1999: 149). She lives in the Netherlands (where 'there is no east and west, and no shadow of the past'), and defines her life as revolving around '[...] art therapy, esoterism, and [her] dogs', with a sense of being, on the one hand, dissociated from her motherland (and forgotten by it), and, on the other, continuously affected by her past, as if *stuck in it* (ibid.: 149, 234). She says that Frank Dietzel's 'perfidy [and] cruelty' towards her has irreversibly changed her social being. For her, any encountered person is 'her [potential] murderer' (ibid.: 235).

This chapter has suggested that an important aspect of narrative self-disclosure of women involved in sexpionage was the eradication of the ambiguity that they had come to embody as both betrayed and betraying subjects. Quoirin (1999: 9–11) describes the *indistinction* between 'victim' and 'perpetrator' inscribed within the figures of these women. It appears as if it was that indistinction (or indefiniteness) that causes disquiet within the transitional setting. In order to be accommodated (and made *legible*) within its 'regime of truth', and thus useful for the reconciliatory politics, these figures need to be stripped of that transgressive ambiguity that resists the institutional-discursive moulding.

The problem with conceptualizing the testimonies of their experiences, as an endeavour that asserts the public validity of their stories and subjectivities, and is potentially emancipative, is that they are produced with (and submit to) a specific (hegemonic) socio-cultural discourse, which operates with reconciliatory-therapeutic-theological categories, and, as such, has yet to demonstrate its commitment to progressive social change and to the facilitation of freedom of political subjects. In this context, what is interesting in Kristeva's theorizing of abjection (Kristeva, 1982: 34–41), is her ambivalence on the association between orality and liberation. She turns to Sigmund Freud's Little Hans and the little girl from Anna Freud's seminar (both figures were characterized by particular skills in, and inclinations towards, verbalization) to suggest that their linguistic activity centred on developing 'counterphobic objects'. The act of naming of phobic thus becomes an attempt at 'devouring' or 'introjecting' (appropriating) its '"oral" object that slips away'. As such, verbalization is motivated by the fear of the 'unnameable'. Self-narrative, therefore, does not necessarily entail the possibility of subjective empowerment, or, for that matter, enhanced self-reflexivity. Rather, verbal activity is linked, for Kristeva, to *passivation* (*I* narrate *myself* through *what was done to me*) and *aggressivity* (*I* narrate *myself* as the only available outlet for the hostility I experienced, having recognized my own subjugation).

The conclusion, therefore, brings this chapter's argument closer to Wendy Brown's suggestion to explore the subversive and political aspects of silence. Here, silence is not an indication of suppressed verbal presence, but signifies a form of resistance to the hegemonic 'regimes of truth'. In other words, in silence, the imagined subject *abstains from action* complicit with this hegemony. Politically, and perhaps ethically, this silence frames a domain of difficult subjective negotiations. The gendered abjection, as an amorphous and polluted body, remains *suspended between* the condition of a 'victim' and a 'perpetrator', and is reducible to neither. As such, it bespeaks an important quality of an *ambiguity within* – the subject not only escapes any singular identification, and remains unruly vis-à-vis the regime of transitional justice and reconciliation, but is also internally conflicted and non-transparent to themself.

In the context of the debates on gendering transitional justice and reconciliation, what, then, are the political consequences of *abstaining from speaking*? Or, for that matter, of abstaining from acting in the capacity of a 'forgiving victim'? If, in some situations, silence can indeed become a 'practice of freedom' (Brown, 1998: 317), then its subversive workings mean not merely rejection of the normative presuppositions of reconciliation, but, rather, such reframing of reconciliation and transitional engagements with the past that renders subjective 'ambiguity within' central to their pursuits of justice.

Notes

Many thanks to Davina Bhandar, Lois Harder, Catherine Kellogg, and Nikolas Kompridis, as well as Susanne Buckley-Zistel for their comments on the earlier drafts of this text.

1. See for example Handrahan, 2004; DeLaet, 2006; Nesiah, 2006; Ní Aoláin and Turner, 2007.
2. For discussions of specific cases on gender and reconciliation see contributions to Pankhurst, 2008.
3. A noteworthy exception is the work of Rothfield (2007a; 2007b; 2006).
4. For overview and critique see Chapter 5 in Ball, 2008.
5. The term transitional justice encompasses a plethora of post-conflict and/or post-authoritarian situations and their accompanying legal and socio-political projects of 'doing justice for' and 'coming to terms with' the past. As for reconciliation, its working definition here is that of 'cancellation of estrangement [...] and enmity' in post-conflict contexts (Bhargava, 2000: 45). The 'gendering' of the transitional justice debates means thus bringing to the surface how the categories of gender have been implicated in the conflict and/or authoritarian situations, and how they accordingly need to be involved and acknowledged in the performance of justice. In this chapter, 'transitional justice' and 'reconciliation' are often referred to together. This is *not* to imply that they are synonymous or reducible to one another. Rather, the author views reconciliation as one of the transitional justice projects. On the other hand, however, reconciliation also exceeds the category of transitional justice projects insofar as (i) its complex ideational and conceptual history has been for a long time separate from transitional contexts *sensu stricto*; and to the extent that (ii) reconciliatory goals often go beyond those of justice-doing.
6. Brudholm (2008: 6) writes, in this context, about the 'alchemies of reconciliation', thus connecting the reconciliatory imperative with the almost magical occurrences of personal and communal metamorphoses.
7. This means that (i) the gendered subjects in focus do not easily fall under the category of being victims of sexual violence; (ii) their very identification as 'victims' is problematic, and (iii) the context of unifying Germany does not seem to match the violent genocidal occurrences of, for instance, Rwanda or the Balkans, that have been in focus of the recent transitional justice debates. It is important to acknowledge, however, that the German unification after the collapse of the GDR has been widely recognized as a case of (post-communist) transitional justice (Miller, 1998).
8. See 'Law About the Documents of the State Security Service of the Former German Democratic Republic' §6 (4)2, 20 December 1991, *author's translation*.

9. *Das Leben der Anderen*, 2005, dir. Florian Henckel von Donnersmarck.
10. See for example p.142 where Douglas writes, 'We cannot possibly interpret rituals concerning excreta, breast milk, saliva and the rest unless we are prepared to see in the body a symbol of society, and to see the powers and dangers credited to social structure reproduced in small on the human body.'
11. Quoirin (1999: 150) makes a point about the psychological and mental problems of most of the women involved in sexpionage whom she interviewed. While she explicitly identifies their cases of depression, neurosis, anxiety attacks, alcoholism, and a variety of psychosomatic disorders as the traumatic *effects* of their involvement in sexpionage and the subsequent trials, she also weaves into their stories the history of mental and emotional instability. In their narratives, it becomes shorthand for their particular vulnerability, and, potentially, also problematization of responsibility.
12. Confer Michel Foucault's theorizing of pastoral power as a Christian-inspired 'art of "governing men"', or one that requires the subject's subordination, obedience, and renunciation (of passions). In pastoral power, thereby, 'we have a mode of individualization that not only does not take place by way of affirmation of the self, but one that entails destruction of the self, [...] a mode of individualization by subjection' (2007: 165, 178, 184).
13. Confer Teitel (quoted in Brudholm, 2008: 7), 'Transitional justice histories are redemptive stories, of return, of wholeness, of political unity.'

References

A. Acorn (2004) *Compulsory Compassion: A Critique of Restorative Justice* (Vancouver: University of British Columbia Press).

B. Rajeev (2000) 'Restoring Decency to Barbaric Societies' in R. I. Rotberg and D. Thjompson (eds) *Truth vs. Justice. The Morality of Truth Commissions* (Princeton: Princeton University Press), pp.45–67.

K. Ball (2008) *Disciplining the Holocaust* (New York: State University of New York Press).

BBC 4 (2004) 'Sleeping with the Enemy' Part 2, *BBC 4*, 22 November 2004.

W. Brown (1998) 'Freedom's Silences' in R. C. Post (ed.) *Censorship and Silencing: Practices of Cultural Regulation* (Los Angeles: Getty Research Institute), pp.313–27.

T. Brudholm (2008) *Resentment's Virue. Jean Améry and the Refusal to Forgive* (Philadelphia, PA: Temple University Press).

J. Butler (2006[1990]) *Gender Trouble. Feminism and the Subversion of Identity* (New York: Routledge).

J. Butler (2005) *Giving an Account of Oneself* (New York: Fordham University Press).

V. Das (2000) 'The Act of Witnessing: Violence, Poisonous Knowledge, and Subjectivity' in V. Das, A. Kleinman, M. Ramphele and P. Reynolds (eds) *Violence and Subjectivity* (Berkley: University of Chicago Press), pp.205–25.

D. DeLaet (2006) 'Gender Justice: A Gendered Assessment of Truth-telling Mechanisms' in T. A. Borer (ed.) *Telling the Truths: Truth Telling and Peace Building in Post-conflict Societies* (Notre Dame: University of Notre Dame Press), pp.151–80.

M. Dennis (2003) *The Stasi: Myth and Reality* (London: Pearson).
M. Douglas (2004[1966]) *Purity and Danger. An Analysis of Concept of Pollution and Taboo* (London: Routledge).
M. Foucault (2007) *Security, Territory, Population. Lectures at the Collège de France 1997–1978* (Basingstoke: Palgrave Macmillan).
L. Handrahan (2004) 'Conflict, Gender, Ethnicity and Post-Conflict Reconstruction', *Security Dialogue*, Vol. 35 No. 4, 429–45.
J. Herman (1997) *Trauma and Recovery* (New York: Basic Books).
M. Kelsall and S. Stepakoff (2007) '"When We Wanted to Talk About Rape": Silencing Sexual Violence at the Special Court for Sierra Leone', *International Journal of Transitional Justice*, Vol. 1 No. 3, 355–74.
J. Kristeva (1982) *Powers of Horror. An Essay on Abjection* (New York: Cambridge University Press).
J. Lechte (2003) 'Abjection' in J. Lechte (ed.) *Key Contemporary Concepts: From Abjection to Zeno's Paradox* (London: SAGE), pp.10–11.
D. Lewis (1976) *Sexpionage. The Exploitation of Sex by Soviet Intelligence* (New York: Harcourt).
H. K. Melton (2002) *Ultimate Spy* (New York: DK Publishing).
C. N. van der Merwe and P. Gobodo-Madikizela (2007) *Narrating Our Healing. Perspectives on Working Through Trauma* (Newcastle: Cambridge Scholars Publishing).
B. Miller (1999) *Narratives of Guilt and Compliance in Unified Germany. Stasi Informers and their Impact on Society* (London: Routledge).
N. Pillay (2007) 'Editorial Note', *The International Journal of Transitional Justice*, Vol. 1 No. 3, 315–7.
V. Nesiah (ed.) *Truth Commissions and Gender: Principle, Policies and Procedures* (New York: International Center for Transitional Justice).
F. Ní Aoláin and E. Rooney (2007) 'Underenforcement and Intersectionality: Gendered Aspects of Transition for Women', *International Journal of Transitional Justice*, Vol. 1 No. 3, 338–54.
F. Ní Aoláin and C. Turner (2007) 'Gender, Truth and Transition', *UCLA Women's Law Journal*, Vol. 16, 229–79.
M. Fulbrook (1995) *Anatomy of Dictatorship: Inside the GDR 1949–1989* (Oxford: Oxford University Press), pp.129–50.
D. Pankhurst (ed.) (2008) *Gendered Peace. Women's Struggle for Post-war Justice and Reconciliation* (New York: Routledge).
D. Pankhurst (1999) 'Issues of Justice and Reconciliation in Complex Political Emergencies: Conceptualising Reconciliation, Justice and Peace', *Third World Quarterly*, Vol. 20 No. 1, 239–56.
S. Pfaff (2001) 'The Limits of Coercive Surveillance. Social and Penal Control in the German Democratic Republic', *Punishment and Society*, Vol. 3 No. 3, 381–407.
L. Pressly (2004) 'The Spy Who Loved Her', *The Guardian*, 18 November 2004.
M. Quoirin (1999) *Agentinnen aus Liebe. Warum Frauen für den Osten spionierten* (Frankfurt am Main: Eichborn).
P. Rothfield (2007a) 'Resistance and Reconciliation: Antinomies of Post-Traumatic Justice' in M. Sharpe, M. Noonan and J. Freddi (eds) *Trauma, History, Philosophy* (Newcastle: Cambridge Scholars Publishing), pp.164–85.

P. Rothfield (2007b) 'Surviving Reconciliation, from the Social to the Singular', *Radical Psychology*, Vol. 6 No. 1, 1–9.

P. Rothfield (2006) 'Sarajevo Beyond the Mirror Image', *Local-Global*, Vol. 2, 23–32.

J. W. Scott (1992) 'Experience' in J. Butler and J. W. Scott (eds) *Feminists Theorize the Political* (New York: Routledge), pp.22–40.

K. Theidon (2007) 'Gender in Transition: Common Sense, Women and War', *Journal of Human Rights*, Vol. 6 No. 4, 453–78.

M. Wolf (1997) *Man without a Face. An Autobiography of Communism's Spymaster* (London: Jonathan Cape).

S. Žižek (2000) 'Class Struggle or Post-modernism? Yes, please!' in J. Butler, E. Laclau and S. Žižek (eds) *Contingency, Hegemony, Universality. Contemporary Dialogues on the Left* (London: Verso), pp.90–135.

10
Transitions to Justice

Nikita Dhawan

Deconstruction *is*, according to Derrida (2002: 243), justice, infinitely deferred, always 'to come' (à-venir), the 'experience of the impossible' (2002: 244). Furthermore, '[j]ustice without force is powerless...force without justice is tyrannical', whereby it is a challenge to 'combine justice and force; and for this end make what is just strong, or what is strong just' (Blaise Pascal cited in Derrida 2002: 238).

The postcolonial world is caught in a dilemma, which is not easily resolved. The formal attainment of independence by colonies and protectorates in Asia and Africa following the Second World War has not ushered in the end of Western imperialism. The epistemic and material conditions that underpinned European colonialism persist to shape our world, so that postcolonial nation states continue to be confronted with the legacies of empire. From development politics to peace and security issues, from human rights to foreign trade policies, from climate change to intellectual property rights, colonial relations still inform how problems are perceived and what solutions are offered. This is also the case in the context of our discussion regarding transitional justice.

Since the 1990s, there has been increasing focus on transitional justice as a means toward undoing past violence and injustice, and toward ensuring world peace and security, particularly for vulnerable groups and communities at risk of violence and persecution. With the emergence of international criminal tribunals, and, more recently, the International Criminal Court (ICC), as well as numerous truth commissions, memory projects, and reconciliation initiatives, the normative impact of transitional justice has been both expansive and, according to many, pervasive. In the face of growing global interdependence, there is rising expectation that powerful actors, organizations, and nation states have an ethical responsibility towards the more vulnerable sections of the world population – especially during conflict and in post-conflict situations. The demand that transnational elites act beyond narrow territorial-based understanding of self-interest in order to 'protect' victim-survivors, and to make perpetrators accountable, seems convincing, at first glance. However, given the long and violent history of colonial intervention in the non-Western world, current attempts to act in the 'interests' of the distant others often invoke suspicion and distrust. Euro-American supremacism and paternalism are reinstated once again with them acting as dispensers of rights and justice.

Justice is commonly understood as the creation of egalitarian societies that guarantee freedom, liberty, and equality, while safeguarding the dignity of every human being. Based on concepts such as human rights, justice involves achieving material and discursive equality of opportunity. In the last few decades there has been an intensive debate regarding what is just, and what are the best means to achieve justice in general, and in particular after violent conflicts and oppressive regimes. The idea of an objective standard of justice has been challenged and critiqued by many scholars including feminists, critical race theorists, as well as queer and postcolonial theorists. This entails a critical engagement with the normative dilemmas of Western notions such as transitional justice, equality, and restitution; namely to what extent are they enabling for disenfranchised communities, and if and how they reinforce hegemonic norms and power relations between those who are constituted as dispensers of justice and those who are simply the receivers of justice. Most theories of justice have been criticized for being Eurocentric and Androcentric, a criticism that can also be extended to transitional justice since it is firmly grounded in a Western (hetero)normative framework. This raises the following questions: Are there objective standards of (transitional) justice that apply universally regardless of culture, race, gender, religion, nationality, or other factors? And if not, what implication does this have on the global distribution of transitional justice and its mechanisms? Who authorizes our norms of justice, and what do we do with those who do not see themselves as objects of our benevolence?

This chapter presents a postcolonial-feminist reading of discourses of justice in general, and transitional justice in particular, to unpack how neo-colonialism is being justified in the name of righting wrongs (Spivak, 2004). In the context of this volume, the objective is to pose a series of questions regarding the historical and cultural situatedness of (transitional) justice, and its applicability in mainly postcolonial contexts. To this end, the chapter is structured in five sections, ranging from the need to overcome the unidirectional flow of norms from the global North to the global South, to interrogating how gender functions as an alibi in legitimizing neo-colonial interventions. By addressing these varied, but interrelated, issues, the aim is to decolonize our epistemologies and practices of (transitional) justice. The chapter begins with a brief interrogation of the colonial continuities of current discourses of justice, peace, and human rights. The second section engages with the challenges of overcoming the Eurocentric bias via a reading of justice and human rights as 'travelling concepts'. The third section focuses on how there is more to gender justice than equality between the sexes; rather an intersectional approach helps augment our understanding of gender relations as power relations. This complicates our analysis of gender violence in conflict and post-conflict contexts. The fourth section unpacks the importance of the notion of 'normative violence' (Butler, 1999, vii-xxvi), in order to understand the simultaneous enabling and disempowering function of norms like justice, both judicially and socio-culturally. The concluding section proposes a reading of justice as a utopian concept, perpetually deferred, never achieving closure, and, thereby, always open to that which it overlooks or silences. This calls for permanent vigilance from dispensers of (transitional) justice in their efforts to right wrongs.

Decolonizing justice

In his book 'The Other Heading: Reflections on Today's Europe', Jacques Derrida observes that Europe has always tended to consider itself as the 'cultural capital' (from *caput*, head) of the world, namely, as providing a lead for 'world civilization or human culture in general' (Derrida, 1992, 24ff.). The role of 'norm-producers' (whether legal or socio-cultural) that Euro-America has historically arrogated itself implies that what is considered to be good for Euro-America is good for the rest of the world. This conviction is accompanied with a pronounced sense of mission that Euro-Americans have the responsibility to dispense justice worldwide. Euro-America, as a guarantor of the exercise of justice, marks a continuity of the 'white man's burden', namely, the responsibility and obligation of the Europeans to 'save' and 'enlighten' the rest of the world. According to this logic, European intervention was, and is, legitimized as a liberating process, and any form of resistance is read as a sign of barbarity against the forces of justice, a rejection of European enlightenment, and as an expression of ingratitude vis-à-vis the good-heartedness of transmitters of peace and justice, which further justifies brutal suppression of any resistance. Racial discrimination, cultural subordination, and economic exploitation of non-Europeans was, and is, legitimized in the name of doing good for the world, in the name of promoting progress, development, and democracy as well as protecting equality, freedom, and liberty. According to this reasoning, natives who are moral and rational are automatically favourably inclined toward Western intervention.

Euro-American claims to leadership in the areas of justice and human rights are based on the assertion of moral and military superiority – especially in post-conflict contexts, whether they be Sierra Leone, Timor Leste, or Bosnia and Herzegovina. This claim to leadership is at the heart of most Western countries' foreign policy legitimacy, which determines the standard for what is right and righteous. The dispensers of justice arrogate themselves the 'normative power' to decide what is 'just' and 'good', with those at the receiving end of justice and rights being simply reduced to 'norm consumers'. A notion of ethical responsibility emerges at the juncture between acting and being acted upon, whereby Euro-America monopolizes agency in the name of protecting and exerting responsibility. In turn, the gratitude that is expected (and sometimes received) from those whose wrongs have been righted by moral do-gooders from above, is a cruel reminder of how the formal transfer of power from colonial rule to native elites has not resulted in the decolonization of the global South or North.

A particularly controversial site where the entangled legacy of European enlightenment and imperialism is negotiated is in the context of discussions regarding international law. This debate is particularly relevant for transitional justice with its increasing focus on judicial provisions to prosecute human rights abuses based on international law. In his canonical work 'Imperialism, Sovereignty, and the Making of International Law', Antony Anghie proposes an alternate history of international law, which challenges conventional accounts that locate the consolidation of the sovereignty doctrine in the Peace of Westphalia of 1648, and unpacks the constitutive role of colonialism in discourses on sovereignty and international law (2007: 310). He argues that, while the Westphalian definition of sovereignty ensured equality amongst Western states, the non-Western world was not granted the same status. He investigates the continuities of this historical relation in contemporary international law, which has failed to overcome this constitutive asymmetry, even as it claims universality. 'Law', remarks Anghie, 'in the name of security, reproduces a new form of imperialism' (2007: 302).

Anghie argues that the legitimization strategy of colonialism as a civilizing mission, and the 'dynamic of difference' (2007: 4) between 'civilized' and 'barbaric' is reproduced in contemporary categories such as 'developed' and 'developing', leading to the distinction between 'developed' and 'developing' legal systems. 'Developing legal systems' are conceded the possibility of becoming developed, but, of course, guidance by Europeans is necessary. This is the infamous colonial pedagogic project of helping 'backward' societies overcome their 'civilizational infantilism'. The supposed political and legal incompetence of the colonized can be corrected through colonial education that offers them the possibility of developing requite capacities to learn to reason, and thereby exercise consent, which is central to the legitimacy of political authority. And those who are not in the position to reason and exercise consent may be governed without their consent (Mehta, 1999: 59).

Anghie gives the historical example of the jurist and theologian Francisco de Vitoria (1492–1546), who was the founder of the School of Salamanca, and who is reputed as the 'father' of international law and for his theory on the law of war (2007: 13). According to de Vitoria, the difference between Spaniards and Indians was that the latter, on account of their barbarian cultural practices and lack of legal personality, were not capable of being sovereign (ibid.: 27). By not being able to fulfil the norms of universal law, specifically Spanish laws, the indigenous people forfeited their autonomy, whereby the Spaniards were justified in imposing their norms, practices, and identity on the Indians (ibid.: 29). Anghie demonstrates how Vitoria's arguments significantly informed the development of international law on three counts. Firstly, certain groups of people could be justifiably excluded from the sphere of sovereignty by virtue of not fulfilling the European norms, which were declared to be universal. Secondly, those who possessed sovereignty were then justified to dominate the non-sovereign. Thirdly, resistance to domination provided further justification for colonialism (ibid.: 31).[1]

The construction of 'the West' as a normative power has left a trail of violent and exploitative systems in the name of modernity, progress, rationality, emancipation, rights, justice, and peace. Any non-Western individual, group, or state wanting to qualify as 'civilized' and modern can only comply and imitate the European norms, or risk the violence of being forcibly 'civilized' and modernized against their consent (which they are in any case not authorized to exercise). The European norms are supposedly worth emulating on the grounds of their superiority. However, even as the native can only attempt to be like the European, s/he is inevitably set to fail. Thus the attempts to imitate European norms can only produce 'bad', 'weak', or 'failed' copies, which once again confirms the authority of the European 'original'.

In the current situation, Anghie's arguments gain significance in the context of the recently established ICC, which so far has only pursued prosecutions in African countries. Amongst the ICC's stated objectives lie the improvement of national justice systems and the rule of law in 'developing countries'. That this can be in conflict with more culturally situated, restorative justice systems becomes apparent in the case of Northern Uganda, for instance, where critics argue that the prosecution by the ICC undermines local justice systems, and thus any form of long-term stable peace. The legitimacy and efficiency of 'local' mechanisms and practices are eroded through the 'top-down' models of transitional justice, which ignore the singularity of the context in which it is to be operationalized. Moreover, the increasing shift of focus from the socio-economic to the psychological aspects of conflict has resulted in pathologization of post-conflict societies. Discourses of trauma justify continued intervention and paternalism as these societies are deemed to be unable to govern themselves because of the trauma of conflict (Harrington, 2010).

In the context of transitional justice, this is inter alia apparent in the rapidly growing networks of experts who parachute into post-conflict or post-authoritarian societies to advise representatives of governmental or non-governmental organizations on how to set up programmes and instruments to deal with the violent past (Kandiyoti, 2004; Al-Ali and Pratt, 2009). Although the tool kits of 'dispensers of justice' might be comprehensive and adaptable to different contexts, the attitude of 'one size fits all' implies that transitional justice is understood as an imperative, without consideration of the social context in which it is applied. This is particularly pertinent when the cornerstone concepts of transitional justice like 'justice', 'truth', or 'reconciliation' carry different historical meanings in different socio-political contexts. Ignoring this diversity of interpretation and negotiation leads the pursuit and application of transitional justice to be perceived as an alibi for neo-colonialism. On the other hand, as has been pointed out, a critique of universal notions of (transitional) justice entails the danger of cultural relativist legitimization of human rights abuses and injustices being defended and upheld as 'local practices'. This raises the dilemma: How can one address issues of justice while avoiding the trap of universalism on the one hand and cultural relativism on the other?

Justice as a travelling norm

Even as the 'origin' (*Genese*) of a theory does not determine its validity (*Geltung*), nevertheless, the Eurocentric bias in the idea of justice cannot be simply overcome by 'provincializing Europe', which is an important aspect of the process of decolonization (Chakrabarty, 1992). The dilemma, however, is that even as Eurocentrism needs to be critiqued, the European intellectual tradition often provides the tools for critique. Hence a postcolonial-feminist theory of justice should not merely entail rejecting ideas of justice that emerge in the West, nor can the aim be to recover 'pure', 'uncontaminated', authentic non-Western notions of justice. Justice may be understood, rather, as a 'travelling norm', which raises questions such as: How do norms travel among the asymmetrical spaces of postcoloniality? How are they translated from one idiom into another, and who is authorized to function as 'cultural translator'? The production of theories and the reception accorded to them are shaped by the specific contexts in which they emerge and are received. But under conditions of globalization, both theorists and theories are increasingly mobile, and are constantly engaged in the process of translation. James Clifford (1989: 177), exploring the etymological roots of the Greek term *theorein*, informs us that it is a practice of travel and observation, wherein someone was sent by the polis to another city to witness a religious ceremony. Thus 'theory' becomes a product of displacement and comparison through a certain distancing; whereby to theorize, one must leave home. But unlike the Greek theorist, whose beginning and ending was the home, this is not applicable for contemporary global circulation of theories and theorists. Moreover, if theory is no longer naturally 'at home' in the West, with this privileged place being increasingly contested by 'other' trajectories of knowledge articulating racial, gender, and cultural differences, this move raises questions of how theory can be appropriated and resisted, located and displaced (ibid.: 178).

Edward Said's (1983) invocation of *Travelling Theory* raises a series of important questions regarding the sites of production, reception, and transmission of theories. Challenging unidirectional flows that do injustice to the ambivalent appropriations and resistances that characterize the travels of theories and theorists between places in the 'First' and 'Third' world, Clifford, following Said, traces the unexpected routes taken by theories as they migrate, observing how they move in and out of discrepant contexts, addressing different audiences (Clifford, 1989: 185). This brings us to the related notion of 'travelling concepts' as designated by the feminist cultural theorist, Mieke Bal (2002). As tools of discourse, concepts enable dialogue and exchange, even as the meaning and significance of concepts differ and are continually negotiated between diverse cultural contexts and historical periods. This calls for critical analysis of the conditions within which specific concepts emerge, how their 'import' and 'export' occur, the transformation concepts undergo as they circulate between different contexts, and an examination of the methodological consequences that the travel of concepts have for transnational analysis of normative orders. And because concepts travel, often without reliable maps, it becomes necessary to trace the trajectories of their journeys and arrivals.

In her seminal work, the Chinese cultural theorist, Lydia Liu, addresses the question of what it means to translate concepts from one language into another on the basis of commonly perceived equivalences (1995: xv). She asks whether it is possible to talk of conceptual flows across the East-West divide without subjecting the experience of the one to representations, translations, or interpretations by the other. What happens when norms 'travel' from one language to another? What is the means of transportation? Are the borders easily crossed? Who fixes and polices the borders (ibid.: 21)? Is it possible to have reliable comparative categories on universal or transhistorical grounds (ibid.: xv)? Liu invokes the notion of 'translated modernity' to raise the possibility of rethinking cross-cultural interpretation, and forms of linguistic mediation between the East and the West. This raises related questions of what it means for theorists and practitioners to cross the 'language barrier' between cultures and linguistic communities (ibid.: 1). Every time the question is raised, 'What is the Hindi or Mandarin word for "Human rights", "Justice" or "Retribution"', the non-existence of an equivalent in vernacular language is either immediately interpreted as a 'lack', or the vernacular term is measured against its Western counterparts (ibid.: 6). The implications of language interaction between East and West are manifold, and the crossing of language boundaries stops being 'merely' a linguistic issue.

In his recent book, *The Idea of Justice*, Amartya Sen (2009) offers two different concepts of justice in ancient Indian jurisprudence, namely, the classical Sanskrit terms *niti* (organizational propriety) and *nyaya* (realized justice), as an antidote to the parochiality of contemporary Western theories of justice by exploring non-European intellectual history (2009: 20). And yet, the question remains: How hospitable is the West to non-Western ideas? The Derridian term 'hospitality' unpacks how hospitality carries its contradiction, namely, hostility inscribed in it (Derrida, 2000: 3). What does the Western intellectual tradition do with the undesirable guest? Do non-Western concepts and practices of justice have a right to be treated hospitably, not to be treated with hostility?

If language politics was at the heart of colonialism, then any attempt towards decolonization must take translingual practices seriously. What happens when a 'Western' concept gets translated into a non-European language, and vice-versa? Can the power relationship between East and West be reinvented? If so, how? It is important to note that a non-European language does not automatically constitute a site of resistance to Eurocentrism; rather, the task of undoing the unilinear flow of concepts and norms would at once entail acknowledging the historicity and contextuality of Western concepts, and facilitating the travel of non-Western concepts and theories. This brings us to the next step in the process: Once norms have travelled into other worlds, how are they negotiated? In the following section we shall analyse the process through a postcolonial-feminist lens: How Third World women are constructed as 'victims'; how their agency is disregarded, eroded, and undermined so as to necessitate 'external' intervention, especially in conflict contexts, which once again strengthens Euro-American paternalism and 'positional superiority'.

Gender justice in a postcolonial world: 'saving third world women'

One of the most challenging fields where issues of justice are debated – in transitional justice and beyond – is in the realm of 'gender justice' (Mukhopadhyay, 2007: 1). The aim here is to examine the role of gender in processes of material and epistemic exploitation, domination, and exclusion, combined with envisioning strategies to provide access to, and control over, resources as well as strengthening the agency of vulnerable persons. Moreover, it also aims to make social institutions set out to dispense justice more accountably and responsibly (ibid.: 5). In negotiating the challenges that arise in enforcing ideals of justice, gender justice seeks to move beyond the mere legal act of conferring rights. For instance, access to justice through legal reform on education or sexual violence has certainly protected and empowered vulnerable women, but often this has been at the cost of reinforcing gender difference (ibid.: 13). On the other hand, even if law does not guarantee justice, one cannot *not* want rights (Kapur, 2005: 37).

Contemporary discourses on gender justice seek to address multiple aspects including philosophical discussions of agency, autonomy, rights, and capabilities; political discussions involving participation, democratization, and citizenship; economic debates about access to and control over resources; and discussions in the field of law about judicial reform and practical matters of access to justice (Goetz, 2007, 27ff.). As illustrated in various chapters in this volume, gender justice in the field of transitional justice does not solely refer to the prosecution of gender-based violence against women (and men) but also to more equitable gender relations after a violent conflict or authoritarian regime. The challenge remains: How to set standards for determining what is just?

Different understandings of the means for achieving gender justice impose competing roles and expectations on national and international actors and organizations (Goetz, 2007). On the one hand, the state is increasingly being replaced by non-state actors – such as international NGOs and representatives of social movements, namely international transitional justice networks, who enjoy a high level of legitimacy in the international public sphere – to globally monitor issues of human rights abuses and their prosecution through tribunals, truth commissions, and the like. On the other hand, it is argued that the state is indispensible for retributive and redistributive justice even as it should be held responsible for protecting its citizens. Against the background of the historical legacy of colonialism and imperialism, military or humanitarian intervention in the name of promoting or protecting gender justice clashes with the sovereignty of postcolonial nation states. There are no easy resolutions to this dilemma.

Varying interpretations of the role of governments, international organizations, and international civil society actors produce very different strategies for implementing gender justice, such as empowerment of vulnerable persons through enabling political participation, or economic self-sufficiency by provision of micro-credits or gender mainstreaming. Similarly, the constitution of gender injustice is located in a range of interconnected socio-political institutions like the family, community, market, and the state. Understanding the ideological and cultural justifications for subordination of vulnerable groups within each arena can help identify how to challenge patterns of injustice.

Current discussions on justice are increasingly employing the model of intersectionality, which seeks to explain and demonstrate how different forms of discriminations overlap and intersect and thereby produce 'vulnerable' subject positions. Power is understood, herein, to have multiple sources, and these diverse forms of power interact, manifesting themselves in context-specific ways. An intersectional approach unfolds how justice in the realm of gender politics is not just a question of equality between the sexes; it also includes other factors like race, class, religion, and able-bodiedness, to name a few. This implies that women (or men) cannot be identified as a coherent or homogenous group. Instead, gender cuts across all social categories, producing different conceptions of justice. What becomes clear, despite the controversy, is that gender justice is more than equal treatment of women and men. In the context of conflict and post-conflict situations, it is a challenge to define and understand the complex manifestations of violence; namely, how economic, sexual, racial, and gender violence are deeply entangled and intersect to generate particular conjunctures of oppression.

Although feminist organizing is increasingly transnational, racial and class domination is still reproduced and perpetuated among feminist discourses and practices. The notion of 'women's interest' shared by all women regardless of race, class, religion, and nationality has led to advocating for general solutions to various perceived problems, which are seen to apply to all women universally. Gender programmes for transitional justice and beyond often represent Third World women as 'in need of help', and thereby, external intervention is legitimized. Insofar as Western feminists have participated in these kinds of 'universalizing' political discourses, and denied the possibility of non-Western forms of gender justice, they have contributed to reinforcing the Eurocentric bias in the pursuit of justice. There is no better example of the cooptation of 'women's rights' for imperialist purposes than the US war on Afghanistan being justified on the grounds that it promoted gender justice for Afghan women. Along similar lines, the recent focus on victims of gender-based violence during the conflicts in the Democratic Republic of Congo led to an outcry in the West, and demands for justice in the form of criminal prosecution – despite the fact that this was by no means a new phenomenon, but has been a frequent occurrence in violent conflicts in the global North and South (Harrington, 2010). Carol Harrington points out how peacekeeping operations, as a means to prevent (sexual) violence against women in contexts of conflict, obscure how peacekeepers perpetuate violence. For instance, the arrival of peacekeeping troops has been associated with a rise in child prostitution, for example, in Bosnia and Kosovo. Harrington warns us to take seriously the relation between the violence and peace industries (Harrington, 2010).

This confirms the assessment of the postcolonial-feminist, Gayatri Chakravorty Spivak, of how (neo)colonialism instrumentalizes the 'women's question'. As a civilizing mission where 'the white man saves the brown woman from the brown man' (Spivak, 1999: 287), the key manoeuvre is to construct the native woman as a 'victim', which, in this logic, justifies the imposition of the 'modernizing', 'liberating', and 'progressive' regime of empire – a process which also consolidates imperial Europe's self-image as civilizationally superior. The Third World woman, as an 'abject victim object' (Kapur, 2005: 98), needs to be liberated by the colonizing powers. This kind of 'victim talk' justifies 'rescue narratives' in which native subjects are constituted and depicted as in need of deliverance. The fact that this continues to be employed to legitimize contemporary interventions proves that gender persists to function as an alibi for neo-colonialism. Malathi de Alwis (2010) highlights how the 'injured body of the Third World woman', especially in the case of 'rape narratives' in conflict and post-conflict contexts, becomes a site of 'victim spectacle' and focuses on how national and international elites consume the pain of others. The production of transnational solidarity functions through identification with the Third World woman's pain. De Alwis asks if we are truly capable of empathizing with the pain of others. Or should we even be allowed to witness their pain if it only serves to affirm our humanity and our capacity to care. This is, of course, accompanied with the need for 'authentic victim subjects' (Kapur, 2005: 95), who truly deserve our benevolence. What do we do with our 'will to empower' the 'weak and the vulnerable'? How is the distance between the victim-survivors and the 'saviours' to be negotiated?

Imperialism mobilized, and continues to mobilize, specific gender norms to legitimize itself. Furthermore, the ideological conflict and collaboration between colonial and native patriarchies are equally important to consider. Similarly, the complicity of Western feminism in colonialism, as well as neo-colonialism, risks being obscured by discourses of 'global sisterhood'. Herein, it is particularly important to investigate the processes by which specific gender norms in transitional justice become hegemonic and thereby frame the discourses of emancipation, freedom, justice, and human rights. Normative ideals of gender structure the social, political, and cultural worlds – not just discursively, but also materially – through institutions such as courts or truth commissions. As has been pointed out by the queer feminist philosopher, Judith Butler (1999: 23), hegemonic gender norms allow certain practices and actions to become recognizable as understandable or natural, while stigmatizing, marginalizing, or rendering invisible – making unintelligible – those behaviours, relationships, and practices that deviate from the norm. Such non-normative subjects and practices fall outside the purview of legitimacy and the project of rendering (gender) justice after systematic human rights abuses.

Frames of justice

In her recent book 'Frames of War: When is Life Grievable?' (2009), Butler explores how the prevailing (Western) norm of 'the human' determines the distinction between those lives that are recognized as grievable and those that are not. Butler explains how our epistemological frames determine what may be recognized as a liveable life, and delimits the sphere of emergence. Thus, what we are able to comprehend is facilitated and limited by norms of recognition. In this context, it is worth highlighting Butler's notion of 'normative violence' (Butler, 1999, vii-xxvi), namely, the violence of particular norms that not only determine who ultimately counts as human, but also regulate what is legible and intelligible within a specific framework. In our everyday understanding, violence is seen to be exerted on an autonomous subject, whereby it is condemned precisely because it violates the subject's sovereignty. In contrast, normative violence is not exerted on preformed subjects, but exercised in the formation of subjectivity. The body does not exist prior to violence; instead it is constituted through it, thereby being an effect rather than simply a recipient of violence. Furthermore, Butler's notion of normative violence attributes the agency of violence to the norms themselves, so that normative violence both enables typical physical violence, while simultaneously erasing the trace of the violence (Chambers and Carver, 2008: 76). Thus, the capacity of norms to exert violence is twofold: On the one hand, there is the occasional and incidental violence that relates to the particular manifestation of the norm; on the other hand, the violence is internal to norms by virtue of their constitutive 'world-making' and 'reality-conferring capacity' (Mills, 2007: 140).

In the context of our discussion, human rights violations can only be redressed by transitional justice apparatuses according to the accepted norms of the human rights discourse. Those subjectivities and practices that fall outside the purview of this framework remain illegible and unintelligible. One of the biggest challenges lies in the difficulty of making normative violence visible by unfolding how norms of recognition function to make certain lives 'impossible' and 'unliveable'. Normative intelligibility is deeply linked to survival, whereby certain forms of violence are deemed as legitimate and permissible, since those at the receiving end fall outside the hegemonic norms of recognition.

Instead of the common sense understanding of the normative as a guiding action, Butler unfolds the nexus of violence, norms, and subject constitution (Mills, 2007: 134). Norms enable and hinder survival through normative constitution of 'lives worth living'. Political contest resides in exceeding and reworking the norm; it rests on negotiating normativity. The capacity to challenge hegemonic norms presupposes an ability to re-imagine our relation to norms. A critical engagement with this hegemonic framing entails not just more inclusive politics of recognition, but a debate regarding the terms of recognition (Butler, 2009: 139). If norms condition and orchestrate the subject, then hegemonic norms of recognition are proven to rely on a failure of recognition (ibid.: 141). According to Butler (in an indirect critique of Rawls), 'the normative framework mandates a certain ignorance about the 'subjects' at issue, and even rationalizes this ignorance as necessary to the possibility of making strong normative judgments' (ibid.: 143). One could conclude that 'a veil of ignorance' is at the heart of normative claims. Butler speaks of a mode of non-thinking that informs restrictive normative models whose aim is to 'map a reality that can secure judgment even if the map is clearly false' (ibid.: 144). However, Butler does not aim to undermine all normative claims, rather she recommends devising 'new constellations for thinking about normativity' (ibid.: 145) and 'expanding the existing normative concepts' (ibid.: 146), so as to enable individuals and communities struggling for enfranchisement (Butler, 2009). By focusing on the coercive and orchestrating dimensions of normative frames, she unpacks the statist as well as non-statist operations of power. The desire for epistemic certainty calls for a commitment to normative judgments within an established and knowable framework – despite ignorance of the contexts and practices that are judged. Thus normative judgments precede the matter of judging, whereby judgment is built into the normative framing which produces a 'judging before knowing' (ibid.: 155). Butler remarks, '[w]e judge a world we refuse to know, and our judgment becomes one means of refusing to know that world' (ibid.: 156). We are predisposed towards certain kinds of normative conclusions, whereby 'parochialism passes itself off as universal reason' (ibid.: 161). Butler proposes that to take distance from the 'ready-made' is a critical task, which calls for new criteria and new forms of judgment, and necessitates new vocabularies.

Butler's critique is crucially relevant for discourses of transitional justice as a process of undoing past wrongs, and also for ensuring peaceful and just futures. Our norms of recognition determine what qualifies as unjust and violent, what mechanisms and instruments are deemed appropriate and legitimate to right wrongs, who is listened to, and who has the power to listen.

This calls on us to critique norms of recognition and to explore how recognizability is historically constituted and articulated. The aim is not merely how to transform existing norms in an effort to make them more inclusive, but rather to investigate how it may be possible to enable new norms to emerge that will lead to a shift in the norms of recognizability (Butler, 2009: 6). Norms are haunted by that which they do not include, the constitutive outside, 'every normative instance is shadowed by its own failure' (ibid.: 7). Butler explains that 'to call the frame into question is to show that the frame never quite contained the scene it was meant to limn, that something was already outside, which made the very sense of the inside possible, recognizable' (ibid.: 9). This unfolds both 'the frame's efficacy and its vulnerability to reversal, to subversion, even to critical instrumentalization' (ibid.: 10).

'Justice to come': the discontinuity between law and justice

So what does it mean when it is claimed that justice must be done? Challenging universal blueprints of implementing justice, this chapter concludes by addressing the inherent moment of undecidability of justice, the 'not yet'. Here we can be particularly inspired by Derridian deconstruction. In his famous article 'Force of Law' (2002) Derrida insists on the discontinuity, the slippages, the incommensurability between justice and law (*loi* and *droit*, *Gesetz* and *Recht*). Even as one is necessary for the operation of the other, and even as they are co-implicated, each is distinct from the other.

Law, as the exercise of justice, is a system of regulated and coded prescriptions – both closed and calculable – that thereby ensures stability, regularity, and consistency (2002: 250). Drawing on Kant, Derrida unfolds how there can be no law without force (2002: 233). Justice compels us to persistently engage with the law for the particular situation, which differs from case to case, to engage with that which is overlooked, excluded, erased, and silenced by the law. This demands a permanent revision, reinvention, rejustification of law in its effort to exercise justice (2002: 251). For instance, the inclusion of sexual violence as a crime against humanity and a crime of genocide since the transitional justice processes for Rwanda und Yugoslavia is a case in point. This revision and inclusion came as a response to demands of inadequacy of previous laws to implement justice by survivors of sexual violence, which testifies to their agency (see Mageza-Barthel in this volume). Law cannot insulate itself from the ethical interventions of justice, of the call to respond to the specific and singular. The challenge is how to reconcile the act of justice that concerns itself with the singular with the imperative of justice, which entails the generality of a norm. It is not only about being within legality or right, but also within justice (2002: 245).

As Derrida remarks, 'Law is not justice' (2002: 244). Justice, according to him, is never done, it never achieves a moment of closure, rather it is permanently deferred, always 'to come', a utopian moment of anticipation. Justice cannot be a temporal event that can be periodized; rather it is always a unique contingent act, which responds to the ethical singularity of the other despite its pretence of universality (Derrida, 2002: 248). Derrida proposes that even as law and justice are inextricably linked, law as an 'authorized force' 'justified in applying itself' (ibid.: 233), is persistently interrupted by justice, which is elusive and incalculable. In every instance of legal decision, there is an effort to enforce justice, but this is inevitably haunted by the undecidable (ibid.: 252) and thus must be permanently revised to attend to the call of that which it excludes, silences, disregards. Justice exceeds law, even as it cannot be materialized without the regulatory framework of law. This calls for deconstructive vigilance and patient, painstaking work on behalf of 'dispensers of justice'. Deconstruction *is*, according to Derrida, justice (ibid.: 243), infinitely deferred, always 'to come' (*à-venir*), the 'experience of the impossible' (ibid.: 244).

In her text 'The Violence of the Masquerade: Law Dressed Up As Justice' (1992), the feminist political theorist, Drucilla Cornell, explains how power struggles and violence masquerade as the rule of law. Taking inspiration from Derrida, she argues that we need to understand that, even as law aspires to be just, it can never 'catch up' with justice, which always exceeds law. This inescapable paradox makes justice an aporia. Cornell, following Walter Benjamin (1965 [1921]), warns that what is 'rotten' in a legal system is its erasure of its violent origins, so that it dresses itself up as justice (Cornell, 1992: 167). This is particularly instructive in the context of the discussion about the genealogy of international law and its involvement in the continued disenfranchisement of postcolonial states, which – even after the achievement of formal independence – continue to be caught in a relation of structural inequality with their former colonizers. Because this historical complicity in colonial violence is erased, it is possible for international law to 'dress up' as a mechanism for justice, and subsequently as judicial approaches to transitional justice. On the one hand, ideals of progress, development, and rights, which are promoted by international institutions, continue to provide justification for intervention in the non-Western world by the West, and may be read as neo-colonialism by other means. On the other hand, fragile postcolonial states often abdicate their responsibility of protecting their most vulnerable citizens in the name of their powerlessness vis-à-vis the growing clout of international institutions.

Against this background, decolonization becomes particularly challenging because the post-colony is caught in a double bind with the legacies of European enlightenment. Eurocentric conceptions of (transitional) justice risk reproducing violent structures even as the goal is to overcome injustice, especially in post-conflict contexts. However, this does not entail a rejection of norms of justice or human rights for their Eurocentric bias, but, rather, the challenge is how to negotiate these norms in order to make them work in postcolonial and post-conflict contexts. There is an urgent need to explore the ways in which postcolonial perspectives push the limits of ideas of justice. Despite claims of 'tolerance' and 'openness', current paradigms often inhibit alternative non-canonical perspectives from emerging, and unwittingly contribute towards Eurocentric epistemic domination.

At the same time, a categorical rejection of European norms in favour of 'pure' non-Western epistemologies is misleading because there are no 'uncontaminated' native perspectives that can be recovered to replace hegemonic systems. As has been the experience in many postcolonial contexts, the critique of modernity has strengthened conservative and fundamentalist nationalist political orders. Thus postcolonial-feminist theorists of (transitional) justice are faced with the paradox that the enlightenment, in spite of its white, bourgeois masculinist bias, is eminently indispensable. The 'western' intellectual tradition is simultaneously indispensable *and* inadequate (Chakrabarty, 1992: 16) in understanding the realities of postcolonial contexts. The challenge is how can enlightenment be taken beyond the confines of Europe and be made to work for the 'Other'? How can we undo the historical dualism between the dispensers of justice and rights and those who are simply the receivers? And, in our particular context, how can transitional justice be translated in mechanisms or initiatives beyond the Western context?

One of the key tests to determine the legitimacy of collectively enforced norms is to assess whether those subject to the arrangements consent to it and have a say in the decision-making process. And because direct participation is not always possible, the issue of representation becomes crucial; namely, someone is entrusted with the responsibility and authority to represent a group of people. In the last few decades, theories of justice have primarily focused on either redistributive justice or politics of recognition, sometimes trying to think both of them together, on other occasions pitting one against the other.[2] An important contribution by postcolonial-feminist theorists has been to insert the issue of representation in the discussion; namely, the necessity to supplement redistribution and recognition with a politics of representation, whereby we need to confront the criteria which pre-determine what will count as a plausible claim for justice and what will not. Who is authorized to speak for those at the receiving end of justice and from where does one draw this authority? Which voices are heard by whom?

Postcolonial-feminist critique seeks to focus on the silencing and exclusion of vulnerable groups from claims of justice. This is a key aspect within political processes that seek to extend legitimacy to victim-survivors in transitional justice. Because the 'norms of recognition' are not in their favour, the political claims of disenfranchised groups appear unintelligible and illegible. As a participant in critical processes, the postcolonial-feminist seeks to recover and represent their interests, thereby articulating the perspectives of those who cannot speak for themselves. However, the postcolonial-feminist, who speaks in the name of the 'silenced Other' is susceptible to being 'co-opted', for even as she interrogates 'Eurocentric' and 'Androcentric' ideals of justice, she 'inhabits intimately' (Spivak, 1999: 191) the structures she is trying to critique. This brings us to the intrinsic paradox in the relation between the *representing* postcolonial-feminist and the *represented* subaltern whose claims cannot be heard. The efforts to give marginalized perspectives a voice in history by the postcolonial-feminist are open to dangers of the representatives essentializing the experiences of a heterogeneous group of people, whose perspectives she is trying to make visible and audible. The solution is not an 'end of representation', but the persistent interrogation of one's complicity in the continued silencing of marginalized perspectives. Postcolonial-feminist goals risk failure if they refuse to acknowledge the constitutive powers of their own representational claims. How is one to ethically and imaginatively inhabit the narratives of the silenced subaltern without appropriating it, without doing violence to it? How can one bridge the distance between those who 'right wrongs' from above, and those below who are wronged? (Spivak, 2004) In representing the interests and voices of others 'over there', careful scrutiny is needed 'over here'. The task of the postcolonial-feminist, as critic, would be to do a genealogy of these 'silences'; to make transparent the structures of power that block, inhibit, and invalidate these fragmentary 'counter-narratives', cognizant of the risk that every attempt to say the 'unsaid' is fraught with the danger of imposing the logic of speech onto it, and the ironical reproduction of endless spirals of silences and of violence. Our speech is parasitical on the subaltern's silence, even as our silence is no guarantee that the subaltern will be heard. Our efforts to do justice to the 'Other' are necessary, and yet insufficient. Here lies the risk and responsibility of our politics of justice – and by extension of transitional justice – in a postcolonial world.

Notes

Sincere thanks to Susanne Buckley-Zistel, Rirhandu Mageza-Barthel and Izmira Aitch for their comments and suggestions.

1. As we know, this reasoning continues to be employed to legitimize present wars in the name of spreading democracy.
2. The famous exchange between Nancy Fraser, Iris Marion Young, and, subsequently, Judith Butler has greatly enriched the discussion on justice. Refer to 'Adding Insult to Injury: Nancy Fraser Debates her Critics: Debating Redistribution, Recognition and Representation' (2008).

References

N. Al-Ali and N. Pratt (2009) *What kind of Liberation? Women and the Occupation in Iraq* (Berkeley: University of California Press).

A. Anghie (2007) *Imperialism, Sovereignty and the Making of International Law* (Cambridge: Cambridge University Press).

M. Bal (2002) *Travelling Concepts in the Humanities: A Rough Guide* (Toronto: University of Toronto Press).

W. Benjamin (1965 [1921]) 'Zur Kritik der Gewalt', in W. Benjamin *Zur Kritik der Gewalt und andere Aufsätze* (Frankfurt/M: Suhrkamp), pp.29–65.

J. Butler (2009) *Frames of War. When is Life Grievable?* (London and New York: Verso).

J. Butler (1999) *Gender trouble: Feminism and the subversion of identity* 10th ed. (London: Routledge).

D. Chakrabarty (1992) *Provincializing Europe. Postcolonial Thought and Historical Difference* (Princeton: Princeton University Press).

S. A. Chambers and T. Carver (2008) *Judith Butler and political theory: Troubling politics* (London: Routledge).

J. Clifford (1989) 'Notes on Travel and Theory' in J. Clifford and V. Dhareshwar (eds) *Traveling Theories, Traveling Theorists* (Santa Cruz: University of California), pp.177–88.

D. Cornell (1992) *The Philosophy of the Limit* (New York: Routledge).

M. De Alwis (2010) *The Apparition of Rape and the 'Sisterhood' of International Feminists*, Keynote, at the conference 'Reimagining Gender and Politics. Transnational Feminist Interventions', Goethe University Frankfurt, 27–28 November 2010.

J. Derrida (2002) 'Force of Law: The Mystical Foundation of Authority' in G. Anidjar (ed.) *Acts in Religion* (London and New York: Routledge), pp.228–98.

J. Derrida (2000) 'Hospitality', *Angelaki: Journal of the Theoretical Humanities*, Vol. 5 No. 3, 3–18.

J. Derrida (1992) *The Other Heading: Reflections on Today's Europe* (Bloomington: Indiana University Press).

N. Fraser (2008) *Adding Insult to Injury: Nancy Fraser Debates her Critics: Debating Redistribution, Recognition and Representation* (London and New York: Verso Books).

A.-M. Goetz (2007) 'Gender Justice, Citizenship and Entitlements: Core Concepts, Central Debates and New Directions for Research' in M. Mukhopadhyay and N. Singh (eds) *Gender Justice, Citizenship and Development* (New Delhi: Zubaan), pp.15–57.

C. Harrington (2010) *The Politicization of Sexual Violence and Post Cold War Feminist Politics*, Paper presented at the conference 'Reimagining Gender and Politics. Transnational Feminist Interventions', Goethe University Frankfurt, 27–28 November 2010.

D. Kandiyoti (2007) 'Political fiction meets gender myth: post-conflict reconstruction, "democratization" and women's rights' in A. Cornwall, E. Harrison and A. Whitehead (eds) *Feminisms in development: Contradictions, contestations and challenges* (London: Zed Books), pp.191–200.

R. Kapur (2005) *Erotic justice: Law and the new politics of postcolonialism* (Leiden: A. A. Balkema).

L. Liu (1995) *Translingual Practice: Literature, National Culture, and Translated Modernity-China, 1900–1937* (Stanford: Standford University Press).

U. S. Mehta (1999) *Liberalism and empire: A study in nineteenth-century British liberal thought* (Chicago: University of Chicago Press).

C. Mills (2007) 'Normative violence, vulnerability, and responsibility', *Differences: A Journal of Feminist Cultural Studies*, Vol. 18 No. 2, 133–56.

M. Mukhopadhyay (2007) 'Gender Justice, Citizenship and Development: An Introduction' in: M. Mukhopadhyay and N. Singh (eds) *Gender Justice, Citizenship and Development* (New Delhi: Zubaan), pp.1–14.

E. W. Said (1983) 'Travelling Theory' in E. W. Said *The World, the Text and the Critic* (Harvard: Harvard University Press), pp.226–47.

A. Sen (2009) *The Idea of Justice* (Cambridge: Harvard University Press).

G. C. Spivak (2004) 'Righting Wrongs', *The South Atlantic Quarterly*, Vol. 103 No. 2/3, 523–81.

G. C. Spivak (1999) *A Critique of Postcolonial Reason: Toward a History of the Vanishing Present* (Calcutta: Seagull).

Index